C0-FYR-130

ENTERED MAY 1 3 2002

Textual Responses to German Unification

Textual Responses to German Unification

Processing Historical and Social Change in Literature and Film

Edited by

Carol Anne Costabile-Heming,
Rachel J. Halverson,
Kristie A. Foell

COLUMBIA COLLEGE LIBRARY
600 S. MICHIGAN AVENUE
CHICAGO, IL 60605

Walter de Gruyter · Berlin · New York
2001

∞ Printed on acid-free paper
which falls within the guidelines of the ANSI to ensure
permanence and durability.

830.9 T355c

Textual responses to German
unification

Die Deutsche Bibliothek – Cataloging-in-Publication Data

Textual responses to German unification : processing historical and social change in literature and film / ed. by Carol Anne Costabile-Heming .... – Berlin ; New York : de Gruyter, 2001
ISBN 3-11-017022-1

© Copyright 2001 by Walter de Gruyter GmbH & Co. KG, D-10785 Berlin

All rights reserved, including those of translation into foreign languages. No part of this book may be reproduced or transmitted in any form or by any means, electronic or mechanical, including photocopy, recording or any information storage and retrieval system, without permission in writing from the publisher.

Printed in Germany
Printing and Binding: Hubert & Co., Göttingen
Cover Design: Christopher Schneider, Berlin

Table of Contents

Multiple Voices—Generational Views

Cinematic Responses

Acknowledgements

We began our collaborations several years ago, when we organized a special session on recent German literature at the AATG annual meeting in 1997. At that meeting we encountered other colleagues who were working on similar projects, and we first discussed the idea of such an anthology. The following year, after another successful session, this time at the GSA conference, we began to plot out the project in earnest. Thanks to technological advances allowing us to solicit and review proposals and manuscripts electronically, we were able to pull this project together in a mere 2.5 years.

This has been a collaborative project from the very beginning, as each editor (when time permitted) took over large portions of the work. In general, the editors are grateful to all of the contributors for their cooperation and ability to comply with deadlines, and to the Walter de Gruyter Verlag, especially Susanne Rade with whom we worked closely on this project. Specifically, we appreciate the support we received from our institutions, colleagues, friends, and family members, who have stood by us during this entire process.

Carol Anne thanks the Department of Modern and Classical Languages and the College of Arts and Letters at Southwest Missouri State University in particular for technological support. She is grateful to Angelika Hermann at Walter de Gruyter Verlag for her assistance in preparing the final manuscript copy. Her husband, Ralf Heming, was steadfast in his support of this endeavor.

Rachel acknowledges the Department of Foreign Languages and the College of Liberal Arts at Washington State University for awarding this project an Initiation and Completion Grant to cover the initial printing, copying and mailing costs associated with approaching publishing houses. Her partner, Cecil Williams, displayed great tolerance for yet another academic project, which has become a part of their shared life.

Kristie is indebted to her colleague, Dr. Margy Gerber, who provided valuable impetus through her own work and through the New Hampshire symposium she organized for many years. Her current research would not have been possible without her graduate training at UC Berkeley and the time she spent teaching and studying film in the German Department at Vassar College. Finally, for vital support of many kinds, she is grateful to her husband, Christopher Williams, and her parents, Darrell and Sally Foell.

Springfield, Missouri   Pullman, Washington   Bowling Green, Ohio
Late February 2001

Introduction

CAROL ANNE COSTABILE-HEMING
RACHEL J. HALVERSON
KRISTIE A. FOELL

"Schreiber, was siehst du?"[1] Processing Historical and Social Change

Heralding the collapse of authoritarian regimes in Eastern Europe and the triumph of liberal democracy, the fall of the Berlin Wall and the subsequent unification of the two German states are defining images of the late 20th century. A decade beyond formal unification seems an appropriate time to reflect on the historical and social changes that have impacted life in the now-unified Germany. Indeed, interest in the former GDR, as well as the *Wende* and the unification process, has not waned in the ensuing years, but rather has led to what Konrad Jarausch termed an "academic boom" (3). The opening of archives, the greater willingness of writers, artists, and scholars to speak about their experiences has certainly made the study of the former GDR a fruitful academic endeavor. The unification process has been of interest to historians, economists, and cultural theorists. Furthermore, a wealth of scholarly studies has examined German culture and society after unification. It is not only the scholars, however, who grapple with the historical and social changes in Germany; writers and filmmakers have been equally active in contributing to discussions and the processes of change. And so we ask, "Schreiber, was siehst du?" as we investigate how intellectuals have chosen to respond to the challenges of German unification in text and film.

The poem from Peter Rühmkorf, whose title serves as our point of reference, begins with a historical résumé that touches on the horrors of German history, both the Nazi regime and the Stalinist tyranny of the GDR:

> Schreiber, was hast du gesehen?
> Ich sehe, sah:
> zwei für unumstößlich gehaltene Reiche
> sah ich zu Grunde gehen,
> eins steht noch da.[2] (267)

1 Peter Rühmkorf, "Schreiber, was siehst du?" "Writer, what do you see?"

2 "Writer, what did you see? I see, I saw: two empires that were once deemed invincible, ruined, one still remains." There are, of course, other possible interpretations for this citation,

What Rühmkorf views as the remaining empire, is actually an amalgam of the former Federal Republic of Germany and the German Democratic Republic. Somehow these two political enemies, two divergent economic and social systems, have combined to form a nation that has earned the respect of former allies and enemies, a nation which has taken on a leadership role in the New Europe. This is, however, not the image that Rühmkorf conveys in the remaining stanzas of his poem that bemoan the current state of the world: overpopulation, environmental destruction, unfulfilled promises. Rühmkorf's poem (like all of those in this collection) is accompanied by a commentary. In his remarks, Wolfgang Thierse chooses not to share Rühmkorf's apocalyptic vision, and focuses on the positive. He stresses that Germany's long journey towards democracy has reached a new quality that lies in the sovereignty of the citizen: for the first time in the post-World War II era, the people, the voters, have chosen democracy directly. Thierse is also astute in recognizing, as do the German people, that a successful democracy, a successful economy, indeed, a successful society, requires plurality: Germany's success depends, too, on the success and help of its European neighbors and its friends and foes in the global community. This, Thierse views with optimism, asserting: "Kassandra is not always right" (270). This anthology seeks to contribute to this dialogue about Germany, how it has evolved since November 1989, how the people have coped with change.

Political reactions to the possible unification of the two Germanys included fear, in particular the fear that Germany could develop into a new superpower and forget the lessons of its history. Even the reactions of intellectuals focused on negatives: the loss of the dream of a "socialist" alternative to the capitalist FRG. Thus, unification faced prejudice before it even happened and attempts to cope with it were confronted with many challenges. Because Germany has a long tradition of writers whose literary works were packed with political and social commentary (Lessing, Goethe, Büchner, Thomas Mann, Heinrich Böll, Günter Grass, to name only the most obvious), it is logical to look to the literary community for its take on this whole process. Yet, the first published "post-*Wende*" text, Christa Wolf's *Was bleibt*, did not portray the contemporary social, political and economic changes, but rather looked back some twenty years. Wolf's protagonist is eerily reminiscent of the author, and the novel's plot, detailing the Stasi's surveillance of a woman writer, mirrors Wolf's experience following the expatriation of Wolf Biermann when she herself was placed under surveillance. Wolf had originally penned the story in 1979, but delayed its publication until after the collapse of the GDR. Critics chided Wolf for postponing publication, claiming that the book's appearance after the fall of the Berlin Wall was almost meaningless. The ensuing

---

including Kaiser and Führer as the empires that were toppled, even the US as the sole remaining empire.

controversy in the *Feuilleton* unleashed a literary debate about the nature of "critical" East German literature. This *Literaturstreit* was an initial indication of the type of controversy that writers and their texts in the post-*Wende* period would endure.

In the period since the fall of the Berlin Wall, intellectuals have confronted a number of challenges. Indeed, the term intellectual has come under considerable scrutiny, firstly because of the role ascribed to them in the toppling of Eastern European regimes in general; secondly for the increasing number of controversies that arose, particularly on unified German soil, that allied intellectuals with countless negative aspects of the GDR regime. As a result, Ian Wallace has noted an overall tendency in Europe to write "their [intellectuals'] political obituaries" (87). Particularly after such proclamations as "Für unser Land" (signed by Christa Wolf, Volker Braun and Stefan Heym among others), it became clear that GDR intellectuals were out of step with the will of the people. Thus, leftist intellectuals were left behind as the momentum of the unification process increased. Controversies and repeated revelations about the collusion between writers and the Stasi, from the highly-respected Christa Wolf and Heiner Müller to the darlings of the Prenzlauer Berg counter-culture, Sascha Anderson and Rainer Schedlinski,[3] did nothing to help the intellectuals' causes.

As the 1990s progressed, writers and filmmakers faced the task, of coming to terms not only with historical developments like unification, economic crises brought on by the currency reform and the switch to a market economy, but also with the Stalinist past. This often occurred in a very public way through the media, but the struggles also raged internally, coming to a climax as the East and West PENs merged. Former GDR writers such as Günter Kunert could not, in good conscience, sit at the same table with Stasi spies.

There was a challenge on another level, subconsciously among the people. Although the citizens on both sides of the German-German border were Germans, they had, through 40 years of separation, grown apart. Indeed, Peter Schneider's statement in 1982 that it will take longer to dismantle the wall inside one's head (*die Mauer im Kopf*) than it will to tear down the physical barricade was unforeseeably prophetic. For even after the concrete barrier, the Berlin Wall, had almost completely disappeared, *die Mauer im Kopf* remained.

We are certainly not the first to broach the topic of literature and unification.[4] In *Germany after Unification: Coming to terms with the Recent Past* (1996), social scientists explore the unification of Germany five years after the fact. They focus on how unified Germany views its past, particularly how the former GDR must adapt and re-evaluate its prior outlook on history.

3 Perhaps most disturbing was the continued collusion between Anderson and the Stasi after Anderson moved to the West, making the Stasi story not just an East German affair.

4 In addition to those treated here, see Alter and Monteath, Brockman, Bullivant (1994), Durrani, Good and Hilliard, Hahn, Lewis and McKenzie or Welzel.

This volume also questions the relationship between Germany and its geo-political neighbors to the East and West. In *Beyond 1989: Re-Reading German Literature since 1945* (1997), Germanists re-evaluated earlier approaches to post 1945 German cultural studies through the lens of a newly unified Germany. Stephen Brockmann's study *Literature and German Unification* (1999) draws on the idea of the *Kulturnation* (Germany as both a cultural and national unity) and examines the literary consequences of unification in this light.

At countless conferences, symposia and literary readings, new literary works were put under the microscope, as scholars and journalists sought the elusive unification novel or *Wenderoman*. Only time will tell if there is such a thing as the definitive *Wenderoman*. Writers and playwrights from both sides of the German-German border have treated the fall of the Wall, the unification of Germany, and the political, economic, and social problems that these historical events have caused. Authors and filmmakers of former East and West Germany have responded in a variety of textual forms (fiction, autobiography, drama, film) to the changes they have experienced in their immediate surroundings as well as in their perspectives on the lives they have lived in a divided Germany. This anthology, *Textual Responses to German Unification*, presents a collection of essays dealing with various approaches taken to events, which occurred before, during and after the opening of the Wall on 9 November 1989, and exemplifies the integral contribution texts have made to dismantling the *innere Mauer* (internal wall) separating the two Germanys.

In the section "Authors and Their Worlds," scholars focus on individual authors and their literary responses to German unification. In "The Journey Eastward: Helga Schütz' *Vom Glanz der Elbe* and the Mnemonic Politics of German Unification," N. Ann Rider launches her analysis of Schütz' novel with the observation that German unification has occurred on Western terms. She opens her treatment of Schütz' novel with the statement that: "Helga Schütz' 1995 novel, *Vom Glanz der Elbe*, works on multiple levels to explore the tropes and realities of Western domination after unification." Key to Rider's examination of *Vom Glanz der Elbe* is the novel's exploration of the levels of Western colonialism and the role of public memory. In *Vom Glanz der Elbe* Schütz presents a unification scenario that runs counter to the assumption that unification means bringing the East up to the social, economic and political standards found in the West. Schütz' concern with the reciprocal movement towards the East is represented by the protagonist's return to the East Germany he left thirty years ago and his search for the sister he left behind. In the course of her analysis, Rider demonstrates that Schütz uses her protagonist's journey to call for a new approach to German identity. Rider demonstrates that Schütz undermines the polarized thinking that has governed the understanding of German identity since 1949 to suggest not a unifying of

East and West Germans, but rather a Germany in which both can exist harmoniously.

In "'ob es sich bei diesem Experiment um eine gescheiterte Utopie oder um ein Verbrechen gehandelt hat': Enlightenment, Utopia, the GDR and National Socialism in Monika Maron's Work from *Flugasche* to *Pawels Briefe*," Stuart Taberner focuses on Maron's work against the backdrop of pre- and post-*Wende* literary discussions. Taberner's comprehensive reading of Maron's work, including *Flugasche* (1981), *Die Überläuferin* (1988), *Stille Zeile Sechs* (1991), *Animal Triste* (1996), and *Pawels Briefe* (1999), ties Maron's voice in the post-*Wende* literary scene to her earlier literary statements on East Germany to demonstrate the author's development (or dismissal) of themes found in her earlier work.

James Reece turns his attention to East German authors and their autobiographies, briefly exploring autobiographical works by both Christa Wolf and Hermann Kant and focusing primarily on Günter de Bruyn's theoretical writings on autobiography and his *Zwischenbilanz. Eine Jugend in Berlin* (1992) and *Vierzig Jahre. Ein Lebensbericht* (1996). Given de Bruyn's extensive publications on autobiography following unification, Reece analyzes his texts to reveal de Bruyn's statement on "both the problems and the possibilities of autobiographical writing from the former GDR." In the course of his analysis, Reece shows that de Bruyn affirms autobiography as a literary form capable of enlightening both its author and its readers.

In "'*Gefälle* in der Landschaft'—On the Critique of Real Existing Capitalism in Volker Braun's Texts," Rolf Jucker takes an unusual approach to texts by Volker Braun to reveal that the significance of Braun's texts extends beyond the narrow perspective of German unification. For Jucker and his reading of Volker Braun, it is not post-unification literature that should be put under the microscope but also post-unification literary scholarship and even the capitalist West as a whole. "Good literature" should serve as a legitimate source of insights into the conundrum of our present human condition. Listing the current weaknesses plaguing capitalist systems, Jucker turns for answers to Braun's recent publication *Das Nichtgelebte. Eine Erzählung* (1995), whose main character, Georg, finds himself both professionally and personally challenged. References to Braun's *Die Zickzackbrücke. Ein Abrißkalender* (1992), *Ist das unser Himmel? Ist das unsre Hölle?* Rede zum Schiller-Gedächtnis-Preis (1992), *Wir befinden uns soweit wohl. Wir sind erst einmal am Ende. Äußerungen* (1998), and *Tumulus. Gedichte* (1999) allow Jucker to show the extent to which Braun's work speaks to the challenges facing the capitalist world. In conclusion, Jucker's analysis of Braun's work and its statement on the future calls for a world in which "dematerialization, restraint, respect, deceleration, restriction" will allow the members of Western societies to achieve equality.

Rachel Halverson's "Comedic Bestseller or Insightful Satire: Taking the Interview and Autobiography to Task in Thomas Brussig's *Helden wie wir*" dissects Brussig's novel to expose the double-edged sword of its satire. The hilarity of Brussig's novel tempts readers simply to enjoy it for its pure comedic value. Such a reading risks missing the greater significance of the novel and its popularity. Halverson's close examination of the novel's autobiographical frame, its interview format, and the narrator's statements on his role in German unification and on history reveal the novel's pointed message on literature and the historicization of Germany's past. As a representative of a new generation of German writers, Brussig offers his readers an explanation for the fall of the Berlin Wall which speaks for a Germany undivided by the *innere Mauer*: *Helden wie wir* (1996), written by a young former East German, implicitly reflects the unified German character apparent in German youth today, rather than the division embedded in the hearts and souls of the older generation. The novel thus belies its retrospective narrative and speaks for a growing group of Germans who know a divided Germany only from their history books.

The second section of the anthology, "Multiple Voices—Generational Views," proceeds from the insight that authors and their work cannot exist in isolation, but rather are products of the historical and social conditions around them. Here literary scholars focus on authors and their responses to unification within the context of the broader literary community. Karoline von Oppen, in her treatment of the older and established generation of writers in East and West Germany, undertakes a thorough analysis of journalistic texts from summer 1989 through late summer 1990. This essay maps out three different phases of the unification debate. She thus fills a gap in critical scholarship that has paid more attention to high-profile writers like Christa Wolf, while ignoring signs that the silencing of critical writers had begun well before the publication of *Was bleibt*. Von Oppen looks first at Stefan Heym, who, through essays in *Die Zeit*, *Süddeutsche Zeitung* and *Der Spiegel*, was highly visible during the *Wende*. Following the proclamation "Für unser Land," Heym gradually vanishes from the West German press. Walter Jens, typically grouped with Günter Grass as a representative critical West German voice, is, in von Oppen's view, virtually silent throughout the fall of 1989. When Jens does speak out in support of Christa Wolf, he is vilified in the press. The case of Helga Königsdorf is the opposite, as she is able to publish in both East and West simultaneously. Von Oppen highlights how all three authors, though initially opposed to unification, grow to accept it despite the constant undermining of their positions through their critics in the press.

In "Everyday Stories of Hope and Despair in East Germany: Kerstin Hensel and Ingo Schulze Write About Life After the *Wende*," Alisa Kasle focuses on the youngest generation of East German writers, who face a second Zero Hour as they struggle to grasp the demise of the GDR and the ensuing political, economic, social and cultural turmoil brought about by unification with the Federal Republic. This generation, she argues, does not focus on political messages, as did earlier generations, but looks to the struggles and issues of everyday people for the thematic basis of their works. Works by these younger authors break through the stigma of providing moral lessons by their sheer avoidance of themes that try to explain past history. Through an examination of Hensel's *Tanz am Kanal* (1994) and Schulze's *Simple Storys* (1998), Kasle highlights how these writers portray the confusing complexity of life after unification, offering that their characters suffer from *Wendeschmerz* ("pain"). She concludes that the strength of these works lies in replacing national and historic events with the subjective experience of individuals as they struggle to come to terms with unified Germany. She further suggests that though both Hensel and Schulze situate their narratives in Eastern Germany, the perspective is not necessarily typically "East German." Instead she proposes that the characters in *Tanz am Kanal* and *Simple Stories* evince a type of *Lebensgefühl*, the sense that life has become complex and even unmanageable. This feeling permeates the younger generation living in post-unification Germany, and can, to varying degrees, be felt on both sides of the German-German border.

Jill Twark also focuses on Eastern German authors, but she examines the tendency of these authors to respond to the unification process with humor and satire. In her examination of Thomas Rosenlöcher's *Die Wiederentdeckung des Gehens beim Wandern. Harzreise* (1991), Bernd Schirmer's *Schlehweins Giraffe* (1992), and Jens Sparschuh's *Der Zimmerspringbrunnen* (1995), she argues that it is difficult to express unification experiences in words. The resultant satirical texts are defensive literary responses to the rapid changes occurring in society. All three authors choose a first-person comic narrator trying to adapt to the political, economic, and social upheaval. While the East-West portrayals in each text may at first seem stereotypical, Twark views them as a necessary expression of the authors' messages. She reasons that the satirical portrayal of West Germans is contrary to the much touted slogan *Wir sind ein Volk* ("we are one people"), thus allowing the authors to assert their own identity against the dominance of West German culture. Because all three narratives are set in the East and deal with East German problems, (Eastern) readers can readily identify with the protagonists. Thus satire can help individuals as they try to come to terms with their new circumstances. Finally, Twark argues that through satire it is also possible for "outsiders" to gain a greater appreciation for the difficulties that ordinary East Germans have had to face in the years immediately following reunification.

Gerald A. Fetz turns to the theater for portrayals of the *Wende* and post-unification existence since 1991, examining the theatrical works of Botho Strauß, Klaus Pohl, and Christoph Hein. Strauß's *Schlußchor* (1991) portrays West Germans unable to understand the significance of recent German history, while East Germans appear out of place in the new Germany. In this early example of a dramatic treatment of post-unification Germany, it remains unclear whether the new situation is to be greeted with joy or concern. Klaus Pohl has brought three plays to the stage, each representing a different perspective on unification. While both *Karate-Billi kehrt zurück* (1991) and *Die schöne Fremde* (1991) fall prey to stereotypical portrayals of East and West, Fetz argues that *Wartesaal Deutschland StimmenReich* (1995), though less dramatic in form, convincingly highlights the very real dramatic upheaval experienced on both sides of the German-German border. It is, however, Christoph Hein's *Randow* (1994) that paints perhaps the bleakest picture of Germany today. Fetz even reasons that the characters in this play provide the most accurate depictions of East Germans in the *neuen Bundesländern*, and speak to the incomprehensible nature of the changes that Germany has endured since 1989. Each of these three playwrights conveys the message that the unification process has been a difficult one, and in many instances remains unresolved. Throughout, Fetz demonstrates that *die Mauer im Kopf* has not been completely dismantled.

Both German film scholarship and production of the past ten years (aside from the "new comedy" wave) seem preoccupied with coming to terms with the past. Perhaps it would be better to speak of "pasts" in the plural: to the always-problematic Nazi past has now been added the past of the GDR (with its many stereotypes) and the past of the Cold War itself. In many cases, the coming to terms with the past (*Vergangenheitsbewältigung*) of German film serves now as a coming to terms with the present (*Gegenwartsbewältigung*), terms that both appear throughout the essays of the section, "Cinematic Responses." Repeating, reciting, reinterpreting, or reclaiming the past in an effort to come to terms with the present: this is the repertoire of narrative strategies pursued by *Wendefilme* and *Mauerfilme* in the past ten years.

Levy and McCormick draw parallels between the post-war period and the post-wall period, pointing out that issues of German identity, racial and otherwise, were not dealt with once and for all in the post-war period, but continue to plague unified Germany today. They argue that the 1947 film *Ehe im Schatten* was a precursor of the later GDR "Antifa" films with a decided difference. While the GDR genre privileged the heroism of Communists as "fighters against fascism," erasing the biologically based victimization of Jews and others, director Maetzig clearly thematizes the Jewishness of his tragic female protagonist. At the same time, "it is Hans' failure to grasp the implications of the political situation until it was already too late that becomes the focus of the film's identification with the victims of the Nazi state." There is thus a tension between seeing and erasing the racial victims of Nazism; later GDR "Antifa" films would choose the latter alternative. Levy and McCormick go on to show that ex-GDR director Helke Misselwitz both continues and inverts these questions in her 1992 film *Herzsprung*. The plot of this film centers on the doomed attraction between an East German woman and an Afro-German man in post-unification Germany; the film directly addresses issues of racism and skinhead violence that broke out with renewed force after, some would claim, forty years of repression in East Germany. Levy and McCormick argue, however, that Misselwitz's narrative and its filmic portrayal defy simplistic reductions into victim and perpetrator, good and bad. Instead, the dichotomies of power and powerlessness seem to bifurcate each character in the film. Since no single character can become an object of undivided identification or criticism, the film forces the viewer to confront the complexities of real life. Levy and McCormick reason that this is a more subtle and perceptive film, but that it nonetheless demonstrates the extent to which there is a great deal of continuity in the "German question" in the post-war and post-wall periods.

Massimo Locatelli's "Ghosts of Babelsberg" examines a series of *Wendefilme* against the backdrop of the DEFA style and concludes that this style and its preoccupations lived on after the demise of the GDR. He claims that East German film exhibited "an openly word-obsessed cultural discourse" that privileged the authorial enunciation. Thematically, he says, GDR films and their successors were preoccupied with provincial locations as sites of identity construction (the *Heimat* idea refigured for a socialist and post-socialist Germany), the hypostatization of the female body as an emblem of the country itself, and the "Socialist Holy Family" consisting of the Worker, his Wife, and their Child. The continuation of these topoi in post-*Wende* film is evident in the films *Erster Verlust* (1990), *Stilles Land* (1992), *Jana und Jan* (1992), *Abschied von Agnes* (1993), *Neben der Zeit* (1995). *Letztes aus der DaDaR* (1991) is presented as a positive exception to the rule for its confrontation with the GDR chronotopy and invitation to active viewing.

Jenifer Ward looks at Margarethe von Trotta's oeuvre from the perspective of her "Wall Movie," *Das Versprechen* (1995). This tale of two lovers separated by the Berlin Wall, who conceive a son in Prague, "on neither West German nor East German soil," evokes the theory of hybridity. Ward argues that "some of the building blocks of hybridity—borders and complicated identities—have been present in German cultural production in the earlier films of von Trotta since the late 1970s." She reviews von Trotta's frequent use of incomplete identities: pairs of female friends who complement one another, German protagonists who find their own culture lacking and "shop" for characteristics in non-Western cultures. Ward concludes that *Das Versprechen*, while evoking hybridity, cannot embrace it, since "German-German hybridity [. . .] is of no use at the advent of a (re-) unified Germany, which so desperately wants to see itself as a unitary culture finally put together again.

Kristie Foell revisits theories of melodrama and claims that it is the commensurate genre for the portrayal of German division and unification, which is, after all, a family story. She analyzes two post-*Wende* melodramas—*Nikolaikirche* (1995) and *Das Versprechen*—against the background of traditional versus "sophisticated" melodrama. *Nikolaikirche* effectively employs traditional melodramatic ingredients, including easy identifications of characters with preexisting cognitive schema, to present an emotionalized account of the Leipzig Monday demonstrations leading up to the opening of the German border. The film's adherence to traditional melodramatic formulae invites the viewer to identify with the German project of unification as well. In contrast to other critics, Foell finds that *Das Versprechen*, while employing many of the stock ingredients of melodrama and inviting strong personal identification, resists indulging traditional melodrama's formulas of closure. In refusing the traditional melodramatic happy ending (a wedding), the film opens a critical space for reflecting on the grand German "marriage" as well.

Helen Cafferty analyzes Leander Haußmann's recent film *Sonnenallee* (1999), the screenplay for which he wrote with Thomas Brussig, and asks why this light comedy touched such a nerve. Not only was the teenage romance set in 1970s GDR a box-office hit in both East and West; it also inspired a lawsuit against Haußmann under Paragraph 194 of the German penal code on the basis that the film represented an insult to those whose escape attempts at the wall resulted in injury, imprisonment, or death. Cafferty examines how the filmmakers used comic techniques to correct discourses on the GDR past that theorize deformation of GDR citizens or that erase the GDR past altogether. Varying degrees of satire are used, from gentle to mocking, in order to establish sympathy with some characters and critical distance to others. Hard-edged satire is reserved for GDR functionaries while "ordinary" GDR citizens, i.e. those without power within the system, are portrayed sympathetically. The film also demonstrates solidarity with these ordinary citizens by citing aspects of GDR life and culture that would be most recognizable to former East Germans. Cafferty further argues that "the film may have knocked a small chunk out of *die Mauer im Kopf*" precisely by normalizing aspects of the GDR past through the genre of romantic comedy, while reclaiming the legitimacy of personal memories of former East Germans. "The comedy works to obliterate 'otherness' for a West German viewer while preserving the 'difference' that makes visible the memory of lived experience in the GDR." At the same time, Cafferty argues, the film resists simplistic nostalgia for an idealized GDR past by celebrating the end of the GDR system in the opening of the Wall.

In its totality, this anthology reflects the multifarious points of view that comprise the unification experience for both East and West Germans. Its strength lies in its treatment of both print and visual media, its inclusion of both younger and older generations and their respective viewpoints, and its incorporation of both West and East German responses to events that have radically altered the worlds in which all Germans live. Just as unifying Germany is taking place on multiple levels in German society, our anthology provides a forum for the critical voices contributing to the unification process; as such it can serve as a valuable resource for students and scholars of contemporary German literature, film, cultural studies, and intellectual history.

Works Cited

Alter, Reinhard and Peter Monteath, eds. *Rewriting the German Past: History and Identity in the New Germany.* Atlantic Highlands, NJ: Humanities Press, 1997.

Arnold, Heinz Ludwig, ed. *Einigkeit aus Ruinen: eine deutsche Anthologie.* Frankfurt/M: Fischer, 1999.

Brockmann, Stephen. *Literature and German Reunification.* Cambridge: Cambridge UP, 1999.

Bullivant, Keith. *Beyond 1989: Re-Reading German Literature since 1945.* Providence: Berghahn Books, 1997.

---. *The Future of German Literature.* Oxford: Berg, 1994.

Durrani, Osman, Colin Good and Kevin Hilliard, Eds. *The New Germany: Literature and Society after Unification.* Sheffield: Sheffield Academic Press, 1995.

Glaeßner, Gert-Joachim, Ed. *Germany after Unification: Coming to Terms with the Recent Past.* German Monitor 37. Amsterdam: Rodopi, 1996.

Hahn, H. J., Ed. *Germany in the 1990s.* German Monitor 34. Amsterdam: Rodopi, 1995.

Jarausch, Konrad. "Beyond Uniformity: The Challenge of Historicizing the GDR." *Dictatorship as Experience: Towards a Socio-Cultural History of the GDR.* Ed. Jarausch. Trans. Eve Duffy. New York: Berghahn Books, 1999. 3-14.

Lewis, Derek and John R. P. McKenzie, Eds. *The New Germany: Social, Political and Cultural Challenges of Unification.* Exeter: University of Exeter Press, 1995.

Rühmkorf, Peter. "Schreiber, was siehst du?" Arnold. 267-268.

Thierse, Wolfgang. Arnold. 269-271.

Wallace, Ian. "German Intellectuals and Unification." Glaeßner. 87-100.

Welzel, Klaus. *Utopieverlust—die deutsche Einheit im Spiegel ostdeutscher Autoren.* Würzburg: Königshausen & Neumann, 1998.

Authors and Their Worlds

N. ANN RIDER

The Journey Eastward: Helga Schütz' *Vom Glanz der Elbe* and the Mnemonic Politics of German Unification

As the euphoria of 1989 subsided and the realities of economic, political and national unification emerged, images in the German public sphere frequently reproduced old ideological subtexts of the West-East relationship particularly through a patriarchal discourse that providentially legitimated the West.[1] Unification was portrayed as a marriage, and a mismatch at that. The groom was handsome, virile and of good social standing; the bride was homely and without a dowry. This marriage metaphor, popularized in media cartoons as well as public discussion, was a link to other tropes of dominance in public discourse as well. Thus, the image of the East was alternately the stepchild, the poor cousin, and the second-class citizen, but also something akin to the unspoiled native, while the West was portrayed as the teacher, the rich uncle, but also the colonialist aggressor and the patriarch.[2] Unification was indeed characterized in terms of the victor and the vanquished, the colonizer and the colonized.[3] The production of these tropes can well be understood within the matrix of signifying social practices that propelled unification and asserted the power and superiority of West German capital and culture over that of the former GDR.

Helga Schütz' 1995 novel, *Vom Glanz der Elbe*, works on multiple levels to explore the tropes and realities of Western domination after unification. On one level, the novel is an investigation of the patriarchal psychological drama behind the post-*Wende* discourse of hegemony. On another level, the novel probes the public memory that is at the very heart of Western hegemony. Contemporary German memory is revealed as a construction containing crucial absences. The novel is also prescriptive. It posits the possibility of German-German reconciliation through the motif of the journey. To heal Germany's cultural, psychological and literal schizophrenia, to transcend Cold War misunderstanding, Schütz' novel implies, one must be willing to enter a foreign territory, to undertake both a geographical and psychological journey. The very nature of

1 For a more detailed analysis of various aspects of the gendered representation of the two Germanys, see Sharp, "Male Privilege."

2 East Germans are "unworldly: non-materialistic, innocent and naïve" in this scenario, according to Sharp ("Male Privilege" 100).

3 See especially Rosenberg.

unification ensured that East Germans make the journey westward. The focus of Schütz' novel, then, is the journey to the East.

Much historical research has been done that legitimates the implicit claim of Schütz' novel, namely that West German identity as exhibited in 1990 was based on absences in public memory that resulted from Cold War ideology. Jacques Derrida's work suggests that all memory is a presence dependent on an absence. The absences in West German memory resulted from a particular construction of history, the fulcrum of which is the foundational narrative of a *Stunde Null* (Zero Hour). Even into the 1980s, the popular belief that West Germany was without history continued, as exemplified in Michael Stürmer's oft-quoted claim, "in einem geschichtslosen Land die Zukunft gewinnt, wer die Erinnerung füllt, die Begriffe prägt und die Vergangenheit deutet" (36).[4] Few scholars would dispute the claim that the Adenauer era emphasized the needs of democracy for the present and future over the memory of the past. That is not to say that the lapses in German memory have not been continually challenged and critiqued. But the particular memory, or "usable past" as Robert Moeller termed it, of the post-war period cast West Germans not in the role of perpetrators, but as victims and victors.[5] This approach was not unlike the foundational narratives of the GDR, which also posited GDR citizens as *de facto* victims and victors. The difference lies in the enemies and allies: unlike in the East where the enemy was fascism, and thus a historical connection could be drawn, the enemy in the West was communism.[6] We know that the American vision of West Germany as a bulwark against communism meant pushing rapid economic recovery at the expense of denazification. In lieu of real denazification, the United States offered symbolic denazification in the form of democracy.[7] However, unlike the foundational narratives of the GDR, which drew on a lively history of socialist antifascism, West Germany was without what Rudzio called a "historical myth" of its democracy.[8] Thus, in the context of the Cold War, democracy frequently became

4 "in a land without history the future belongs to those who fill memory, shape concepts, and determine the meaning of the past." [Translations are my own.]

5 In his excellent essay on the construction of history in West Germany of the 1950s, "War Stories," Moeller argues that the 1950s images of German soldiers or refugees from the Eastern Front as victims had the effect of masking a past of Germans as perpetrators with a victim's version of history. The resurrection of those images in the 1980s, most notably at the Bitburg cemetery, served much the same purpose. See especially page 1041.

6 To be fair, East German Cold War ideology simplistically equated capitalism with fascism, and thus the West Germans were labeled fascist enemies as well. Much of the East German citizenry, however, overcame the ideology and familiarized themselves with West German culture. A similar reversal took place on only a limited scale in West Germany in the 1960s. The majority of the country maintained its anticommunism and therefore, remained virtually uninterested in the East.

7 Contemporary additions to the discussion on U.S. policy in Germany have come from Carolyn Eisenberg and from Rebecca Boehling, both of whom see the problems of pushing reform almost solely through economic institutions, which ultimately reinforced a conservative, anticommunist agenda.

8 Betz suggests the extent to which West Germany's new, usable history created problems of identity. Of particular interest is his mention of Wolfgang Rudzio (41).

coterminous with the immediate needs of postwar anticommunism; German westernization was hence equated with an anticommunist worldview.[9] The fall of the Berlin wall provided the final legitimation of the latent victors' mentality, which emerged triumphant in1990.

As the philosopher, Agnes Heller, points out, both memory and forgetting are involved in rendering meaning. "Memory also involves forgetting, and thus the decoding of the relation to long-term information, and so memory also constitutes *involvement in rendering meaninglessness*" (*General Ethics* 25). Since West German identity as a Western, liberal democratic country depended so strongly on its anticommunism, it is not surprising that East German conceptions of history were jettisoned altogether after unification.[10] Gone, too, were common German memories of the immediate post-war period, and of Germany's relationship to Eastern Europe prior to 1949.[11] *Vom Glanz der Elbe* is implicitly relevant to this discussion of the politics of public memory for it essentially thematizes the westernization of German mnemonic politics of 1945 and 1990.

I

On the first level of the novel, Schütz was interested in the psychological drama underlying the relationship of the West to the East. The novel begins with a geographical journey. The American professor of physics, Adam Brühl, takes his sabbatical year in Germany, the land of his birth. One of the goals for his sabbatical year is to search for his sister, Anna, whom he left behind 30 years ago in East Germany. Proceeding like the Freudian psychoanalyst, Schütz turns the geographical journey into a psychological one, tapping the psychic structures at the source of current German national identity by unlocking absent memories of the German past.[12] As these memories are restored through the figure of Adam,

---

9 West Germans could adopt post-war anticommunism wholeheartedly since it complemented existing fascist anticommunism according to Boehling (277).

10 I make this claim advisedly, since much historical work has since been done that attempts to reclaim and reassess East German history from a more objective standpoint. However, I would argue that the perspective from which this material was assessed is integrally important to whether this work merely substantiated the West German historical construction, i.e. its inherent anticommunism, or not. See for example some discussions surrounding the application of the term "totalitarianism" to the GDR, which tended to simplistically equate the GDR with the Third Reich (Friedrich). Further, anticommunist logic continues to manipulate the critical assessments of research into the nature of East German antifascism so as to dismiss East German antifascism *in toto*. See Herf, for example, who reduces the polyvalence of fascism to one primary component, namely anti-Semitism, thereby reducing antifascism to a pro-Jewish stance.

11 Kohl's gaff during the unification discussions that the borders with Poland might be in question reminds one that the lack of a material border with Eastern Europe from 1949-1990 resulted in a tangible mental distance of West Germany from its historical neighbors.

12 Applying psychological inquiry by personifying the state is indeed a risky business. On one hand,

the symbolic images of domination that perpetuate the image of the GDR as second-class citizen are exposed by Schütz as psychic images in which a particular identity—a Germany fully integrated into Western ideology—is invested. At the outset Schütz seeks to decenter the site wherein collective memory is constructed. First, the text problematizes the assumption of an essentialized German identity. Adam Brühl is a *Findelkind*, a foundling who was discovered in a carriage in the aftermath of the bombing of Dresden together with a presumed twin sister. The two children were given the name of the prince whose name adorned the famous Dresden landmark where they were found, the Brühl Terrace. Thus, from birth the identity of the main character of the novel is an adopted one, tenuously linked to the places he inhabits and the people who seemingly by accident share with him geographic space. The topos of adoption reveals the artificiality of Adam's current national identity as an American citizen and serves in the novel to symbolize the fortuitous nature of personal identity.

Geographic space, too, becomes a site of contested German identity in the novel. The Germany to which Adam returns in the early 1990s is not the Germany of his birth (Dresden 1945), nor the Germany he fled as a young man (the GDR of the early 1960s). Adam's identity is precariously spread across past and present national boundaries, across ideologies, and across histories. He is like the vast majority of Germans of his generation upon whom historical circumstances have at various times foisted a new citizenship and, hence, national identity. Adam's adopted identities and apparent "homelessness" distance the reader from self-evident definitions of *Heimat* as a national boundary embodying a fixed identity.

The novel, then, aspires to widen the notion of national identity to multiple positionalities while postulating the psychological forces working against such expansion at a time when German collective memory was being ossified by the politics of the *Wende*.[13] This ossification was often justified by the presumed need to defend a unitary national identity.[14] Thus, though Adam's historical identity is

---

Schütz' method partakes of the self-same problematic method which reifies the image of the GDR. Typically, the trend toward applying psychological analysis to unification led to questioning the mental health of GDR citizens in the immediate post-*Wende* period. Sharp has succinctly captured this trend. "As one might expect, West Germany's value system is taken as the norm and assumed to be healthy, and the GDR is pronounced deviant, sick, traumatized in numerous articles and texts. The diagnosis is made easier by the long-standing belief that madness is essentially female and it is only the GDR's mental health which is called into question" ("Male Privilege" 178). Joachim Maaz popularized the psychological portrait of East Germans as traumatized and unable to get in touch with their feelings (*Der Gefühlsstau*). On the other hand, Schütz applies the method in order to question the construction of West German national identity and to overturn the heretofore established clichés about East-West identity.

13 Sheehan defines national identity as issuing from "shared experiences, values and institutions" (31). However, Adelson's understanding of positionality helps us to negotiate the "social and discursive relations" that conjoin in such an identity construct (What is shared? How is it shared?) as well as the "given historical moment" wherein these relations are produced and produce power relations (64).

14 Huyssen argues that any discussion of national identity (let alone attempts to widen that identity) lead to a dead-end in Germany because liberals are unwilling to discuss the notion of nation at all

multiple, his psychological identity is narrowly premised on his identification with Western ideology.[15]

A further consequence of the novel is to remind the reader that just as the bride of the patriarch-dominated marriage is banished from the public realm, so, too, the unification process threatened to summarily remove GDR narratives from German public memory. This delegitimation of the GDR is symbolized by Schütz in the figure of a woman, Anna. Who is Anna? The reader experiences Anna only as Adam's composite image of her, an image that partakes of the gendered ideology of unification and embodies the provincial, second-class characteristics commonly associated with the denigration of the GDR. Adam recalls the first time the two foundlings were reunited as teenagers:

> Adam hatte auf seinen Touren gehofft, daß sie, die Gesuchte, neben seinem wunderbaren Rennrad würde bestehen können. Er mußte mit dem ersten Blick erkennen: sie konnte es nicht. Es war zum Heulen. Zöpfe. Ein Geruch nach Erde und Staub. Eine Trachtenjacke mit aufgestickten Eichenblättern [. . .]. Er ärgerte sich über ihren Husten, das dauernde Gebell ohne Taschentuch [. . .]. Statt ja sagte sie nu, statt nein sagte sie ä oder ä gorne. (30)[16]

Her provincial appearance is outmoded and silly, her demeanor evokes in him disgust rather than sympathy, and even her simplest utterances disturb him. Schütz exaggerates Adam's disappointment through the comparison of the girl to his bicycle, a reaction that already foreshadows the disparities between them. In Adam's memory these disparities are measured in terms of his escalating material advantages (the bike, popular clothing, a home, a medical education, the chance to go West) versus her privation (typically eastern clothing, malfunctioning typewriter, eschewing a career for the early responsibility of motherhood). Thus, his memory of this initial meeting is emblematic of his subsequent image of Anna as a personification of the less successful GDR.

Paramount in Adam's primary memory of Anna is his disgust. Beneath this disgust Schütz portrays Adam as riven with guilt. The basis of this psychological insecurity is a repressed knowledge of the fortuitous nature of his historical fate.

(believing a postmodern Germany to be beyond that). Conservatives "take nation and national unity for granted," and both leave hegemony over the definition of the term to the "rabid nationalist" discourse of the right wing (74-78).

15 It is important to note that though Adam might be labeled an East German, his self-understanding has jettisoned that label and memory. As a chiffre for Western influence, Adam's character represents the Germany that moved from post-war unity through the upheaval of division to the ideological turn westward. Viewed in this way, the fact that he left the East in the 1960s, and not in the 1940s or 1950s becomes insignificant.

16 "Adam had hoped that she, the one he sought, would measure up against his wonderful racing bike. He knew at first glance that she could not. It was awful. Pigtails. A smell like dirt and dust. A knitted jacket with oak leaves stitched into it [. . .]. He was bothered by her coughing, the constant barking, always without a handkerchief [. . .]. Instead of 'ja' she said 'nu,' instead of 'nein' she said 'ä' or 'ä gorne.'"

There were two abandoned children in the carriage: she ended up in an orphanage, while he was placed with the family of a well-respected scientist. The unconscious but emotionally present bond of their sibling relationship pierces the dualism of his worldview, by the undeniable intertwining of their origins, and by his subconscious fear that her fate might well have been his.

Their fates were not left to chance, however. While Schütz' text seeks to reveal the misnomers of patriarchal discourse, it does not overlook the gendered structures of German society that have relegated women throughout history to a sphere in which their public opportunities were limited. Schütz adds a sociohistorical dimension to Adam's memory by invoking famous brother/sister hierarchical pairs of German cultural history: Johann and Cornelia von Goethe, Heinrich and Ulrike von Kleist, the Mozart and Nietzsche siblings (210).[17] The relationship to his sister recounted in Adam's memory reverberates with that of Goethe to his sister Cornelia. Like the revered German poet, who insisted that his sister Cornelia write her letters to him in such a way that he might correct them, Adam corrected Anna's letters written to him in English when he took up residence in the United States and returned them to her. Like Cornelia, who was hardly allowed to leave the home and who only vicariously experienced travel through her brother, so, too, was Anna left behind when her brother was allowed special dispensation to travel to Heidelberg, a trip from which he never returned. In this historical pair, the brother's relationship to the sister is frequently characterized by his subconscious guilt for the privilege that his gender has accorded him in society and a concomitant sense of responsibility toward his sister, which Goethe assuaged through attempts to remake her so that she would be pleasing to other men.[18] Such attempts, however, created a conflict for Goethe and Cornelia, for in pleasing her brother and assuming her female role in society, Cornelia could never be viewed by her brother as an equal.[19] Adam's relationship to Anna takes on similar, though not identical, characteristics. In Adam's memory, he recalls Anna as his victim. "Er brauchte das Mädchen als Gesellschafterin für den Alten, und dazu hatte er es so gefädelt, daß sie es als Gunst verstehen mußte. Sie verstand es als Gunst" (33).[20] Thus, Schütz creates a relationship marked by

---

17 The rediscovery of the sisters of famous German men began in earnest in the 1980s, following studies of the women active in the Jena Romantic Circle. In the GDR, the scholar Sigrid Damm published *Cornelia Goethe*. The seminal Western study, *Schwester berühmter Männer* (ed. Luise Pusch), contains biographical portraits of twelve women (not all German).

18 It is frequently cited that Goethe attempted to create Cornelia as his own "Werck" by proscribing her daily activities, including her reading and writing, in his absence. In a letter to her he wrote, "wirst du nun dieses alles, nach meiner Vorschrift, gethan haben [. . .] du sollst in einem kleinen Jahre das vernünftigste, artigste, angenehmste, liebenswürdigste Mädgen, [. . .]. Ist das nicht ein herrliches Versprechen!" (Damm 75). ("If you have done all this according to my instructions, within one year you will become the most reasonable, charming, agreeable and loveable girl [. . .]. Is that not a splendid promise!").

19 Prokop comes to a similar conclusion (105).

20 "He needed the girl as a companion for the old man, and he had arranged it in such a way that she would have to see it as benevolence. She did see it as benevolence."

political and sexual metanarratives and by subconscious drives to control otherness. The resurfacing of these memories provokes guilt in Adam for his former behavior; however, his guilt does not change his relationship to her as one of benevolence to a lesser other, for he still presumes he is searching for a needy East German sister.

It is significant for our purposes that Schütz shifts the patriarchal metaphor from a marriage to a sibling relationship. The marriage relationship assumes that wife and husband do not necessarily share a common parentage or history. The metaphor as applied to German unification requires the bride to abandon, even renounce, her past and embrace that of her husband. As Ingrid Sharp has correctly noted, the image of the marriage:

> sets the tone for the relationship, normalizing the kind of inequality between the states which is taken for granted in an old-fashioned marriage: as well as taking on the name, value system and allegiances of her new partner, the GDR is expected to develop those feminine virtues suitable for a wife, patience, compliance and gratitude, while West Germany displays the male characteristics of leadership, rationality and arrogance ("To the Victor"175).

While I wish to argue that Adam's memory of his sister is in collusion with the gendered personification of the state described here by Sharp, Schütz' jettisoning of the marriage image offers both the possibility of exploring the gendered social structures of unification and imagining unification beyond patriarchal assumptions.[21] In the sibling relationship, Schütz finds a metaphor that more closely reflects the structure of the German past: Germany as separated twins, raised apart under different socioeconomic and ideological circumstances. The gendered personification of both states as siblings also allows a psychological analysis that legitimates differences rather than creating a hierarchy of values. Thus, Schütz can explore both the effects of hierarchical thinking while also illuminating the ways in which that hierarchy is manufactured, suggesting it might be overcome.

I have suggested that the reemergence of Adam's memories of his sister exposes a subconscious guilt: guilt for his privilege, yet also guilt for the disdain he felt toward the figure of the other. True to the Freudian psychoanalytical method, Schütz adds a further level to Adam's guilt, that of sexual tension and incestuous longing for his sister.[22] Involuntary memory forces Adam to re-experience the ambivalence of his relationship to Anna, namely the sexual tension. Adam's exploration of the sexual tension and its repression in his relationship to

---

21 The sibling relationship in modern Western European culture, while psychologically charged and not necessarily equal, is not immediately a social (or economic) relationship in which the brother has control over the sister, as is the case in a marriage relationship. Thus, a possibility at least exists for this relationship to proceed from a position of equality.

22 Again, the parallel is made with the psychological relationship of Goethe and his sister (Eissler, especially 45-46).

his sister is paramount to this novel.[23] As the object of his desire, he sought to control her; since he could not actualize his sexual desires, he pushed her away, and ultimately fled. The insoluble dilemma of the sibling relationship is expressed by Kleist in a letter to his sister Ulrike: “Wärst Du ein Mann oder nicht meine Schwester, ich würde stolz sein, das Schicksal meines ganzen Lebens an das Deinige zu knüpfen” (Pusch 237).[24] Adam’s benevolent desire at this late date to find and perhaps help his presumably needy East German sister is unveiled as an impossible drive for reunification with the object of his desire. “Pflicht, Verantwortung—vorauseilendes Mitleid. Er wollte nun endlich auf die Suche nach seinen Angehörigen gehen” (Schütz 198).[25] That drive is ultimately an egotistical one of *self*-reunification.

The psychological profiles depicted in the novel parallel the historical relationship of West Germany to East Germany produced by the Cold War. Since the end of World War II the self-identity of each German state was based to a large degree on the very “otherness” of the other German state. The competing national identities of the Federal and Democratic Republics of Germany thusly were built upon intractable dualism; each claimed its validity as the righteous protectorate of German tradition and culture, and of the contemporary world order; each saw the other unsympathetically as its diametric opposite. These national identities and their political relationship to one another solidified in their legitimatory discourses. In the case of West Germany, its identity was based not only on East Germany’s “otherness,” but also on the necessity of what was dubbed “*re*-unification.” Even the Basic Treaty engineered by Willi Brandt’s *Ostpolitik* allowed West Germany to maintain its self-described constitutional prerogative over East German citizens through the wording “Two German states in one German nation.” For West Germans, then, unification embodied a psychological ego celebration of wholeness, played out in the reuniting of families and the portended return of West Germany’s rightful geographic property.

The novel suggests that movement beyond this psychology of ego-unification requires a journey in which difference is confronted. Schütz thematizes this problematic in the portrayal of the East Germans Adam meets in the community of Steinstücken where he spends his sabbatical year.[26] For example, Amely, a

23 Readers of Schütz’ earlier novel, *In Annas Namen* (1987), will be intrigued by coincidences between the characters in that novel and here. The biographies of the two Annas coincide, yet the information the first Anna gives about her brother does not coincide with the Adam of *Vom Glanz der Elbe*. Schütz even deliberately makes references to the other Anna (see page 42). One could posit several theories about the discrepancies, most of which would revolve around the problematic nature of telling about someone else’s life.

24 “If only you were a man or not my sister, I would be proud to link the fate of my entire life to yours.”

25 “Duty, responsibility—anticipatory sympathy. He wanted to finally get started with the search for his own kind.”

26 Steinstücken is a significant site for the Cold War period, since this Zehlendorf suburb, though historically part of Potsdam, was part of Western territory. It was virtually cut off from West Berlin when the wall was built, requiring its 200 inhabitants to cross GDR territory to reach West Berlin.

cleaning woman, is Adam's first encounter with the East. This character functions on several levels as a model of the relationship of the West to the East. The young, Western artist for whom Amely cleans wants to portray her in a chapter of his novel: *Amely in Men's Clothing* (108). The cross-dressing motif describes both the desire to recreate Amely as a man, and also to recreate the Easterner as Westerner. Amely indeed acts out the fantasy for herself. However, the literary project fails when Amely's East German memories do not coincide with Western cultural memory. Her character should find a sled, the self-same sled of *Citizen Kane* fame.[27] But the Easterner Amely has never heard of *Citizen Kane*, and Amely has sled memories of her own. They are memories of war, of hunger, of wartime justice and a miserable sled she calls a *Käsehitsche*. Since war, cold, hunger and the quaint provincialism of GDR historical memory do not fit the artist's image; the project fails (123). Thus, *Vom Glanz der Elbe* thematizes the resistance of GDR recollections to Western cultural dictates.

The prescription merely to confront difference has its limitations, however. There is the propensity of the character of Adam to engage the East primarily on the level of psychosexual drives. For example, in addition to the functions of Amely's character already described, she acts as well on the psychoanalytic level where Adam's relationship with the other is primarily sexual. He enjoys Amely's sexual company fleetingly as part of his new adventure. But he becomes annoyed when it appears she might demand more of his time and space, suggesting Adam's unwillingness to engage her beyond a superficial level (220).[28] Adam turns his attention to another East German woman who fulfills his sexual and psychological needs in a different way: he believes she looks just like Anna (202).[29] Thus, his relationship with the East, though productive in confronting difference, is still limited by its determination through psychosexual drives. An authentic reconciliation, born of mutual recognition, requires more.

The character of Amely also points the reader to another level of the novel by revealing Adam's past. Adam knows what a *Käsehitsche* is. This common vocabulary establishes the mnemonic link to Adam's German identity that predates his move westward. But the significance of these memories only slowly becomes apparent to him. Adam's sojourn in Germany begins like the Parzivalian

---

In a 1971 territory exchange, a thoroughfare allowed the area's integration into West Berlin.

27 Of course, the movie *Citizen Kane* is also significant in this regard both as a quintessentially American, hence Western, movie and as the story of brutish capital's rise to power in the United States.

28 To be fair, Amely admits to herself that she is not in love with Adam. Therefore, their separation is mutual, and Amely should not be viewed as a victim.

29 Again, readers of *In Annas Namen* will be intrigued, for the title character does indeed give birth to a daughter, though the chronology here does not quite fit. However, it is her likeness to Anna that is paramount here. The character does bring Adam closer to Anna's world, namely her professional world of GDR film. Not coincidentally, it is also where the author Schütz is at home, having produced several documentary films for DEFA.

quest, which at first is no quest at all, only chance meetings and happenings.[30] Their significance is not apparent until Adam is willing to embrace the absences in his personal history, that is, to undergo self-reflection and self-critique.

II

The novel thereby thematizes the structure of contemporary German public memory. It suggests that this mnemonic structure, based as it is on significant absences, occasions a stagnant understanding of history, which is both self-deluding and precludes an East-West reconciliation. The next leg of Adam's journey precipitates a correction to that understanding.

The experience of history is physical. Repressing the memory of that experience brings physical manifestations as well. Adam's attempt to repress memory originally took the form of flight. The United States functions on one level of the novel as Adam's refuge from history. Schütz carefully constructed this image of the United States as a "verwandlungssüchtige Welt" (40), a world addicted to change where the past is nowhere noticeable. Americanization is understood at this level as a move into the post-modern, *post-histoire* future. Thus, the *Geschichtslosigkeit*, or lack of history, that Stürmer ascribed to West Germany takes on multiple meanings here, for Americanization is not only a sign of Germany's westernization, it is also a convenient means by which to escape the responsibility of historical reflection. Adam's earlier self-reproach makes clear the active renunciation of that responsibility: "Einen Knaben, der sich selbst so vor ein Gericht stellt, wollte Adam nicht kennen. Ich bin es nicht. Vorläufig kein Erinnern. Haben als hätten wir nicht" (73).[31] The final line, "Haben als hätten wir nicht," recurs throughout the novel like a mantra for Adam's drive to create an identity without history.

The United States further functions on this level as the origin of a particular Western identity construction based in anticommunism. The fictive Adam at first returns to a unified Germany the emissary of a Western ideology issuing

30 This is underscored by the fact that Adam's life in Steinstücken is not structured around the search for his sister at all; in fact, at times he seems rather helpless in this regard for he has not even bothered to look in the phone book. His sister lives in Potsdam and his nephew but not a few subway stops away. Since Adam's profession as a scientist would preclude his ineptitude in doing research, a psychological reason for his inability to "progress" in his search makes the only logical sense.

31 "Adam was not interested in any boy who subjected himself to self-criticism. It's not me. For the time being, no remembering. Have as if we had not." The leitmotif of the Parzivalian quest figures here, too. The recognition of the suffering of others is a prerequisite for the recognition of and empathy for the "other." In the novel, Adam's inability to recognize the "suffering" of his foster father (he suppresses a translation of the Russian term *stradanije* or "suffering") forebodes both his personal fallacy as well as his stance toward his foster father's rejection of a fixed progression of time (85-87). The significance of his understanding of time will be addressed later.

ultimately from the United States, the lone surviving super-power whose culture so radically influenced Western Germany after 1949. Adam's American consciousness of history is one of "historical past" (Heller 44) that is, a socio-cultural understanding which suppresses his personal linkages with that history.[32] The ascription of meaning and values to that history comes from the ideology of the Cold War. The novel illustrates this point by recounting a previous trip to Dresden in which Adam repressed his memories of Dresden as his home and divested himself of all identity with his past and the GDR (39-40). Shorn from this memory, too, are the identification of the United States as the coconspirator in the bombing of Dresden, the significance of Adam's birth during the Third Reich and his youth in the GDR. He experiences Dresden only through the sanitized public memory of the Cold War: the gray atmosphere, the decay, the blandness of new socialist construction.

A leitmotif throughout the novel is the equation of Adam's public memory with a particular kind of science, which is identified through the structure of crystals: orderly, symmetrical and homogeneous. Such a structure echoes the Cold War construction of history. The Cold War understanding of history bears the markings of the "social rationalization" process—the attempt to order and regulate the chaos of modern societies—of the late 20th century.[33] Adam's East German foster father, portrayed in the novel as the discoverer of the structure of crystal, became a victim of the symmetrical thinking of the Cold War in East Germany as well. When he discovered that his scientific work would be used against his will to support the Soviet military build up of the late 1950s, he stood fast (79). Later he prophesied the coming age of containment (*Einmauerung*) of the GDR and was quietly divested of power. He then organized Adam's escape to the West. But rather than save Adam from the Eastern manifestations of Cold War ideology, Western ideology merely fashioned a new symmetrical thinking for Adam.

Schütz deftly weaves further strands of the scientific leitmotif throughout the text; prior to his sabbatical trip Adam had sent ahead an envelope containing the theory generated by his scientific research to the organizers of a world climate conference in Berlin. In it he claims that the last Ice Age will soon make its final appearance and cover the European continent (233). This is indeed a curious claim, and it seems completely out of place for Adam's character. It makes sense,

32 Unlike other German emigrants Adam meets in the US, he does not mourn for his passport. He eventually takes on the opinion of his American wife, namely that it is better to leave the past behind (42).

33 Atina Grossmann defined the use of the term "rationalization" by social historians of Germany as "organized efforts—by the state, by business, by social, political, and labor movements—to order and regulate the chaos of modern societies, to govern behavior and structure social relations, and hence the effects of industrialization and urbanization" (14). She argues that rationalization efforts in the United States were not limited to external discipline, but also strove toward internalization of the mores which would occasion "good" behavior. I would argue that historical understanding could indeed figure into this social rationalization process, wherein a complicated, contradictory history would be viewed as inefficient, and therefore, irrational and useless.

however, as the logical conclusion of a symmetrical, homogeneous understanding of history; the crystalline structure of ice represents stasis, time frozen.[34]

The past for Adam, who has imbibed American culture these thirty years, is likewise saturated with the specter of death as he begins his journey. A dime-store novel Adam purchases before his flight to Germany sets the historical stage: "Die Geschichte erzählte von den Toten Berlins. [. . .] Die Toten lebten in Jahres- und Tageszeiten und hatten ihre Häuser, Quartiere und Geschäftigkeiten. Die Toten lebten?" (6).[35] The dead are forgotten, are an absent memory from a past that has been marginalized by the politics of the present. Because Adam has repressed his past, and thereby lost touch with his sister, he forebodes that she must have died in his absence. The novel again provides a symbol of Western ethnocentrism; the preclusion of the existence of the other beyond the consciousness of Western perception. However, the brush with European history that the dime-store novel imparts to Adam is the first suggestion of viewing history not as dead, but as living; hence his question, "The dead lived?" The notion of a living past sets the narrative stage for the novel's denouement, that is, Adam's quest to reclaim his past.

III

The denouement unfolds from Schütz' invocation of another traveler and American witness to the past, Kurt Vonnegut's Billy Pilgrim from *Slaughterhouse Five*. Just as Schütz widens the notion of identity to include multiple positionalities, so too she posits a multivalent understanding of time by juxtaposing Adam's theory of orderly structure with thermo-dynamic time in which "das Chaos wächst," chaos grows (146). The American Pilgrim—with his manner of becoming "unstuck" in time and his intense reexperiencing of moments of the past—becomes an intertextual model for Adam's rediscovery of his absent memories. Pilgrim's experience of Tralfamadorian time, that all moments are permanent and exist simultaneously in another moment, is superimposed on the novel's historical understanding and juxtaposed to Adam's earlier paradigm of monological time. The more Adam confronts the past–his past–the more his static notion of time and identity, like the end of the Ice Age, literally melt. His wife sends a newspaper clipping reporting that a large piece of ice had broken from the Arctic glacier, which suggests that Adam's theory about the coming Ice Age is

34 A nod to Kurt Vonnegut cannot be overlooked here, for it is Ice Nine that freezes the oceans and causes the end of the world in *Cat's Cradle*. The arms race, which was a direct result of Cold War thinking, indeed brought the world to that brink. The influence of Vonnegut's work will be discussed further.

35 "The story told of the dead of Berlin. [. . .] The dead lived in the spans of years and days and had their houses, their quarters, their concerns. The dead lived?"

wrong (231). When the news reaches him, he is beyond caring, for his own understanding of time and history is in flux.[36] It is at this point that Adam's return to Dresden sets memory in motion. The figure of Adam, thus, accepts the challenge to the West implicit in Eastern culture, and in so doing, embarks on a journey of historical self-reflection.

For Schütz, obtaining access to moments absent in memory requires recognition of the physical nature of historical experience. Typically in Schütz' work physical geography—notably, architecture and landscape—becomes the medium through which the physical body engages history. Place stimulates the sense perception which, in a Proustian manner, activates involuntary memory. Such memory, speaking with Proust, is stripped of the manipulations of the conscious mind and "guarantee[s] the truth of the past" (Proust 205).[37] The special quality of involuntary memory is both its dependence on the re-experiencing of a lost memory and its ability to situate the "truth of the past" outside of monological time. Now returning to Dresden for the second time, Adam revisits the places of his childhood, the Brühl Terrace which protected the infants and which now stands as witness to history. Its secrets, however, are not immediately apparent and remain locked in memory: "Die Steine reden nicht mehr von der Hölle, sie reden ganz allgemein vom Zeitvergehen" (239).[38] Rather it is the smells of the Brühl Terrace which activate Adam's involuntary sense memory: "Echtes Zeugnis, das persönlichste Angebinde war dieser Grottengeruch. Ein Lockduft des Mutterschoßes" (240).[39] Involuntary sense memory brings Adam outside of monological history to the site where events exist simultaneously. Symbolically, this memory brings Adam to his home in the novel; not a unified romantic notion

---

36 Numerous encounters set this process in motion, which cannot all be recounted here. However, the appearance of his friend Andrew, an historian, plants the first seed of historical reevaluation. Andrew is an authentic German-American mix: he is part Prussian and part Native American. His interest in the historical figure Otto the Great becomes a leitmotif of the overlapping of past and present. He further represents an understanding of historical time that extends far beyond the recent German past.

37 Proust describes this phenomenon in *The Past Recaptured*: "But it was precisely the fortuitous, unavoidable way in which I had come upon the sensation that guaranteed the truth of a past which that sensation revived and of the mental images it released. [. . .] That sensation is the guarantee of the truth of the entire picture composed of contemporary impressions which the sensation brings in its train, with that unerring proportion of light and shadow, emphasis and omission, remembrance and oblivion, which conscious memory and observation will never know" (205-206).

38 "The stones no longer speak of that inferno, they speak more generally of the passing of time." Adam takes a tour of the landmark, and other members of the group speculate as to whether the stones of the terrace could have withstood the firestorm enough to offer protection. Adam keeps to himself his own testament to the walls of the terrace. Also hidden from the tourists are the chambers where bodies were never recovered, or were burned in a mass grave. Vonnegut describes such a scene as well. Thus, the history to which the terrace bears witness is not immediately visible, and can only be revealed through memory.

39 "This grotto smell was genuine proof, the most personal gift. The tempting fragrance of the mother's womb."

of *Heimat*, but reunion with a memory site that is the most personal and also forms a link with German historical experience.

Involuntary sense memory functions in the novel to posit a place outside of monological history where multiple and even contradictory images can coexist as German history. The notion that history is multifarious and often contradictory is a leitmotif throughout the novel. For example, Adam's sabbatical year in Steinstücken is spent in the literal no-man's land between East and West, among the people who lived the division of Germany daily. This geographical space becomes the site of possible mutual recognition as characters from both the East and West, from Germany's past and present, coexist and cross Adam's path.

Potsdam itself, the former "second capital" of Prussia and now *Landeshauptstadt* of Brandenburg, provides a variegated historical landscape in which "court history" and the peasant history written by GDR historians coexist in the architectural remnants.[40] No less significant for understanding the novel is the city of Adam's birth, Dresden. This former "Florence of the Elbe" now reproduces in its skyline the fractured German memory. Despite the vestiges of its regal past (the Zwinger and Semper Oper), new modern buildings mark the sites of its scars. Here, more than anywhere else in unified Germany, the solid lines of historical ideology are blurred, for hero and enemy, victim and perpetrator are not easily distinguished in Dresden history. The river Elbe itself becomes a protagonist, impartially reflecting the diversity of the German historical landscape.[41] These landscapes are the tactile link to German history, disinterested witnesses testifying to the multicolored fabric of the German past. Thus, Adam's journey reveals his forgotten memories, but also exposes him to a new conceptualization of history, one that might allow for the side-by-side existence of difference and historical contradiction.

The motif of the journey raises the question of mutual recognition. Why does Schütz focus solely on the recognition of the East by the West if mutual recognition is the prerequisite for reconciliation? Let us turn to the post-*Wende* conversation between Christa Wolf and Jürgen Habermas published in Wolf's *Auf dem Weg nach Taboo* (1994). Even the left, liberal intellectual Habermas is clearly marked by a Western bias. Though he admitted to knowing little about the

---

40 A visitor to Sanssouci or the Neue Palais during the GDR period, for example, would have been struck by the contrast between the typical court history of the Prussian monarchy and the GDR emphasis on the peasants and artisans whose talents and hard work made such splendors possible. However, this history, too, was marginalized in the post-*Wende* historical context.

41 The Elbe was a recurrent theme in GDR literature in which the problematic of articulating the landscape of memory and the horrors of the Dresden bombing are played out. Schütz' novel might well be read as part of the intertextual dialog between Heinz Czechowski, Karl Mickel and Volker Braun about this problematic of articulating history in the Elbe landscape. Volker Braun's lines "Nun ist die Wüste bewässert, aber Sachsen liegt öde. / Eine Zeile nur gießt (diese) noch Glanz auf die Flur!" ("Now the desert is irrigated but Saxony lies dry/ Only one line waters the splendor in the hall") echo in the novel's title, *Vom Glanz der Elbe* (Braun, "Berlinische Epigramme" in *Langsamer kirschender Morgen*). See Berendse.

East, he seemed to view this as an unproblematic difference. The degree to which the exclusionary nature of West German culture made knowledge of the East useless, and therefore unworthy of pursuit, seems to have escaped Habermas. Wolf labeled this disposition a "Verengung" ("narrowness"), particularly when juxtaposed to the East, where access to Western thought was of course partially limited, but nonetheless sought after and more readily available than Eastern thought was available in the West (152). Thus, even those with a critical disposition toward the Federal Republic seemed in need of self-reflection. The self-critique that East Germans had been forced to undertake was evident. Schütz' novel suggests that West Germans, too, needed to have the humility to undertake their own self-critique for there to be the possibility of reconciliation.

It is significant, then, that Anna remains throughout only a constructed image in the text; the reader never meets her.[42] Reports about Anna place her in Hollywood in her capacity as a film archivist where she is collaborating with a female American director on a film about the East. Thus, Anna, for her part, has undertaken a journey westward. And, unlike Adam, she has chosen a place in United States culture in which historical memory is least compromised, namely documentary film. She is portrayed as literally a keeper of the memory of the past, of the history of the East. This information about Anna not only dissipates the image constructed by Adam, it gives a fleeting view of the self-confident, productive East German woman.[43]

Though mutual recognition is the prescription for reconciliation of the novel, the novel is not about Anna. It is about Adam's journey, about the necessity of dismantling the fixed image of the East constructed in Western identity. As long as Adam remained caught in the gendered economy of post-war ideology, as long as he denied historical memory, he needed Anna/the East to define himself. The journey, which Adam finally undertakes, to his credit, allows the possibility for transcending the fixed identities he created for himself and for Anna by reclaiming personal and historical memories.

---

42 A former landlord and part-time painter remarks that Anna moved out as soon as he had completed a portrait of her, "Tatsächlich, als hätte sie mit dem Bild nicht unter einem Dach leben wollen" (275) [Really, as if she did not want to live under the same roof as that picture.], suggesting further the problematic nature of attempting to construct an image of Anna. Schütz dealt with this issue in a quite different way in *In Annas Namen*. There, the narrative voice contemplates the act of literary creation. The fictitious Anna, whose past is interwoven with the memories of the narrator, is a repository for a particular zeitgeist, the GDR of the 1980s. The narrator is conscious of the enticement of overlapping the real and the fictional world it has created, but is content with the act of creation itself: "Am Ende aber freut mich mein schöner, mein listiger Aufenthalt, mein sonnenbeschienenes, wortreiches Versteck" (*In Annas Namen* 11) [But in the end I like my beautiful, my cunning sojourn, my sun-drenched, word-rich hiding place.].

43 Simone Shoemaker's film, *My Second Life*, and the collection of interviews, *The Wall in My Backyard*, both present the diversity among East German women and problematize a monolithic understanding of women post-*Wende*.

IV

In contrast to Schütz' ideal of a non-contemporaneous history, contemporary German national history is portrayed through the figure of Adam as a bi-polar construct of homogeneous memories isolated from a multivalent history filled with contradictions and seemingly irreconcilable oppositions.[44] The history of Germany, Schütz suggests, cannot be understood by choosing one version and rejecting another (as in the world view of the Cold War), nor even through accommodation (the liberal standpoint of Brandtian *Ostpolitik*). Rather the novel demands the dignity of difference. A leitmotif from Vonnegut's novel *Slaugther House Five* echoes throughout the novel's conclusion: "I suppose they will all want dignity" (184), and in fact, this is precisely what is demanded in the novel. Schütz is not interested in defining East Germans, but in allowing them the dignity to define themselves. Furthermore, the novel suggests that the construction of identity in the post-war period left a wall in the German psyche that precluded an ability to humbly embark on self-reflection and self-critique. Schütz' concept of history brings the reader to the end of the Cold War dualism, to the end of the gendered symbolization of the West/East relatioship, and posits a space in which the tolerance of an undecidable, multifarious and contradictory history actually heralds reconciliation: the ability to embrace German differences, to accept the contradictions of the past and to construct a national identity with multiple positionalities. In the final scene of the novel, Adam is picking mushrooms with Anna's son, Rainer.[45] In a gesture that bespeaks surrendering oneself to the flow of history as it moves into the future, Adam instinctively moves toward Rainer, that is eastward. It is a hopeful image, but not without its tension. The possibility of German reconciliation is no less fraught with ambiguities than the German past, and for Helga Schütz, that is as it should be.

Works Cited

Adelson, Leslie A. "Torkan's *Tufan: Brief an einen islamischen Bruder.* Inscriptions and Positionalities: Some Particulars." Adelson. *Making Bodies, Making History. Feminism and German Identity.* Lincoln: U of Nebraska P, 1993. 57-86.

Alter, Reinhard & Peter Monteath, eds. *Rewriting the German Past. History and Identity in the New Germany.* Atlantic Highlands: Humanities Press, 1997.

---

44 Concerning the West German museum debates Maier argues, "Part of the German debate has been a dispute over whether there can even be a coherent museum, that is whether a unified visible presentation of a problematic history is possible at all" (123).

45 Mushroom picking functions as a leitmotif both for the East German character (Amely picks mushrooms) and for Adam's search for an organic attachment to his past.

Alter, Reinhard. "Cultural Modernity and Political Identity: From the Historians' Dispute to the Literature Dispute." Alter and Monteath. 152-74.
Berendse, Gerrit-Jan. "Zu neuen Ufern: Lyrik der 'Sächsische Dichterschule' im Spiegel der Elbe." *Studies in GDR Culture and Society 10* (Lanham: U of America P, 1991): 197-211.
Betz, Hans-Georg. "Perplexed Normalcy: German Identity after Unification." Alter and Monteath. 40-64.
Boa, Elizabeth and Janet Wharton. *Women and the Wende. Social and Cultural Reflections of the German Unification Process.* Amsterdam: Rodopi, 1994.
Boehling, Rebecca. *A Question of Priorities. Democratic Reform and Economic Recovery in Postwar Germany.* Providence: Berghahn, 1996.
Damm, Sigrid. *Cornelia Goethe.* Berlin/Weimar: Aufbau, 1987.
Eisenberg, Carolyn. *Drawing the Line. The American Decision to Divide Germany, 1944-1949.* Cambridge: Cambridge UP, 1996.
Eissler, K. R. *Goethe. As Psycholanalytic Study, 1775-1786.* Vol. I. Detroit: Wayne State UP,1963.
Friedrich, Wolfgang-Uwe, ed. *Totalitäre Herrschaft--totalitäres Erbe.* Special issue of *German Studies Review* (Fall 1994).
Fulbrook, Mary. "Reckoning with the Past: Heroes, Victims, and Villains in the History of the German Democratic Republic." In *Rewriting the German Past.* 174-96.
Grossmann, Atina. "Remarks on Current Trends and Direction in German Women's History." *Women in German Yearbook 12* (Lincoln: U of Nebraska P, 1996): 11-25.
Heller, Agnes. *A Theory of History.* London/Boston: Routledge & Kagan Paul, 1982.
---. *General Ethics.* Oxford: Basil Blackwell, 1988.
Herf, Jeffrey. *Divided Memory. The Nazi Past in the Two Germanies.* Cambridge: Harvard UP, 1997.
Huyssen, Andreas. *Twilight Memories. Marking Time in a Culture of Amnesia.* New York: Routledge, 1995.
Maaz, Joachim. *Der Gefühlsstau.* Berlin: Argon, 1991.
Maier, Charles S. *The Unmasterable Past. History, Holocaust, and German National Identity.* Cambridge: Harvard UP, 1988.
Moeller, Robert G. "War Stories: The Search for a Usable Past in the Federal Republic of Germany." *American Historical Review* 101 (1996) 4: 1008-1048.
Pape, Walter. "Cultural Change and Cultural Memory: The Principle of Hope in the Times of German Unification." *1870/71-1989/90: German Unifications and the Change of Literary Discourse.* Ed. Pape. Berlin: de Gruyter, 1993. 1-21.
Prokop, Ulrike. "Cornelia Goethe: Die Melancholie der Cornelia Goethe." Pusch. 49-121.
Proust, Marcel. *The Past Recaptured.* Trans. F. Blossom. New York: Random House, 1932.
Pusch, Luise, ed. *Schwestern berühmter Männer. Zwölf biographische Portraits.* Frankfurt aM: Insel, 1985.
Rosenberg, Dorothy. "The Colonization of East Germany." *Monthy Review* (September 1991): 14-33.
Schütz, Helga. *Vom Glanz der Elbe.* Berlin: Aufbau, 1995.
---. *In Annas Namen.* Berlin: Aufbau, 1986.
Sharp, Ingrid. "Male Privilege and Female Virtue: Gendered Representations of the Two Germanies." New German Studies 18.1/2 (1994): 87-106.

---. "To the Victor the Spoils: Sleeping Beauty's Sexual Awakening." Boa and Wharton. 177-88.

Sheehan, James. "National History and National Identity in the New Germany." In *1870/71-1989/90: German Unifications and the Change of Literary Discourse.* 25-36.

Stürmer, Michael. "Geschichte in einem geschichtslosem Land." *Historikerstreit.* München:Piper, 1987. 36-38.

Vonnegut, Kurt. *Slaughterhouse Five or the Children's Crusade. A Duty-Dance with Death.* New York: Delacorte Press, 1969.

Wolf, Christa. "Vom Gepäck deutscher Geschichte–Briefwechsel mit Jürgen Habermas." In *Auf dem Weg nach Tabou. Texte 1990-1994.* Köln: Kiepenheuer & Witsch, 1994. 140-155.

STUART TABENER[1]

"ob es sich bei diesem Experiment um eine gescheiterte Utopie oder um ein Verbrechen gehandelt hat"[2]: Enlightenment, Utopia, the GDR and National Socialism in Monika Maron's Work From *Flugasche* to *Pawels Briefe*

The centrality of the theme of biography to Monika Maron's fiction is axiomatic. Nor should this be surprising given the extraordinary degree to which the author's own history intersects with the traumas of the German past. Maron is a quarter Jewish—her grandfather was murdered by the Nazis—and part of the "progeny" of the GDR, having been raised as the stepdaughter of the SED member and sometime Minister of the Interior, Karl Maron. She was an uncompromising, perhaps even inflexible critic of East German politics and society, and—shortly before the *Wende*—a writer-in-exile following her move to Hamburg in 1988. The theme of gender also plays a marked role in Maron's writing as a meditation upon the relationship between power, patriarchy and the oppression of women in a state outwardly committed to full equality. Finally, her trivial involvement with the East German security services between 1976 and 1978 made her vulnerable to accusations of selective amnesia during the round of exposures of writers' *Stasi* activities that followed unification.

In the decade since the demise of the GDR, Maron has emerged as a scathing opponent of those who defend it even after its demise:

> Über die DDR herrschte eine unkontrollierte Geheimpolizei; die DDR betrieb die Militarisierung des Staates bis in die Schulen und Kindergärten, in der DDR wurden Bücher, wenn nicht verbrannt, so doch verboten; nicht die Bundesrepublik war eine Diktatur, sondern die DDR. ("Das neue Elend" 87)[3]

---

1 I am grateful to the Alexander von Humboldt-Stiftung for assistance during a year of research at the University of Konstanz when this essay was written.

2 "The question of whether, when talking about the experiment that was GDR, we're talking about a failed utopia or a crime." All translations are my own.

3 "The GDR was controlled by an unaccountable secret police; the state pursued a policy of militarization even in schools and kindergarten; it's certainly true that books were not burned,

In particular, Maron has been caustic in her verdict upon those authors who stayed in the GDR and supported its ideals if not its reality. In a *New German Critique* essay (published in English), she berates GDR intellectuals as a "particularly spoiled group," lambastes their vainglorious conviction that they had the "right, even the duty, to speak in the name of a majority condemned to silence," and claims that "a mere half-truth was sufficient to lend its announcer the reputation of a prophet in a milieu full of stupid and shameless mendacity" ("Writers" 38). Maron also denounces the "craving for action of West German utopian thinkers" (41), and indicts the inability of the left-liberal consensus to acknowledge the moral bankruptcy of the state that had embodied its dreams of an alternative to capitalism.

In an interview with Gerhard Richter, Maron notes: "Die Kritiker holen aus einem Buch heraus, worüber sie selber gerade nachdenken" (4).[4] This is perhaps true of Elizabeth Boa's discussion of Ingeborg Bachmann and Maron. Thus the British critic's approach to the two authors is set in the context of her ruminations on the post-modern deconstruction of the Enlightenment. For Boa, recent thinking in Germany and elsewhere challenges fundamental precepts of the Enlightenment, including:

> die aufklärerischen Glaubenssätze, die erstens besagten, daß die Befreiung eines autonomen und einheitlichen Subjekts aus unverstandenen und deshalb unwiderstehbaren sozialen Mächten möglich ist, und zweitens, daß eine solche Befreiung einen universellen und transkulturellen geschichtlichen Prozeß darstellt. (128)[5]

The wars in the Balkans, the rise of nationalism, research into genetics, human psychology and sociology, and the rise of religious fundamentalism have certainly conspired to undermine the (western) belief in the educability of human actors. Yet Boa is determined that the fundamental bulwark of Enlightenment, that is, the concept of *Kritik* as a transcendent reimagining of the existent, should be defended. For this, she looks to art for an imaginative space in which emancipation is furthered by the utopian critique of the "really existing":

> Daß der Krieg ewig dauert, heißt auch weniger dramatisch ausgedrückt, daß die Politik ewig vonnöten ist und damit auch, daß die Aufklärung der sich immer

---

like under Hitler, but they were banned; it wasn't West Germany that was a dictatorship but East Germany, the GDR."

4 "Critics discover in a book whatever they happen to be thinking about at the time."

5 "those Enlightenment principles which stated, firstly, that emancipation of an autonomous and unified subject from social conditions which seem impenetrable and thus immutable is possible, and, secondly, that emancipation itself is a historical process that is universal and cross-cultural."

ändernden Machtverhältnisse zwischen sich ändernden Gruppen nötig bleiben wird. Solche Aufklärung bieten die Werke Bachmanns und Marons. (143)[6]

Maron is aligned with a generation of women writers, including Bachmann, Christa Wolf, and most probably Irmtraud Morgner. Nancy Lukens makes explicit the Maron-Wolf-Morgner parallel and their shared interest in "gender, rationality, and the self-destructive cycle in which industrial society finds itself" (67-68). Brigitte Rossbacher includes Helga Königsdorf, and notes the use by GDR women writers of "narrative techniques such as dreams, fantasy, and myth to subvert the realist paradigm and rational discourse and create an aesthetic realm, which allowed for the (free) play of possibilities for social change" ("The Status of State" 194).

There are certainly comparisons to be made. Yet Maron could also be likened to male authors, most obviously Uwe Johnson, whose need for absolute integrity brought about his withdrawal from public life.[7] Indeed, this comparison might serve to accent the single-mindedness, intrusion of autobiography and tendency towards a more severe (but equally reflective) argumentation that may distinguish Maron from Bachmann, Wolf and Morgner. Equally, the incorporation of Maron into a female canon rooted in an Enlightenment critique of the perversion of its own original humanist goals via "male" instrumental reason obscures this author's questioning of the very possibility of *Aufklärung* (Enlightenment) in the first instance.

Maron's novels from *Flugasche* (1981) to *Animal Triste* (1996) display an ever-intensifying pessimism about the possibility of such a transcendent position of Enlightenment *Kritik*, beyond history and personal experience, as it were. Before *Pawels Briefe* (1999), the author's work increasingly suggests that dissent and rebellion are situated within the "excess" of an individual's personality, within the surplus not susceptible to social and historical determination and which represents the untamed, the uncivilized, and perhaps also the imaginative and artistic. This causes a crisis of integrity following the not-to-be-suppressed suspicion that dissent derives from the essential amorality of an ego lacking a powerful superego rather than from a higher principle. It is a crisis that becomes more marked following the events of 1989. In the 1990s there is no *transparently* unjust opponent against which one might—without too much hesitation—fight the righteous fight.

The situation in Maron's *Pawels Briefe* is somewhat different. In this novel, the Holocaust paradoxically, offers a form of utopia, enabling a critique of the aberrations of the present, and specifically the GDR, that cannot be

6 "To say that the struggle continues, and will continue forever, simply means that politics will always be required and that it will always be necessary to investigate and expose the constantly shifting power relationships between ever-different groups. Enlightenment of this kind is offered in the work of Bachmann and Maron.

7 Maron chose to write on Uwe Johnson in her contribution to a *neue deutsche literatur* special edition in which authors discussed the writers that had influenced them most.

refuted. Yet the fact that this is once again a utopia, a non-place, means that Maron must struggle with her awareness that the Holocaust cannot be concretely imagined, that the story of her murdered grandfather cannot be reconstructed, and that its appropriation as a departure point for her criticism of her mother's complicity in the GDR diminishes its sanctity. In the end, however, Maron prefers to ignore these problems, thereby weakening the novel's persuasive power.

From *Flugasche* to *Animal Triste*

The 1981 novel *Flugasche* thematizes the clash between individual and society. Conformity is pitted against authenticity. Josefa's refusal to ignore the environmental costs of the outdated industrial practices in the town of B. (most likely Bitterfeld) which contribute to the death of the worker Hodriwitzka brings her into conflict with the editors of the journal for which she writes. She is cajoled, patronized, infantalized, and finally dismissed from the party and her job. Ultimately, she suffers a case of split personality, resolving, or rather avoiding the conflict between acquiescence and authenticity by means of a schizophrenic division. This is manifest in the substitution of the first person narrator—who laments: "Ich werde um mich selbst betrogen. [. . .] Alles, was ich bin, darf ich nicht sein. Vor jedes meiner Attribute setzen sie ein "zu": du bist zu spontan, zu naiv, zu ehrlich, zu schnell im Urteil" (78)[8]—by a third person narrator. The "real" Josefa nonetheless breaks through in a number of flights of fantasy (in an otherwise realistic text) during which she imagines her escape from convention.

Critics have tended to read *Flugasche* exclusively as a critique of the GDR. Certainly, its debunking of socialist realism—Hodriwitzka's fate belies the glorification of the "positive hero"—the attacks on the practice of *Selbstkritik* ("self-criticism"), and the emphasis upon the subjectivity of its protagonist support this. Yet Josefa's disenchantment exceeds what might be expected of a dissenting journalist in conflict with the party. Nor is her struggle solely defined by her efforts to achieve emancipation and self-realization in the face of patriarchy. Her alienation is thus not only socially and politically conditioned, or even determined primarily by her gender. It is also self-alienation, deriving from her inability to reconcile her poetic vision of the world with its banal reality. As Martin Kane notes: "the immediate trigger for this reprehensible and culpable move is not her reformer's zeal—the rational, crusading journalist side of her—but her fatal tendency to view a highly

8 "I am being cheated of my own sense of who I am. Everything that I am, I am not allowed to be. In the case of each of my attributes, they add a 'too': you're 'too' spontaneous, 'too' naïve, 'too' honest, 'too' quick to judge."

prosaic world in poetic terms" (229). Kane's stress upon the word "fatal" invokes the definition of tragedy as an inevitable outcome following from an excess of a single, otherwise positive, trait. Josefa's protest is not willed, deliberate, or even intended. She can do no other, and thus what she cannot claim is ethical superiority. Kane's suggestion that her poetic disposition pre-exists reality, moreover, is just as suggestive. The propensity for dissent is entirely contingent. As long as the predilection for nonconformity encounters an obstacle it is easy to rationalize it as a *consequence* of circumstances. Once oppression disappears, lessens, or becomes more diffuse, however, the individual may begin to doubt the existence of a higher principle conferring "objective" legitimacy upon dissent.

If *Flugasche* is primarily a "realist" text interrupted by intermittent flights of fantasy, *Die Überläuferin* (1988) is the opposite. This novel picks up where *Flugasche* left off, this time, confining Josefa's successor, Rosalind, to a "room of her own." Ostensibly paralyzed and unable to leave the house, Rosalind revisualizes the world in accordance with her own highly individual perspective. The characters that oppress her in "real life"—party officials, superiors and colleagues—appear in her fantasies as gross caricatures, thereby rendered comic. She also invents a friend, or more likely an alter ego, Martha, who functions outside of social convention, indulging in petty theft, indecency and disrespect. Above all, this character, with whom the protagonist sometimes merges, represents Rosalind's wish for self-identity. As in *Flugasche*, it is a quest for authentic biography unpolluted by the pressure to conform.

Yet Martha does not emerge as a wholly positive counter-example to the "real" world of social orthodoxy. Her rejection of social niceties, her disregard for the sanctity of property, and her sexual immoderation occasionally alienates even Rosalind. As Ricarda Schmidt argues, "the radicalness of Martha's refusal to conform either to social rules or to Kant's categorical imperative would pose a threat to any society." Moreover, Schmidt continues, "Maron refuses here to construct her novel on the simple opposition between a repressive order, which is to be viewed negatively, and a rebellious individual, who is to be viewed positively" ("From Surrealism" 248). Given the evident overlap, both biographical and temperamental, between Martha and Rosalind (and Maron), this refusal of a simple polarity is significant. On the one hand, Martha's "excess" of personality—viewed by the "Assoziation dichtender Männer," that is, by the GDR literary establishment, as "Romantizismen, Lyrismen, Pathos, Selbstmitleid, Infantilismus und modisches Femininisten-geplapper" (*Die Überläuferin* 156)—offers opposition to an unjust status quo.[9] At the same time, however, her nonconformity may be motivated less by critique than by an animalistic amorality and directionless hedonism.

9 "The association of verse-making men" (i.e. the *male* GDR literary establishment) condemns her poetry as "excessively romantic, trivial lyrics, full of pathos, self-pity, infantilism and trendy feminist waffle."

The intimation that dissent is located in personality rather than principle removes the illusion of objectivity that lends social criticism its legitimacy. This realization leads to the disintegration of her self-image, moreover, as she imagines alternative interpretations of her past behavior:

> Obwohl mir die Einzelheiten meines Lebens natürlich vertrauter sind als die anderer Leute, bleiben mir seine wirklichen Zusammenhänge in vielem verborgen, und ich finde zu verschiedenen Zeiten sehr unterschiedliche Erklärungen für seinen Verlauf, während mir Idas oder Clairchens Leben in ihren sich selbst verursachenden Folgen einen klaren, zuweilen sogar eindeutigen Zusammenhang offenbaren, was, wie ich befürchte, nichts als eine Täuschung ist. (72)[10]

Rosalind concedes that her construction of an "outer" reality premised upon the apparent stability of relations of cause and effect she perceives within the behavior of her acquaintances is simply a means of compensating for the arbitrariness of her own history: "wogegen das eigene, nur erlebte Leben als ein rätselhafter Haufen von Knoten und Schlingen vor einem liegt und es der jeweiligen Stimmung oder auch nur der Willkür überlassen bleibt, das Hin und Her eines Details zu bestimmen" (73).[11] This insight relativizes Josefa's quest in *Flugasche*: "Das Eigentliche, nach dem sie suchte, war die ihr gemäße Biografie" (99).[12] Rosalind can no longer be certain that such a biography, one that fits her life, exists.

Maron's first post-*Wende* novel, *Stille Zeile Sechs* (1991), appears, on first reading, as a triumphalist reckoning with GDR totalitarianism. Set in the mid-1980s, the work depicts the relationship between Rosalind, who has resolved no longer "to think for money," and a retired party member, Beerenbaum, whose biography, Brigitte Rossbacher notes, "meshes with that of such political personages as Walter Ulbricht, Wilhelm Pieck and her own stepfather, Karl Maron" ("(Re)visions" 16). Rosalind is now employed to type up the memoirs of the former top party member. Notwithstanding her apparent social and political resignation, she challenges his version of the past and refuses to let him repress communist crimes. For Frauke Lenckos, therefore, Rosalind's disruption of his narrative represents resistance to GDR totalitarianism:

> Not only does she passively manipulate Beerenbaum who varies and times his accounts according to her reactions and dictates so as to arouse her wrath or her

10 "Although the details of my life are, of course, more familiar than the details of other peoples' lives, the way in which all these facts hang together remains a mystery to me, and at different times I find very different explanations for the way my life has gone, whereas the meaning of Ida's life, or Claire's life, the way in which cause leads to effect in their lives, occasionally even unambiguously so, appears obvious to me. I fear that this is simply an illusion.

11 "Whereas your own life, on the other hand, which after all you have simply 'experienced' not understood, lies before you like an unfathomable pile of knots and coils, and it depends on your mood, or perhaps it is simply arbitrary, as what sense you make of the details in their ever-shifting combinations."

12 "What she was actually looking for was a biography to fit her life."

> admiration, she also actively changes his text. In the beginning, Rosalind reliably records five pages per session. Soon, however, she interrupts Beerenbaum's dictations with sighs, hiccups, and remarks about spelling mistakes. At other times, she omits aspects, which she finds unimportant. She offers unwanted comment, and refuses dictation. After her outburst, Rosalind spends more time arguing with Beerenbaum than recording his memoirs. (112)

The outburst in question comes when Rosalind denounces Beerenbaum and the author Victor Sensmann (a.k.a Christoph Hein) for their complacent refusal to concede the misery of the Berlin wall. The Stalinist excesses that Beerenbaum witnessed in his youth but now wishes to suppress are presented as the pre-history of the GDR, and both states are further paralleled with National Socialism. For Rosalind, therefore, "Sibirien liegt bei Ravensbrück" (142).[13]

Stille Zeile Sechs appears to reverse the self-doubt that had begun to emerge in *Die Überläuferin*. History, it seems, has vindicated Rosalind's dissent. Furthermore, the novel participates in controversies of the early 1990s concerning similarities, or otherwise, between Nazism and the GDR. Yet *Stille Zeile Sechs* is more than just a statement of Maron's impressions of the GDR as a totalitarian state. Instead the text revolves around the uneasily equivocal relationship between "Opfer und Unschuld" ("sacrifice and innocence"). The novel is thus structured around an question derived from Ernst Toller's *Masse-Mensch*, a play that reflects on the revolutionary situation of 1919: "Muß der Handelnde schuldig werden, immer und immer? Oder, wenn er nicht schuldig werden will, untergehen?"[14] (41). On the one hand, this refers to the older generation of communists, including Beerenbaum, whose anti-fascism was exploited as a justification for the widespread abuse of human rights in the GDR. At the same time, Rosalind's own complicity is insinuated. Her transcription of Beerenbaum's biography, however subversive, not only lends the moribund GDR an air of respectability, perhaps turning her—as an author—into his "Mittäter" (77), his accomplice. It also induces her to move from victimhood to guilt. If she is not to remain passive, she must act. Her revolt is transmitted in her verbal attacks on Beerenbaum, yet these, in part, at least, cause his heart attack and his premature death. The narrative "I," as Rossbacher notes, is "both victimized and implicated," forcing the question: "Is she not, like Beerenbaum, driven to act, finally to be the victor, not the victim?" ("(Re)visions" 21-22). Yet Schmidt's claim that Maron attempts to mitigate Rosalind's guilt, "in order to preserve her as a figure of identification," does not ring true ("From Surrealism" 252). The switch between first-person and third-person narration in Rosalind's account of her violence, certainly indicates, as Schmidt suggests, that she "has experienced a temporary split of identity into a passively observant self, an acting self, and a

13 "Stalin's Siberia is next to the GDR's Ravensbrück detention camp"

14 "Must he who acts be then guilty, for evermore? Or, if he chooses not to be guilty, must he fail to survive?"

self acting in the imagination, thus making the appearance of the repressed Other in her both an easily recognizable and safely contained temporary event" ("From Surrealism" 253). Yet the more powerful, and more lasting impact derives the animal aggression of her fantasy: "Sie trat ihn gegen die Rippen, den Kopf, in die Hoden, beidbeinig sprang sie auf seinen Brustkorb. Er rührte sich nicht. Als das Blut aus seinem Ohr lief, gab sie erschöpft auf" (*Stille Zeile* 208).[15] What remains is a strong sense of the frailty of the civilized conventions insulating Rosalind from instinct.

The interaction of personality and historical context is pivotal within Maron's 1996 novel *Animal Triste*. Here, the nameless narrator has removed herself from society following a failed affair with a married man and recounts, insofar as she is able or willing to remember, the story of this relationship. On the one hand, she refuses to locate her narrative in any particular period, frequently referring improbably and vaguely to the past as "vor vierzig oder fünfzig Jahren" (17).[16] Her indifference to historical context appears to frame the novel as a psychological investigation into "der Liebe Fluch und Segen,"[17] to cite Marcel Reich-Ranicki, who praised Maron for finally having found "her theme" (185-190). Yet the novel presents a full-frontal attack on the GDR and communism. The narrator extemporizes:

> Darum weiß ich nicht, welche Meinung man sich inzwischen über diese Zeit gebildet hat und wie man über sie spricht. Ich kann mir aber nicht vorstellen, daß heute noch irgend jemand verstehen kann, wie es damals einer als internationale Freiheitsbewegung getarnten Gangsterbande gelingen konnte, das gesamte osteuropäische Festland einschließlich der Binnenmeere, einiger vorgelagerter Inseln und der okkupierten Hoheitsgewässer von der übrigen Welt hermetisch abzugrenzen und sich als legale Regierungen der jeweiligen Länder auszugeben. (30)[18]

This passage, by no means unique within the novel, participates directly in the current debates concerning the evaluation of the GDR past. It exploits the supposed benefit of hindsight in order to delegitimate efforts to defend the GDR as a failed, but well-intentioned experiment.

---

15 "She kicked him in the ribs, head, testicles, jumped on his chest, using both legs. He did not move. Only when the blood was running out of his ears did she finally stop."

16 "forty or fifty years ago."

17 "the curses and blessings of love"

18 "That's why I have no idea what the agreed view of that time is and how people talk about it. I can't imagine, however, that there's anybody left today who claims to be able to understand how a band of gangsters, disguised as an international liberation movement, managed completely to cut off from the rest of the world the whole of the East European mainland, including several land-locked seas, a couple of nearby islands and the territorial waters of the countries it had occupied, and to pass itself off as the legal government of each of these countries."

The relationship between historical context—condemnation of the GDR from the perspective of the mid-1990s—and personality is examined by Ricarda Schmidt:

> While on the overtly political level Maron's novel is a fairly simplistic satire of GDR socialism, as an examination of the psychic consequences of life in the GDR the novel develops a critique of idealism as such. In that sense, *Animal Triste* is not a *sentimentalisch* novel [. . .] but rather one which combines post-modern relativism (the renunciation of the telos of harmony) with an impassioned rejection of GDR socialism. ("The Gender" 230)

Idealism here may be taken to refer not only to the utopian illusions of the older generation in the GDR, or the self-deceptions of the left-liberal intellectual classes in the West, but also to the protagonist's unfulfilled hopes of reaching harmony with her past. Post-modern insights, Schmidt implies, reject not only the master narratives of historical materialism and capitalism, but also any notion of the self. Certainly, there is little progress in the narrator's self-awareness, despite the ever-increasing encroachment on her consciousness of the reality principle in the form of previously repressed memories, culminating in her suspicion that Franz's death may have been her doing. Hence the novel comes to an end with her inability to recall whether or not she deliberately pushed him under the bus that killed him.

Alison Lewis argues that it is misleading "to see love as in some way displacing the concerns of history and politics or as effecting a clean break with the past" (30). For this critic, the consequences of social and political reality "are everywhere and undeniably present, most palpably in the narrator's obsessive and fateful denial of the reality principle" (43). The narrator thus erases her GDR biography, and looks to Franz to "give meaning to years of frustrated hopes and longing" (32). Her effacing of the past initiates a denial of her own corporeality, Lewis argues, as "symptomatic of a blocked or repressed identification with the mother and with the "castrated" position of normative femininity" (36). Her refusal of the "female role," combined with her rejection of her father, leaves her no "satisfactory point of identification," and predicts her inability to conform to social and sexual norms and her regression to "narcissistic, infantile strategies" (38). This entails a re-visioning of Freud's primal scene in which she imagines Franz and his wife copulating on holiday in Scotland.

The difficulty with Lewis' argument arises once the Australian critic endeavors to link her insights into the narrator's psychic state with the latter's GDR past. Lewis argues that the only position available to the protagonist is that of "barbarian" allocated her by Franz after her rude interruption of his marital holiday: "Ultimately, Franz cannot compensate for the 'Willkür des Absurden'" (*Animal Triste* 32) ['the arbitrary absurdity'] under the rule of the gang, it seems he can only exacerbate the inferiority of her past. Instead he can bring civilization to the barbarians, as did the Romans who built Hadrian's

Wall" (40). Lewis thus parallels Franz' inability to understand his lover's past, and his perceived civilizing mission, with the western take-over of the GDR and the eradication of its culture. The narrator's place within this scheme, Lewis argues, is to "embrace the return of the repressed in becoming West Germany's uncivilized other" (40). According to this reading, the narrator "enacts a regression through the stages of individual history, even through the stages of evolutionary history becoming prehuman, an 'Äffin with a 'dichtes kurzes Tierfell' and a 'stumpfes Tiernase,' or the 'verirrtes Insekt' looking for an escape" (40).[19] Yet, quite apart from the fact that Hadrian's Wall was built to keep the barbarians out, not civilize them, there is no compelling reason why the narrator's instinct-driven personality must necessarily be associated with any particular system or period. She feels at home in New York, since this city represents simply the "Inbegriff des Maßlosen" (219)—the very incarnation of a lack of proportion. No attempt to verbalize—render civilized and capable of logical exposition—can succeed against the primal urges that are allegorized by the narrator's involvement with dinosaurs, a species condemned to extinction by its inability to adapt: "Ich begriff, daß es das Saurierhafte an mir war, das so liebte, etwas Uraltes, atavistisch Gewaltsames, jede zivilisatorische Norm mißachtend, und nichts, was Sprache brauchte, konnte recht haben gegen meine Liebe zu Franz" (131).[20] This primitive self pre-exists social and historical conditions. The protagonist's dismissive judgment of the GDR should be taken at face value: "Das meiste war auch zu absurd, als daß man es sich hätte merken können" (31).[21] There is no need then to reconcile the novel's overt attacks on the GDR with its seemingly unrelated explorations of individual psychology. The efforts of critics to establish a connection between these two strands may, in truth, point to a desire to explain away unconscious drives by subordinating them to "social reality."

Animal Triste incorporates a "philosophical surplus," a quality of abstract rumination on human nature. The narrator's frequent self-description as an animal and her preference for being surrounded by flesh-eating plants predict the close of the novel:

> Immer mehr Tiere kommen, große und kleine, und setzen sich still zwischen die anderen. Ich liege in ihrer Mitte und fürchte sie nicht. Ich bin eins von ihnen, eine braunhaarige Äffin mit einer stumpfen Nase und langen Armen, die ich um mein Tierleib schlinge. So bleibe ich liegen. (238)[22]

---

19 "'a female ape' with a 'thick, short fleece' and the 'stubby nose of an animal' or the 'confused insect' looking for an escape."

20 "I understood that it was the prehistoric reptile in me that loved so, something that was age-old, primitive and violent, something that took no notice of the norms of civilization, and nothing that needed words to express it could ever win against this primitive love I had for Franz."

21 "Most of it was too absurd for one to remember."

22 "More and more animals arrive, some large, some small, and sit down amongst the others. I am lying in the middle of them and am not afraid. I am one of them, a brown-haired ape with

This confirms that the animal motif is not simply a metaphor for the narrator's love for Franz, but rather an act of biological and anthropological self-recognition. She has accepted her essential nature as a beast. Any attempt to claim otherwise reveals a misunderstanding of nature: "Wer die Macht der Natur über die Menschen leugnet, hat nicht mehr aufzubieten als seinen Wunsch und einen Glauben, der in der Verkleidung eines Unglauben daherkommt" (176).[23] The Enlightenment is wishful thinking, an act of faith posing as doubt.

Pawels Briefe

In the opening pages of *Animal Triste*, the narrator determines that memory is overrated and forgetting unduly stigmatized:

> Ich weiß nicht, wie man heute darüber denkt, aber vor vierzig oder fünfzig Jahren, als ich noch mit den anderen Menschen lebte, galt das Vergessen als sündhaft, was ich schon damals nicht verstanden habe und was ich inzwischen für lebensbedrohlichen Unfug halte. (17)[24]

These lines contain a number of allusions. Firstly, they verify the narrator's surrender to her instinctual self. Animals, as Nietzsche notes, have no memory and thus no ethical insight. Furthermore, the passage may point to the rumpus surrounding the revelations of Maron's brief involvement with the state security services. More generally, however, it may also refer to the fixation on the past that spawned the legend of anti-fascism in East Germany and *Vergangenheitsbewältigung* (coming to terms with the past) in the FRG, and, after unification, initiated renewed discussion of the parallels between the GDR and National Socialism. Thus, the narrator's dismissal of the notion that forgetting is "sündhaft" undermines the discourse of vigilance based in the fact of the Holocaust. This paradigm has sustained Enlightenment thinking in the post-war period.

Given the hostility to the fetishization of memory in *Animal Triste*, and indeed elsewhere in her fiction, it seems surprising that Maron's latest novel, *Pawels Briefe* (1999), should focus upon the author's investigations into the history of her family, involving an account of her grandfather, murdered by the

---

a stubby nose and long arms, which I wind around my animal's body. That's how I remain lying."

23 "Whoever denies the power of nature over mankind can prove no evidence of this other than his desire that it should be so, and a kind of faith that comes disguised as an enlightened lack of faith."

24 "I don't know what people think about all that these days, but forty or fifty years ago, when I still lived in the company of other human beings, to forget was seen as sinful. I never really got that, even at the time, and now I think it's nonsense, maybe even life-threatening."

Nazis, and an exploration of her mother's activities as a communist in the post-war years and later in the GDR. On the surface, this autobiographical work appears to subscribe to a belief that it is possible to interrogate the past, make sense of it, and draw lessons that can have an impact on the individual's journey towards self-realization. The inclusion of family photographs, Maron's visit to Poland to her grandfather's village, and, first and foremost, Pawel's letters to his wife and children from the ghetto in Belchatow endow the composition with an aura of biographical authenticity that seems to contradict the skepticism prevalent in the earlier fiction. The images of trees inside both front and back covers further embed the narrative within the supposed site of Pawel's execution, although the storyteller cannot be certain that he was killed in these forests and not in a camp. These prints pre-empt challenges to the authenticity of the narrative.

This new focus upon memory and the past is striking, raising the question of what has changed since the earlier novels. The issue of motive, in fact, introduces the narrative: "Seit ich beschlossen habe, dieses Buch zu schreiben, frage ich mich, warum jetzt, warum erst jetzt, warum jetzt noch" (*Pawels Briefe* 7).[25] Three questions are posed, although, significantly, the sentence lacks a question mark, as if the answers are known in advance. Firstly, what has happened in the present to make the telling of this story so urgent? This is closely related to the second question of why the tale was not told previously. Thirdly, what continued relevance does it have? Scattered throughout the text are a number of responses. Hence, the reason why Maron writes now, and not earlier, has to do with the events of 1989: "Manchmal denke ich, daß ich erst in diesem Herbst erwachsen geworden bin; ich war achtundvierzig Jahre alt" (131).[26] The collapse of the GDR has removed the object of her detestation and forced her to review her life and past in a new light. This has an essential bearing on her relationship to her mother and stepfather, both leading figures in the Communist state:

> Ich mußte aufgehört haben, meine Eltern zu bekämpfen, um mich über das Maß der eigenen Legitimation hinaus für meine Großeltern und ihre Geschichte wirklich zu interessieren. Ich mußte bereit sein, den Fortgang der Geschichte, die Verbindung zu mir, das Leben meiner Mutter, einfach nur verstehen zu wollen, als wäre es mein eigenes Leben gewesen. (13)[27]

---

25 "Since I decided to write this book, I've been asking myself why now, why not before, why now after all this time."

26 "Sometimes I think that I only really grew up in the autumn of 1989; I was forty-eight years old."

27 "I must have finally given up fighting my parents. Now I could be truly interested in my grandparents and their history, rather than just in asserting my own legitimacy as a person. I had to be prepared to simply understand the way things happened, the way it related to my life, the life of my mother. I had simply to try to understand it, not challenge it—as if it had been my own life."

This account will be unencumbered by self-justification or censure. The instinctive revolt that infused Maron's earlier fiction appears to be absent, as does the attendant self-doubt.

Yet these lines may also be read differently. Apprehension about a lack of clarity in the past is associated with an urgent, perhaps even obsessive need for unequivocal interpretations. Here, the "I" is not only a rhetorical strategy, an imagined adjunct to the "we" in conversation with itself, but the narrator's "I," for whom precise knowledge of the past is not a luxury but an imperative. Thus, the novel incorporates a contradiction. On the one hand, the narrator strives to persuade the reader that this biographical inquiry is the product of a more mature self. Maron has transcended biography, and her personality, and achieved impartiality. At the same time, *Pawels Briefe* is motivated by an omission on the part of her mother that renders true objectivity impossible for Maron as narrator. Shortly before his death, therefore, Pawel had written a letter, to be translated from Polish by Hella, Maron's mother, and later to be bequeathed to Monika. Yet Pawel's farewell letter had remained forgotten—and thus denied to its intended recipient—until 1994. Only then was it discovered during a search for old photographs and documents instigated by a Dutch television documentary on the subject: "Wann werden die Deutschen endlich normal?" (10).[28]

Pawel's letter is the real reason for the composition of the novel. The connection to the past, the history within which Maron might have found the "biography that fits her" sought by her protagonists from *Flugasche* onwards, had been severed. Maron's sense of loss is evident: "Vor diesem Vergessen stehe ich ratlos, so ratlos wie Hella selbst" (113).[29] Yet this carefully constructed phrase offers only illusory sympathy to the mother. Indeed, Hella had also forgotten other missives, including those she wrote to the Nazi authorities in an attempt to convince them that her father's conversion to Baptism was valid. The narrator initially wonders whether these were written in order to secure official permission for Hella to marry a non-Jew. At first this cynical interpretation is rejected. Subsequently, however, the problem of memory reappears:

> Hätte Hella nicht ein ungewöhnlich gutes Gedächtnis, so gut, daß sie in meinen Augen manchmal in den Verdacht gerät, nachtragend zu sein, ließen sich ihre Erinnerungslücken durch die überlagernde Zeit und Hellas Alter erklären. So aber stehen sie als ein erklärungverlangendes Warum über den Jahren nach 1939. (17)[30]

28 "When will the Germans finally be normal?"

29 "This failure to remember leaves me at a total loss, as much at a loss as Hella herself."

30 "If it weren't for the fact that Hella has an unusually good memory, so good, in fact, that I sometimes suspect her of bearing grudges, the gaps in her recollection could be explained away as a consequence of her age and the time that has passed since. But, because her memory is so good, we need to know why she seems to have forgotten so much from the years after 1939."

The fact that Hella's memory is typically so good makes her forgetting appear as repression. This undermines her version of her biography, in which she insists that her loyalty to communism was free of any desire for personal gain. It also indirectly answers the question at the heart of the work: "ob es sich bei diesem Experiment um eine gescheiterte Utopie oder um ein Verbrechen gehandelt hat" (129).[31] The entire East German experiment appears to have been based on an act of forgetting. Anti-fascism is revealed as a myth, as an attempt to garner legitimacy for a system that, Maron suggests, in fact repeated many of the crimes of its predecessor. Hence, the narrator speculates that Hella's neglect of Pawel's letter is linked to the atmosphere of 1945, and the building of socialism in the GDR:

> Das Jahr 1945 sei für sie wie eine Wiedergeburt gewesen, hat Hella gesagt. Eine Wiedergeburt ohne Eltern, ein Neuanfang ohne die Vergangenheit? [. . .] Und später, als das Leben längst weitergegangen war, als die Zeitungen "Neues Leben," "Neuer Weg," "Neue Zeit" und "Neues Deutschland" hießen, als die Gegenwart der Zukunft weichen mußte und die Vergangenheit endgültig überwunden wurde, wurde da auch die eigene Vergangenheit unwichtig? (113-114)[32]

Hella's enthusiasm for the GDR is sustained at the price of repressing the parallels between it and the regime that murdered her father. This act of betrayal causes an unbridgeable rift between the generation that founded the GDR and its rebellious children, "weil die Kinder das Pathos des antifaschistischen Widerstands ernst genommen haben, während ihre Eltern schon dabei waren, sich aus Widerstandskämpfern in Machthaber zu verwandeln" (170).[33]

In its focus on generational conflict, *Pawels Briefe* appears to fit into the wave of literature exploring parental, although most often paternal, involvement in National Socialism that began in the FRG and Austria in the early 1970s. This genre includes novels such as Peter Handke's *Wunschloses Unglück* (1972), Brigitte Schwaiger's *Lange Abwesenheit* (1980) Christoph Meckel's *Suchbild: Über meinen Vater* (1980), Peter Härtling's *Nachgetragene Liebe* (1980), and Peter Schneider's *Vati* (1987). Thus, *Pawels Briefe* seems to owe less to an East German tradition, including Ulrich Plenzdorf's *Die neuen Leiden des jungen Ws* (1973), Volker Braun's

31 "The question of whether, when talking about the experiment that was GDR, we're talking about a failed utopia or a crime."

32 "The year 1945, she said, was like a rebirth. I said: A resurrection without parents, a new start without the past [. . .]. And later, I said, once life had long become routine again, once the newspapers had titles like "New Life," "New Path," "New Time" and "New Germany," and the present gave way to the future, and the past was finally overcome, did your own history suddenly become unimportant?"

33 "Because the children took seriously the whole pathos surrounding the legend of the anti-fascist resistance, whereas their parents were in the process of transforming themselves from resistance fighters against Hitler into the new bosses in communist East Germany."

Unvollendete Geschichte (1977), or Christoph Hein's *Drachenblut* (1982), in which parent-child conflicts are fictionalized rather than based on the author's biography, and in which the focus is on the present rather than the past. Similar to Meckel and Härtling, moreover, Maron's inquiry begins with the shock discovery of previously unseen personal documents. In *Suchbild*, the son discovers a notebook recording his father's increasingly enthusiastic attitude towards Hitler, his naïve adoption of a heroic *Blut und Boden* mythology, and his attempts to reconcile his aesthetic sensibilities with Nazi ideology. Härtling's novel begins with the inadequacy of the paternal records with which the son hopes to gain an insight into his father's real, yet subdued opposition to Nazism. The similarity between Maron's novel and these texts may suggest her desire to parallel Nazism and the GDR.

Common to all these novels, however, from both East and West, is a belief in the necessity of enlightenment. In all cases, the commitment to reason, tolerance, and self-realization makes it possible to attack the failings of the older generation. In the West German novels, this attitude derives its moral force from revulsion at Nazi crimes, and, ultimately, the Holocaust. In the East German texts, legitimacy is derived from "true" anti-fascism and from frustration at the state's betrayal of socialist ideals. Maron's book echoes both the western focus on the Shoah—the fact of Pawel's murder—and eastern critiques of the GDR's corruption of its founding goals. Yet the emphasis is very much on the mass murder of Jews. In the post-1989 era, left-wing utopias cannot bear close scrutiny—if, for Maron, they ever could—whereas the Holocaust cannot be challenged. Evidence for this is supplied by the respect rightly paid to survivor accounts, and the authenticity imputed to recent bestsellers such as Ruth Klüger's *weiter leben* (1992), Victor Klemperer's *Tagebücher 1933-1945* (1995), and, following its publication in 1999, Marcel Reich-Ranicki's *Mein Leben*.

Pawel's fate provides Maron with a position from which she can criticize her mother's commitment to communism free of the fear that her protest might simply derive from petty resentment or her own "excess" of personality. Animosity towards the mother is, of course, a frequent motif in Maron's writing, as is the glorification of the grandfather. Thus, her 1989 essay, entitled "Ich war ein antifaschistisches Kind," directly contrasts her grandfather's victimhood with her mother's supposed complicity in order to frame the question: "warum Leute, die in ihrer Jugend gegen Ungerechtigkeit und Unterdrückung gekämpft und ihr Leben dafür eingesetzt haben, in Jahrzehnten unangefochtener Macht ihr eigenes Volk mit den Mitteln von Gangstern betrogen und beherrschten. Und andere es duldeten" (28).[34] Yet *Pawels*

34 The essay is called: "I was an anti-fascist child." The quotation asks "why people, who fought against injustice and oppression in their childhood, and who risked their lives, came to betray their own people in the course of decades of unchallenged power and using gangster methods. Und why other people tolerated it."

Briefe—incorporating aspects of this essay some ten years later—intensifies the idealization of the grandfather, and, indeed, both grandparents. Most obviously, Pawel offers an example of resistance: "nur indem er sich von anderen unterschied, konnte er mir gegen sie beistehen" (*Pawels Briefe* 63).[35] More generally, the fate suffered by Maron's grandparents endows them with a significance that extends beyond the purely biographical: "Vor allem aber gab es ihren Tod, der sie immer mehr sein ließ als meine Großeltern" (8).[36] They offer deliverance from the past—"Sie waren der gute, der geheiligte Teil der furchtbaren Geschichte" (8)[37]—and exist outside of history and social context. Thus, they are "nicht nur aus einem anderen Jahrhundert, sondern aus einer anderen Welt" (15).[38] They represent the hope of messianic redemption insofar as traces of their lives in the present suggest that good may occasionally survive evil—"das nicht getilgte Wort, der nicht gelöschte Name Iglarz, wie eine Erlösung für uns" (104)[39]—and to the extent that they embody genuineness: "Trotzdem suggerieren die Bilder meiner Großeltern dem Betrachter das Gefühl, etwas Gültiges, nicht Austauschbares zu sehen" (30).[40] This authenticity transcends the ambiguous and equivocal blurring of innocence and complicity, dissent and oppression that obtains within immanent social and historical circumstances, and, since it is grounded in pure victimhood, engenders a critique of present-day reality that seems to be unassailable.

The narrator's unabashed exaltation of her grandparents' lives invests their deaths with retrospective meaning. This substitutes teleology for contingency. The anxiety that a biography might represent nothing more than a series of random traumas and experiences—consisting, in Niklas Luhmann's words, as quoted by Maron, of "'Wendepunkten, an denen etwas geschehen ist, das nicht hätte geschehen müssen. Das beginnt mit der Geburt'" (153-154)[41]—is repressed within the narrator's need to infuse Pawel's murder with supra-historical significance. At the same time, she is uncomfortably aware of her self-deception:

> Ich neige dazu, den Zufällen und spontanen Entscheidungen der Vergangenheit zu unterstellen, sie seien insgeheim schon immer einem sich viel später offenbarenden Sinn gefolgt, und ich befürchte, es könnte ebenso umgekehrt sein: weil man das Chaos der Vergangenheit nicht erträgt, korrigiert man es ins Sinnhafte, indem man

35 "Only by being different from other people could he be of any help to me."

36 "It was above all the manner of their deaths that made them more than just my grandparents."

37 "They were the good, sacred part of the whole terrible story."

38 They were "not only from another century, but another world."

39 "It was kind of redemption for us: the word that has not been erased, the name Iglarz that has not been wiped away."

40 "Yet the pictures of my grandparents gave the person looking the feeling that this was something genuine, irreplaceable and non-exchangeable."

41 "Turning points, when something has happened that should not have happened. That starts with the fact of being born."

> ihm nachträglich ein Ziel schafft, wie jemand, der versehentlich eine Straße ins Leere gepflastert hat und erst dann, weil es die Straße nun einmal gibt, an ihr beliebiges Ende ein Haus baut. (13)[42]

The key terms are "sich offenbaren," "Sinnhafte" and "Ziel," once more suggesting Hegelian and Enlightenment concepts of history. Maron cannot accept this portrayal of historical processes, much as she would like to do so. Indeed, she consistently rejects her mother's conviction that everything that happened in the older woman's life was an inevitable outcome of social and historical processes, explainable, therefore, by the laws of historical materialism. Hella thus disputes her daughter's suggestion that she might have become a supporter of the SPD if she had only fallen in love with a social democrat rather than a communist, and insists that her path was pre-programmed. Hence, Monika speculates what might have become of her mother if she had not gone to work for Karl Maron, and argues "daß sie mir auch diesmal widersprechen und behaupten würde, wenn nicht der Weg ins Stadthaus, hätte ein anderer Weg sie in eine ähnliche Richtung geführt" (154).[43] For Hella, biography is a product of social class and historical circumstances.

The narrator's compulsion to refer to the Shoah as the ultimate source of legitimacy for her rebellion against her mother and the GDR is further undermined by her awareness that she is reading meaning into an event that is essentially incomprehensible. Auschwitz cannot be truly imagined. Its reality remains impossible to grasp, and this forms an obstacle to its appropriation in the battles of the present. The attempt to render the circumstances of her grandparents' deaths plastic, ends in either banality or mysticism: "Im Schatten ihres wirklichen Todes hat kein Detail Bestand, es wird banal oder mystisch" (23).[44] If the Holocaust is made commonplace or everyday it loses it redemptive power. If it is presented as mystical, on the other hand, it remains abstract, ahistorical and removed from reality.

The narrator's difficulties are compounded by the fact that the documentary evidence she possesses of her grandparents' existence is incomplete. Maron's postmodern sensibilities subsequently surface to frustrate her desire for a historicization of the past. Hence, her image of Pawel and Josefa is securely tied to the few photographs that remain of them. Yet her

42 "I tend to imagine that chance happenings and spontaneous decisions in the past all along, in secret, possessed some meaning that would be revealed much later. At the same time, I was scared that the opposite might be just as true: because we can't cope with the chaos of the past, we 'correct' it, make sense of it, by giving it a goal in retrospect, just like the someone who has built a road to nowhere by mistake and then builds some random house at its side—after all, the road is there now."

43 "she would contradict me this time as well and insist that even if this path hadn't taken her to where she ended up, another path would have taken her in a similar direction."

44 "No details could survive in the shadow of the reality of their death, they just seem banal or mystical."

attempts to recreate the texture of their lives—to add color to her black and white image—achieve only the most fleeting success: “Immer schieben sich in Sekunden die schwarzweißen Fotogesichter über die farbigen Fragmente” (18).[45] The reality of their experience is too far removed from the present, and Monika’s biography too different:

> Zwischen der Geschichte, die ich schreiben will, und mir stimmt etwas nicht. Welches Thema ich auch anrühre, nach fünf oder vier, machmal sogar nach zwei Seiten schmeißt mich die Geschichte oder schmeiße ich mich aus dem Buch wieder raus. Als hätte ich darin nichts zu suchen; als wäre meine Absicht, aus den Fotos, Briefen und Hellas Erinnerungen die Ahnung vom Ganzen zu gewinnen, vermessen für einen Eindringling wie mich. (52)[46]

The narrator cannot piece together the lives of her grandparents in order to reinstate a “whole” that would redeem her own contradictory biography. Her efforts to reassemble the events suffered by her grandparents represent, moreover, an appropriation of their history. She is an intruder, whose vision of family history posits a specious contrast between past and present: “Das einfache Leben meiner Großeltern und ihrer Kinder, von welcher Seite ich mich ihm auch nähere, gerinnt mir zur Idylle, und schon verbietet sich der nächste Satz” (52-53).[47] Her idealization is unintended, yet inescapable. In addition, she further describes the gulf between her sentimental longing for the seeming harmony of her grandparents’ existence and the reality of her own life: “Vielleicht ist es meine eigene Rührung, die mir verdächtig erscheint, denn nichts von dem, was mich am Leben meiner Großeltern bis zu Tränen rührt, schien mir brauchbar für das, was ich im Leben vorhatte” (53).[48] The narrator also admits that she desires neither the “vier Kinder, denen ich mein Leben gewidmet hätte” nor “die Gläubigkeit in die Worte des Herrn,” and queries: “Welche Rolle maß ich mir an, indem ich eine Lebensform preise, die ich für mich selbst verwerfe?” (53).[49]

---

45 “Time and time again their black and white faces, their faces as they appear on the photographs, wash over the color fragments in seconds.”

46 “Between the story that I want to write and myself something is wrong. Whatever topic I start to write about, after four or five, perhaps even after two pages, the story throws me out of the book, or I throw myself out of the book. As if I had no business being there in the first place, as if it were my intention to gain an impression of the whole from the photographs, letters and Hella’s memories. That would be going too far for an intruder like me.”

47 “The simple life of my grandparents and their children seeps away into pure idyll, however I approach it, and then I cannot write another sentence.”

48 “Perhaps it is my own emotion that appears suspect to me, because nothing of that which moves me to tears about the lives of my grandparents seems applicable to what I intended to do with my life.”

49 “four children to whom I would have devoted my life,” nor the “faith in the Lord’s word.” “What do I think I am doing when I praise a way of living that I would never want for myself?”

The most serious difficulty Maron encounters in her many efforts to secure her grandparents' lives as a redemption of the post-1945 era is presented, however, by Pawel's membership in the communist party. His affiliation is introduced in a brief yet revealing sentence: "Pawel war Mitglied in der Gewerkschaft, im Bund deutscher Radfahrer, später trat er in die Kommunistische Partei ein" (55).[50] The narrator's aspiration to relativize Pawel's sympathies is apparent in her lengthy listing of the grandfather's *other* activities. In addition, the subject is not mentioned again for another five pages, until the narrator asks: "Wie soll ich mir meinen Großvater als Mitglied der Kommunistischen Partei vorstellen?" (59).[51] She determines that she might view his communism as an extension of his adopted Christianity: "An der unbeirrten Gläubigkeit ihres Vaters zweifelt Hella aber nicht, und somit habe ich keinen Grund, etwas anderes anzunehmen, als daß mein Großvater nicht seine Überzeugung gewechselt hat, sondern nur die Gemeinschaft, mit der er für sie eintreten wollte" (60).[52] Yet the strength of Monika's conviction here is undermined by the complexity of her syntax—which is tellingly formal, suggesting a lack of inner certainty—by the fact that she has no direct evidence of his continued religiosity, and by a previous discovery: "Von dem Pfarrer der Neuköllner Baptistengemeinde erfahre ich aber, daß Paul Iglarz am 1. Mai 1929 auf eigenen Wunsch aus dem Gemeinderegister gestrichen wurde" (59).[53] Monika's association of her grandfather with extra-historical notions of justice, equality and tolerance—implied by his Baptism—is thus weakened by his fraternization with a movement contaminated by its criminal actions in the Soviet Union and the GDR.

Pawels Briefe meditates then on the dilemmas that run throughout Maron's fiction. The narrator's utopian proclivities—"ein Mischmasch aus kindlicher Paradiessucht, christlicher Moral und individuellem Freiheitsdrang" (62)[54]—predict her desire for the redemption of the past. Yet this deliverance cannot come from the great political movements of the twentieth century. The artist's affinity for transcendence clashes with her skepticism towards *grands récits*, a mistrust of attempts to historicize the past, and an insight into the contingency of history and personality. In short, a naïve longing for authenticity collides with a postmodern sensibility. This generates the predicament that is so typical of the earlier novels: "Aber wer weiß schon genau, wie und warum sich bestimmte Eigenschaften in uns entwickeln und warum andere verkümmern"

---

50 "Pawel was a member of a Trades' Union, a member of the association of German cyclists. Later he became a member of the Communist party."

51 "How am I to imagine my grandfather as a member of the Communist Party?"

52 "Hella had no doubts about her father's unchanging religiosity, and I have no reason to assume anything other than that my grandfather changed not so much his convictions but rather the team with which he hoped to realize them."

53 "I found out from the vicar of the Neukölln Baptist church that Paul Iglarz was taken off the registry of members on 1 May 1929, at his own request."

54 "A mixture of childish longing for paradise, Christian morality and a drive for personal freedom."

(126).[55] It is impossible to know why an individual possesses one set of qualities rather than another. The dream of self-realization is replaced by the suspicion that self-knowledge is a deception that merely reflects the needs of the present moment. Hence, the narrator concedes that she has often asked "warum ich wohl geworden sein könnte, wie ich bin" and found different answers "zu verschiedenen Zeiten" (166).[56] The search for self-knowledge is simply an attempt to give meaning to a biography that might otherwise appear random: "Wenn ich meiner Biographie eine Gestalt suche, kommt ein dürres eckiges Gebilde zusammen, mit willkürlichen Streben nach rechts und links, als hätte da etwas werden sollen, was dem Rest seinen Sinn hätte geben können" (70).[57] This is a life without elegance and full of contradictions. Hella's vision of her life is, perhaps predictably, quite different: "Wenn Hella die Skulptur ihres Lebens beschreiben sollte, würde sie vermutlich ein harmonisches kompaktes Werk vor Augen haben, mit einigen Schrunden und Scharten, vielleicht ist irgendwo sogar ein ganzes Stück rausgehauen, aber insgesamt erscheint es gelungen" (70).[58] For Hella, therefore, her life retains its purpose and harmony, despite the revelation of the GDR's moral and political bankruptcy.

The narrator's ruminations on self-knowledge beg the question of what predisposes an individual to happiness or melancholy:

> Was entscheidet darüber, ob wir uns eher an die glücklichen Momente unseres Lebens erinnern oder an die unglücklichen; ob uns unsere Triumphe vor den Demütigungen einfallen oder umgekehrt? Liegt es in unserer Natur, im ererbten Temperament oder an den Umständen unserer Geburt oder an dem ersten Eindruck, den die Welt uns macht? Oder gräbt sich solche Eigenart nur langsam in unseren Charakter? Ich kann mir vorstellen, daß ein früherer, nicht erinnerbarer Schreck uns für lange Zeit das Glück unzugänglich machen kann. (69)[59]

What influences a person to view his or her biography in negative rather than positive terms? The hypothesis that a single trauma might be responsible for

55 "Who knows exactly how and why certain qualities develop in us and why others simply fade away?"

56 "How it is that I came to be who I am." She finds different answers "at different times."

57 "Whenever I try and give my biography some shape, I end up with a withered form with sharp edges, with arbitrary offshoots to the right and the left, as if something was supposed to take shape that would have given the rest some meaning."

58 "If Hella were to describe the architecture of her life, she would probably have a mental picture of a harmonious, compact work of art, with a few cracks and chips, perhaps a whole piece might have been hewn out somewhere, but on the whole it is a success."

59 "What determines whether we remember the happy moments of our lives rather than the unhappy times, whether we remember our triumphs before our humiliations, or the other way around? Is it a question of our 'natures,' of the temperament that we have inherited from our parents, or does it have to do with the circumstances of our birth or the first impression that the world makes on us? Or do such qualities simply build up slowly in our characters, over time? I can quite easily imagine that an early shock, even one that we no longer remember, can make it impossible for a long time for us to be happy."

unhappiness is superficially attractive. Yet the phraseology that introduces this theory is revealing: "Ich kann mir vorstellen." The words "I can imagine" disclose a desire that it should be so even as they admit a paucity of evidence. The narrator is avoiding the issue, refusing to decide between natural predisposition or social context as the root of dissent. The supposition of a sole trauma, moreover, generates a new mythology, which cannot be challenged, since it is, by definition, "ein früherer, nicht erinnerbarer Schreck." It is a shock that cannot be remembered, thus it cannot be questioned. The victimhood she had attributed to her grandfather, but which his Communist Party affiliations had inhibited, can now be conferred upon her own person.

The suggestion of an "original trauma" recalls the Freudian notion of fetishization—the primal scene which cannot be remembered but which causes the individual's obsession with objects contiguous with the place or time of the shock—and the centrality of the Holocaust to post-war Enlightenment thinking. In *Pawels Briefe*, the two are linked. Maron's postmodern sensibilities thus undermine the Shoah as the site of authenticity in which her critique of the present, the GDR and her mother might be located. She is forced to concede that Pawel's victimhood was neither redemptive, nor transcendent. It was a result of historical circumstance and contingency. Maron's grandfather did not choose his life. Nor was his death a protest, against Nazism, or anything else. He was as passive as the workers in the 1930s, or the population of the GDR. He was murdered, moreover, because he was a Jew, and this he did not choose. The narrator cites one of her grandfather's letters: "'Es muß doch ein zu ungeheuerliches Verbrechen sein, Jüdischer Abstammung zu sein, aber glaubt es mir, liebe Kinder, ich hab es nicht verschuldet. Wenn mir die Eltern zur Wahl gestellt worden wären, ich hätte mir womöglich auch andere Eltern gewählt aber ich mußte es auch so nehmen, wie es mir geboten wurde'" (98).[60] These lines do not suggest the redemption of history, but rather resigned acceptance of it. The narrator's wish that the Holocaust legitimate her protest is left unfulfilled. A substitute legend emerges therefore: "ein früherer, nicht erinnerbarer Schreck." This shock, which is perhaps more imaginary than real, is fetishized in order to disguise the narrator's inability to resolve the doubts she has concerning her dissent. It further distracts from the disillusionment engendered by her present, more precise analysis of her grandfather's biography

Pawels Briefe is an autobiographical text that invites the reader to draw conclusions about its author. Maron, it seems, would like her audience to receive the novel as the product of mature reflection, an indication of the degree to which the events of 1989 forced her to become an adult, birth at age forty-eight so to speak. Framed thus, the motifs that overdetermine the author's

60 "It must be a gross crime to be of Jewish descent, but, believe me, dear children, I am not to blame. If I could have chosen my parents, I might well have chosen different parents, but I had to take it as it came."

earlier work—her rage at the GDR, her questioning of the motives for her dissent, and the nexus of personality and social context—dissolve within yet another interpretation of her biography. These issues are now attributed to generational conflict. Thus, Maron appears to concede that the anger she felt at the repression of the past enacted by the GDR's counterfeit anti-fascism, while doubtlessly genuine, also provided a convenient means of prosecuting her antagonism towards her mother. A similar idea emerges from recent examples of *Vaterliteratur* by West German authors. In Peter Schneider's *Vati* (1987), for instance, the narrator describes a friend's attacks on his father as a generational conflict thinly disguised as a reckoning with the past: "Es gab ja, Ende der sechziger Jahre Kommilitonen wie Dich, die von ihren Erzeugern nichts mehr annahmen als Geld und nur ein Lebensziel zu verfolgen schienen: nicht so werden wie ihre Väter" (28).[61] Bernhard Schlink's protagonist in *Der Vorleser* (1995), likewise, declares: "Manchmal denke ich, daß die Auseinandersetzung mit der nationalsozialistischen Vergangenheit nicht der Grund, sondern der Ausdruck des Generationskonflikts war, der als treibende Kraft der Studentenbewegung zu spüren war" (161).[62] In each case, the focus is on the protagonist's own relationship (rather than that of his/her parents) with the past, including both National Socialism and personal history.

In broad terms, therefore, Maron's novel echoes the discourse of "growing up" attached to the generation of '68 in the west and the realization by the same generation of dissidents in the east that criticism within a liberal democracy is more fraught than opposition under totalitarianism. It also appears to resolve the problem of where dissidence comes from by presenting the narrator as a more mature figure—still a "difficult" personality, but one now more adapted to her social environment. Yet there is still too much resentment of the mother, the GDR, or the failings of her own biography, and too much attempt at self-justification. In this novel, Maron simply invents a new myth of victimhood, with herself at the center.

Works Cited

Boa, Elizabeth. "Schwierigkeiten mit der ersten Person: Ingeborg Bachmanns *Malina* und Monika Marons *Flugasche*, *Die Überläuferin* und *Stille Zeile Sechs*." *Kritische Wege der Landnahme. Ingeborg Bachmann im Blickfeld der neunziger Jahre*. Ed. Robert Pichl and Alexander Stillmark.Vienna: Hora-Verlag, 1994. 125-145.

---

61 "After all, I had friends at university at the end of the 1960s just like you. Friends that didn't want anything from their parents, except money, and whose only goal in life seemed to be not to become like their fathers."

62 "Sometimes I think that the whole process of confronting National Socialism was not the reason for the generational conflict that was behind the student movement of the late 1960s, but an expression of it."

Härtling, Peter. *Nachgetragene Liebe*. Darmstadt und Neuwied: Luchterhand, 1980.
Kane, Martin. "Culpabilities of the Imagination: The Novels of Monika Maron." *Literature on the Threshold. The German Novel in the 1980s*. Ed. Arthur Williams, Stuart Parkes and Roland Smith. Oxford: Berg, 1990. 221-234.
Lenckos, Frauke E. "Monika Maron: *Stille Zeile Sechs*." *New German Review* 8 (1992): 106-116.
Lewis, Alison. "Re-membering the Barbarian: Memory and Repression in Monika Maron's *Animal Triste*." *The German Quarterly* 71.1 (1998): 30-46.
Lukens, Nancy. "Gender and the Work Ethic in the Environ-mental Novels of Monika Maron and Lia Pirskawetz." *Studies in GDR Culture and Society 8*. Ed. Margy Gerber. London: University Press of America, 1988. 65-81.
Maron, Monika. *Animal Triste*. Frankfurt am Main: Fischer, 1996.
---. *Flugasche*. Frankfurt am Main: Fischer, 1981.
---. "Ich war ein antifaschistisches Kind." *Nach Maßgabe meiner Begreifungskraft*. 9-28.
---. Interview with Gerhard Richter. "Verschüttete Kultur—Ein Gespräch mit Monika Maron." *GDR Bulletin* 18.1 (1992): 2-7.
---. "Nach Maßgabe meiner Begreifungskraft." *Nach Maßgabe meiner Begreifungskraft*. 103-111.
---. *Nach Maßgabe meiner Begreifungskraft*. Frankfurt am Main: Fischer, 1993.
---. "Das neue Elend der Intellektuellen." *Nach Maßgabe meiner Begreifungskraft*. 80-90.
---. *Pawels Briefe*. Frankfurt am Main: Fischer, 1999.
---. *Stille Zeile Sechs*. Frankfurt am Main: Fischer, 1991.
---. *Die Überläuferin*. Frankfurt am Main: Fischer, 1988.
---. "Verspätete Lektüre. Über Uwe Johnson." *neue deutsche literatur* 46:2 (1998): 158-170.
---. "Writers and the People." *New German Critique* 52 (1991): 36-41.
---. "Zonophobie." *Nach Maßgabe meiner Begreifungskraft*. 112-120.
Meckel, Christoph. *Suchbild: über meinen Vater*. Düsseldorf: claassen Verlag, 1980.
Reich-Ranicki, Marcel. "Der Liebe Fluch." *Der Spiegel* 2 Dec.1996: 185-190.
Rossbacher, Brigitte. "(Re)visions of the Past: Memory and Historiography in Monika Maron's *Stille Zeile Sechs*." *Colloquia Germanica* 27.1 (1994): 13-24.
---. "The Status of State and Subject: Reading Monika Maron from *Flugasche* to *Animal Triste*." *Wendezeiten. Zeitenwende. Positionbestimmungen zur deutschsprachigen Literatur 1945-1995*. Ed. Brigitte Rossbacher and Robert Weninger. Tübingen: Stauffenburg Verlag, 1997. 193-214.
Schlink, Bernhard. *Der Vorleser*. Zürich: Diogenes, 1995.
Schmidt, Ricarda. "From Surrealism to Realism: Monika Maron's *Die Überläuferin and Stille Zeile Sechs*." *Women and the Wende. Social and Cultural Reflections of the German Unification Process*. Ed. Elizabeth Boa and Janet Wharton. Amsterdam: Rodopi, 1994. 247-255.
---. "'The Gender of Thought': Recollection, Imagination, and Eroticism in Fictional Conceptions of East and West German Identity." *Whose Story?—Continuities in Contemporary German Language Literature*. Ed. Arthur Williams, Stuart Parkes and Julian Preece. Frankfurt am Main: Peter Lang, 1998. 219-247.
Schneider, Peter. *Vati*. Darmstadt and Neuwied: Luchterhand, 1987.
Walser, Martin. "Die Banalität des Guten." *Süddeutsche Zeitung* 10 Dec. 1998, sec. *Feuilleton* 17.

JAMES R. REECE

Remembering the GDR: Memory and Evasion in Autobiographical Writing from the Former GDR

In the opening lines of the 1990 essay "Zur Erinnerung. Brief an alle, die es angeht," Günter de Bruyn makes the following ironic appeal to his unnamed readers:

> Dieser Brief, sehr geehrte Herren, möchte Sie dazu bringen, die Arbeit des Umwälzens, mit der Sie beschäftigt sind, für einige Minuten ruhen zu lassen und den stetig nach vorn, in die Zukunft, gerichteten Blick kurz zurück oder nach innen zu wenden—sich also zu erinnern, bevor das Vergessen beginnt. (7) [1]

As soon becomes clear, the "sehr geehrte Herren" of de Bruyn's salutation are the countless functionaries of the GDR's extensive bureaucracy and security apparatus, many of whom in November and December of 1989, as de Bruyn was writing, were already in the midst of a personal *Wende* of their own. It is they, de Bruyn goes on to argue, who are now in the best position to offer some insight into the "heimlichen oder auch unheimlichen Mächte, die unser aller Leben bewegten oder tangierten"(8).[2] They had been, after all, the visible agents of those very forces that, at one time or other, had left their mark on the lives of virtually all of the GDR's citizens.

To this audience de Bruyn facetiously proposes the establishment of a "Zentralen Erinnerungsbüros," the *ZEB*, an office for the purpose of collecting memory. Here a computer would carefully catalog, cross-reference and store the individual memories of the GDR's citizens from the past forty years, such that at the touch of a button one might learn "wer, wo und wann für wen Schicksal spielte" (14).[3] Far from the threatening prospect one might at first imagine, de Bruyn suggests that such an office would be welcomed by large segments of the population. And he assures his readers that any attempt to assign blame would be senseless: "[. . .] denn jeder hatte der schlechten Sache ja guten Glaubens oder

1 "This letter, most honored sirs, is written in the hope you might pause for a few minutes in the work of upheaval with which you are busy and briefly direct your glance—now trained so intently forward, into the future—backwards or inwards—that is, remember before the forgetting begins." All unattributed translations are my own.

2 "secret or even sinister powers that moved or touched upon all of our lives."

3 "who, where and when, had determined whose fate."

der Not gehorchend oder mit Widerwillen, auf jeden Fall aber der Pflicht nachkommend, gedient" (14).[4] As the place where all citizens could rid themselves of or, as the case might be, "correct" their memories, the *ZEB* would play a crucial role in the psychic healing of the GDR's population, while allowing historians to document conclusively: "daß hier ein fleißiges und gutgläubiges Volk, in dem jeder für jeden nur immer das Beste gewollt hatte, von einer Handvoll Unfähiger und Korrupter, die den Staat durch den Bau luxuriöser Jagdhäuser zugrunde gerichtet hatten, unterdrückt worden war" (15).[5]

De Bruyn's sardonic proposal works simultaneously on two levels. As satire, the "letter" anticipates the actions of many who will attempt to avoid accountability for their part, whether active or passive, in what the GDR had been and become over its forty-year existence. On this level, de Bruyn mocks his fellow citizens and the anonymous "geehrte Herren" of the infamous *Staatssicherheit* (secret police) for their hasty retreat from any official association with the GDR. At its most essential core, however, the proposal is, despite its obvious irony, a serious call for "remembering the GDR"; that is, for individual accountability and a truthful coming to terms with the totalitarian state and its legacy. For de Bruyn, remembering is an essential and necessary task that must be undertaken immediately, "bevor das Vergessen beginnt" (7).[6]

---

4 "for each person had, after all, served the bad cause in good faith, or out of necessity, or with reluctance, in any case, however, in keeping with (his) duty."

5 "that here an industrious and credulous nation, in which each person had only ever wanted the best for his fellow citizens, had been oppressed by a handful of incompetents and reprobates who had led the country into ruin through the building of luxurious hunting lodges."

6 "before the forgetting begins." In remarks made following a reading of this essay in Berlin during the summer of 1990, de Bruyn stressed "die Notwendigkeit, sich zu erinnern—und zwar kritisch" ("the need to remember—and to remember critically")—a need which, in his view, was all the more urgent as the two German states rushed toward unification. Before the same audience, the poet Heinz Czechowski struck a similar note in his essay "Anmerkungen zur Trauerarbeit in der DDR" (broadcast earlier in 1990 by the *Norddeutscher Rundfunk*). In discussion with the audience, Czechowski expressed concern, not unlike de Bruyn's, over what he called the danger of a "Verflachung der Trauerarbeit" ("lack of depth in grieving"). For Czechowski, it remains a central task of literature to counteract the impulse to forget. This task took on added urgency during this transitional year of 1990: "weil das Volk mehr Interesse an der Bewältigung der Zukunft hat" ("because the people are more interested in coming to terms with the future"). Czechowski's formulation "Trauerarbeit" ("work of grieving"), with its implicit reference to the legacy of Nazi dictatorship in 1945, suggests a reflective and inward "coming to terms" with the GDR. In place of an aggressive attack against those assumed to be responsible, Czechowski calls for "die anständige Aufarbeitung unserer zwiespältigen Vergangenheit" ("the decorous clearing up of our divided past") and the need for writers to explore why the GDR had taken the path it had. In his view, not least of all writers have the responsibility to ask what role they played both individually and as a group in the GDR's failed history. De Bruyn and Czechowski were among several GDR writers who gave readings before and participated in discussions with a group of North American Germanists at the 1990 Loyola College Berlin Seminar: "Literatur und Gesellschaft der beiden deutschen Staaten" July 16-21, 1990.

Four years later in 1994, Christa Wolf commented on the difficulty that the work of remembering entails. In the speech "Abschied von Phantomen. Zur Sache: Deutschland," Wolf dismisses as illusion any idea of an easy break with the GDR's troubling legacy, either for herself or, indeed, for any of her fellow citizens: "So leicht und heiter, wie es am 4. November 1989 auf dem Alexanderplatz schien, können wir uns von unserer Vergangenheit nicht verabschieden."(335).[7] Here she notes also the troubling tendency among many ex-GDR citizens to turn away from any honest attempt at dealing with the past. For many in the East, unification has brought with it a new sense of psychological dislocation and estrangement; too often East Germans have had to discover that openness in discussing the past is used against them. She continues that this experience serves all too readily in turn as a "Vorwand für die Abwehr jeder kritischen Selbstbefragung oder sogar für die Umdeutung der eigenen Biographie"(335).[8]

The reluctance and even active resistance among GDR citizens to examine honestly their own past is clearly reminiscent of the situation confronted by an earlier generation of German authors and intellectuals. In the 1950s and 1960s a new generation of post-war writers in the West used their writing to hold up a mirror to the Nazi past at a time when their fellow citizens were more disposed to leave the past behind and "move ahead" with the project of rebuilding Germany. In the wake of German unification and the often startling revelations of the *Gauck-Behörde*—an almost eerie, real-life imitation of de Bruyn's *Zentrales Erinnerungsbüro*—it is not surprising that during the past ten years writers in the East should have become agents and advocates for remembering.

In the 1990s autobiography in various guises has figured prominently in the large body of writing devoted to remembering the GDR. Perhaps quite naturally,

---

7 "We cannot say goodbye to our past as easily and cheerfully as we thought we could at the Alexanderplatz on November 4, 1989" (van Heurck 301). Wolf's essay is the concluding piece in the collection of letters, essays, and other texts published in 1994 under the title *Auf dem Weg nach Tabou* (English translation by Jan van Heurk under the title: *Parting from Phantoms*). While not autobiography per sé, the collection of texts nonetheless offers both a probing self-interrogation and, ultimately, a self-defense, as Wolf's response to her critics and the controversy over her role as a leading writer in the GDR.

8 "a pretext to avoid any critical self-questioning and are even revising their life histories" (van Heurck 301). Wolf is one of several writers to note the disturbing tendency to "reinterpret" one's biography in light of the *Wende*. In the satirical poem "Kollektiver Abgesang," one of "Fünf sarkastische Sonette" published together in 1992, the poet Yaak Karsunke has his "chorus" declare its collective innocence in all things having to do with the GDR while regretting that its (silent and passive) "heroism" during the dictatorship has gone unnoticed. Hence the sonnet's concluding lines: "das einzige, was uns dabei geniert: / dass unser heldentum nun niemand honoriert" ("the only thing that bothers us about this: / that no one now honors our heroics"). As suggested also (if somewhat less directly) in de Bruyn's and Wolf's essays, in Karsunke's poem the socialist dictatorship serves as the convenient excuse of the "average citizen" for forty years of "getting along" and "getting by." Thus the collective "wir" of the poem excuses itself from the very sort of critical and self-critical reflection that de Bruyn, Czechowski, and Wolf are calling for in the early 1990s.

writers who had lived part or all of their creative lives in the shadow of a restrictive and coercive state turned to autobiographical writing, whether as a simple act of self-defense and self-definition, or as the means to interrogate their lives as former citizens of the GDR. As might be expected, the approaches to autobiographical writing and the forms it has taken have been varied, and the results have been mixed.[9]

In the traditional view of autobiography as a literary form there is an implicit claim to truth: the autobiographer recalls his or her own story, a story which only he or she can completely know and, perhaps, adequately tell; it is to be a "true" account of one's life, based on "facts" and free of invention. The literary-theoretical debate of the last 30 years has challenged this seemingly naïve claim to "truth," pointing to the unreliability of such categories as authorial intention and calling the very language of the text itself into question. And yet, despite the apparent "impossibility" of autobiography, the form continues to attract both writers and readers alike who find in it a way of approaching some measure of truth about "self" and its place in time and history.[10]

The telling of the "facts" of one's own story is at once both attractive, in the straightforward simplicity of its intention, and fraught with unexpected pitfalls in its actual execution. In the opening pages of his 1991 autobiography *Abspann. Erinnerung an meine Gegenwart*, Hermann Kant is confident in the knowledge that he writes "im Schutze von Tatsachen" ("under the protection of facts" 5). He appears oblivious to the precarious nature of the "facts" of one's existence, filtered as they are through individual memory; similarly, he prefers to ignore his own shaping and selecting presence in the text as the author of his life story. Thus Kant writes of his longstanding intention to record those parts of his life story that had not found a place in his other books and realizes that his memories will serve well in the place of fictional invention, which he readily forsakes.[11] But as Kant's book illustrates, writing "under the protection of facts" does not

9 As Wolfgang Emmerich and others have pointed out, the flood of autobiographical texts that began to appear after the *Wende* had important antecedents in the mid-1980s. For an informative discussion of autobiographical writing both before and after 1989-90, see Emmerich, 479-487. See also Andress's discussion of the autobiographies by Stefan Heym, Hermann, Kant, Heiner Müller, and de Bruyn (*Zwischenbilanz*) in "Neue Autobiographien von DDR Schriftstellern."

10 By way of introduction to his discussion of the autobiographies by Kant and de Bruyn, Andress provides a useful summary of the challenges to autobiography in the work of Paul de Man and Philip Lejeune. It is Lejeune who concludes that "in spite of the fact that autobiography is impossible, this in no way prevents it from existing." As Andress goes on to observe, despite the "impossibility" of the project, writers are drawn to autobiography and the notion that it can serve as an avenue to self-discovery. See both "Kants *Abspann*" (137-138) and "Mittel der (Selbst-)Erkenntnis" (1-2).

11 Kant comments: "Von den Konflikten, durch die man kam, darf keiner als ausgedacht und ertüftelt geschmäht werden; man schreibt im Schutze von Tatsachen, wenn man von seinem Leben schreibt" (5-6). ("None of the conflicts that one has endured may be rejected as made-up or contrived; one is writing under the protection of facts when one writes of one's life")

guarantee either good autobiography or, necessarily, a truthful book. For while his book is full to overflowing with facts, the "whole truth" of Kant's life is sadly absent. Indeed, as others (among them, Günter de Bruyn) have previously observed, the abundance of facts, delivered in countless often digressive anecdotes, ultimately obscures and distorts rather than reveals the man behind these experiences.[12] Kant's less-than-straightforward *Erinnerungen* (memories) belie his naïve reliance on the "facts" of his life to speak for themselves; they illustrate well the problematic relationship between memory and truth, between truthfulness and evasion in autobiographical writing, which shall be at the center of the discussion below.

Kant's easy confidence in his ability to relate the facts of his life stands in sharp contrast to Christa Wolf's self-questioning uncertainty when confronting "diese verdammte Wahrheitsfrage" ("Antwort" 197)[13] as she calls it in her 1992 correspondence with the Russian writer and critic Efim Etkind. In Wolf's formulation:

> Wie kommt es, daß, je näher man an "die Wahrheit," das heißt an sich selber, die multiplen Wesen in sich und besonders an jenes Wesen herangeht, mit dem man sich am wenigsten identifizieren möchte: wie kommt es, frage ich, daß sich in den Text, der sich auf die Spur dieses Wesens und seiner Wahrheit begibt, auf dem Weg vom Kopf über die Hand bis aufs Papier immer ein Hauch von Unaufrichtigkeit einschleicht? (197) [14]

As Wolf suggests in her response to Etkind, writing truthfully about oneself is an extremely difficult if not impossible task: not so much due to the fragile nature of the "facts" themselves as to "die Leichtigkeit zu lügen und die Unmöglichkeit, die Wahrheit zu sagen" (197),[15] especially when exploring the least likeable and most problematic aspects of oneself. That Wolf is attempting to write truthfully of her life and actions as a writer (i.e., a person of status and privilege) in a repressive state merely magnifies the difficulty and complicates the task of interrogating one's life.

Among the writers who spent most or all of their creative lives prior to 1990 in the GDR, Günter de Bruyn has written perhaps most extensively on the questions posed by autobiographical writing in general and by the overlapping

12 There is broad agreement among critics that Kant's book "fails" the test of good autobiography. See Andress's "Kants *Abspann*" for a careful analysis of this failure.

13 "this damned question of the truth" (van Heurck 158).

14 "In other words, how is it that the closer you get to the truth—that is to yourself, to the multiple beings inside you, and especially to the one of these beings with whom you would least like to be identified—how is it, I ask, that a tinge of insincerity always sneaks into any text in which you try to track down this being and its truth, somewhere along the way from the head to the hand to the paper?" (van Heurck 158).

15 "On the Ease of Lying and the Impossibility of Telling the Truth" (van Heurck 158). Here Wolf is using Etkind's formulation, who in his letter to her expresses great affinity with the narrator of Wolf's controversial book *Was bleibt* ("Von den multiplen Wesen in uns" 194).

problems of memory and truthfulness when writing of one's life in a totalitarian state. De Bruyn's views on autobiography are articulated in three dissimilar but complementary texts that appeared in the 1990s: First of all, in a critical review of Hermann Kant's autobiography *Abspann* published in 1991; secondly, in a lengthy theoretical essay in which he explores the nature and purpose of autobiography; and finally, by example, in his own autobiography, the first two volumes of which have appeared under the titles *Zwischenbilanz. Eine Jugend in Berlin* (1992) and *Vierzig Jahre. Ein Lebensbericht* (1996). Taken together, the sharply critical review, the theoretical essay, and the carefully told account of his forty-year career as a writer in the GDR offer a coherent and insightful view into both the problems and the possibilities of autobiographical writing from the former GDR.[16]

Following the completion of *Zwischenbilanz* in 1992 and during the work on *Vierzig Jahre*, de Bruyn took time to collect his thoughts on the nature and function of autobiography and to reflect on the problems and challenges of the genre in a series of lectures given in 1993 at the University of Vienna and published later as a small book with the title *Das erzählte Ich. Über Wahrheit und Dichtung in der Autobiographie*. Here, he writes of the strong attraction and the formal challenge for a writer of fiction like himself "Faktisches zu erzählen," that is, "unter Verzicht auf Fiktionen Tatsachen zu erzählen" (16).[17] He goes on to differentiate between various aspects of the impulse to write factually about oneself. It is, first and foremost, a means of confronting oneself, of "Selbstauseinandersetzung," of "Selbstforschung und Selbsterklärung" but also a means of "Rechenschaftsablegung" (18); it is, utimately, "der Versuch, mich über mich selbst aufzuklären," the attempt to discover "wer ich eigentlich sei" (19).[18] Autobiography also involves examining one's relationship to history and to the time in which one has lived; it is the opportunity "das Ich in die historischen Geschehnisse einzuordnen, es aus ihnen erklären, durch sie vielleicht auch bewerten zu können" (19-20).[19] De Bruyn elucidates: "Das Ich

16 Halverson similarly considers the two parts of de Bruyn's autobiography and the theoretical essay as "a triad" in which the essay provides "the framework within which to understand *Zwischenbilanz* and *Vierzig Jahre*, including how de Bruyn chose to narrate his life story and how he constructed his identity" (1).

17 "to narrate factual things," that is, "to tell facts without recourse to fiction."

18 de Bruyn's terms translate roughly as "self-confrontation," "self-discovery and self-explanation," and "accounting for oneself"; it is, as he summarizes further, "the attempt to enlighten myself about myself" and to discover "who it is that I actually am." Cf. Andress' discussion of Lejeune's *pacte autobiographique* "in dem sich Autobiographen nicht zu einer historischen Genauigkeit verpflichten würden, was ohnehin unmöglich sei, sondern eher zu dem Versuch, sich aufrichtig mit dem eigenen Leben auseinanderzusetzen und es zu verstehen" ("Kants *Abspann*" 137). ("in which autobiographers would not be held to a standard of historical accuracy, which is anyhow impossible, but rather to the attempt to analyze one's own life openly and to understand it.")

19 "to place the self in the context of historical events, to elucidate it from them and to be able to evaluate it with reference to them."

und die Zeitläufte müssen aufeinander bezogen werden, in der Hoffnung, daß beide dadurch Konturen gewinnen und daß aus dem Einzelfall so etwas wie eine Geschichtsschreibung von unten entsteht" (20).[20] Finally, to construct a narrative only from "the facts" of one's life is a challenge for the writer of fiction, "ein Wirtschaften im Mangel" ("managing scarcity") that has a formal attraction of its own. But restricting oneself to "the facts" does not spare the autobiographer from struggling with the "question of truth" which will merely present itself in a different, subtle way in the form of the narration itself (20).

In de Bruyn's view, a central difficulty of autobiographical writing lies in the fact that, by its very nature, it claims the status of "truth," even "the whole truth," for itself. It is, in fact, a "Dichtung"—used by de Bruyn in Goethe's sense of the word—an ordered and shaped collection of "partial truths" ("Teilwahrheiten") that together represent an attempt to write, "die ganze Wahrheit über das schreibende und beschriebene Ich" (31-32).[21] The trouble is, of course, that each of us has her or his own "truth," a truth that of necessity is determined by both the moment in which it is written and the limits of the author's self-knowledge. As de Bruyn sees it, the writer begins with an image of his or her present self and must attempt to show just how this self came to be (35). In this context, he draws upon his own experience to caution against "false memories," for memory can enlarge and diminish, reduce and enhance; it can reshape reality according to its needs (39). With some chagrin he recalls the Stasi's attempt many years earlier to secure his cooperation as an informant, an episode that, as he remembered it, had lasted but a few weeks before he had seen through their ruses and refused any further contact with them. When, in the early 1990s, he was able to read his Stasi files, he was startled to find a significantly different portrayal of the events:

> Was sich mir in der Erinnerung fast zum Ruhmesblatt des Widerstands gestaltet hatte, wurde mir nun zum Schandblatt verwandelt, sieht man von meiner tatsächlich konsequenten Weigerung am Ende ab. Zwischen den Belästigungen der Stasi-Leute hatten nicht, wie ich mich erinnert hatte, wenige Wochen, sondern zwei Jahre gelegen; sie waren mehr als zweimal in meine Wohnung gekommen und hatten mehr von mir erfahren, als mein Gedächtnis bewahrt hatte. Offentsichtlich hatte die Demütigung vor den gehaßten und gefürchteten Leuten, die ich mir nicht vergeben konnte, einen Verdrängungsmechanismus in Gang gesetzt, der es mir erlaubte, als ich selbst weiterzuleben, und die Erinnerung hatte zusätzlich manches zu meinen Gunsten verkehrt. (*Das erzählte Ich* 45-46)[22]

---

20 "The self and the times must be examined in relation to one another in the hope that both thereby become clearer and that out of individual experience there is something like history writing from below."

21 "the entire truth about the self (the 'I') who is writing and who is being portrayed."

22 "What in my memory had nearly become a glorious example of resistance was transformed into its disgraceful opposite, if one disregards my refusal in the end, which was in fact consistent. In between the harassments of the people from the Stasi there had not been, as I

The lesson to be drawn from this revealing example of repression is clear to de Bruyn: one must cultivate a healthy "mistrust" of one's own memory and be willing to question the contradictions that may result from its subjective and "self"-defensive reshaping of past events (45).

Nevertheless, the inherent subjectivity of autobiography and the questions of authenticity and truthfulness that it raises do not, in and of themselves, trouble de Bruyn. Indeed, *Zeitbezogenheit* (i.e. that the autobiographer writes in a particular era and from the temporal perspective of a particular point in his or her life) and *Subjektivität*, subjectivity, are in his view integral to the whole project. What ultimately distinguishes autobiography and gives it its particular interest and contour is "daβ hier jemand sich so beschreibt, wie er sich selbst sieht und beurteilt. Interessanter als die mitgeteilten Fakten über eine Person ist die Art, wie sie von dieser Person mitgeteilt werden. Objektivität, die auch nicht möglich wäre, wird gar nicht verlangt" (62).[23]

Yet, one can and should distinguish between "good" and "bad" autobiography. Midway through the essay, de Bruyn points in passing to the greater likelihood of poorly realized and dishonest autobiographies in times of abrupt political change. In clear reference to the German *Wende*, he notes that many of the memoirs appearing in Eastern Germany in the early 1990s provide ample evidence for intentional omissions, self-deception and plain dishonesty (*Ich* 41-42). Precisely because the need to justify and acquit oneself is so strong in times of radical political change, there is, de Bruyn seems to suggest, an even greater need for reader and writer alike to be wary: to mistrust

had remembered, a few weeks but two years. They had come into my home more than twice and had learned more from me than my memory had preserved. Apparently, the humiliation before these hated and feared people—a humiliation that I could not forgive myself—had set in motion a process of repression that allowed me to continue to live as the 'self' I was accustomed to, and my memory [of the events] had additionally changed some things to my advantage." In an earlier article in the *Frankfurter Allgemeine Zeitung*, de Bruyn had commented on feeling both "Schuld" ("guilt") and "Betroffenheit" ("perplexity") at this discovery. Although his and other *Stasi* files were clearly full of false information and were to varying degrees "ein Phantasieprodukt" ("a fantasy product") of their many authors, they nonetheless provided an important check for one's memory and its sometimes more comfortable version of events. Here, as is also the case in his later analysis of this episode in *Vierzig Jahre* (cf. the chapter "Streng geheim." 190-202), de Bruyn is characteristically hard on himself for not having lived up to his own high standards of behavior ("Dieses Mißtrauen" 163).

23 "that here someone is describing himself just as he sees and judges himself to be. More interesting than the facts that are communicated about a person is the manner in which they are communicated. Objectivity, which wouldn't be possible anyway, is not even expected."

memory, to watch for obvious omissions and evasions, and to question the text for signs of self-delusion and dishonesty.[24]

De Bruyn's view of what constitutes good and bad autobiographical writing can be found in nascent form in his 1991 review of Hermann Kant's *Abspann*. The unflattering title of the review, "Scharfmaul und Prahlhans" captures de Bruyn's response to the author's narrative stance, a stance that, in his view, is fundamentally at odds with Kant's announced autobiographical purpose. De Bruyn summarizes: "immer entsteht der Eindruck: Er prahlt. Immer ist er auf Beifall aus oder auf dessen Gegenteil. Immer macht sich der Drang bemerkbar, im Mittelpunkt öffentlicher Aufmerksamekeit zu stehen" (17).[25] This tendency is most apparent to de Bruyn in the countless anecdotes that interrupt the flow of Kant's narrative. In one aside after another, Kant digresses to provide some interesting and cleverly told tidbit from his many encounters with well-known and influential personalities of our time. In the process, the life story that ought to emerge is overwhelmed and eventually lost in the extraneous detail. This is true even of Kant's engaging account of his childhood and youth in Hamburg and Parchim that de Bruyn considers the best of the "three books" contained in this one long one.[26] Here Kant introduces his readers to the working class milieu in which he grew up and to a large and interesting cast of characters from his family, the neighborhood, and the family's extended circle of friends. These passages, which offer some insight into the influences that shaped Kant's social and political consciousness, are undercut by the intrusive presence of Kant's digressive and ironic narrative voice (17).

Similarly, the second of the "three books," consisting largely of "nostalgische Nichtigkeiten" contained in "eine über den ganzen Band

---

24 Under the chapter heading "Historisches," de Bruyn comments on the difficult balancing act required of the autobiographer when looking back at one's actions in public life. On the one hand, a writer must be scrupulously honest and exacting when questioning his own past actions. De Bruyn speaks in this regard of "der Grundsatz der Schonungslosigkeit" ("the principle of pitilessness") (*Ich* 56). On the other hand, examining one's role in contemporary public life brings with it a danger of becoming entangled in current polemics and self-justifying arguments, all of which can detract from the main task of being a "möglichst genauer Chronist seiner Selbst und daraus folgend, der Zeitläufte [. . .]" (59-60). ("as accurate a chronicler of one's self as possible, and as a result, of the times as well")

25 "one always has the impression: he is boasting. He is always looking for applause or for its opposite. The need to be at the center of public attention is always apparent."

26 De Bruyn begins his review with the following general characterization: "Dieses hastig geschriebene Buch besteht eigentlich aus dreien, einem überflüssigen, einem ärgerlichen und einem guten, die mehr oder weniger geschickt ineinander verwoben sind" ("This hastily written book actually consists of three [books]: a superfluous one, an irritating one, and a good one, that are more or less adeptly intertwined with one another") (17). In addition to the account of Kant's childhood and youth (the "good" and "best" book of the three), de Bruyn finds two other less appealing and far less successful books, which he refers to collectively as an "Enthüllungs- und Rechtfertigungswälzer" ("a huge volume of revelations and self-justifications") and which earn, respectively, the approbations "überflüssig" and "ärgerlich" (17).

verstreute Sammlung von Anekdoten,"[27] would not be worth mentioning were it not for the fact that it represented one of the ways in which Kant seeks to avoid confronting himself and his actions: "Denn statt sein Verhältnis zur Macht zu klären, macht er aus seinen Begegnungen mit den Mächtigen niedliche Geschichten, in denen von Gefahr und Drohung nichts mehr zu spüren ist" (17).[28] Here is, in succinct form, both de Bruyn's main criticism of Kant's book and, implicitly, the standard against which he would judge all serious autobiography. Kant's recollections lack any honest attempt at self-interrogation, something that de Bruyn holds to be central to the autobiographical impulse. Where readers might rightly expect a thoughtful coming-to-terms with his well-documented public life, perhaps even self-revelatory insights into the pressures he was subject to during his long presidency of the *Schriftstellerverband* (Writers' Union), Kant is strangely reticent to provide clarification. Where de Bruyn demands that an author be "pitiless" (*Ich* 59) in his interrogation of his own public persona, Kant prefers to divert his readers with self-important anecdotes and witty asides.[29]

Nowhere is this failing clearer than in the large portion of Kant's *Erinnerungen* devoted to his life as a writer and cultural functionary in the GDR. In short vignettes, in which both friend and foe are introduced and, accordingly, either celebrated or dispatched, he recounts his literary successes as well his own early difficulties with the GDR's unrelenting cultural bureaucracy; and he mounts an aggressive defense of his leadership of the *Schriftstellerverband.* Kant claims to have spoken his mind when it counted and points to his interventions on behalf of colleagues and their books as well as to what he considered to be the development of democratic procedures during his time as president of the *Verband.* It is these claims that lead de Bruyn to suggest the appellation "Großmaul" ("big-mouth") in place of Kant's own usage "Scharfmaul" ("sharp-tongue"), for Kant's account of this most public part of his career is in large part "eine Aufzählung von Heldentaten" (17).[30]

At the same time, Kant only reluctantly admits responsibility for the darker moments of the organization's history, such as in the case of the controversial and much-publicized expulsion of nine critical writers from the

27 "little bits of nostalgia" contained in "a collection of anecdotes strewn throughout the entire volume."

28 "For instead of clarifying his relationship to those in power, he uses his meetings with the powerful as the stuff of nice stories in which there is no trace of danger or threat."

29 Cf. Andress, "Kants *Abspann*" 139.

30 "a catalog of heroic deeds." De Bruyn summarizes Kant's presentation with skeptical irony: "Denn er hat immer, intern versteht sich, das Maul aufgerissen, immer Mut vor Sekretärsthronen bewiesen und damit nicht nur Schlimmeres verhütet, sondern auch viel Gutes erreicht" ("For he always spoke up–privately, of course–he always displayed courage before the thrones of the party big-wigs and had not only prevented worse things from happening but had often done some good in the process.") (17).

Schriftstellerverband in 1979.[31] And here, too, Kant's grudging apology for his role in these events is undercut by an involved justification that seeks to spread the blame evenly among all who were involved, including the nine colleagues who were among those who "[. . .] uns so in die Ecke trieb, daβ wir nur noch wütend um uns schlagen konnten" (490).[32] In these passages, Kant does not so much tell his own story as his side of the story; he is not engaged–as we might expect of the serious autobiographer, in the process of interrogating his past, but is occupied instead with answering his critics.

De Bruyn's review suggests that Kant's autobiography fails in two important ways. First, Kant's account of his life and particularly that of his very public life as a writer and cultural functionary lacks the truthful candor ("Aufrichtigkeit") that is a given in the relationship of trust between the writer and reader of autobiography. For de Bruyn, this lack of truthfulness has less to do with the facts themselves than with Kant's apparent unwillingness to question his long-rehearsed and "self"-defensive version of his public life. Kant's reluctance to examine this public life against the historical record of the GDR's repressive cultural policies and well-documented machinations against critical writers and others–policies which he implicitly and explicitly represented in his role as one of the GDR's foremost cultural spokesmen—undermine the credibility of his narrative and can only lead the informed reader to distrust and eventually discount Kant's voice. Secondly, whether as a conscious strategem or not, Kant's failure to reign in his "Erzähl- und Verzierlust" ("Scharfmaul" 18) leaves the reader with a diffuse and unclear image of the man and the times in which he lived.[33] By failing to give shape and focus to the abundant material of his life, Kant fails also to lend it the representative "truth" that individual life stories can, in de Bruyn's view, attain as a kind of "history from below" (*Das erzählte Ich* 20).

In both of these respects de Bruyn's own narrative of his life as a writer and citizen in the GDR offers an instructive contrast to Hermann Kant's. For, if Kant's book fails in part because of his inveterate "Erzähllust" and the seeming inability, if not unwillingness, to give shape and meaning to this abundant

31 See especially Chapter XX of *Abspann* (465-490).

32 "[who] drove us into such a corner that we had no choice but to strike out furiously in all directions."

33 "delight in telling stories and embellishing them" Andress summarizes Kant's underlying strategy with the term "Legendenbau" ("legend-building"), concluding his article with the judgment: "In *Abspann* bietet uns Kant die Legende, die er der Nachwelt überliefern will" ("In *Abspann* Kant presents us with the legend that he wants to pass on to posterity") ("Kants *Abspann*" 147). De Bruyn suggests a dual strategy at work in Kant's narrative: on the one hand Kant employs a successful marketing strategy by serving up to his audience witty stories about his comings and goings with a large cast of influential contemporaries ("Scharfmaul" 17); at the same time his profuse anecdotes serve to obscure the real man behind the stories ("Scharfmaul" 18).

content, de Bruyn's is successful in its scrupulous honesty, its relative spareness, and its clear focus.

Of the writers who stayed in the GDR until the *Wende*, de Bruyn is something of an exception. He was neither, like Kant, a writer loyal to the party line nor was he an openly active dissident. And, if he gradually became better known in the West as a "critical" writer in the 1980s, it was not, as readers of *Vierzig Jahre* learn, because he wished to place himself in the limelight. To the contrary, had circumstances allowed, he would gladly have remained in his preferred role of a somewhat distant and always skeptical outsider, a role that to varying degrees he was able to maintain over most of the forty-year existence of the GDR.

Although the "forty years" of de Bruyn's title correspond to the "Lebensjahre der DDR" ("lifetime of the GDR"), it is not his intention to write a book about the GDR. Rather, as he explained in the essay *Das erzählte Ich*, his intent is to describe his own adult life "das sich zwar in der DDR abspielte und von ihr beeinflußt wurde, aber doch *mein* Leben blieb" (17-18).[34] Hence, the book accompanies de Bruyn more or less chronologically through the various stages of his adult life—as a student at the *Bibliothekfachschule* and as a young librarian, later as an independent writer—pausing along the way at important markers in the history of the GDR: most notably in June of 1953 (the workers' uprising in East Berlin), August of 1961 (the building of the Berlin Wall), November of 1976 (the expulsion of the dissident poet Wolf Biermann) and again in November of 1989 (the opening of the Berlin Wall and the borders between East and West). By linking his own development as a writer to the events that shaped his relationship to the state, de Bruyn is able to provide a psychologically revealing self-portrait that also provides his readers with a glimpse of what life in a broader sense was like in the totalitarian state.[35]

At the center of de Bruyn's narrative is the question of how an individual can maintain his or her integrity in the face of a powerful and coercive state, or more directly stated: how does one remain true to oneself without doing unnecessary harm to one's life and career? Throughout *Vierzig Jahre*, he describes in ever-new variation the difficult balancing act between "Mitlaufen

---

34 "that took place in the GDR and was influenced by it but still remained *my* life" [de Bruyn's emphasis]. Later in the essay de Bruyn adds the qualifying "hope" nevertheless "[daß] sich [...] aus dem erzählten Leben mit wenig Kommentierung ein Zeitbild ergibt" (56). (" that from the narrated life story with little commentary a picture of the times emerges.")

35 Tate observes that readers expecting information about important cultural and political events are likely to be disappointed by de Bruyn's book; his perspective remains throughout "that of the fallible observer whose memory may fail him at crucial moments and whose personal preoccupations often place these great historical moments in a curiously distanced light" (210). Andress also emphasizes the inherent subjectivity of de Bruyn's insights into life in the GDR and suggests that de Bruyn's successful autobiography is but one of many individual accounts that are needed before we will have a full and accurate picture of the GDR ("Mittel" 9).

und Distanzhalten" (204),[36] an act that he found himself required to perform again and again in his life as a citizen of the GDR. And at each repetition of this demanding "trick" he interrogates himself once again, measuring the damage, the inevitable "Schaden an Geist und Seele" that he and his friend Herbert had agreed must eventually result from living in the "Zwangsklima" (72) of the GDR.[37]

The state's coercive presence is evident at each new stage in de Bruyn's career. When his decision to become a librarian is frustrated in West Berlin by the lack of the *Abitur*, he is able to secure a place at the *Büchereischule* in East Berlin by agreeing to take part in the activities of the "youth organization": "Diese Nachgiebigkeit hatte zur Folge, daβ ich kurzzeitig als FDJ-Mitglied geführt wurde, aber nie Gebrauch davon machte, geschweige den Beitrag zahlte oder mich im blauen Hemd sehen lieβ" (10).[38] After several months of making excuses for not being able to attend the next official function, his pursuers finally lose interest and leave him to himself. In de Bruyn's response to this early example of coercion we can see both his strong impulse to remain on the outside and, in embryonic form, his most basic stratagem of "giving in" where he must, but never committing himself to more than the situation absolutely requires.[39]

As de Bruyn discovers later on, "keeping one's distance" as a means of maintaining one's integrity is not always as unproblematic as it was for the clever and stubborn 23-year old. Thus, when recalling one of his first library positions, he is ashamed at the role he was given to play on the library's *Bestandskommission*, in his words, "eine Art Volksgerichtshof für Bücher" (34)[40], whose task it was to rid the collection of "suspicious" books of bourgeois leaning. Now his memory zeroes in on the folded pamphlet of

36 "going along and keeping one's distance"

37 "damage to one's spirit and soul" resulting from the "coercive climate" of the GDR. Streul notes with reference to the dilemma faced by de Bruyn and other East Germans who found themselves at odds with the GDR's political system but were nonetheless dependent on it for educational and professional opportunities, that it was not so much a matter of choosing between "Anpassung oder Widerstand" ("conformity or opposition") as negotiating a position between "Anpassung *und* Widerstand" (963; my emphasis). Streul concludes, perhaps somewhat narrowly, that it is de Bruyn's primary purpose in *Vierzig Jahre* "diese Zwangslage zu beschreiben und Rechenschaft über seine Handlungen und Versäumnisse zu geben" ("to describe this coercive environment and to provide a justification for his actions and omissions") (961).

38 "This pliability had as its result that I was listed for a short time as a member of the Free German Youth, but I never made use of it (membership status) much less paid dues or let myself be seen in a blue shirt (of the FGY)."

39 Halverson finds examples of this tension throughout both volumes of de Bruyn's autobiography; thus she refers to de Bruyn's "double identity," consisting of the external "public identity" required of his positions as a soldier, teacher, or librarian and of a "private inner self [. . .] attached to his world of writing and reading" (3).

40 "a kind of 'People's Court' for books" Here de Bruyn is referring to the notorious *Volksgerichtshof* of the Third Reich.

guidelines "zur Verbesserung der Buchbestände" (35)[41] in the introduction of which his name appeared as one of several contributors. De Bruyn finds only limited comfort in the fact that he and some of his colleagues were able eventually to save some of the "questionable" books, and is mildly amused at his own idealistic naiveté some forty years earlier:

> Für mich aber war und ist dieses Papier ein Grund zur Beschämung, doch zog ich damals daraus nicht die Lehre, daβ Mitmachen Mitverschulden bedeutet, sondern hielt an der Meinung, daβ man, um Schlimmeres zu verhüten, schlimme Posten wenn möglich besetzen sollte, noch lange Zeit fest. (35-36)[42]

This simple realization, "daß Mitmachen Mitverschulden bedeutet," accompanies de Bruyn throughout his narrative; it, more than any other single aspect of the text, sets de Bruyn's autobiography apart from many post-*Wende* examples of the genre that, like Kant's, disavow responsibility and succumb to self-justifying rhetoric.

If, as a beginning writer, de Bruyn still believed that, with occasional concessions, he would be able to protect his own and his work's integrity. Later, following his first successes, he could no longer be so sure. Writing of the success of his first novel, *Der Hohlweg*, he refers to it now as a "Holzweg" (116),[43] for it was written with an eye to the censor who would have to approve its publication. That the novel was awarded the GDR's *Heinrich Mann Preis* and enjoyed several reprintings was a source of embarrassment and many sleepless nights for the young de Bruyn, for he knew even then that it was his "flexibility" and "compliance" that were being honored and rewarded. "Sich willig und wendig zeigen" (95), "willfährig"(116, 186, 198), "nachgiebig" (186)—this is the vocabulary of pliability and of "going along," of "Mitlaufen," and de Bruyn searches his past for signs of it at each stage in his career.

From the perspective of the 1990s, it is easier for de Bruyn also to see the role that ambition played in the compromises that he struck along the way. Success was crucial to the independent life as a writer that he sought; it was the key to maintaining his precarious position as an outsider. Now it seems clear to de Bruyn that a combination of fear of the unknown and ambition (i.e. the possibility of continuing literary success in the GDR) was, together with his mother and his strong ties to the landscape of his native Brandenburg, the

41 "for the purpose of improving the library collection"

42 "But for me this paper was and remains a cause of shame; at the time I did not draw from it the lesson that participation is complicity, but rather held the view for a long time to come that, when possible, one ought to take on despicable tasks in order to prevent even worse things from happening."

43 Literally "a cart-path in the woods" but meaning here "the wrong track."

crucial factor in his decisions, both early and late in his career, not to go to the West.[44]

Success within the context of the GDR presented other difficulties for de Bruyn:

> Kritische Bücher wollte ich schreiben, aber die sollten in der DDR gedruckt und gelesen werden können. Auch Erfolg wollte ich damit haben, nicht aber durch diesen von einem Staat anerkannt werden, der von mir nicht anerkannt war. Daß diese Anerkennung Annehmlichkeiten brachte, vergrößerte noch mein Unbehagen. (144)[45]

De Bruyn's ambivalence regarding his success is a recurring motif in the text: with success came greater "freedom," whether in the form of travel privileges, increased material security, or simply in the possibility of being left in peace. Yet success brought with it also pressures, both from within and without, to cooperate and conform.[46] All of this changed abruptly for de Bruyn with the Stasi's attempt to recruit him as an informant in December of 1973.

The chapter in *Vierzig Jahre* devoted to this episode ("Streng geheim" 190-202) illustrates especially well the scrupulous rigor with which de Bruyn examines his actions for signs of personal weakness and self-compromising behavior. As noted previously, this episode, more than any other, encouraged in de Bruyn an enduring "Mißtrauen in mein Erinnerungsvermögen" (192), a "mistrust" that he has referred to elsewhere more broadly as "dieses Mißtrauen gegen mich selbst" ("Mißtrauen" 162).[47] Here, as throughout his narrative, de Bruyn adheres unflinchingly to "pitilessness" (*Das erzählte Ich* 59) as a guiding principle in examining what he now sees as his weakness when faced with Stasi intimidation. His judgment is characteristically severe: he writes of a personal sense of "Schmach" and "Scham" (*Jahre* 192) and of "die Tragödie meines Versagens" (201).[48] Upon reviewing his Stasi-file, he concludes

---

44 See especially the chapters "Gesamtdeutsches" (97-106) and "Westwärts, aufwärts" (122-132) in which de Bruyn describes his decisions on two occasions not to remain in the West when he had the opportunity and instead to return to the GDR. In an interview with Ingo Hermann in 1993, de Bruyn suggests another reason as well: he recalls there that in the 1980s he became uncomfortable with the fact that so many "critical" writers were leaving the GDR, and that this contributed to his resolve to stay. See *Was ich noch schreiben will* 52-54.

45 "I wanted to write critical books, but they ought to be able to be published and read in the GDR. I also wanted to be successful at it without being recognized for it by a State that I did not recognize. That this recognition brought amenities only increased my discomfort."

46 In such conflicts Halverson finds further evidence for the "incongruity between de Bruyn's internal and external identity," an incongruity which is summarized finally, she argues, in the fact that de Bruyn sees himself as "a German author and scholar" while the reading public and literary institutions in both East and West Germany insist upon categorizing him as an East German (6).

47 "mistrust in my ability to remember" and "this mistrust of myself."

48 "disgrace" and "shame" and of "the tragedy of my failure."

harshly: "Geheimnisse hatte ich nicht verraten, aber dem Wissen der Stasi Bestätigung gegeben und mich dabei in beschämender Weise als willfährig erwiesen. Ich war mir untreu geworden aus Angst" (198).[49] Elsewhere in the text, de Bruyn's rigorous self-judgment extends to "sins of omission" as well. Thus he recalls that his much-publicized speech at the tenth *Schriftstellerkongreß* (Writers' Congress) in 1987 calling for an end to censorship—a modest but significant "victory" in the context of the GDR's often unpredictable cultural politics and, justifiably, reason for some degree of personal satisfaction—was undercut by his and his colleagues' failure the very next day to protest the arrest of a group of citizens' rights activists in a church just blocks away from their meeting hall (230-31).

Following shortly after the Stasi episode, the expulsion of Wolf Biermann from the GDR in November of 1976 was to mark the end of de Bruyn's increasingly precarious balancing act between "Mitlaufen und Distanzhalten." For de Bruyn, the *Biermann-Affäre* was a critical watershed and an intellectual emancipation. For the first time critical writers and others in the GDR joined in common protest: "Das stärkte das Selbstbewußtsein und klärte die Fronten" (212).[50] In the group protest of 1976, the outsider de Bruyn moved beyond merely "keeping his distance" and joined with others in "resistance" to the state.

In the final chapter of his book, de Bruyn relates the mixed feelings that he felt at the opening of the Wall on 9 November 1989. Together with the dominant feeling of elation that the news brings, he reports "dunklere Melodien":

> Was sich störend unter dem Jubel regte, nährte sich auch aus Selbstvorwürfen, mangelnde Aktivität im Befreiungsprozeß betreffend, aus der Sorge, daß mit der Freiheit auch Dummheit und Bosheit freigesetzt würden, und aus einer Art Abschiedsschmerz. (255)[51]

The "pain of parting" has nothing to do with the hated repressive state; rather it is for the circle of friends, "der sich unter dem Druck von Bedrohung und Einschränkung gebildet hatte und nun zerfiel" (255).[52] He is quick, however, to allay our fears that he has fallen victim to false romanticism and *Ostalgie*. With characteristic calm clarity, he sees these alliances for the "Notgemeinschaften"

---

49 "I had not betrayed any secrets, but I had offered corroboration of the Stasi's information and had shown myself to be compliant in a shameful way. I had been untrue to myself out of fear."

50 "That strengthened [our] self-assurance and clearly drew the battle lines."

51 "darker melodies" and "What made itself disturbingly present amidst the rejoicing arose partly from self-recriminations having to do with [my] lack of involvement in the liberation process, from the concern that with the arrival of freedom stupidity and meanness would also be set free, and from a kind of pain at parting."

52 "That had formed under the pressure of threat and restriction and was now dissolving."

("communities of necessity") that they were, not as a political framework for the future. With the end of the GDR, it is only natural that they end as well.

Here, as throughout his book, de Bruyn remains a somewhat detached and skeptical observer of his time and of himself. As Dennis Tate has observed, de Bruyn succeeds in carefully preserving a "balance between the personal and the political" (212) without succumbing to "the temptations of playing to the (Western) gallery" (209). This two-fold success is closely tied, as we have seen above, to de Bruyn's scrupulous and uncompromising self-interrogation and to his healthy distrust of simple, black-and-white answers to the complex questions posed by the forty-year existence of the GDR. In *Vierzig Jahre*, de Bruyn reaffirms the promise and possibility of autobiography both as an avenue of self-discovery and a window to history.

Works Cited

Andress, Reinhard. "Hermann Kants Erinnerungsbuch *Abspann*: ein Beispiel von Legendenbau." *Seminar* 34.2 (May 1998): 137-148.

---. "Neue Autobiographien von DDR Schriftstellern. Beiträge zur Aufarbeitung der DDR?" *GDR Bulletin* 20.1 (Spring 1994): 1-12.

---. " Mittel der (Selbst-)Erkenntnis in Günter de Bruyns zweiteiliger Autobiographie *Zwischenbilanz* und *Vierzig Jahre.*" *glossen* 7 (1999): 12 pp. <http://www.dickinson.edu/departments/germn/glossen/heft7/andress.html>.

de Bruyn, Günter. *Das erzählte Ich. Über Wahrheit undDichtung in der Autobiographie*. Frankfurt am Main: Fischer Verlag, 1995.

---. "Dieses Mißtrauen gegen mich selbst. Schwierigkeiten beim Schreiben der Wahrheit: Ein Beitrag zum Umgang mit den Stasi-Akten." *Frankfurter Allgemeine Zeitung* 18 February 1993. Excerpted with the title "Selbstprüfung" in *Die Mauer fiel, die Mauer steht. Ein deutsches Lesebuch 1989-1999.* Ed. Hermann Glaser. Munich: deutscher taschenbuch verlag, 1999. 162-63.

---. "Scharfmaul und Prahlhans. Der 'Abspann' des Hermann Kant: der ehemalige Präsident des DDR-Schriftstellerverbandes hat seine Erinnerungen geschrieben." *Die Zeit* 34 (North American Edition, 27 September 1991): 17-18.

---. *Vierzig Jahre. Ein Lebensbericht.* Frankfurt am Main: Fischer Verlag, 1996.

---. *Was ich noch schreiben will. Gespräch mit Ingo Hermann.* Ed. Ingo Hermann. Göttingen: Lamuv Verlag, 1995.

---. "Zur Erinnerung. Brief an alle, die es angeht." *Sinn und Form* 3 (1990): 453-458. Rpt. in *Jubelschreie, Trauergesänge. Deutsche Befindlichkeiten.* Frankfurt am Main: Fischer Verlag, 1994. 7-15.

---. "Zur Erinnerung. Brief an alle, die es angeht." Reading and discussion. The Loyola College Berlin Seminar: "Literatur und Gesellschaft der beiden deutschen Staaten." Berlin. 17 July 1990.

Czechowski, Heinz. "Anmerkungen zur Trauerabeit in der DDR." Reading and discussion. The Loyola College Berlin Seminar: "Literatur und Gesellschaft der beiden deutschen Staaten." Berlin. 21 July 1990. Originally recorded and broadcast by the Norddeutscher Rundfunk. Hamburg. Germany. Spring, 1990.

Emmerich, Wolfgang. *Kleine Literaturgeschichte der DDR.* Leipzig: Kiepenheuer Verlag, 1996.

Glaser, Hermann, ed. *Die Mauer fiel, die Mauer steht. Ein deutsches Lesebuch 1989-1999.* Munich: deutscher taschenbuch verlag, 1999.

Halverson, Rachel. "Unifying the Self: Günter de Bruyn's Autobiographical Response to Post-Unification Germany."*Glossen* 9 (2000): 6pp. <http://www.dickinson.edu/departments/german/glossen/heft9/debruyn.html>.

Kant, Hermann. *Abspann. Erinnerung an meine Gegenwart.* Berlin: Aufbau, 1991.

Kaarsunke, Yaak. "Kollektiver Abgesang." *Kursbuch* 109(1992): 98.

Streul, Irene Charlotte. "Anpassung und Widerstand–Günter de Bruyn als Chronist." *Deutschland Archiv* 29.6 (1996): 961-966.

Tate, Dennis. "Günter de Bruyn: The 'Gesamtdeutsche Konsensfigur' of Post-Unification Literature?" *German Life and Letters* 50.2 (1997): 201-213.

Wolf, Christa. "Abschied von Phantomen. Zur Sache: Deutschland." *Auf dem Weg nach Tabou. Texte 1990-1994.* Köln: Kiepenheuer & Witsch, 1994. 313-339. Originally given as a speech in the series "Dresdner Reden" at the Dresden State Opera, 27 February 1994.

---. *Parting from Phantoms. Selected Writings, 1990-1994.* Trans. Jan van Heurck. Chicago: University of Chicago Press, 1997.

- - - "Von den multiplen Wesen in uns. Efim Etkind an Christa Wolf. Christa Wolf an Efim Etkind." Wolf. 194-201. Originally published as "Von den multiplen Wesen in uns–Briefwechsel mit Efim Etkind." *Frankfurter Allgemeine Zeitung.* 3 February 1993.

ROLF JUCKER

"*Gefälle* in der Landschaft"—On the critique of real existing capitalism in Volker Braun's texts

The main enemy of the open society, I believe, is no longer the communist but the capitalist threat. (*George Soros*)

Es ist doch klar, daß der Kapitalismus keine Lösung für die Probleme der Welt hat. (*Heiner Müller*)

Alles sollte so einfach wie möglich gemacht werden, aber nicht einfacher. (*Albert Einstein*) [1]

At the end of the second millennium (according to the Christian calendar), we have entered paradise on earth. Quite contrary to Volker Braun's former hopes and aspirations, we have managed to do so without relying on any outlandish socialist ideas. Only the radical negation of this tradition has enabled us to reach previously unimagined heights in the evolution of mankind. The collapse of the Eastern Bloc socialist countries has finally brought the centuries-old speculation over various political systems to an end. We have reached the "end of history": western liberal democracy and capitalism have, in an evolutionary process, emerged as the only practical, meaningful and desirable systems of social order. Francis Fukuyama—who, with the help of millions of dollars from the American Olin corporation, ensured that the world heard his message, whether it wanted to or not (George 11)—argues in his article "The End of History?" that liberal democracy represents the "end point of mankind's ideological evolution" and

---

1 George Soros: "Capital Crimes." *Atlantic Monthly* (January 1997), quoted in Robertson 54.
"It is quite clear that capitalism offers no solution to the problems of the world." (Müller, *Gesammelte Irrtümer 3* 85) Compare also the following passage from the poem "Fernsehen" (1990): "Wegmarken durch den Sumpf, der sich schon damals zu schließen begann über dem vorläufigen Grab der Utopie, die vielleicht wieder aufscheinen wird, wenn das Phantom der Marktwirtschaft, die das Gespenst des Kommunismus ablöst, den neuen Kunden seine kalte Schulter zeigt, den Befreiten das eiserne Gesicht seiner Freiheit." (*Die Gedichte* 233). ("Tracks through the marsh, which even then began to close over the temporary grave of utopia and which might reappear when the phantom of the market economy, which replaces the specter of communism, gives the new customers the cold shoulder and shows the liberated the iron face of its freedom.")
"Everything should be made as simple as possible, but no simpler."
Unless otherwise noted, all translations are my own.

"final form of government" (4). In the current phase of globalization, the only remaining issue is to convert the rest of the world to this faith so that it may share in the blessings of such a state of grace. The capitalist revolutionary was therefore correct in recognizing 1989 as that "Chock," through which the events, according to Walter Benjamin, "sich als Monade kristallisier[en]," i.e. as "das Zeichen einer messianischen Stillstellung" which triggers the longed for revolution. 1989 is thus "die kleine Pforte" in the course of history "durch die der Messias treten konnte" ("Über den Begriff" 703-704),[2] in the unexpected guise of the "liberal free market economy."

I must apologize for being unable to repress my sarcasm in my brief attempt to mislead you. This claim that we have turned into the final straightaway of history following the events of 1989 is simply too absurd to be convincing.[3] Moreover, may Walter Benjamin forgive me for misusing him to play this joke on you, the reader. I have analyzed and criticized this way of thinking—which now seems to have been accepted as "common sense" in the form of the conviction that a market economy and liberal democracy are supposedly unsurpassable,[4] even if not as far as the "end of history" is concerned—in detail elsewhere.[5] I would therefore just like to summarize the most important points here.

Before I do so, however, I must briefly explain my reasons for addressing this subject. I am of the opinion that literature fails if it only satisfies our aesthetic requirements. It undoubtedly fails if it does *not* fulfill these aesthetic needs, but conversely, the manner in which reading functions makes it impossible for us to disregard all the other dimensions of a literary text. We are forced to form an opinion, be it positive, negative or indifferent, of the world view which every text—whether consciously or not—imposes on us: what do we make of its historical, political and social parameters, of its conception of the human race?[6]

---

2 That "shock, by which it crystallizes into a monad", i.e. as "the sign of a Messianic cessation of happening". 1989 is thus "the strait gate through which the Messiah might enter" (Benjamin "Theses" 264-266).

3 Compare also Heiner Müller: "Das Ende der Geschichte ist ein Wunschtraum saturierter Eliten" (*Gesammelte Irrtümer 3* 121). ("The end of history is a pipe-dream of wealthy elites.")

4 The notorious *Neue Zürcher Zeitung* speaks to this day of the "Unabänderlichkeit ökonomischer Gesetze" ("irrevocable economic laws"), as though it were referring to the laws of nature rather than the ideas of a pseudo-science (Schwarz 27).

5 See Jucker "Zur Kritik." Compare also Robertson 17, and: "The apparent recent victory of world capitalism and market economies poses severe challenges for the third world. While capitalism can produce a variety of consumer products and generate wealth for some, it is accompanied by problems, including growing inequality, that render it a highly questionable force for improving the lives of the world's poor" (Franke and Chasin i).

6 "Somit konfiguriert [der Leser beim Lesen] einen *möglichen Ablauf von Ereignissen oder einen möglichen Zustand der Dinge* [. . .] wagt er eine Hypothese über Weltstrukturen. In einem Großteil der gängigen Literatur über Textsemiotik ist es üblich geworden, im Hinblick auf diese vom Leser vorhergesehenen Zustände von *möglichen Welten* zu sprechen" (Eco 143). ("In this way [the reader] constructs a *possible course of events or a possible state of affairs*; [. . .], he hypothesizes structures for the world. In much of the current literature on textual semiotics it has become customary, with regard to these conditions projected by the reader, to speak of *possible worlds*.")

This applies to all possible texts, from reports in the mass media, light fiction, novels and concrete poetry, to, say, Paul Celan's hermetic aesthetics.[7] Literature, therefore, always takes a standpoint regarding our world; it is a commentary—whatever form it may take: surrealist, escapist, affirmative, subversive, etc. Good literature—and here I am once again treading on thin ice, since in postmodern times, when everything is supposed to be equally valid,[8] the very phrase is unacceptable—should open up our world to us, it should challenge and develop our understanding of the complex interrelations between things. Literature can only truly function if it provides us with a contrasting, alternative world, a world that holds up a mirror in front of us. This idea is, of course, not remotely new, but I believe it is worth reiterating today in these times of ideological ossification. To bear witness to this, I would like to call upon two very different observers, who come from different periods and conceptual backgrounds. In 1916, Viktor Schklowski wrote:

> Um nun die Empfindung des Lebens wiederzugewinnen, die Dinge wieder zu fühlen, den Stein steinern zu machen, gibt es das, was wir Kunst nennen. Ziel der Kunst ist es, ein Empfinden für die Dinge zu vermitteln, das sie uns *sehen* und nicht nur wiedererkennen läßt [. . .]. [Die Kunst versucht also] die Dinge dem Wahrnehmungsautomatismus zu entziehen. (17-18; my emphasis)[9]

And, in 1983, Paul Feyerabend, critic of modern scientific thinking, formulated it as follows:

> Aber—wie kann man etwas überprüfen, das man die ganze Zeit anwendet? [. . .] Wie kann man entdecken, welche Welt man voraussetzt, wenn man in üblicher Weise vorgeht? Die Antwort ist klar: man kann das nicht von *innen* her auffinden. Man braucht einen *äußeren* Maßstab der Kritik, ein System alternativer Annahmen, oder, da diese Annahmen sehr allgemein sind und gewissermaßen eine ganze Gegenwelt konstituieren: *Man braucht eine Traumwelt, um die Eigenschaften der wirklichen Welt zu erkennen, in der wir zu leben glauben.* (36-37)[10]

---

7 In her study *Vom Engagement absoluter Poesie* Marlies Janz showed succinctly that it is quite simply impossible *not* to read Celan's verse politically.

8 Compare: "Im Westen die 'postmoderne Verbissenheit', die Fronten auszulöschen, die Positionen zu vermengen." "In the West the 'postmodern determination' to destroy the fronts, to mix up the positions." (Braun, *Wir befinden* 97).

9 "Now, in order to regain the sensation of life, to feel things again, to make the stone stone again, there is what we call art. The aim of art is to convey a feeling for things, so that we *see* rather than just recognize them [. . .]. [Art, therefore, tries] to withdraw things from the automatism of perception."

10 "But—how can one examine something that one uses all the time? [. . .] How can one discover which world one presupposes if one acts in the normal way? The answer is clear: one cannot find it from the *inside*. One needs an *external* yardstick of criticism, a system of alternative assumptions, or, as these assumptions are very general and, to a certain extent, constitute a whole alternative world: *one needs a dream world in order to recognize the characteristics of the real world in which we believe to live.*"

If literature can be such an alternative world, it also means that literary studies should analyze these texts with regard to what they have to offer in this respect. In other words, do contemporary texts have anything remotely useful to say in response to the important global problems with which we are confronted? Can they offer us any assistance in seeing and breaking through the ideological *idées fixes* of public discourse and the uniform stodge of the mass media?

That would mean, however, that the texts have something to say about today's real existing capitalism. In this article, I will examine some of Braun's texts with a view to precisely this, for he says himself: "Die Literatur hat, in unklaren Verhältnissen... Ermittlungen zu führen, Erkundungen zu machen" ("Ein Fall von monströser Banalität" 69).[11] I am particularly interested in this since a great deal of literary studies seems, to me at least, to be primarily retrospectively oriented. The principal question seems too often to be whether certain texts take a valid standpoint regarding the GDR. What these texts have to say about the capitalist present and future is rarely acknowledged.

It is now, after the collapse of a system that could never have been seriously considered an alternative model for society—not least because it rested on the same basic premises of an industrial society (see Kurz)—that the work really begins. Now that one need not hide behind feigned dichotomies of friend and foe any longer, it is finally possible to ignore the shadow-boxing in the political arena and worry about reality once again; now—as Volker Braun, using a thought from Walter Benjamin, formulated it—there is "wieder ein *Gefälle* in der Landschaft," "an dem die Kritiker ihre Kraftstationen errichten [können]" ("Volker Braun im Gespräch" 25).[12]

Let us make only a relatively uncontroversial demand of human societies, namely, that any exploitation of inner and external nature, as well as of other people, is illegitimate, unless it can be specifically justified. The appropriateness of Heiner Müller's words, quoted at the beginning of this essay, is thus immediately clear. I would just like to summarize briefly the main points where our real existing capitalism, understood as an economic and political system of organization, fails:

a) Inner nature:

The most diverse indicators—from the divorce rate to child abuse, from different addictions to eating disorders, from crime statistics to the demand for all kinds of psychotherapies, to dissatisfaction in the workplace—suggest, even with careful interpretation, that very few people in our societies are happy and fulfilled in the long term.

---

11 "Literature should, in unclear circumstances [. . .] lead investigations and make reconnaissance missions."

12 "A difference of altitude in the landscape at which critics can build their power stations."

b) Social organization:

1. Social fairness: the gap between rich and poor is constantly widening. Between 1960 and 1991, the share of global income of the richest 20 per cent of the population rose from 70 per cent to 85 per cent, while the share of the poorest fell from 2.3 per cent to 1.4 per cent. The ratio between the share of the richest and the poorest therefore increased from 30:1 to 61:1 (*Human Development Report 1996* 2). This ratio rose exponentially to reach 82:1 in 1995: "New estimates show that the world's 225 richest people have a combined wealth of over $1 trillion, equal to the annual income of the poorest 47% of the world's people (2.5 billion) [. . .]. The three richest people have assets that exceed the combined GDP of the 48 least developed countries." (*Human Development Report 1998* 29-30)

2. Fifty-years after the United Nations' Declaration of Human Rights in 1948, many of these rights are still unattainable for large sections of the population, even in the richest and supposedly most highly developed countries. Even in Western countries Article I ("All human beings are born free and equal in dignity and rights.") has fallen prey to commercialization: constitutionally, all these rights are indeed guaranteed, but in practice they are generally only accessible to those who can afford to buy them. (see Chomsky in Peck 189)

3. Liberal democracy does not even function properly in its traditional area, namely the *polis*, as the USA or Switzerland exemplify. In both cases, which are much cited as model democracies, there is little evidence of democratic self-determination and participation, but instead direct dependence on the "democratic" influence of wealth, education, gender, race, etc. (see Jucker, "Zur Kritik" 46-50 and Ferguson).

4. The state of affairs looks yet more desolate when one considers the sphere in which most people who have a job spend the majority of their time: the world of work. This is still organized in a dictatorial manner, and increasingly so in times of globalization, mostly without any right to self-determination or participation for those involved. In many areas dominated by multi-national corporations, brutal exploitation is used. One need only think of the sweatshops of the Third World's textile industry, of those who work in the mining, coffee and banana industries, or of the forced laborers in China or Burma who manufacture our children's toys and other goods (see Madeley).

c) Relationship to external nature:

Most obvious is perhaps the failure of capitalism with regard to its relationship with nature. The progress paradigm, faith in science—which, in the so-called "life sciences," such as genetic engineering, is coming back with a vengeance, cleverly marketed by extensive public relations, i.e. propaganda campaigns—has led to a hubris which believes that the economic system can function independently, as it were, of the earth's eco-system, and that this eco-system is, in addition, available free of charge as a store of materials. For a society that places so much trust in science, this is somewhat surprising, as the scientific facts are so clear: the earth's eco-system is a limited, closed, non-materially-growing system. As every human activity, including all economic activities, is dependent on this eco-system as the indispensable life-support

> system, such activity is only possible within determinable boundaries (Costanza 2). This quite clearly means that our whole ideology of growth and consumption, which still measures economic success in increased GNP and/or personal success in terms of material goods, completely by-passes the physical realities of our existence.

In his theses on the philosophy of history, Walter Benjamin has previously explained very clearly where the problem with the mentality of this approach lies:

> Die Arbeit, wie sie nunmehr verstanden wird, läuft auf die Ausbeutung der Natur hinaus, welche man mit naiver Genugtuung der Ausbeutung des Proletariats gegenüber stellt [...]. Zu dem korrumpierten Begriff von Arbeit gehört als sein Komplement *die* Natur, welche, wie Dietzgen sich ausgedrückt hat, "gratis da ist." ("Über den Begriff 699)[13]

The thorny aspect of this Benjamin quotation is that his criticism was directed against Social Democracy. In today's Europe, where 13 of the 15 EU states are currently governed by or with the participation of Social Democrats, the true content of this assertion has no better illustration: even where, as in Germany, the Greens form part of the government, the Social Democrats have still been unable to overcome this in the long run self-destructive concept of nature.

In other words, there is quite enough need for action and knowledge. We are by no means at the end of history—on the contrary, we have only just begun to tackle the realities of our world. And it is for precisely this purpose that we need the challenge, the incentive offered by literature, to help us, at best, truly to grasp our circumstances. For, in spite of the fact that our world is increasingly complex, I consider the cynical assurances that it can no longer be explained and understood as lies, which (Western) intellectuals expound to justify their complacency. It is very often the case that matters are relatively transparent and easy to comprehend if one only tries. Therefore, Einstein's motto, quoted above, can be read in two ways: on the one hand, he exhorts us to make sure that we can see the woods for the theoretical trees, and, on the other, he warns us not to simplify away complexity where it really does exist.

So what does all this have to do with Volker Braun's texts? The first text with which I would like to illustrate my point is a story published in 1995, entitled *Das Nichtgelebte*. The text is a dense parable about what it means to be alive rather than simply to vegetate. It skillfully links all the levels that make up a human being: body, feelings, sexuality, identity, work, politics and sense of community, by narrating two events in Georg's life. Braun uses a language, which on the one hand has the intense clarity we know from his verse and on the other progresses almost nimbly. These two events are set before and after unification and are separated by the big Alexanderplatz demonstration of 4 November 1989.

---

13 "The new conception of labor amounts to the exploitation of nature, which with naive complacency is contrasted with the exploitation of the proletariat. [...] Nature, which, as Dietzgen puts it, 'exists gratis,' is a complement to the corrupted conception of labor." ("Theses" 251).

Moreover, they are represented in a parallel or contrapuntal fashion, even to the extent that the language used is mirrored.

The first level, namely Georg's brief relationship with the much younger Luise, reveals the ground Georg still has left to cover before he will be able to love according to his abilities and needs. We experience his empathy, his tenderness and his respect when he spends two days first merely observing the sleeping Luise, who has returned from the nightshift, and then—naked and aroused—touching her. He does not, however, abuse her, although she is defenseless and at his mercy: "Er hätte Luise, um aus seiner armen Lage zu kommen, Gewalt antun müssen, aber es hatte ihm der rohe Mut gefehlt" (13).[14] Interestingly, these exact words, "Es hatte ihm der rohe Mut gefehlt", are later repeated (27), and, indeed, in the context of a failure on Georg's part. Schaber, his superior, gives an "eklen Vortrag" ("horrible talk") which fills Georg with loathing: he cannot, however, find the "rohe[n] Mut," "aufzustehen" and "zu speien" ("to get up and spit") (27). While this courage would be injurious and presumptuous in the private sphere, its absence is certainly considered positive—"Er hatte nur ihren Schlaf bewacht, und, bei dem Gedanken, Zärtlichkeit empfunden, die er wie einen Raub aus der Höhle trug" (13).[15] Georg's lack of courage in the public domain of work is already clearly linked with the feeling of a lost chance, a feeling that dominates the end of the text.

In any case, Georg does sleep with Luise—by mutual consent, while his protest against Schaber never takes place. Yet, in his relationship with Luise, even while having sex, Georg fails to break through to a self-determined, fulfilled life; he loses her before he has really won her. However, during their joint trip, which ends in the "Doppelzimmer des Strandhotels" ("room at the beach hotel"), there is a moment of fulfilled present that merits analysis because of its utopian nature. By chance, Luise and Georg reach a now obsolete strip of no man's land along the former German-German border. This "nirgends. Kein Ort," this nowhere area, this lost and forgotten region is the "innerste Afrika" (innermost Africa) of which Braun speaks elsewhere.[16] This "Unort" (non-place) has escaped the "process of civilization" and the ideological constructs of West as well as East, even though admittedly these are embedded in its history, recalled in its "Todesstille" (deadly silence). Here Georg is thrown back to a bare existence and finds: "Und entsetzlicherweise hatte er sich jetzt gänzlich zuhause gefühlt, in der Heimat, es hatte nichts gefehlt" (18).[17]

---

14 "He would have had to harm Luise in order to escape his wretched situation, but he lacked the raw courage."

15 "He had only guarded her sleep, and, with this thought, felt tenderness, which he carried like a thief from the den."

16 Compare the poem "Das innerste Afrika" (from *Langsamer knirschender Morgen*. Braun, *Texte in zeitlicher Folge*, Vol. VIII. 87-90; the 10 volumes of the *Texte* published between 1989-1993 will henceforth appear as: volume number page number), as well as the scene of the same name in *Transit Europa* (IX 135-7). Also: "Arbeitsnotiz 5.5.85" (IX 143).

17 "And, horrifyingly, he now felt totally at home, in the homeland; there was nothing missing."

The equivalent moment during coitus is again only a brief instant, which is quite clearly declared as an ideal. After Georg lets sexual intercourse wash over him passively, distanced and with an acute awareness of his age—"elendes Dasein" (20), it says—, the "sixty-nine," which is forced upon him, catapults him into the open: "so daß Georg [. . .] verzweifelt alle Rücksicht aufgebend, zu handeln begonnen hatte. Wie ein freier Mann, in einem glücklichen Leben, das vor ihm lag" (20-21).[18] When Luise then bites him passionately on the neck, he endures the pain: "ein brausendes Gefühl von Angst und Lust; er war zu seiner Bestimmung gekommen" (21).[19]

Human purpose is therefore, we can perhaps extrapolate: to act, as free beings, self-determinedly. Only this leads to a fulfilled life and opens up the future. However, the text simultaneously makes clear that this is Georg's purpose, to which he aspires to develop, but it does not yet describe his reality. It is not self-determination and freedom that trigger him to act but desperate self-defense, and it is initially only simulation, role-play.

Yet on the second narrative level, the argument with Schaber, Georg reaches just such a paradigmatic point. In the boiler room of Schaber's block of flats Georg gives him his newest manuscript. Schaber reads aloud from it, with the following result:

> Sie hatten ja, der Suada folgend, gefühlt, daß sie an eine Grenze kamen, hinter der die Wahrheit lag; vor den Palisaden ihrer Gewißheiten die rohen nackten Tatsachen. Sie waren ins unbewachte Offene hinausgeraten, ängstlich bewußt ihres herrlichen Vergehens [. . .]. Auf die verstaubten Säulen Altpapier gestützt [. . .] war er [Georg] plötzlich in einer Fremde gewesen, dem eigenen Denken; Schaber gleichgültig; er, er elend vorhanden. (32)[20]

Here, the reader is confronted with some extremely interesting points. It is plainly obvious, as it is in the love scene, that the text is not concerned with an ideology, such as "socialism," with a fixed construct of ideas, a utopian blueprint, which needs only to be translated into practice. It is not about any given, but about what each individual must first work out without "Palisaden [der] Gewißheiten," in conceptual openness with no ideological safety net. Interestingly, the postmodern attitude of "anything goes," relativism or subjectivism are not the issues in this context. The outside world is not a linguistic game, dependent on intellectual fashions—it is real and recognizable; conceptual openness only succeeds if it is

18 "So that Georg [. . .] desperately giving up all deliberations, had begun to act. Like a free man, in a happy life, which lay before him."

19 "A thunderous feeling of fear and desire; he had found his purpose."

20 "Following the torrent of words, they had felt that they were coming to a frontier, behind which lay the truth: before the palisades of their certainties the raw, naked facts. They had come out into the unguarded open, anxiously aware of their glorious misdemeanor [. . .]. Leaning on the dusty piles of old paper [. . .] he [Georg] had suddenly been in a foreign land, in his own thoughts; Schaber indifferent, he, he wretchedly present."

prepared to accept the "nackten rohen Tatsachen." And this process of realization can, it seems, take place intersubjectively: "*Sie* waren ins unbewachte Offene hinausgeraten" (my emphasis). However, these "eigene" thoughts, as opposed to heteronymous ones, are a "Fremde" because we must first tear down "Palisaden" of our preconceived opinions and find the courage to venture into the unknown, the "Offene," in order to be able to truly perceive reality again, in Schklowski's sense as cited above. Anyone who closely examines the public discourse of politics, economics or the media will surely find more than a grain of truth in such a perspective, a fact which inspired more than 30 British non-governmental organizations in 1996 to publish a book entitled *The Politics of the Real World*, with the objective of prompting official politics finally to abandon its ritual self-admiration.[21]

There is something more that merits consideration here, to which I shall return at the end of this essay. The word "elend" appears for the second time; after the "elende[n] Dasein" in the love scene, Georg is now "elend vorhanden." This word becomes a cipher for what we should strive for. In Middle High German, *ellende* means "foreign, exiled" and originates from the Old High German *elilenti* or the Anglo Saxon *eli-lendi*, which both mean "in a foreign land, expelled."[22] In other words, "elend" describes the necessity of giving oneself over to the strangeness of one's own thinking, of the truth, of the examination of the facts, of self-determined action, things that seem foreign to us because of our preconceived ideas and palisades, even though they are at the center of our existence.[23]

The end of the text is also interesting. Georg asks himself what the cause could be of the threefold failure that the text recounts: the collapse of the relationship with Luise, the inability to break away from Schaber, as well as the ineffectiveness of the big demonstration on Alexanderplatz on 4 November, of the "großen berühmten Menge" ("the great famous masses") (36) which was searching for the "Möglichkeit" ("possibility") (39). The answer to all three questions is one and the same, and no class enemy or unfavorable circumstances play a role: "Wir haben es nicht gewollt. [. . .] Es ist uns nicht ernst gewesen. Wir hatten Zeit genug" (36).[24] This thought, "der ihm ins Herz schnitt," is described as a "glücklicher," "ein unausweichlich wahrer" (36)[25]. It is important to bear in mind that the thought, and not the result of the unwillingness, was "glücklich." This is emphasized by the portrayal of this result as negative: "Es geschieht uns recht. Nun

21 Compare also, for instance, Richard von Weizsäcker's analysis of the 'Politikverdrossenheit" in the FRG, in which such motives play an important role (*Richard von Weizsäcker im Gespräch* 137-182).

22 *Duden »Etymologie«: Herkunftswörterbuch der deutschen Sprache*. Mannheim: Bibliographisches Institut, 1989. 152.

23 Ernst Jandl, in his lectures on poetics, also speaks at one point of the "*Fremde*," "die sein eigenes Leben war" "*the strangeness*, which was his own life" (123).

24 "We did not want it. [. . .] We did not take it seriously. We had enough time."

25 "cut through his heart" "happy" "an unavoidably true [thought]"

müssen wir damit leben, in diesem Universum des Nichterlebten [. . .] und die Zukunft wird immer kleiner" (36-39).[26]

This thought makes Georg happy, because he immediately realizes that it is in keeping with a fundamental insight. The future only opens up in self-determined desire, only then does the longed for experience transform itself into life, possibility into reality. Only then can one enter the foreign land of facts. Only then, to comment on the epigraph of the book, can one be "lebendig" "in diesem brennend sehnsüchtigen Leib," *without* "zu ersticken vor Traurigkeit." (5)[27]

Volker Braun once plausibly explained the problem of real existing socialism, with reference to the industrialization of the GDR and open-cast coal-mining: "Jeder Handgriff [war] durchdacht, jede Tätigkeit rational, die des Maschinisten, des Dispatchers, des Schichtingenieurs, jedes Gewerk hatte seine Logik, aber das Ganze war womöglich Wahnsinn" (Jucker, *Volker Braun* 17).[28] Real existing capitalism seems to me to be suffering from an identical structural problem, and this also explains why we have such difficulties recognizing the insanity of what we do. The individual activities that we carry out—whether driving in the car to the supermarket, purchasing clothes, making holidays in the South, or working as a stockbroker, a lecturer, a car mechanic etc.—seem to make sense in themselves: we can derive satisfaction from them, be proud of the professionalism with which we carry them out and of the importance that we attribute to them. Only when we consider all these activities together and in a global context, do the consequences become visible. Only then do we notice that, within the confines of our life-support system called planet earth, they no longer make any sense at all and in reality become destructive. In Braun's own words: "Dieselbe Arbeit, die die Gattung auseinanderreißt, zerreißt die Natur. Das ist die Dimension der Macht, als menschlicher Anmaßung" ("Müdigkeit" 119).[29]

The reason for this—as Hannah Arendt[30] and Günther Anders[31] were quick to point out—is that people can and do produce much more (with exponentially

---

26 "It serves us right. We must now live with it in this universe of the inexperienced [. . .] and the future is becoming smaller and smaller."

27 "alive," "in this burning, longing body" *without* "suffocating from sadness."

28 "Every movement was thought through, every activity was rational—that of the engine-driver, the dispatcher, the shift engineer, every trade had its logic, but as a whole it was probably madness."

29 "The very same work that tears people apart rips nature to shreds. That is the dimension of power, in the form of human presumption."

30 "But it could be that we, who are earth-bound creatures and have begun to act as though we were dwellers of the universe, will forever be unable to understand, that is, to think and speak about the things which nevertheless we are able to do. [. . .] If it should turn out to be true that knowledge (in the modern sense of know-how) and thought have parted company for good, then we would indeed become the helpless slaves, not so much of our machines as of our know-how, thoughtless creatures at the mercy of every gadget which is technologically possible, no matter how murderous it is" (3).

31 "Die drei Hauptthesen: daß wir der Perfektion unserer Produkte nicht gewachsen sind; daß wir mehr herstellen als vorstellen und verantworten können; und daß wir glauben, das, was wir können, auch zu dürfen, nein: zu sollen, nein: zu müssen—diese drei Grundthesen sind angesichts der im letzten

multiplied power since industrialization) than they are able to understand and cope with. This is true in almost all areas, in the nuclear industry as well as genetic engineering—the consequences of the latter are not yet even understood scientifically, not to mention its social and environmental effects. It also applies, however, to the conventional chemical industry, which releases thousands of new substances into the environment every year without even a half-decent idea about their long-term impact. Yet the same is true of our decisions as consumers, which we usually make in an utterly naïve manner, without even remotely considering the social and ecological costs that we thus inflict on the so-called Third World (Madeley).

In other words, we are still pitiful beginners when it comes to making everyday decisions and, additionally, determining societal forms of organization and production equal to the complexity of our circumstances. Only very rarely do these decisions and deliberations take into account a comprehensive and full analysis of the consequences and interdependencies of such activities and systems. Such research is done on individual products for ecological reasons, namely in the form of a life cycle analysis, which assesses the ecological impact of a product "from the cradle to the grave," and we need just such analyses and information for every single one of our activities.

This, I believe, is what Volker Braun is talking about in "Notizen eines Publizisten" (Braun X: 167-173; also *Wir befinden uns soweit wohl* 23-28), as well as in *Iphigenie in Freiheit*, where he writes: "Die Frage aller Fragen: nach der friedlichen *anderen* Arbeit, die vertagt scheint" (144).[32] Here we find a radically different interpretation of the present, compared to Fukuyama's quote at the beginning of my essay, which celebrates the "final victory" of capitalism as deliverance.[33] Braun points out that no one is searching any longer for answers to

---

Vierteljahrhundert offenbar gewordenen Umweltgefahren leider aktueller und brisanter als damals" (vii). ("The three main hypotheses: that we are incapable of matching the perfection of our products; that we can produce more than we are able to imagine and take responsibility for; and that we believe we are permitted to, no: that we should, no: that we must, do what we can do—these three basic theories are, in view of the environmental dangers which have become clear in the last quarter century, unfortunately more current and explosive than they were then.")

32 "The question of all questions: where is this peaceful *other* work, which seems to be deferred?"

33 Volker Braun's new volume of poetry *Tumulus* comments on this "deliverance" satirically throughout. Compare, for example: "Das liebe Zimmer der Utopien/ Entläßt den Gast in den Unsinn/ ES GILT ALLE VERHÄLTNISSE stehenzulassen/ IN DENEN DER MENSCH EIN GEKNECHTETES" ("Abschied von Kochberg" 20). ("The beloved room of utopias/ releases its guest into nonsense/ ONE SHOULD preserve ALL RELATIONS/ IN WHICH MAN IS AN ENSLAVED") "Die Teetrinker Marrakeschs sind noch zu bekehren/ Zu den globalen Göttern" ("Das Magma in der Brust des Tuareg" 24). ("The tea drinkers of Marrakech are yet to be converted/ To the global gods.") "Geht, sagte man (jeder kennt die Stimmen), geht uns mit eurer Hoffnung [. . .] Sie ist rot, sie ist blutig, schwört ihr ab. Begrabt diese Fahne. *Es wird nie anders werden.*" ("Die Bucht der Hingeschiedenen" 30). ("Leave, they say (everybody knows the voices), leave us with your hope [. . .] It is red, it is bloody, renounce it. Bury this flag. *It will never be different.*") Also: "Es ist wieder erlaubt, sagt Lord Dahrendorf/ Ohne Scham von Kapitalismus zu sprechen/ Für den Rest des Lebens der Urschleim der Ausbeutung." ("Material XVI: Strafkolonie"

the most important questions of our time, that our system is clearly unable to answer these questions and simply suppresses them. Yet the questions have not become obsolete because of this, on the contrary: in view of the destruction of the environment and growing global inequality, they are becoming increasingly urgent. Braun captures in these words what today is meant by the term sustainability, namely the search for a way of life, which treats nature and fellow humans in a respectful manner such that dignified human life will also be possible in the future. This takes us back to the beginning of my discussion, where I claimed that a society only has a right to call itself human if it can survive without illegitimate power over other people, oneself and nature. The quoted "friedliche *andere* Arbeit" (Braun X: 144) is one that exists without "Kolonisierung" ("colonization"), without obliterating "Individualität" ("individuality") or "Natur" ("nature"), without marginalizing "Frau[en]" ("women"), "Neger" ("Negroes"), and the "arbeitslose Rest der Gattung" ("unemployed remainder"), one that produces things and working conditions which make sense in a global and local context, one that is truly meaningful:

> Eine Gangart, mit der wir zu anderen Zielen kommen, zu sanfteren Technologien, zu einem milderen Markt. Der horizontalen Gesellschaft kann eine soziale Produktion entsprechen, die Erfindungen anderer Art braucht als die der erbarmungslosen Konkurrenz. [. . .] Unser Haushalt wiese sich aus durch Produktion von Vernunft; unser Planziel die Versöhnung mit der Natur, auch unserer eigenen, nicht länger ihre Katastrophe. ("Notizen eines Publizisten" 170)[34]

Or focusing on the political level formulated in the interview "Lösungen für alle": "und die Frage ist, ob es nicht etwas Moderneres gibt als den Zirkus der Parteien, eine Demokratie der Basis, eine Demokratie, die *Lösungen für alle* will. Freizügig und selbstbewußt, solidarisch mit sich und mit der Natur und mitdenkend mit der Welt" (162).[35] As long as this is not the case, there is no reason—other than for a small, ruling, rich minority—to rejoice. This is captured precisely in *Iphigenie in*

31). ("It is permissible again, says Lord Dahrendorf/ To speak of capitalism without shame/ For the rest of our lifetime the primeval slime of exploitation.")

34 "A way of life through which we come to other goals, more humane technologies, a more considerate market. A horizontal society can be in keeping with a social production, which needs inventions of a different kind to that of merciless competition. [. . .] Our budget would be distinguished by the production of sense; our planning goal the reconciliation with nature, also our own, no longer with its catastrophe."

35 "And the question is whether there is not something more modern than the circus of political parties, a participatory democracy, a democracy that wants *solutions for all.* Generous and self-aware, in solidarity with itself and with nature, and caring for the whole world." Heiner Müller makes a similar point in "Plädoyer für den Widerspruch": "Wir sollten keine Anstrengung und kein Risiko scheun für das Überleben unsrer Utopie von einer Gesellschaft, die den wirklichen Bedürfnissen ihrer Bevölkerung gerecht wird ohne den weltweit üblichen Verzicht auf Solidarität mit andern Völker" (*Gesammelte Irrtümer 3* 36). ("We should shy away from neither effort nor risk for the survival of our utopia of a society which fulfils the real needs of its population, without sacrificing solidarity with other nations, as is customary worldwide.")

Freiheit, quoting Bertolt Brecht's *Fatzer*: "Und von jetzt ab und eine ganze Zeit/ Wird es keinen Sieger mehr geben/ Sondern nur mehr Besiegte" (130).[36] Even this minority, even the prospering West, even we belong in this situation to the losers, as Schumacher aptly put it: "Modern man does not experience himself as a part of nature but as an outside force destined to dominate and conquer it. He even talks of a battle with nature, forgetting that, if he won the battle, he would find himself on the losing side" (3).

Logically, however, this also means that—after we have been indoctrinated for decades that growth is the only goal—we must finally accept the greatest challenge to our thinking *and* actions. We must learn to live within the limits of our eco-system: "Und in kein Ausland flüchtet sich die Hoffnung/ Die wüste Erde ist der ganze Raum" (*Iphigenie in Freiheit* 137).[37] The text accepts the serious consequences of this insight. Instead of continuing to deceive itself about the problems with preconceived ideas, it admits: "Jetzt wird es endlich schwer. Ich weiß nichts mehr" (137).[38] This means that we are only at the beginning, not the end of history: "Wir müssen ohnehin zurück bis in die Startlöcher [. . .]" ("3. Oktober 1990" 199)[39]:

> So sehen wir uns in der offenen Landschaft um so mehr in einen ungeheuren Zusammenhang geraten von Arbeit und Krieg, Profit und Bewußtsein, Macht und Hunger, und die Anstrengung der Vernunft ist gefordert wie nie. Welche Täuschung, es würde eine friedliche, einfachere Welt. ("Jetzt wird der Schwächere plattgewalzt" 207-8 [*Wir befinden uns soweit wohl* 59-63])[40]

This is also reinforced by another thread, which runs through *Iphigenie in Freiheit* and reaches a climax in scene 4 ("Antikensaal"): hunger.[41] I have already indicated above that reducing genuine complexity only creates new problems, rather than solving any. This is commonly accepted in environmental studies. Only approaches that include all 4 "E's" are considered worthwhile: Equity [=social equality], Environment, Economy, Empowerment [=participatory democracy].[42] We are therefore fooling ourselves when we speak of progress and

---

36 "And from now on and for a long time/ There will be no more winners/ Only losers." This is a quotation from Brecht 116.

37 "And hope takes refuge in no foreign land/ The desolate earth is the only space." See also: "Wie lange hält uns die Erde aus/ Und was werden wir die Freiheit nennen" ("Nach dem Massaker der Illusionen" *Tumulus* 28). ("How long is the earth putting up with us/ And what will we call freedom.")

38 "Now it is at long last becoming difficult. I don't know anything any more."

39 "We must go back to the starting blocks in any case [. . .]"

40 "So we see ourselves in the open landscape, all the more caught in a tremendous complexity between work and war, profit and convictions, power and hunger, and the effort of reason is demanded as never before. What a delusion, that it would be a peaceful, simpler world."

41 Compare also X 138, as well as the corresponding passage in the poem "Das innerste Afrika" (VIII 88) and in *Böhmen am Meer* (X 74).

42 See Alicia Bárcena, and Diomar Silveria. "Envisioning Sustainable Alternatives within the

development, while more and more people in the world are becoming poorer, and therefore inequality increases—including in industrial countries such as the USA or Great Britain. And this hunger, for which we are partly to blame,[43] and the associated need for justice, will one day return to haunt us. At the end of *Iphigenie*, we find the following: "Sprengsatz der Strukturen, Stoff für den Hunger der Welt, der in die Türen tritt, ein Kinderleib" (143).[44] And the "Leipziger Vorlesung" concludes with the following sentence: "ABER, IHR TRÄUMER, GLAUBT IHR WIRKLICH, DER ZERFALL DES HISTORISCHEN KOMMUNISMUS HABE DEM BEDÜRFNIS NACH GERECHTIGKEIT EIN ENDE GESETZT?" (Braun X 192).[45]

Then, in the "Prolog zur Eröffnung der 40. Spielzeit des Berliner Ensembles" the literal and metaphorical meanings of hunger become one: "Aber bedenkt/ Daß da auch Hunger herrscht/ Mit dem Mandat der Massen, Hunger/ Nach Gerechtigkeit" (*Zickzackbrücke* 38; *Wir befinden uns soweit wohl* 12).[46] Finally, in the 1994 sketch "Karte aus Kairo," Braun writes:

> Der Norden redet, wie Marc Aurel im Drogenrausch, mit dem er die Magengeschwüre betäubte, von der Einen Welt und der Menschenwürde: und grenzt zugleich eine Hemisphäre aus durch Schuldscheine und Sanktionen. Es ist die Komödie der Menschheit, unter ihrem Wissen zu leben. Die Angst des Nordens: ein Leben zu führen, das nicht für alle taugt; die Furcht und Hoffnung der Völker. (*Wir befinden uns soweit wohl* 110-111)[47]

Braun thus pushed his critique of capitalism into the "Fremde" of his "eigenen Denkens": if we accept the "rohen nackten Tatsachen" (*Das Nichtgelebte* 32) and see through the illusion of boundless wealth which the industrial countries and rich Third World elites have been able to indulge in during recent decades, then a different future emerges, a realistic, poorer, lasting one:

Framework of the UNCED Process." Costanza 455 and 460.

43 See also: "Wissend länger als ich/ Wird die Ausbeutung dauern an der ich teilhabe/ Länger als ich der Hunger der mich ernährt/[. . .]/ Die Lügen der Dichter sind aufgebraucht/ Vom Grauen des Jahrhunderts An den Schaltern der Weltbank/ Riecht das getrocknete Blut wie kalte Schminke" (Müller, "Müller im Hessischen Hof," *Gedichte* 253). ("Knowing that longer than myself/ Will the exploitation in which I take part last/ Longer than myself the hunger which feeds me/[. . .]/ The lies of the poets are used up/ By the horrors of the century At the counters of the World Bank/ The dried blood smells like cold make-up.") See also, as a radical contribution to the problem of overpopulation, Müller's poem "Ahnenbrühe" (243).

44 "Explosives for structures, food for the hungry of the world, who enters our doors, a child's body."

45 "BUT, YOU DREAMERS, DO YOU REALLY BELIEVE THAT THE COLLAPSE OF HISTORICAL COMMUNISM HAS BROUGHT AN END TO THE NEED FOR JUSTICE?"

46 "But remember/ That hunger also rules/ With the mandate of the masses, Hunger/ For justice."

47 "The North, like Marc Aurel under the influence of the drugs he used to ease his stomach ulcers, talks of One World and human dignity: and simultaneously excludes one hemisphere with debts and sanctions. It is the comedy of humanity to live below its knowledge. The fear of the North: to lead a life which is not suitable for all; the fear and hope of the peoples."

> Der Mensch muß damit leben, daß er die Zukunft nicht (mehr) kennt, ohne daß er beginnt, bedenkenlos gegen andere und Zukünftige zu leben. Die Lösungen für alle können kein Luxus der Künste bleiben. Das Ideal ist zur elementaren Angelegenheit geworden, es setzt das blutige, hungernde, lebendige Fleisch der Probleme an. Die Idee der Menschheit ist zur Sache der Wirklichkeit verdammt. ("Ist das unser Himmel?" 169; *Wir befinden uns soweit wohl* 87)[48]

Nevertheless, that does not mean the end of all hope, merely the end of hope for salvation. It signals the arrival in the "gewöhnliche[n] Realismus der unheilen Welt, unserer industriellen und kolonialen Lebensform" ("Leipziger Vorlesung" 191);[49] so neither illusions nor resignation, but recognition of the possibilities: "'Es gibt unendlich viel Hoffnung, nur nicht für uns,' sagt Kafka, nein, es gibt wenig Hoffnung, aber für uns" ("Ein Ort für Peter Weiss" 174).[50]

However, this little hope can only manifest itself if we too, in the rich West, acquire completely new, age-old, values by which to orient ourselves: dematerialization,[51] restraint, respect, deceleration,[52] restriction. The aim is—though implicit—equality: equity, justice, and justifiable social relations without exploitation cannot be achieved otherwise.[53] Braun has formulated this most clearly in two notes on his work. I will add nothing more to them, as these passages are unsurpassable in their intensity and urgency: on 29 March 1985 he wrote, with reference to *Transit Europa*: "und das exil kann nur modell sein für die heutige befindlichkeit, für unser aller leben im übergang: die wir den alten kontinent unserer *gefährlichen gewohnheit* und *anmaßenden wünsche* verlassen müssen, ohne doch das neue ufer zu erkennen zwischen uns" (IX 141, my

---

48 "Man must live with the fact that he does not know the future (any longer), without beginning to live thoughtlessly towards others and future generations. Solutions for all cannot remain a luxury of the arts. The ideal has become an elementary matter; it confronts the bloody, starving, living flesh of the problems. The idea of humanity is damned to be an issue of reality."

49 "everyday realism of the ill-fated world, of our industrial and colonial way of life."

50 "'There is infinite hope, only not for us,' said Kafka, no, there is little hope, but for us."

51 See Jucker "Toward Dematerialization."

52 This is a thought that was very important to Heiner Müller: "Revolutionen sind eher Versuche, die Zeit anzuhalten, die Beschleunigung der Geschichte zu bremsen. Solche Versuche wird man heute wohl positiv bewerten: Die totale Beschleunigung führt zum Nullpunkt, in die Vernichtung" (*Gesammelte Irrtümer 3* 154). ("Revolutions are really attempts to stop time, to slow down the acceleration of history. Such attempts may well be regarded as positive today: total acceleration leads to zero, to annihilation.") The idea is evidently derived from Walter Benjamin: "Die Marx-Korrektur von Benjamin: Revolution nicht als Beschleunigung, sondern Revolution als Notbremse." "Benjamin's correction of Marx: revolution not as acceleration but revolution as an emergency brake" (193); see also, on slowing down as a quality in an economic as well as an ecological sense: (80). And, with regard to perception, the following thought is also suggested: "Gerade was über das Fernsehen abläuft, ist ja eine zunehmende Beschleunigung der Wahrnehmung, die effektiv aber eine Reduzierung der Wahrnehmung bedeutet" (*Gesammelte Irrtümer 2* 109). ("Precisely what is shown on television is of course an increasing acceleration of perception, but which effectively means a reduction in perception.")

53 Compare also Karin's dream, revealing now as ever, in *Unvollendete Geschichte* (IV 61-64, especially 64).

emphasis).[54] And in a note to *Die Übergangsgesellschaft*, he pointed out on 25 September 1982:

> wir wissen, es ist die hauptsache, das leben zu ändern, d.h. das eigene [. . .] aber wir wollen uns nicht aus unseren halterungen reißen. weil wir sonst elende wären, verdammte, entlassene, denen niemand die hand gibt, außer den künftigen freien unvorstellbaren menschen. man muß aber in das elend gehn (VIII 164).[55]

Works Cited

Anders, Günther. *Die Antiquiertheit des Menschen. Bd. 1: Über die Seele im Zeitalter der zweiten industriellen Revolution*. München: C.H. Beck, 1988.

Arendt, Hannah. *The Human Condition*. Chicago: University of Chicago Press, 1958.

Benjamin, Walter. "Theses on the Philosophy of History." *Illuminations*. Trans. Harry Zohn. New York: Harcourt, Brace & World, 1968. 255-266.

---. "Über den Begriff der Geschichte." *Gesammelte Schriften*. Vol. I. Ed. Rolf Tiedemann und Hermann Schweppenhäuser. Frankfurt/M.: Suhrkamp, 1977. 691-704.

Braun, Volker. "Ein Fall von monströser Banalität." *Wir befinden uns soweit wohl*. 69-71.

---."Ist das unser Himmel? Ist das unsre Hölle?: Rede zum Schiller-Gedächtnis-Preis (Stuttgart 10.11.1992)." *Sinn und Form* 45.1 (1993): 166-169.

---. *Iphigenie in Freiheit*. *Texte in zeitlicher Folge*. Vol. X. 125-145.

---. "Jetzt wird der Schwächere plattgewalzt." *Texte in zeitlicher Folge*. Vol. X. 203-208.

---. "Leipziger Vorlesung." *Texte in zeitlicher Folge*. Vol. X. 173-192.

---. "Lösungen für alle." *Texte in zeitlicher Folge*. Vol. X. 158-162.

---. "Die Müdigkeit beim Gedanken an die Macht. " *Wir befinden uns soweit wohl*. 117-119.

---. *Das Nichtgelebte. Eine Erzählung*. Leipzig: Faber & Faber, 1995.

---. "3. Oktober 1990" *Texte in zeitlicher Folge*. Vol. X. 199.

---. "Ein Ort für Peter Weiss." *Wir befinden uns soweit wohl*. 164-174.

---. *Texte in zeitlicher Folge*. Vols. I-X. Halle, Leipzig: Mitteldeutscher Verlag, 1989-1993.

---. *Tumulus. Gedichte*. Frankfurt/M.: Suhrkamp, 1999.

---. *Wir befinden uns soweit wohl. Wir sind erst einmal am Ende. Äußerungen*. Frankfurt/M.: Suhrkamp, 1998.

---. *Die Zickzackbrücke. Ein Abrißkalender*. Halle: Mitteldeutscher Verlag, 1992.

Brecht, Bertolt. *Der Untergang des Egoisten Johann Fatzer. Bühnenfassung von Heiner Müller*. Frankfurt/M.: Suhrkamp, 1994.

---

54 "and exile can only be a model for our present state, for all our lives in transition: we, having to leave the old continent of our *dangerous habits* and *presumptuous desires*, without yet being able to make out the new shore between us."

55 "we know the main thing is to change the life, i.e. our own [. . .] but we are loathe to tear ourselves from our habits. because we would otherwise be wretched, damned, expelled, those to whom no-one offers a hand, apart from the future free unimaginable people. yet one must go into wretchedness."

Costanza, Robert et al., ed. *Getting Down to Earth. Practical Applications of Ecological Economics*. Washington, D.C.: Island Press, 1996.

Costanza, Robert. "Integrated Envisioning, Analysis, and Implementation of a Sustainable and Desirable Society." Costanza. 1-13.

Eco, Umberto. *Lector in fabula. Die Mitarbeit der Interpretation in erzählenden Texten*. München: Hanser, 1987.

Ferguson, Thomas. *Golden Rule. The Investment Theory of Party Competition and the Logic of Money-Driven Political Systems*. Chicago, London: University of Chicago Press, 1995.

Feyerabend, Paul. *Wider den Methodenzwang*. Frankfurt/M.: Suhrkamp, 1983.

Franke, Richard W. and Barbara H. Chasin. *Kerala. Radical Reform as Development in an Indian State*. 2nd ed. Oakland: Food First Books, 1994.

Fukuyama, Francis. "The End of History?" *The National Interest* 16 (1989): 3-8.

George, Susan. "Eine kurze Geschichte des Einheitsdenkens." *Le Monde diplomatique [deutsch]* 2.8 (1996): 10-11.

Human Development Report 1996. Ed. by the United Nations Development Programme (UNDP). New York, Oxford: Oxford University Press, 1996.

Human Development Report 1998. Ed. by the United Nations Development Programme (UNDP). New York, Oxford: Oxford University Press, 1998.

Jacobs, Michael. *The Politics of the Real World. Meeting the New Century*. Written and edited for the *Real World* coalition. London: Earthscan, 1996.

Jandl, Ernst. *Das Öffnen und Schließen des Mundes. Frankfurter Poetikvorlesungen*. Darmstadt, Neuwied: Luchterhand, 1985.

Janz, Marlies. *Vom Engagement absoluter Poesie. Zur Lyrik und Ästhetik Paul Celans*. Königstein/Ts.: Athenäum, 1984.

Jucker, Rolf, ed. *Volker Braun*. Cardiff: University of Wales Press, 1995.

---. "'Wir befinden uns soweit wohl. Wir sind erst einmal am Ende.' Volker Braun im Gespräch mit Rolf Jucker." In Jucker *Volker Braun* 21-29.

---. "Zur Kritik der realexistierenden Utopie des Status Quo." *Zeitgenössische Utopieentwürfe in Literatur und Gesellschaft. Zur Kontroverse seit den achtziger Jahren*. Ed. Rolf Jucker. Amsterdam, Atlanta: Rodopi, 1997. 13-78.

---. "Toward Dematerialization: The Path of Ethical and Ecological Consumption." *ON...* 12.1.1998. <http://www.onweb.org /features/new/dematerial/dematerial.html>

Kurz, Robert. *Der Kollaps der Modernisierung. Vom Zusammenbruch des Kasernensozialismus zur Krise der Weltökonomie*. Frankfurt/M.: Eichborn, 1991.

Madeley, John. *Big Business, Poor Peoples. The Impact of Transnational Corporations on the World's Poor*. London, New York: Zed Books, 1999.

Müller, Heiner. *Gesammelte Irrtümer 2. Interviews und Gespräche*. Ed. Gregor Edelmann and Renate Ziemer. Frankfurt/M.: Verlag der Autoren, 1990.

---. *Gesammelte Irrtümer 3. Texte und Gespräche*. Frankfurt/M.: Verlag der Autoren, 1994.

---. *Die Gedichte*. Ed. Frank Hörnigk. Frankfurt/M.: Suhrkamp, 1998.

Peck, James, ed. *The Chomsky Reader*. London: Serpent's Tail, 1992.

Robertson, James. *Transforming Economic Life. A Millennial Challenge*. Dartington: Green Books, 1998.

Schklowski, Viktor. "Kunst als Verfahren (1916)." *Die Erweckung des Wortes. Essays der russischen Formalen Schule*. Ed. Fritz Mierau. Leipzig: Philipp Reclam jun., 1987. 11-32.

Schumacher, E.F. *Small is Beautiful. A Study of Economics as if People Mattered.* London: Vintage, 1993 {Original 1973}.

Richard von Weizsäcker im Gespräch mit Gunter Hofmann und Werner A. Perger. Frankfurt/M.: Eichborn, 1992.

RACHEL J. HALVERSON

Comedic Bestseller or Insightful Satire: Taking the Interview and Autobiography to Task in Thomas Brussig's *Helden wie wir*[1]

Thomas Brussig's satiric novel *Helden wie wir* (1996) has taken post-unification Germany by storm. Written in the irreverent tradition of Phillip Roth and John Irving, as noted on the book's jacket, the novel's rapid rise up the bestseller list is hardly surprising. After several years of dealing with the grim reality of unification, Germans from both sides of the *innere Mauer* ("internal Wall") find that the novel's humor provides much needed comedic relief and that the novel's "hero," Klaus Uhltzscht, with his phallocentric take on the fall of the Berlin Wall, offers plenty of laughs.[2]

In the course of the novel, Brussig demonstrates repeatedly that nothing is too sacred to escape his biting satire. *Helden wie wir* parodies the legitimate pillars of East German society, such as the press, politicians, fashion, and the Stasi. The novel even targets East German literature by including one of the *grandes dames* of the literary scene, Christa Wolf, on Uhlzscht's path to greatness. One chapter is titled "Das 7. Band: Der geheilte Pimmel" ("The Seventh Cassette: The healed Penis"), and Uhltzscht's attendance at a demonstration where Christa Wolf is speaking precipitates his eventual rise to genital grandeur. While he is recovering from surgery to repair the damage from his penis-transforming accident, Uhltzscht even reads Wolf's seminal novel *Der geteilte Himmel*, which he refers to as an "Erektionstöter" ("erection killer"; 307) to prevent any spontaneous erections he might experience.

Given the novel's satiric, almost light tone and its undeniable popular success, it is tempting to regard *Helden wie wir* as a well-timed piece of *Trivialliteratur*, capable of little more than amusing German readers who have grown weary of the heavy, introspective writing style stereotypically expected from most major post-war German authors on both sides of the Wall. Yet, in addition to numerous reviews in newspapers and magazines, the novel has also

1 I would like to thank Dr. Sonja Hokanson, Dr. Susan McLeod, Dr. Julie Wieck, and Dr. Lori Wiest for their insightful reading of this manuscript.

2 A stage adaptation of *Helden wie wir*, which premiered on 27 April 1996, at the Kammerspiele of the Deutsches Theater in Berlin, speaks further for the novel's success. For further insight into the stage version of the novel, see Weber.

attracted the attention of literary scholars. Using Freud's theory of wit, Wolfgang Gabler analyzes the humor in Brussig's *Helden wie wir* and Jens Sparschuh's *Der Zimmerspringbrunnen* to reveal the novels' portrayal of the collective unconscious: "Ich nutze damit das psychoanalytische Verfahren, an Fehlleistungen unbewußte Konflikte erkennen zu können"[3] (148). In the case of *Helden wie wir*, Gabler focuses on the inconsistencies between the novel's seemingly incompetent narrator and his occasional moments of brilliance. Like Gabler, Margrit Frölich also uses Freudian theories to analyze the comic satiric elements in the novel. She supplements this with insights into humor provided by the works of François Rabelais and Mikhail Bakhtin's treatment of the grosteque-comic in Rabelais' work to argue that: "[Brussig] needs to be included in the retrospective reflections on the GDR as the view of someone from a generation of young East Germans alienated by the reality of state socialism" (28). In his "'Das Volk jedenfalls war's nicht!': Thomas Brussigs Abrechnung mit der DDR," Reinhard K. Zachau reviews the novel's reception in newspapers and magazines and Brussig's literary influences to reach the conclusion: "Das Buch kann letztlich nicht literarisch beurteilt werden, da es aus der DDR-Perspektive für DDR-Bürger geschrieben wurde"[4] (394). However, he goes one step further to point to the importance of interpreting the political implications of the text. In contrast to Gabler, Frölich and Zachau, I will move beyond Uhltzscht's comic façade to examine his narration of his life story, including his choice of autobiographical frame, the interview format of the novel, his statements on his role in German unification, and his opinions on history. This examination will dissect and peel away the novel's convoluted absurdity to disclose its statement on literature and the historicization of Germany's past. My analysis of Uhltzscht's story as a satire of both East and West German society will thus ultimately demonstrate how and to what degree demystifying the events leading to German unification is an integral part of understanding Germany's present.

Helden wie wir essentially takes to task two post-unification publishing trends: the autobiography and the interview. On the one hand, the novel falls clearly into the genre of fictional autobiography with Klaus Uhltzscht's fictional narration of his life story. The novel's 1996 publication date positions it after the initial proliferation of East German memoirs and autobiographies between 1989 and 1994. The publication of autobiographies posthaste by major politicians such as Günter Schabowski, Egon Krenz and Erich Honecker and older generation East German authors, Günter de Bruyn, Hermann Kant,

---

3 "For this (i.e. *my argumentation*) I will use a psychoanalytic methodology to be able to discern unconscious conflicts in the novel's inconsistencies." (This is my own translation of this excerpt from Gabler's article.)

4 "The book cannot in conclusion be judged in literary terms, since it was written from a GDR perspective for GDR citizens." (This is my own translation of this excerpt from Zachau's article.)

and Heiner Müller typifies not only the post-unification publishing scene, but the popularity of this genre in the Nineties (Nalbantian viii). Julian Preece in his "Damaged lives? (East) German memoirs and autobiographies; 1989-1994" goes so far as to refer to the sudden surge in this genre following unification as a "publishing phenomenon" (349).

As with autobiographies, interviews with East German citizens have also dominated post-unification publishing. Robin Ostow speculates in a 1993 special issue of *Oral History Review*: "...that citizens of the former German Democratic Republic had become the world's most interviewed population" (1). Just as so many East Germans have recounted their lives in East Germany to both foreign and domestic journalists and scholars, so does Klaus Uhltzscht. In fact, the interview format drives the telling of his life story following the opening paragraph of the novel, which is supposedly Uhltzscht's attempt to write his autobiography. Interestingly enough, Uhltzscht's highly cognizant account of his birth triggered by the rumble of a tank regiment on its way to Czechoslovakia in 1968 is highly reminiscent of Oskar's memory of his birth in Grass' *Die Blechtrommel*, the life story of post-war West German literature's most infamous rascal, and provides a connection to an acclaimed work of post-war West German literature.

Following this first paragraph, which has taken him two years to write, Klaus is interrupted by a call from a Mr. Kitzelstein, a reporter for *The New York Times*. Ultimately, the interview with Kitzelstein organizes the body of the novel which is divided into seven chapters, entitled "Bände" ("volumes"), marking the number of cassettes Kitzelstein uses to record his interview with Uhltzscht and underscoring Uhltzscht's longwindedness. Kitzelstein is a silent interview partner whose sole function is that of a listener and that of the person to whom Uhltzscht directs his rhetorical questions. In this non-interactive mode, Kitzelstein thus mirrors the position of the reader. Although he will transpose the interview from its recorded autobiographical format into a biographical, journalistic statement on Uhltzscht's role in history, the text of *Helden wie wir* remains autobiographical, i.e. it is Uhltzscht speaking on Uhltzscht. As Uhltzscht summarizes quite succinctly in the opening pages of the novel: "Die Geschichte des Mauerfalls ist die Geschichte meines Pinsels" (7).[5]

Not only does the interview with Kitzelstein serve as a framework for Uhltzscht's narration of his life story, it also allows the novel to explore the various modes of interaction possible between the interviewed and the interviewer, running the gamut from Kitzelstein's role as a close confidante to his role as an unsympathetic witness to the injustices in Uhltzscht's life. For

5 "The story of the Wall's end is the story of my penis, [. . .]" (5). (Please note that all English translations of *Helden wie wir* included in the footnotes are taken from John Brownjohn's translation of the novel. The short translations included in the body of the article are my own.)

example, Uhltzscht bets Kitzelstein he can praise his mother three consecutive times (26). While telling of the parental disciplinary measures he suffered when he failed to remember to lock their apartment door, however, he looks to Kitzelstein for sympathy and affirmation (35). In the course of the interview, Kitzelstein often functions as a confidante for Uhltzscht, just as when he explains his frustrations with the commonness of his first name and the impossibility of his consonant-loaded last name (42-43). He, in turn, even taunts Kitzelstein to guess what his mother calls his penis (53) and goes so far as to reproach him for being repulsed by his method of coping with wet dreams, namely sleeping with a scouring pad in his pajamas to prevent the ejaculate from reaching his sheets and ultimately coming to his mother's attention (85). He also despairs to Kitzelstein that his parents still make his penis their business, when he recounts the loss of his virginity, which also resulted in a nasty case of gonorrhea (135-137). Unlike a typical interview in which the interviewer has some modicum of control over the interview and uses his/her questions to steer the course of the discussion, Uhltzscht's perhaps extreme dealings with Kitzelstein lay bare the underlying nature of interviews and exemplify the dominant role of the interviewed. The person being interviewed ultimately controls the discussion in both his/her response to the interviewer and in his/her willingness to speak on certain matters. In *Helden wie wir*, Kitzelstein, the interviewer, is thus reduced to a sounding board for Uhltzscht's agenda, emphasizing the primacy of the "story" to the interview. Within the context of the interviewing frenzy in unified Germany and in the new provinces in particular, Uhltzscht's interview with Kitzelstein is a scathing indictment of the man-on-the-street approach to gathering information to measure the challenges unification has brought with it.

Yet Uhltzscht's motivation in telling Kitzelstein his life story involves more than parodying interviews in general. He intends to revise the publicly acknowledged account of 9 November 1989. In other words, he wants to set history straight. Before he even begins regaling Kitzelstein with his version of the events leading up to 9 November 1989, Klaus sets the tone of the interview: "Lassen Sie mich zuerst ein paar Mißverständnisse klären" (6). [6] The "misunderstandings" to which he is referring are the role of the East German people, the "*Das-Volk-sprengt-die Mauer*-Legende" (*The-People-force-open-the-Wall* Legend"; 6) as Uhltzscht refers to it, and the role of Günter Schabowski in announcing the opening of the Wall in a press conference. In positioning himself from the outset as the maker of and also as the reviser of history, Uhltzscht transforms the telling of his life story into an implicit criticism not only of the tremendous role of interviews with average citizens in explicating the demise of the German Democratic Republic, but also of historical accounts.

6 "First, however, let me dispel a few misapprehensions" (4).

Uhltzscht's opening commentary connects his autobiography directly with history: "Mr. Kitzelstein, wie Sie sehen, habe ich meiner historischen Verantwortung voll bewußt, bereits damit begonnen, die Geschichte meines Lebens aufzuschreiben" (5).[7] Such an opening heralds Uhltzscht's importance or at least his self-importance. As Suzanne Nalbantian points out in her *Aesthetic Autobiography*, "Autobiography, in the popular form, is the rage of our era. Public figures inevitably resort to this form to reveal aspects of their lives after they have been at center stage" (viii). In light of Nalbantian's assertion, Uhltzscht's story is worth following on two counts: he is, or at least he thinks he is, important enough to write his autobiography; and his fame has brought him to the attention of a major foreign newspaper, *The New York Times*. Kitzelstein's telephone call, however, not only interrupts the narrative line of Uhltzscht's autobiography, but also shifts his life story to its true point of reference, i.e. from his birth in a small hotel to an explanation of his role in the fall of the Berlin Wall. In other words, Uhltzscht's life story has a two-fold purpose. It will reveal the details of a new beginning for Germany and also a new phase of growth and notoriety for Uhltzscht's genitalia.

The opening statement by Uhltzscht establishes an equivalency that functions as an advanced organizer and foreshadows the nature of the narrator and of his story which is disclosed as the novel unfolds. As Hayden White points out in his *Metahistory*:

> The historian (*In Uhltzscht's case, he is his own historian, a hobby historian.)* arranges the events in the chronicle into a hierarchy of significance by assigning events different functions as story elements in such a way to disclose the formal coherence of a whole set of events considered as a comprehensible process with a discernible beginning, middle, and end. (7)

Just as Uhltzscht reduces the history of the fall of the Berlin Wall to the story of his penis, he also establishes an equivalency between his life story and the story of his genitalia, i.e. the uniqueness of his male anatomy is the one constant and ever present element in the trials and tribulations of his otherwise rather pathetic life. It also serves to bring coherence to the sum of events that constitute his past. Beginning with his childhood memories of summer camp, including competing in pissing contests, discussing penis size, and sharing stories of seeing their parents having sex, the narrator's male member is the one constant thematic element in his life story.

Uhltzscht's obsession with his penis falls into essentially two categories. Primarily, he is concerned about its size. As he confesses to Kitzelstein: "Ich habe den kleinsten Schwanz, den man je gesehen hat" (101),[8] and he refers to

7 "You see, Mr. Kitzelstein? I'm so fully aware of my historic responsibilities that I've already begun to write the story of my life [. . .]" (3).

8 "*Eh bien*, for my age I had the smallest dick imaginable" (80).

his penis on several occasions as "mein kleines Zipfelchen" ("my little tail"). Secondly, he views mastering his erections as one of life's biggest challenges. As Uhltzscht puts it,"Meine ganze Pubertät über hatte ich nichts anderes zu tun, als meinen Ständer wegzuräumen" (71).[9] Therefore, without his genital escapades, Uhltzscht may simply be reduced to an overprotected child with a domineering mother and a cold, distant father, who grows up in an apartment conveniently located across from the *Ministerium für Staatssicherheit* (Ministry for State Security) in East Berlin. In assigning his genitalia celebrity status, Uhltzscht catapults his life story and his physical being onto the stage of world history.

History and fame run throughout Uhltzscht's story. Even as a child, he is confident that they both will figure prominently in his future. His childhood success at a science fair and his resulting picture on the first page of the *Berliner Zeitung* convince him early on that it is only a matter of time before he wins a Nobel Prize. When the adoption of his plan by the Stasi to halt the production of illegal flyers seems about to become reality, Uhltzscht exclaims: "Dann bin ich endlich bedeutend, dann werde ich (mit Foto) in die Geschichtsbücher eingehen, als der Mann, der dem Flugblattunwesen ein Ende setzte!" (167).[10] Uhltzscht considers his historical significance to be predetermined within a framework of events that are simply waiting to happen. It is as though he has a five-year plan for his greatness and he anticipates at each turn the catalytic event that will set the ball rolling.

Uhltzscht's narrative, however, does not place history in a vacuum. In telling of his grandiose fantasies of fame and glory present in his work for the Stasi, he juxtaposes his preconceptions of his work for the Stasi, which he views as "eine historische Mission" ("a historic mission"), with the mundane priorities of his co-workers (150). Uhltzscht tells of his great disappointment when Major Wunderlich, his commanding officer, makes it clear on his first day of work that a good supply of pretzel sticks and regular runs around the track are essential to their work. The wide gap between Uhltzscht's preconceived "historische Mission" and the details he chooses to share about his work environment places his idealized view of history on the same level of his dreams of greatness, clearly in the realm of fantasy, far removed of the reality of his daily life. Uhltzscht's concept of historical destiny, however, paints him furthermore as a naïve believer when he is forced to rationalize the daily absurdities of his life as contributing forces on his path to greatness. For instance when he breaks his left thumb and right wrist falling down the stairs after masturbating in an apartment building stairwell, he contemplates how he is going to explain his injuries to Major Wunderlich and how perhaps

9 "I spent my entire adolescence trying to banish hard-ons, but only with limited success" (57).

10 "I would be important at last, I would go down in history (with photograph) as the man who put an end to the leaflet scourge!" (135).

Wunderlich ironically would want to employ his masturbatory skills in combating the pacifist movement: "Mit Lizenz für den historischen Fortschritt zu wichsen war schon immer mein Wunsch! Und fünfzig Millionen wären nicht einfach weggeworfen und vergessen, nein, ihr Tod hätte einen *Sinn!*" (201).[11] In juxtaposing his serious hopes for the historical greatness to which he is predestined with the absurdity of daily existence, Uhltzscht doubly undermines the significance of his life story. Not only is his pathetic life clearly at odds with his self-perception, but his understanding of historical significance for the most part contradicts the details of the experiences he chooses to compose his life story.

Contrary to expectation, Uhltzscht's concept of history deviates from the Marxist historiography in which class struggle is the driving force for the inevitable evolution of a society, and it instead more closely parallels the traditional Western cult of the individual. As Uhltzscht exclaims in a moment of professional euphoria: "Ich war über meine historische Mission im klaren und alles, war mir geschah, paßte ins Bild. Denn was ich auch tat, war weltbewegend und geschichtsverändernd – *weil ich es tat*" (255).[12] Uhltzscht's understanding of the interplay between his sense of self-importance and his concept of history structures his rendition of other events in his past. Due to the unique composition of his blood, which is a result of his limiting his fluid intake, one of his methods of controlling his troublesome, spontaneous erections, Uhltzscht is asked to donate blood to save Erich Honecker's life. This incident supplies more food for Uhltzscht's ego:

> Aber weil ich alle sexuellen Regungen unterdrückte, driftete ich in die Perversion ab. Ergo: Nur ein Perverser wie ich konnte der Retter sein, [. . .] Es ergibt auch einen *Sinn*. Und plötzlich tauchten historische Zusammenhänge auf: Wenn ich bisher nur rätselte, was *die* mit meinem so kostbaren Leben vorhaben, und sich herausstellt, daß mit meinem kostbaren Leben ein Generalsekretär gerettet wird. (274)[13]

This statement combines the three elements key to Uhltzscht's understanding of events of historical significance: his sexuality, his ego, and the role of destiny and fate in his justification for living. His dreams of his imminent fame

11 "It has always been my ambition to jerk off legitimately, in the interests of historical progress, and my fifty million microfish wouldn't be simply discarded and forgotten—no, their death would acquire some *meaning*!" (162).

12 "I was conscious of my historic mission, and all that happened to me accorded with it. What I did was earth-shaking and epoch-making *because I did it*" (207).

13 "By suppressing my sexual urges, however, I had strayed into perversion. Ergo, only a pervert like me could have saved the jackstraws player and enabled him to go on playing.
A rather tacky *curriculum vita*, perhaps, but also—whichever way you look at it—imbued with *meaning*. The historical context suddenly dawned on me: I'd wondered what 'they' planned to do with my precious life, and it had transpired that my precious life was ensuring the survival of a General Secretary" (222).

present in his childhood hopes of becoming a Nobel Prize winner come to fruition in the seemingly banal act of donating blood, and in turn convince him of the inevitability of his place in history.

Yet, Uhltzscht's blood donation has greater implications than simply the intersection of his path with that of a major historical figure. The resulting, as Uhltzscht terms it, "Perversenbluttherapie" ("therapy using the blood of a perverse individual"; 276) provides still another connection between Uhltzscht and the Berlin Wall. Not only is he responsible for bringing it down, in his mind he is also responsible for Honecker's behavior in the fall of 1989, the fall in which East Germany celebrated its forty years of existence. Uhltzscht is otherwise at a loss to explain Honecker's insistence on a celebration of great pomp and circumstance in the face of mounting protest demonstrations taking place in cities such as East Berlin and Leipzig, and his longevity given his pancreatic cancer. His knowledge of the blood transfusion inspires him and allows him to position himself prominently vis-à-vis November of 1989: "Ich stehe da und verstehe *alles*, was damals gelaufen ist" (276).[14]

Uhltzscht's understanding of his destiny and place in history reaches its peak at the height of the demonstrations in East Berlin at the beginning of November 1989. As he presses through the masses at a demonstration hoping to reach the speakers' platform, Uhltzscht takes a comical fall down some steps and ends up doing a dangerous tango with a protest sign. In addition to suffering a head injury, Uhltzscht's dance with the protest sign leaves his genitalia hopelessly mangled. Uhltzscht himself compares his damaged penis to a "zertretenen Frosch" ("squashed frog"; 293). This accident gives Uhltzscht another push on his journey to enlightenment. As he is recovering from reconstructive surgery, he reaches a new plateau in his understanding of history:

> Ich entdeckte, daß ich eine *Vergangenheit* habe und daß diese Vergangenheit eine *Bedeutung* hat und daß meine Gegenwart, die Schmerzen und der zertretene Frosch, nicht zufällig in mein Leben hereinbrachen, sondern alles Bisherige nur verlängerten. Daß alles logisch verlief und so enden *mußte*. (293)[15]

Struggling with his pain, Uhltzscht sees the continuity in his life. His accident appears to him at this point as a logical extension of a life that has been dominated and driven by the dictates of his penis. Uhltzscht views his life story as a continuous, linear entity heading "penis-long" towards a destiny whose grandeur he can at this point only accept and await.

---

14 "I understand *everything* that happened at that time" (224).

15 "I discovered that I had a past, and that my present pain and the squashed frog were not fortuitous irruptions into my life, merely a continuation of all that had gone before—that everything was following a logical course and had *had* to end this way" (238).

On 9 November, Uhltzscht realizes the destiny and purpose of his newly created male organ. Escaping from the hospital, Uhltzscht feels a need to right a wrong and sets out to show his newly enhanced equipment to a woman, who during a brief sexual encounter had once laughed mercilessly at its pitiful size. This woman, whom Uhltzscht refers to mercilessly as the "Wurstfrau" ("sausage woman"; 188) due to her short, pudgy stature, lives on a side street of the Bornholmer Straße, a street with a border crossing at its end. On this evening, the masses, inspired by Günter Schabowski's statement, are waiting to cross over the border. Seeing the thousands of people detained by only ten or twelve border guards, Uhltzscht surmises: "[. . .] ein Volk, das ratlos vor ein paar Grenzsoldaten stehenbleibt, ein solches Volk hat einen zu kleinen Pimmel—in diesen Dingen kenne ich mich aus" (315-316).[16] With this statement, the significance of Uhltzscht's penis moves from the physical realm of sexuality to the metaphorical realm of potency, strength, confidence and courage. And with his rallying cry–"*Na los! Ihr müßt mehr drücken, verdammt noch mal! Volle Pulle! Ihr schafft es! Ich weiß, ihr könnt es schaffen!*" (316),[17] Uhltzscht opens the Wall.

In the closing paragraph of the novel following his announcement that he now has a career starring in porno films, Uhltzscht once again emphasizes his historical significance: "Wer meine Geschichte nicht glaubt, wird nicht verstehen, was mit Deutschland los ist! Ohne mich ergibt alles keinen Sinn! Denn ich bin das *Missing link* der jüngsten deutschen Geschichte!" (323).[18] Klaus Uhltzscht, who is the son of a control-freak mother and non-participatory father, a sexually repressed and obsessed member of the Stasi who is guilty of child abduction and attempted rape, the victim of a disfiguring, transformative injury, just happens to be the guy who is in the right place at the right time. In his opinion, it is his life story that is necessary to understand the vagaries and idiosyncrasies not only of the fall of the Berlin Wall but of the current state of affairs in united Germany.

What kind of statement does a novel with this narrator and this conclusion make on Germany today? Klaus Uhltzscht is not a narrator whom one grows to respect in the course of his story. Nor are his story and his convictions highly plausible. In fact, *Helden wie wir* is far removed from the genre of historical fiction, which does provide its readers with personalized, yet believable accounts of historical events. The one thing that *Helden wie wir* does, however, is offer a humorous explanation for an event which even with the distance of

16 "[. . .] people nonplussed by a handful of border guards—people of that kind have undersized dicks, take it from one who knows" (256).

17 "Go on, shove harder, damn you! Give it all you've got! You can do it, I know you can!" (257).

18 "No one who dismisses my story can possibly understand what's wrong with Germany. Why not? Because nothing makes sense without me—because I'm recent German history's *missing link*" (262).

more than a decade, still defies our comprehension on some level. In Uhltzscht's mind's eye, history becomes something inevitable, convoluted, and dependent on individuals, circumstances and timing. His character removes history from the realm of great powers and governments and places it on the human level, the level of the individual. The ridiculousness of Uhltzscht and his story, nonetheless, discredit his claim to fame, but also it leaves in its wake the bare issue of fate. Herein lies perhaps the point that Uhltzscht makes with his story: change can happen and will happen.

Yet to reduce the novel to a commentary on East German society, its people and its values would be shortsighted. Ultimately, *Helden wie wir* is making fun of both East and West Germans by playing not only with the stereotypes of East Germans but also by transferring some of East Germans' stereotypes of the West to the character of Klaus Uhltzscht and his interviewer, Mr. Kitzelstein. After all, it is a major American newspaper, *The New York Times* that is essentially buying into Uhltzscht's story. Even Uhltzscht's egotistical approach to the course of world events is more typical of the West, where the individual, at least ideologically, reigns supreme as the mover and shaker of life-transforming change. Uhltzscht's new found professional career in the porno industry is without a doubt a direct play on the evils of the West. Clearly, the character of Klaus Uhltzscht and his life story essentially embody elements of both East and West Germany, and in doing so may speak more for the similarity of Germans from both sides of the Wall, rather than for their assumed dissimilarity. Thus, *Helden wie wir* written by a young former East German implicitly reflects the unified German character apparent in German youth today, rather than the division embedded in the hearts and souls of the older generation.

Works Cited

Brussig, Thomas. *Helden wie wir*. Berlin: Verlag Volk & Welt, 1995.

Brussig, Thomas. *Heroes like us*. Trans. John Brownjohn. New York: Farrar, 1996.

Frölich, Margrit. "Thomas Brussig's Satire of Contemporary History." *GDR Bulletin* 25 (1998): 21-30.

Gabler, Wolfgang. "Die Wende als Witz: Komische Darstellungen eines historischen Umbruchs." *Literatur* 18.3 (1997): 141-154.

Nalbantian, Suzanne. *Aesthetic Autobiography: From Life to Art in Marcel Proust, James Joyce, Virginia Woolf and Anais Nin*. London: Macmillan, 1994.

Ostow, Robin. "Restructuring Our Lives: National Unification and German Biographies. Introduction." *Oral History Review* 21.2 (1993): 1-8.

Preece, Julian. "Damaged lives? (East) German memoirs and autobiographies; 1989-1994." *The New Germany: Literature and Society after Unification*. Ed. Osman Durrani, Colin Good, and Kevin Hilliard. Sheffield: Sheffield Academic Press, 1995. 349-364.

Weber, Carl. “A Picaresque Tale: East Germany’s Last Act.” *PAJ: A Journal of Performance and Art* 65 (2000): 142-145.

White, Hayden. *Metahistory: The Historical Imagination in Nineteenth-Century Europe*. Baltimore: The Johns Hopkins UP, 1973.

Zachau, Reinhard K. “‘Das Volk jedenfalls war’s nicht!’: Thomas Brussigs Abrechnung mit der DDR.” *Colloquia Germanica* 30.4 (1997): 387-395.

Multiple Voice—Generational Views

KAROLINE VON OPPEN

"Man muß jetzt laut schreien, um gehört zu werden"[1]: Stefan Heym, Walter Jens, Helga Königsdorf: An intellectual opposition?

> Auf dem schwankenden Terrain selektiver Wahrnehmungen haben sich Intellektuelle aus der ehemaligen DDR und der Bundesrepublik ohne Schwierigkeiten treffen können. Stefan Heym wollte "den sozialistischen Traum weiter träumen," hat seinem Unbehagen [. . .] ebenso Ausdruck gegeben wie auf der anderen Seite Walter Jens [. . .] und Günter Grass erklärten, die DDR müsse eine "sozialistische Alternative" bleiben [. . .]." (Noack 63)[2]

In 1991 Paul Noack, academic and former *Frankfurter Allgemeine Zeitung* editor could construct an oppositional grouping of writers that stretched from the GDR writer Stefan Heym to Günter Grass and Walter Jens. They had become the radical voices in the debate about unification, and the differences in their respective positions no longer mattered in his dismissive account *Deutschland, deine Intellektuellen: Die Kunst, sich ins Abseits zu stellen*. What mattered was the exclusion of critical voices from future debate, or as Helmut Peitsch argues, "aus dem Untergang der DDR das Ende der Rolle des bundesrepublikanischen Schriftstellers als öffentlicher Kritiker plausibel zu machen" ("Vereinigung" 43).[3] While few analyses of the period of unification dare ignore the vociferous debate that broke out following the publication of Christa Wolf's *Was bleibt* in June 1990, Peitsch argues that the proclamation "Für unser Land" in November 1989 already marked the beginning of attempts to undermine the role of writer as critic (43). There is little need to reopen the Wolf debate here, for it has by now been well documented and analyzed.[4] It

1 "Today one has to shout loudly to be heard." The title is taken from a comment made by Helga Königsdorf in conversation with Günter Gaus (79). All translations in this text are my own. Many thanks to Katrin Eberbach and Sonja Bernhard for their comments.

2 "Intellectuals from the former GDR and the Federal Republic had no trouble finding each other on the shaky ground of selective perception. Stefan Heym wanted to continue 'to dream the socialist dream' and gave voice to his uneasiness as on the other side Walter Jens and Günter Grass declared that the GDR must remain a 'socialist alternative.'"

3 "to make an argument that the role of West German writers as public critics should cease with the demise of the GDR"

4 In June 1990 Christa Wolf publishes a novella entitled *Was bleibt*. It immediately sparks a controversy in the press that continues throughout 1990. Initially addressing the supposed

must be pointed out, however, that even critics writing more generally on writers in this period have been very judgmental, but at the same time appear not to have explored in any great detail the actual responses, journalistic or otherwise, of writers.[5] This has not prevented many from reaching damning conclusions.[6] While one could argue that all of this is irrelevant today, many years after the event, I argue that such an analysis is still illuminating. By looking back at the earliest attempts to reconfigure the literary sphere it becomes possible to recall a time where definitions are still in flux, where the consensus is not yet established and is thus more open to critique and scrutiny. This in turn can contribute towards an understanding of seemingly separate debates occurring throughout the 1990s (cf. Peitsch, "9. November"; "Vereinigung"). Finally, such a study provides an opportunity to examine the process of negotiation that I argue characterizes an author's intervention in the media in any epoch.

I will re-examine the journalistic responses of three well-known writers from East and West Germany from the summer of 1989 to the late summer of 1990. By re-examining both their contributions and the changing reception of their ideas, it becomes possible to map out phases in the unification debate.[7] As Robert Weninger rightly argues, literary debates are "präzise Seismographen der politischen Gegenwarts-befindlichkeit" (231), but perhaps the reverse is also the case.[8] For it is clear that the process of political unification was accompanied by a concerted attempt to delegitimize the role of author as critic.[9] I will show that this is *as much* in evidence in the changing

---

complicity of Wolf, the debate soon targets authors from both East and West Germany. The debate is launched simultaneously in the two main feuilletons of the Federal Republic, *Die Zeit* and *Frankfurter Allgemeine Zeitung*: (Greiner, "Mangel"; Schirrmacher, "Druck"). A complete overview of the debate can be found in the Thomas Anz volume. Further insights into the text and the ensuing debate can be found in Paul; Kuhn; and Brockmann, "Introduction" and *Literature* 64-80.

5 One explanation for this could be a restrictive reliance on "die Feuilletons der überregionalen Blätter" as Helmut Kreuzer (408-409) has argued. Another is the use of anthologies of contributions, which tends to confirm trends by the necessary selection process.

6 Compare: "And it was perhaps, understandable that the vast majority of intellectuals inside the GDR opposition—now suddenly catapulted into power and prominence—continued fighting for what they had wanted all along: democratic socialism." (Brockmann , "Introduction" 15). "German intellectuals, in both East and West, propounded at the time, and still remain grumblingly attached to the vain, frustrated hope of something called 'the Third Way.'" (Lasky 86). "The fall of Communism was not welcomed here as, [. . .] a victory of liberty; instead it was denounced as the imposition of capitalism and predatory colonization by the western part of the divided nation. This perception is still widely shared by East (and West) German intellectuals and continues to contaminate the political and intellectual life of Germany today" (Joppke viii).

7 In my volume *The Role of the Writer in the Unification of Germany 1989/90*, I have undertaken a detailed study of nine representative authors and their responses to German unification. The results indicate that the majority neither opposed unification nor remained silent (Oppen).

8 "precise seismographs of the political situation."

9 See Bogdal, Oppen, and Pietsch "9. November" for example.

reception of the three authors examined here, as in the Wolf debate. Heym's rise and fall in the West German media, for example, appears to have had little to do with his position on unification, as is generally assumed. I will show that it is at the point that Heym accepts the idea of unification as a possibility for reform in all of Germany, that he becomes dismissed as "a perpetual dissident."[10] Walter Jens's position is decidedly more ambiguous. He is "invisible" in the press for many months, mainly it seems because of his outspoken rejection of unification, but by mid-1990 begins to appear more frequently. His position in debates is more conciliatory than Heym's, yet his legitimacy is also undermined, particularly after his intervention in the Wolf debate. Thus, even before the Wolf debate had really gathered momentum, critical voices such as Jens and Heym had already been silenced.

Within the few analyses that do exist of this period, attention is seldom paid to how an author negotiates his/her role in the press. Contradictions that exist are smoothed out to present a well-formulated, unambiguous position. Thus, a majority of analyses come to the clear conclusion that "... even though their [intellectuals'] positions differed considerably, it was precisely their joint opposition to the course of events which produced their image of failure" (Huyssen 117). What is frequently overlooked is the fact that writers may present an intentionally ambiguous position, may alter their argument or may be deliberately cloaking their argument in ambiguous phrases in order to gain access to a discourse. As Stefan Heym explained: "... man muß Mittel und Wege finden, das, was man für richtig hält, auch zu transportieren. Es kostet eine Menge List, wenn man derlei in den offiziellen Medien machen will, aber wo haben es denn die Schriftsteller, die geistigen Arbeiter und die Leute, die etwas Neues zu sagen haben, je leicht gehabt?" (Liersch 92).[11] Uncovering the "ways and means" used to gain access to discourse is no easy task. It requires an analysis that accepts that subjection to a discourse can be voluntary. By going beyond Foucault and arguing that subjection to a discourse can be motivated by reasons other than an acceptance of the terms of the discourse, resistance becomes possible. As Edward Said argues of foucaultian discourse theory: "Foucault seems to have been confused between the power of institutions to subjugate individuals and the fact that individual behavior in society is frequently a matter of following rules and conventions" ("Foucault" 151). This, according to Said, is the beginning of the difficult task of "formulating the discourse of liberation" (153).

I argue firstly, that the focus on the Wolf debate has led to a neglect of that debate's prehistory, namely of the responses of authors *from the autumn of 1989*. This prehistory is vital to an understanding of the process of cultural

10 I used the term coined by Peter Hutchinson (1992) to describe Heym's lifelong opposition.

11 "one must find ways and means to convey that which one considers right. It requires much cunning if one wants to do this in the official media. But when have writers, intellectual workers and people who have something new to say, ever had it easy?"

reconfiguration that is characteristic for the post-Wende situation.[12] Secondly, few critics have concerned themselves with the strategies of engagement, the "Mittel und Wege" that are employed to gain access to a discourse, the partial conformism that is the cost of retaining discursive visibility and the ambiguities and transformations that may occur within the position of an author. Of course, critics may simply have [deliberately?] failed to scrutinize the texts carefully. Either way, I maintain that there is a significant dislocation between the actual intervention of authors and the dominant perception of authorial responses; a dislocation that has been pivotal in the redefinition of the role of the writer. This is, of course, the crucial aspect of the matter. If the role of authors has been redefined—"Der Bedarf nach politischer Aktivität von Schriftstellern ist unvermittelt erloschen" (Noack 74)—as a result of being presented as "das retardierendste Moment in der deutschen Entwicklung" ("Nötige"), then this analysis is more than an account of events past.[13] It is a necessary attempt to redress the balance in a rather one-sided debate, which has had longlasting effects. But perhaps balance was never at issue. As Frank Schirrmacher later states quite openly, the intention was: "zu zeigen, daß hier im Vergleich zu Kohl oder Engholm oder Bertelsmann keine größere Kompetenz mehr vorlag, über Dinge der Moral oder Politik zu reden" (Anz 257).[14]

Stefan Heym and Walter Jens among others have today come to symbolize intellectual resistance to unification. Jens is probably best known for his outspoken defense of Wolf, although this is not his only public statement of the period, and Heym is known as the incorrigible socialist who dreamt of a third way for the GDR. Helga Königsdorf is also associated with the opposition, although her reception has been less severe. She is however vital here, for I argue that her ability to maneuver her position in the media is exemplary, and is undoubtedly a reason for the more muted reception of her texts. Heym and Jens however feature frequently as representative figures in analyses of the responses of writers. Klaus Scherpe, for example, re-examines Heym's unification texts [in 1995] only to observe that Heym "der moralisierende Ersatzpolitike[r]" (120) is unaware of the redefinition of his role: "Am Beispiel Heyms will ich vielmehr den problematischen Gestus des moralischen Intellektuellen aufzeigen, der an seiner Position festhält, ohne deren Veränderung im sozialen Feld selber zu bemerken" (118).[15] Karl Heinz Bohrer on the other hand chose to target West German authors Walter Jens

12 One of the best overall analyses of this process can be found in the volume *After Unity: Reconfiguring German Identities* (Jarausch).

13 "The demand for the political involvement of writers has come to an end" as a result of being presented as "the greatest delaying factor in German developments."

14 "to show that in comparison to Kohl or Engholm or Bertelsman no greater competence existed to speak about matters of morals or politics."

15 "the moralizing 'Ersatz'-politician"; "Using the example of Heym I will moreover demonstrate the problematic attitude of the moralizing intellectual who holds onto his position without himself recognizing the change in the social field."

(and Günter Grass) in order to dismiss their legitimacy to engage in public debate, particularly vis-à-vis unification: "Denn wer sind Günter Grass und Walter Jens heute? Zwei gewichtige Figuren der Öffentlichkeit, gewiß, habituell 'engagiert' und aller Ehren wert, politisch und intellektuell aber schon seit längerer Zeit überfordert, die die Chance wittern, einer epochal überholten Zivilisation, wie der DDR Stichworte zur Einbringung ihrer Werte zu liefern" (1015).[16]

Stefan Heym

Let me begin with Heym. In a celebrated discussion with Günter Grass in 1984, Heym uses the image of the open wound to describe the division of Germany: "wir können noch so viel Antibiotika darauf streuen, sie wird weiter eitern" (*Einmischung* 40). While rejecting "artificial" cures, Heym expresses his conviction that division is not final: "es kann nicht ewig dauern" (53).[17] So how does this "perpetual dissident," whose preoccupation with division is beyond question, react to the revolutionary events of 1989? Famously, on 4 November 1989, Heym addresses the huge crowds on the Alexanderplatz in revolutionary triumph and earns the rare praise of Frank Schirrmacher (1989): "Doch es gibt Augenblicke, wo Schriftsteller wirklich zu Wortführern werden können."[18] This positive assessment of Heym's role is extremely short-lived. By 1990 a critic could write of Heym's presence at a writers' meeting: "Erstaunlich ist, daß zu so einem Treffen der Schriftsteller Heym eingeladen wird" (Bauer).[19] His surprise rests on the fact that Heym had remained in the GDR, now already defined as a totalitarian state, and could therefore not be regarded as a legitimate critic.[20]

Heym is very visible in the press in the early autumn of 1989 publishing in *Die Zeit*, *Süddeutsche Zeitung* and *Der Spiegel*. As he writes later: "Eine Zeitlang war der 'Spiegel' sozusagen mein Leib-und-Magen-Organ, ich habe eine Menge Themen dort behandeln können; aber dann war zu, absolut zu." (Liersch 93).[21] West German television and press critics give him maximum

16 "Who are Günter Grass and Walter Jens today? Two important figures of public life certainly, regularly politically 'engaged' and deserving of all respect, politically and intellectually however overburdened, who sense the opportunity to introduce their own values into an anachronistic civilization like the GDR."

17 "we can administer as many antibiotics as we like, the wound will continue to suppurate."; "it cannot last for ever."

18 "There are moments where writers can really become spokespersons."

19 "It is surprising that the writer Heym has been invited to such a gathering."

20 The first signs that the GDR was to be compared with Nazi Germany appear in March 1990. Compare Peitsch, "9. November" 216-218.

21 "For a while the 'Spiegel' was my favorite mouthpiece. I was able to discuss many issues there but then it was closed to me, completely closed."

visibility in this period. In many ways he is regarded as a role model dissident author and "Wortführer" until the proclamation "Für unser Land," for which he subsequently bears the sole responsibility, heralds the end of the legitimacy of GDR dissident writers. This proclamation has possibly become the single most cited evidence of intellectual opposition, despite its decidedly more ambitious aims.[22] This period is in any case marked by the beginning of the dominance of the West German elites, as signaled by Helmut Kohl's interventionist "10-Punkte-Plan" ("10-Point Plan") for German unity.

Throughout the late summer of 1989 Heym is undoubtedly concerned about the possibility of a wholesale take-over of the GDR, and he is outspoken in his rejection of immediate unification. Yet in August 1989 he participates in a discussion with Egon Bahr where he refuses to make a definite statement on unification, despite Bahr's clear rejection of the idea (Süskind, "Kuckuckseier"). At this stage Heym has little hesitation in insisting that the existence of one German nation is not sufficient to justify immediate unification: "Wenn man in einem gemeinsamen Haus wohnt, muß man nicht unbedingt im selben Zimmer wohnen" (Scheller).[23] Here Heym is of course prioritizing independence by adapting Gorbachev's famous slogan of the "European house." Nonetheless, Heym remains resolutely opposed to the official GDR state position on GDR identity—"Es gibt keine DDR-Nationalkultur, ebensowenig wie es eine DDR-Nation gibt. Es gibt Deutsche in einem sozialistischen [. . .] Staat" (*Einmischung* 247)—while firm in his opposition to rapid unification.[24] The GDR, he argues, should represent a "Gegengewicht gegen die Daimler-Messerschmitt-Bölkow-Blohm-BASF-Hoechst-Deutsche-Bank-Republik auf der anderen Seite der Elbe" ("Ist die DDR").[25] Several days prior to the opening of the Wall, Heym publishes his last article to contain a clear revolutionary call for independence and reform, which ends with a defiant "Es lebe die Republik" (*Einmischung* 264).[26] In his next public interview he already hints at a revised version of his reform plan. Using exactly the same image as before, he alters the emphasis: "Aber ich bin der Meinung, daß dieses vereinte Deutschland ja nicht unbedingt ein Bonner Deutschlandmodell, Typ Mercedes/MBB sein müßte" (Ihlau).[27] Prior even to

22 Compare, for example, Konrad Wolf's comment on the proclamation: "der Filmmacher Konrad Wolf sprach von einer denkbaren 'neuen Einheit' der Deutschen, die Reformen in beiden Staaten voraussetzte" (dpa). This was reported by the deutsche presse agentur but not included in the newspaper reports. ("the filmmaker Konrad Wolf spoke of a possible 'new unity' for the Germans that pre-supposed reforms in both states.")

23 "Just because one lives in one house does not mean one has to live in the same room."

24 "There is no national GDR culture nor even a GDR nation. There are only Germans living in a socialist state."

25 "counterbalance to the Daimler-Messerschmitt-Bölkow-Blohm-BASF-Hoechst-Deutsche-Bank-Republic on the other side."

26 "Long live the republic!"

27 "But I am of the opinion that this unified Germany need not be based on the Bonn, Germany model, type Mercedes/MBB."

Helmut Kohl's plan for confederative structures, Heym is already contemplating the reform necessary in a *unified* state as opposed to merely in the GDR.

Heym's reception in September/October 1989 is still very favorable: "einer der einflussreichsten Schriftsteller der DDR" (Amü); "[Heym] gehört [. . .] zu den meistbefragten Schriftstellern der DDR" (Mudrich).[28] On 26 November 1989 Heym is a signatory of the proclamation "Für unser Land," and by late November 1989 his legitimacy as "Wortführer der Massen" has ended. The turning point is perhaps most visible in the *Spiegel* of 4 December 1989, which is quick to target Heym for his role in the proclamation, defining it as "die Heym-Initiative" and "Heyms schöner Traum" ("Bleibt"), despite other well-known signatories.[29] Heym's well-known "Aschermittwoch" (Ash Wednesday) article is also published in this edition of *Spiegel*, the fate of which is by now well known. Monika Maron, whose departure from the GDR in 1988 guarantees her a privileged position in this debate, famously attacked Heym in February 1990 for his privileged existence in the GDR comparing him to the party elite. The main effect of her attack was to reinforce the notion that Heym was a recalcitrant socialist; a fact supposedly in evidence in the "Aschermittwoch" article. Ironically, this article possibly represents the most visible evidence of a shift in Heym's position.

The religious allusion in the title is an indication of the disillusionment that will become characteristic of his work, particularly in his refusal henceforth to elaborate concrete proposals. I argue that Heym, aware of the precariousness of his position, partially accepts the consensus on unification, presumably in order to retain the legitimacy to engage in debate. He revokes his previous insistence on independence by linking it explicitly to reform: "Reden wir über die Einheit. Tatsache ist, zwei kapitalistische Staaten sind nicht vonnöten" ("Hurra").[30] This is a clear shift away from his earlier notion of the German house. Without immediate reform, an independent GDR is redundant and unification now provides an opportunity to reform all of Germany. On 9 December 1989 Heym finally accepts the inevitability of unification demanding only consideration for East German values—"Die Frage ist nur, was für ein geeintes Deutschland das dann sein soll: ein Großdeutschland wieder, wie gehabt, durch Anschluß zusammengekommen, [. . .] oder ein anderes, Neues, in das auch die Bürger der DDR ihre Erfahrungen und Werte [. . .] mit eingebracht haben werden. (*Einmischung* 272)—a desire which hardly represents a radical vision for Germany.[31] His only prerequisite is that

28 "one of the most influential writers of the GDR." "[Heym] belongs to the most popular writers of the GDR."

29 "the Heym initiative"; "Heym's beautiful dream." These included Volker Braun, Christa Wolf and the filmmaker Konrad Wolf.

30 "Let us talk about unity. The fact is that two capitalist states are not necessary."

31 "The question remains what sort of Germany it will be: another 'Großdeutschland' brought together through annexation as before, [. . .] or a different new Germany into which the

"Wirtschaft wie Gesellschaft in der DDR jetzt in Ordnung kommen, in eine demokratische Ordnung" (*Einmischung* 272).[32] Clearly, nothing in this speech conflicts with the dominant rhetoric of the time. But again that is not the issue. I argue that Heym is delegitimized not for his support for democratic order, but for his representative role as GDR dissident writer. His partial acceptance of the consensus alters little in his ongoing unfavorable reception.

From this point onward, Heym vanishes from his prominent position in the West German press. He continues to appear throughout 1990 in less mainstream publications including *Der Gewerkschafter*, and *Zeitschrift der Gewerkschaft*, with a longer section in *Stern* and the publication of a short story in *Süddeutsche Zeitung*.[33] While his influence steadily declines, critics of his position become more outspoken. Throughout the early months of the year Heym continues to express his view that Germany will unify, but has only vague formulations for future reform: "Auch ich habe in dieser Lage mehr Fragen als Antworten, insbesondere solche, die die Nation und Europa betreffen. Die Antworten darauf können Ost und West nur gemeinsam finden" ("Überlegungen").[34] Unification has become the only solution to the problems facing the two states, and Heym is more cautious in his position.

In March 1990 Heym is awarded the "Gutenberg écrits et libertés" prize by Jack Lang, the French Minister for Culture, a fact which is only reported in *Neues Deutschland* (Dümde).[35] What is remarkable about his reception from this point onwards is that he not only becomes labeled an intransigent socialist, despite his conciliatory position on unification, but that his literary reputation takes on a new significance. In December 1989 "der revolutionäre Romantiker" is described as being concerned only "ob er den Roman der Revolution noch wird schreiben können" (Hank),[36] while in February 1990, Monika Maron sharpens the tone with her attack on writers, exemplified by Heym, and on their literary works. Her conclusion is clear; dissidence had not existed in the GDR, and opposition to unification was merely an attempt to retain privilege: "Schon für ein bisschen Mut wurde man als Held verehrt, als die leibhaftige Opposition. Sich aus dieser Bedeutung zu verabschieden ist offenbar noch schwer."[37] Heym's declining reputation is also in evidence in

---

citizens of the GDR will have brought their experiences and values."

32 "the economy and society of the GDR be brought in order, into a democratic order."

33 See for example K.-P. Wolf. Also Heym's texts "Überlegungen," "Was wird aus," and "Der Besitz."

34 "In this situation I, too, have more questions than answers, particularly relating to the nation and to Europe. The answers to these questions can only be found by East and West working together."

35 Jack Lang of course also acknowledges Christa Wolf at the height of her most difficult period in the press.

36 "the revolutionary romantic" is only concerned "whether he will still be able to write the novel of the revolution."

37 "Even for a little courage one was honored as a hero, as the opposition in person. To bid farewell to this significance is obviously still very difficult."

reviews of his volume of short stories *Auf Sand gebaut* (1990). Critics refused to recognize the stories as literature, arguing that Heym was still attempting to disseminate his political ideas: "Da Stefan Heym weiß, daß es derzeit keine Chance gibt, wie damals im vorigen Herbst, sich auf Plätzen Gehör zu verschaffen, schiebt er seine Rede kurzerhand der Hauptfigur in den Mund" (Steinert).[38] This, critics argue, has diminished the value of the texts to "Sandkastenspielen, zu Trivialliteratur" (Franke); or to "mitleiderregendem, kolportagehaftem Boulevardjournalismus" (Mohr), because "[d]iese literarische Aktualität hat natürlich ihren Preis" (Mudrich).[39]

Heym's awareness of the constraints on his role, his search for "Mittel und Wege" to retain influence is indicative of a self-consciousness that is, I argue, an effect of the literary debates of the Wende. Equally striking however, is the smug complacency of critics who have no hesitation in boasting about their role in the reconfiguration of the literary sphere of the post-*Wende* period: "Man nehme als Beispiel Stefan Heym, einen Schriftsteller, den die Presse der Bundesrepublik lange Jahre als ziemlich wasserdichten Helden gefeiert hatte, weil er den Honeckers und Hagers so manche Wahrheit sagte, und den man, als er mitten in der Revolution die DDR als eigenen Staat erhalten wollte, all die vielen Treppen seines Ruhms hinunterwarf; da liegt er nun zwischen seinen Büchern, die wir ihm nachgeworfen haben" (Glotz).[40] By October 1990 Heym has been discredited politically and aesthetically for a position that was at best moderate. His insistence on the existence of one German nation, his call for democratic reform and for a more ethical process of unification is ignored, while his literary reputation is undermined. Ironically, for Heym, it was not until he accepted the inevitability of unification that he came to stand as representative for all intellectual opposition in this period: "Heym's position resembles that of the entire opposition" (Brockmann, "Introduction" 15).

---

38 "As Stefan Heym knows that he has no chance today, like last autumn, of finding an audience on public squares, he places his speech into the mouth of his main character." See Kristie Foell's analysis of Stefan Heym's responses for an interesting discussion on Heym's attempts to fictionalize historical events. She underlines the "conscientious distinction" made between fact and fiction "on both stylistic and content levels" (46).

39 "to sand pit games, to trivial literature"; "sympathy-evoking, trashy, popular journalism"; "this literary topicality has of course got its price."

40 "Let us take the example of Stefan Heym, a writer celebrated by the press of the Federal Republic for many years as an unquestioned hero because he presented the Honeckers and Hagers with many a truth. When he tried to retain the GDR as an independent state in the midst of the revolution he was thrown down the many steps of his fame. There he lies now amidst his books that we threw after him."

Walter Jens

GDR dissident writers vanish from the mainstream feuilleton in late autumn 1989. The first phase of the debate had ended, and pro-unification writers such as the West German Peter Schneider, and émigré GDR writers such as Monika Maron and Rolf Schneider took up dominant positions.[41] Within the then still visible grouping of West German critics of unification, Walter Jens and Günter Grass soon become key targets in the press. As President of the Akademie der Künste (West) in 1989/90, Walter Jens enjoyed many advantages in gaining access to the media. He had the Academy's publication *hanseatenweg 10: Zeitschrift der Akademie der Künste* at his disposal, but his public role was necessarily restricted as representative spokesperson of the academy. Jens had long argued in favor of the existence of a "Kulturnation" ("nation united by culture") while recognizing the existence of two states: "Die DDR ist ein Staat, die Bundesrepublik ist ein Staat, aber ich weigere mich, Ausland in dem Augenblick beginnen zu lassen, in dem ich den Bahnhof Friedrichstraße in der einen oder in der anderen Richtung verlasse" (Pankow 319).[42] Yet Jens's response in the autumn of 1989 is described as silence. Even in December 1989 when he takes up a clear position—"Ganz 'entschieden' gehe er von der Zweistaatlichkeit aus"—his response is reported as "keine Antwort" (Kippenberger).[43] On 7 February 1990 the *Tagesspiegel* comments on Jens's absence in the debate: "Was macht Jens eigentlich? Wo steckt er?"[44] But this again is inaccurate. In December 1989, for example, Jens had publicly criticized the call for the GDR to join NATO as "eine unglaubliche Anmaßung."[45] In January 1990, he published an article in *Neue Rundschau* entitled "Nachdenken über Deutschland," where he pondered the triumphalism of capitalism. Here he quite explicitly defines the potential "Deutschland" in positive terms as a state which would incorporate "jene aufmüpfigen Radikaldemokraten [. . .], die, Basis-Rechte einklagend, nicht nur in Leipzig, sondern auch zwischen Kiel und Konstanz erklären: 'Wir sind das Volk'" ("Warnung" 93).[46] Jens's supposed opposition to unification is thus far from clear. The linkage made between Jens and Grass is also disingenuous for they hold very different standpoints in this period. Where Grass famously insists on two states by invoking Auschwitz, Jens rapidly perceives an opportunity for

41 See for example, Oppen and Peitsch, "Vereinigung."

42 "The GDR is one state, the Federal Republic is one state but I refuse to consider myself abroad once I leave Friedrichstraße train station in one or other direction."

43 "He most definitely assumed that two states would continue to exist."; "no response."

44 "What is Jens doing? Where is he hiding?" This citation is taken from *Fachdienst Germanistik* 4 (1990). No title is given for the article, which appeared in *Tagesspiegel* on 7 February 1990.

45 "an unbelievable presumption." As cited in the dpa report of 14 December 1989. The fact that it did not feature in the main feuilleton suggests the untimely nature of his comment.

46 "those rebellious radical democrats who demand basic rights by declaring 'We are the people' not only in Leipzig but also from Kiel to Konstanz."

reform of a unified state.[47] While both initially defend the notion of the "Kulturnation" as the only commonality between the two states, Jens quickly accepts it as the basis for a reformed "Deutschland." What is remarkable about his position is that he soon afterwards rejects the existence of any cultural commonalities between the two states. Jens not only accepts the changing consensus on the existence of the "Kulturnation," he also adopts a conciliatory approach throughout the debates of 1990. He has, I argue, been falsely described as one of the most radical voices, for a position that was at best moderate.

In March 1990, Jens organizes a conference at the Akademie der Künste, to discuss the future of the two states. He admits that unity will take time: "Wir sind weit von einander entfernt, zeigt der Stadtplan" ("Zwei deutsche Staaten" 13), and asks for writers to play a role in this process.[48] Throughout the conference his is a moderate voice calling for co-operation and dialogue between East and West.[49] Jens's subsequent contribution to the Wolf debate however is given maximum coverage by the West German press, and plays a decisive role in his reception. His defense of Wolf, particularly at the Potsdam colloquium in June 1990, results in him becoming associated with the intellectual opposition.[50] At Potsdam, Jens controversially demands "ein wenig mehr Sensibilität statt des Spruchkammerdenkens" calling for tolerance, conciliation and a culture of dialogue between the two cultural traditions ("Plädoyer").[51] In his speech on the development of a specific GDR literary culture, he argues that its role as "Zeitungsersatz" ("substitute journalism") was now exhausted ("Plädoyer"). In the light of the Wolf debate this was undoubtedly an ambiguous, although widespread, view.[52] He also dismisses the notion of the silence of intellectuals: "In Wahrheit haben sie eher zu viel als zu wenig geredet" ("Plädoyer").[53] These two comments seem to me characteristic of Jens's conciliatory position. While he criticizes the tenor of attacks on GDR writers, he is not fully prepared to recognize the quality of the literature, and while he recognizes that authors were far from silent in this period, he is critical of their intervention.

---

47 For a more detailed overview of Grass's response in this period, see Peitsch ("Antipoden").

48 "We are far apart from each other according to the city map."

49 At one stage Christoph Hein broaches the anti-intellectualism of the time, and Jens pleads for moderation: "Wir haben uns vorgenommen, meine Damen und Herren, eine 'andere' Diskussion zu führen: also nicht abfragen." (Jens , "Zwei deutsche Staaten" 17). "Ladies and Gentlemen, our intention is to have a different kind of discussion, in other words without interrogation."

50 The colloquium was organized by Bertelsmann and was entitled "Kulturnation Deutschland: Getrennte Vergangenheit, gemeinsame Zukunft."

51 " a little more sensitivity instead of this ideology of the denazification chamber." The row that is provoked by his use of the term "Spruchkammerdenken" is disingenuous in the light of its previous usage in the *Frankfurter Allgemeine Zeitung* in February 1990. (Maetzke).

52 This was an accepted definition of the "Kulturnation," but is ambiguous in this context (cf. Reid).

53 "In truth they rather talked too much than too little."

His conclusions on the outcome of the Potsdam colloquium, published only in *Neues Deutschland*, are also ambiguous. Entitled "Noch weit entfernt von Streitkultur," Jens bemoans the cultural divide separating East from West and calls for a "culture of disagreement" ("Streitkultur"): "Da sind Vertreter aus zwei Ländern, die sich der gleichen Sprache bedienen, und doch, das wurde hier deutlich, sehr weit voneinander entfernt sind" (Gutschke).[54] The response to this is immediate and harsh: "Nein, wir brauchen keine Streitkultur, sondern Streit" proclaimed Ulrich Greiner ("Potsdamer Abgrund").[55] Yet effectively Jens's assessment of the colloquium is similar to that of his critics. Greiner, for example, argued that only German grammar united East and West ("Potsdamer Abgrund"). It is only Jens's call for tolerance that is openly dismissed. As Jessen (1990) concluded: "In der Tat zeigte die Diskussion, wie bereitwillig auch westliche Teilnehmer sich vom totalitären Geist anstecken und auf schonende Sprachregelungen verpflichten ließen."[56] The reactions of critics revealed that the debate about the GDR had entered a new phase, and that "Spruchkammerdenken" was indeed what was being called for. By defining the GDR as totalitarian any defense of its writers could be dismissed. So, while Jens had moved away from his initial and more critical position, his defense of tolerance was sufficient to place "Jens und seine Gesinnungsfreunde" ("Potsdamer Abgrund") in the storm of the debate.[57] Jens is widely rebuked for his position, and clearly told what is expected of him: "Im Grunde weiß er, daß die DDR-Autoren ihre Vergangenheit noch vor sich haben. Und das, nicht Scheinpolemik würden wir gerne von ihm hören" (Fuld).[58]

Jens and Grass have become representative of the failure of West German writers in this second phase of the debate, and are seen as evidence of the need for a re-evaluation of the role of critical engagement: "daß ihnen dabei auch Autoren wie Walter Jens, Günter Grass [. . .] mit gleicher Empörung sekundierten, zeugt von einer tiefreichenden Verwirrung und Verstörung der Geister und Gemüter in diesem Lande" (Willms).[59] While it is true that both Grass and Jens rejected the facile comparison made between the Nazi regime and the GDR, Jens's position on unification is decidedly more ambiguous. I argue, however, that their individual positions are less significant to their

54 "Representatives from two countries are here speaking the same language and yet it became clear how far apart they are from another." Jens's usage of the term "Streitkultur" indicates his belief in the existence of two distinct political cultures. The term derives from the attempts at rapprochement between the SED and the SPD in 1987.

55 "No, we do not need a culture of disagreement, we need disagreement."

56 "The discussion in fact showed how willingly even western participants allowed themselves to be infected by the totalitarian mentality and adopted conciliatory language."

57 "Jens and his ideological bed fellows."

58 "Deep down he knows that GDR writers still have their past in front of them, and that is what we could like to hear from him, not false polemicizing."

59 "and that authors like Walter Jens and Günter Grass supported them in this with similar indignation is evidence of a deep-rooted confusion and disturbance in the minds and souls in this country."

critics than the fact that both are influential authors who refused to contribute to the demonization of the GDR. Jens and Grass are symbolic figures of critical intellectual activity "Jens ist eine Institution, ein Meinungsführer auf seine Weise" (Halter), and while their positions vis-à-vis unification differed significantly, they are defined as representative of West German opposition to unification, regardless of their respective writings.[60] Jens, like Heym, becomes the target of the critics at a point where he not only accepts the inevitability of unification, but also has moved away from his defense of a "Kulturnation" to a call merely for tolerance and conciliation. It would seem therefore that their position as established critical writers in the Federal Republic figured decisively in their reception. By 1991 the link that Paul Noack makes in my opening citation is easier to understand. Supposedly based on their responses to unification, their critical reception is also a result of their influential position in the West German literary establishment.

Helga Königsdorf

In my final section on the response of Helga Königsdorf, I would like to examine her work in the light of her strategic positioning of texts and selective use of metaphors. While I suggest that this is in evidence in the prose of all three authors examined here, it can be shown most vividly in Königsdorf's writing. Königsdorf, like Heym, publishes the bulk of her articles in the autumn of 1989, and like Heym can be considered a dissident author. She too formulates reform programs, initially for an independent GDR but soon for a unified state. Unlike Heym and Jens, however, the press does not vilify Königsdorf, although she too appears to encounter difficulties in publishing texts that run counter to the dominant consensus on unification. She does however manage to publish in both the *Frankfurter Allgemeine Zeitung* and *Neues Deutschland* at the same time. I argue that she successfully applies the "Mittel and Wege" at her disposal, publishing almost precisely opposing viewpoints in different newspapers at the same time. While one could accuse her of opportunism, or argue about which series of articles reflects her "true" position, it is apparent that the articles published in *Neues Deutschland* follow from her texts of 1989, whereas her articles in other western newspapers conflict with her earlier work.

In 1989 Helga Königsdorf openly defends her membership in the SED with her famous slogan "Ich bleibe in der Partei, damit die Partei nicht so bleibt" ("Partei").[61] Throughout the autumn of 1989 she calls for reform: "Das Wort 'Wende' sollte den Übergang zu einem humanen, den modernen

60 "Jens is an institution, an opinion leader in his own way."
61 "I am staying in the party so that the party does not stay the way it is."

Anforderungen adäquaten Sozialismusmodell bezeichnen" (*1989* 65).[62] Yet she is rapidly aware of the futility of her position "aber es wollte niemand auf mich hören" (79).[63] By December 1989 she expresses her realization that change is unfeasible: "Unmöglich ist es, zu diesem Zeitpunkt mit einem neuen Konzept, das vielleicht wieder nicht funktioniert, aufzutreten" (114).[64] Instead of focusing on the GDR state, she transfers her reform ideas to a united Europe: "Durch unsere Revolution, [. . .] ist zum erstenmal, eine Situation entstanden, die eine europäische Gemeinschaft wirklich real erscheinen läßt [. . .]. Zum erstenmal kann ich auf das Wort 'deutsch' stolz sein" (115).[65] The shift from her support for reform of one state to reform of a potential European community is accompanied by a shift in her self-perception. She begins to distance herself from its conceptualization.

Reviews of the text *1989 oder Ein Moment Schönheit*, Königsdorf's volume of articles, poems and diary entries and letters, are unusually harsh. Critics compare this "überflüssige[n] Buch" (Schwilk) to "das Tränenbuch 'Was bleibt'" only to discover that Königsdorf has managed "Wolf zu untertreffen" (Serke).[66] This critical reception presents Königsdorf as part of the staunch opposition to unification, yet the volume in question contains an article published in *Frankfurter Allgemeine Zeitung*, a newspaper not usually known for its sympathies for radical opponents. That article, however, presents an entirely different side of Königsdorf's writing. Entitled "Bitteres Erwachen" (Bitter Awakening), and thus reminiscent of Heym's "Aschermittwoch" article, Königsdorf presents a public mea culpa: "In diesem Jahr habe ich meine Heimat verloren. In diesem Jahr fiel ich aus der Rolle. Für eine gewisse Zeit wenigstens glaubte ich, in meiner eigenen Inszenierung zu leben. Und das war gut."[67] Her despair at developments, her perceived loss of a "Heimat," which is no longer conceived of in a united Europe, is paradoxically what may have secured her publication. For her acceptance that events can no longer be

62 "The word 'Wende' was meant to describe the turning to a humane socialism capable of meeting modern demands."

63 "but no one wanted to listen to me."

64 "It is impossible to show up now with a new concept that might not work either." This awareness seems to have resulted from observing the failure of the proclamation "Für unser Land."

65 "Through our revolution a situation has for the first time occurred that allows a European community to seem possible. For the first time I can be proud of the word 'German.'" Compare Brinkler-Gabler who argues that Königsdorf recognizes the impossibility of utopia but retains a "project of collective identity and collective rhetoric" (279). Brinkler-Gabler also notes the shifting identities adopted by Königsdorf arguing that this represents her identity as a "post-unification subject" (281).

66 "superfluous book"; "that tear jerker 'Was bleibt'" has managed "to do worse than Wolf."

67 "In this year I lost my home. In this year I forgot myself. For a while at least I believed that I was acting in my own production. And that was good." The suggestion of awakening from sleep appears in a variety of guises in this period. It implies the awakening to "truth" but also contains the more sinister notion of Germany awakening (Süskind, "Midlife"; Maron). It does, of course, naturalize the process of division and unification, and hence does not conflict with the consensus on the nation at this point.

influenced, that the hope for reform has run its course, is, I argue, a clear indication of her attempts at conciliation. In the light of the perceptiveness of her earlier writing, her bitter awakening is in any case disingenuous.

In February 1990 she again publishes in *Frankfurter Allgemeine Zeitung,* this time on writers in the GDR. Her first-person plural ("wir") for the first time represents a literary grouping as opposed to a political identity, and her definition of the future role for GDR writers has been often cited: "Es (das Volk) leidet und braucht unsere Liebe. Wir dürfen es nicht verachten [. . .]. Wir sind sogar von Berufs wegen für Gefühle zuständig" ("Spektakel").[68] The reduction of the role of writer to emotional crutch for GDR citizens represents a new departure in Königsdorf's work. She effectively rejects her own role as critic and reformer, yet at the same time continues to assert that role in *Neues Deutschland.* In this *Frankfurter Allgemeine* article she also accepts that the exodus of 1989 acted as the main catalyst to events, whereas she sees herself as belonging to a group of "Weltverbesserer[n]" or "improvers of the world" ("Spektakel"). But this opposition between reform and unification had clearly not been in evidence in her work in 1989. Effectively, Königsdorf is accepting the dominant consensus, which regarded the exodus as symbolic for unity, while isolating those whose reform ideas had now become redundant. Consequently, she no longer makes any reference to the potential for reform in a unified state.

While one could argue that Helga Königsdorf's bitter awakening had led her to revoke much of what she wrote in 1989, this does not explain why she continued to publish critical articles throughout 1990 in *Neues Deutschland.* Her reaction to the March election of 1990, for example, is far from disillusioned: "Die Zeit, öffentlich zu trauern is vorbei: Ehe die schwarzen Kleider modisch werden, müssen wir sie notgedrungen ablegen [. . .]. Es ist höchste Zeit sich auf die Realitäten mit einer gesunden Portion Realismus einzustellen" ("Gedanken").[69] In July 1990 she analyzes the economic costs of unification (again in *Neues Deutschland*) and arrives at a highly critical assessment of the situation ("Es lebe"). Around the same time, she publishes an article in *Die Zeit,* which mourns the loss of a sense of "DDR-Verbundenheit" or "allegiance to the GDR" ("Schmerz").[70] Yet Königsdorf's writing of the autumn of 1989 had not been characterized by such a loyalty. It is not until after the Wolf debate in August 1990 that she welcomes [in the West German press] the potential for critique in a unified state, perhaps aware of her own contribution to the polarization of East and West authors: "Nun

---

68 "The people are suffering and need our love. We are not allowed to despise them. We are, in fact, responsible for feelings by profession."

69 "The time for public mourning is over. Before black clothes become fashionable, it is vital that we discard them [. . .]. It is high time that we adapt to realities with a good portion of realism."

70 Compare a later interview where she regrets this publication in the light of its timing. She argues that she had not intended it as a contribution to the Wolf debate (Dietrich 284).

darf ich mich plötzlich in ganz Deutschland einmischen. Warum bin ich nur nicht früher darauf gekommen?" ("Deutschland").[71]

Reviews of Königsdorf's publications in this period reflect the ambiguity in her writing by varying between praise and contempt of her work.[72] The key problem with her own fluctuating position is perhaps best illustrated by a review of her epistolary text *Ungelegener Befund*. Martens praises Königsdorf's contributions to public debate: "[H.K.] gehört zu jenen Intellektuellen, die [. . .] auch öffentlich reflektieren. Besonders über die Rolle der Kultur und der Künstler im alten System."[73] This is clearly false, and I argue that it is not until Königsdorf adopts a more conciliatory approach that she is "heard" making a contribution to public debate. The price of being heard appears to include accepting that writers had failed because of their futile defense of independence and reform. That this is not in fact the case is clear from the writings of all three writers analyzed here, *regardless of their own statements to the contrary*. Königsdorf in many ways best exemplifies the difficulties of intervention in this highly charged debate on the nation. While Heym becomes more circumspect in his interventions, she appears to accept a partial conformism in the West German press, while continuing to publish more critical accounts in *Neues Deutschland*; an option that Heym would not presumably have entertained. Jens in the end resorts to historical allusion, ironically perhaps a strategy associated with GDR writers, to present a more critical analysis of unification than his writings here would suggest (Jens/Vitzthum 1). All three authors, therefore, accept the inevitability of unification and even welcome it as a chance to reform both states. They thus accept the consensus, and in the cases of Königsdorf and Jens, adopt a moderate tone calling for co-operation and a reappraisal of the critical role of writers. This in itself is not problematic. What must be emphasized, however, is that this aspect is ignored by critics who continue to undermine their position on the basis of their supposed relentless opposition.

It is clearly difficult to assess what effect such a narrowing of debate has had on the process of unification and the newly formed state. What is clear is that if Heym, Königsdorf and Jens are representative of opposition to unification, then those voices that diverged more radically from the consensus, the actual opposition in other words, faced enormous resistance.[74] Furthermore, the narrowing of debate may well have facilitated the rush to

71 "Now I am suddenly allowed to intervene in all of Germany. Why didn't I think of that earlier?"

72 She publishes four texts within a short period of time: *1989 oder Ein Moment Schönheit*; *Ungelegener Befund; Adieu DDR: Protokolle eines Abschieds; Aus dem Dilemma eine Chance machen: Reden und Aufsätze.*

73 "[HK] belongs to those intellectuals who also intervene publicly. Particularly on the subject of the role of culture and artists under the old system."

74 My own analysis of the responses of Joseph von Westphalen and Michael Schneider suggests that their initial rejection of any belief in the unity of the two states led to their rapid disappearance from the press (Oppen 181-221).

unity. As Helmut Peitsch argues: "Weil Kritik entlegitimiert wurde, konnten die Situationsdefinitionen in Schlagworten und Bildern rasch wechseln, ohne daß deren problematische Beziehung zur Realität der zwei vierzigjährigen Gesellschaften gesehen wurde, die in einen Staat nach vorgegebenem Muster vereinigt werden" ("Vereinigung" 44).[75] As far as the intervention of the authors themselves is concerned, the ephemerality of their positions and their willingness to alter their standpoint accepting a redefinition of their own role suggests that the desire to avoid isolation is perhaps greater than assumed. Authors however seem aware of the constraints, negotiating their position by publishing more critical accounts outside the mainstream feuilleton. So Heym could reassess the situation in 1991 in *Freitag*, and come to this final and somewhat pessimistic conclusion:

> Schon in grauester Antike beseitigten die Sieger bei den Besiegten zuerst die Sänger und die Schreibkundigen, denn deren Wort barg Gefahr. So radikal geht man heut nicht mehr vor, zumindest in Mitteleuropa: man mordet nicht mehr die Person, nur ihren Ruf ("Seelenschmerzen").[76]

Works Cited

Amü. "Für kluge Kinder. Eine Lesung von Stefan Heym." *Neue Zürcher Zeitung* 26 September 1989.

Anz, Thomas (ed.). '*Es geht nicht um Christa Wolf*'. *Der Literaturstreit im vereinten Deutschland*. Munich: Spangenberg, 1991.

Bauer, R. "Träume und Klagen helfen den neuen Ländern nicht weiter. Erstaunliche Worte von Stefan Heym, Christa Wolf und Bärbel Bohley." *Rheinische Post* 7 November 1990.

"Bleibt die Avantgarde zurück?" *Der Spiegel* 4 December 1989.

Bogdal, Klaus-Michael. "Wer darf sprechen?: Schriftsteller als moralische Instanz—Überlegungen zu einem Ende und einem Anfang." *Weimarer Beiträge*. 37 (1991): 597-603.

Bohrer, Karl-Heinz. "Kulturschutzgebiet DDR?" *Merkur*. 10/11 (1990): 1015-1018.

Brinkler-Gabler, Gisela. "Exile, Immigrant, Re/Unified: Writing (East) Postunification Identity in Germany." *Writing New Identities: Gender, Nation and Immigration in Contemporary Europe*. Eds. Gisela Brinkler-Gabler, Sidonie Smith. Minneapolis: University of Minnesota Press, 1997. 264-92.

Brockmann, Stephen. "Introduction: The Reunification Debate." *New German Critique*. 52 (Winter 1991): 3-30.

---. *Literature and German Unification*. Cambridge: Cambridge University Press, 1999.

---

75 "Because criticism was delegitimized, the slogans and pictures defining the situation could rapidly change. This left unclear their problematic relationship to the reality of two forty-year-old societies that are now being united in one state according to a predetermined pattern."

76 "Already in age-old times the victors first eliminated the poets and writers amongst the defeated because their words were dangerous. Today one does not go about it so radically: one no longer destroys the person, just their reputation."

Dietrich, Kerstin. *"DDR-Literatur" im Spiegel der deutsch-deutschen Literaturdebatte: "DDR-Autorinnen" neu bewertet*. Frankurt am Main: Lang, 1998.

dpa. "Aufruf von Prominenten zur Bewahrung der Eigenständigkeit der DDR.' 28 November 1989.

Dümde, C. "'Erstaunt, erfreut und auch schockiert' Stefan Heym bei Preisverleihung in Paris." *Neues Deutschland* 26 March 1990.

Foell, Kristie A. "Shaping History: Stefan Heym's Responses to German Unification." *Colloquia Germanic.* 27 (1994): 37-48.

Franke, K. "Sandkastenspiele. Stefan Heyms Wende-Stories." *Süddeutsche Zeitung* 29/30 December 1990.

Fuld, Werner. "Kleinere Brötchen. Walter Jens, gegen sich selbst verteidigt." *Frankfurter Allgemeine Zeitung* 20 July 1990.

Gaus, Günter. "Züruck in die Alltagsgeschichte: Helga Königsdorf im Gespräch mit Günter Gaus." *neue deutsche literatur*. 497 (1994): 78-92.

Glotz, Peter. "Das Riesenkadaverlein." *Frankfurter Allgemeine Zeitung* 2 October 1990.

Greiner, Ulrich. "Mangel an Feingefühl." *Die Zeit* 1 June 1990.

---. "Der Potsdamer Abgrund. Anmerkungen zu einem öffentlichen Streit über die 'Kulturnation Deutschland.' *Die Zeit* 22 June 1990.

Gutschke, I. "Walter Jens: Noch weit enfernt von Streitkultur. Vom Kolloquium 'Kulturnation Deutschland.'" *Neues Deutschland* 13 June 1990.

Halter, Martin. "Walter hier, Jens da. Hans Dampf in allen Geistesgassen—und drei Zeitschriften." Badi*sche Zeitung* 5 November 1990.

Hank, R. "Stefan Heyms romantischer Sozialismus. Eine Diskussion bei der IG-Metall." *Frankfurter Allgemeine Zeitung* 13 December 1989.

Heym, Stefan. "Aschermittwoch." *Der Spiegel* 4 December 1989.

---. *Auf Sand gebaut. Sieben Geschichten aus der unmittelbaren Vergangenheit und vierzehn Zeichnungen von Horst Hussel*. München: Bertelsmann, 1990.

---. "Der Besitz. Oder: Jetzt, wo sich alles ändert. Eine Erzählung." *Süddeutsche Zeitung* 28/29 July 1990.

---. *Einmischung: Gespräche, Reden, Essays*. Munich: Bertelsmann, 1990.

---. "Hurra für den Pöbel." *Der Spiegel* 6 November 1989.

---. "Ist die DDR noch zu retten? Aus dem real existierenden muß ein wirklicher Sozialismus werden." *Die Zeit* 13 October 1989.

---. "Nach den Jahren der Stagnation. Aus der Rede Stefan Heyms auf dem Alexanderplatz." *Frankfurter Allgemeine Zeitung* 6 November 1989.

---. "Seelenschmerzen." *Freitag* 13 December 1991.

---. "Überlegungen eines Querdenkers. DDR-Autor Stefan Heym: 'Ein Volk, ein Reich, ein ..?'" *Zeitschrift der Gewerkschaft* 2 (1990).

---. "Was wird aus Deutschland? Deutschland nach der Wahl in der DDR: Die Währungs-, Wirtschafts- und Sozialunion ist greifbar nahe. Wie schnell kommt die ganze Einheit, was bringt sie den Menschen? Deutsche Nation—was heißt das überhaupt? Der DDR-Schriftsteller versucht eine Deutung. Prominente von hüben und drüben geben ihre Antwort." *Stern* 29 March 1990.

---. "Zwischenbericht." *Der Spiegel* 23 October 1989.

Hutchinson, Peter. *Stefan Heym: The Perpetual Dissident*. Cambridge: Cambridge University Press, 1992.

Huyssen, Andreas. "After the Wall: The Failure of German Intellectuals." *New German Critique*. 52 (1991): 109-143.

Ihlau, O. "SZ-Gespräch mit Stefan Heym. 'Es ging immer unmoralisch zu in dieser Partei'. Nach Überzeugung des DDR-Schriftstellers werden beide deutsche Staaten nach einer gewissen Zeit zusammenfinden." *Süddeutsche Zeitung* 25/26 November 1989.

Jarausch, Konrad H. *After Unity: Reconfiguring German Identities*. Providence: Berghahn, 1997.

---. *The Rush to German Unity*. Oxford: Oxford UP, 1994.

Jens, Walter. "Nachdenken über Deutschland. Warnung vor den Winken aus dem Zuschauerraum." *Neue Rundschau* 101 (1990): 91-93.

---. "Nachdenken über Deutschland. Zwei deutsche Staaten—eine gemeinsame Geschichte, Kultur und Verantwortung? Unter der Leitung von Walter Jens diskutierten Volker Braun, Peter Härtling, Christoph Hein, Wolfgang Kohlhaase und Egon Monk." *hanseatenweg 10. Zeitschrift der Akademie der Künste* 1 (1990): 8-36.

---. "Plädoyer gegen die Preisgabe der DDR-Kultur. Förderungen an die Intellektuellen im geeinten Deutschland." *Süddeutsche Zeitung* 16/17 June 1990.

Jens, Walter/ Graf Vitzthum, Wolfgang. *Dichter und Staat: Über Geist und Macht in Deutschland: Eine Disputation zwischen Walter Jens und Wolfgang Graf Vitzthum*. Berlin: de Gruyter, 1991.

Jessen, Jens. "Auch tote Götter regieren. Streit der Intellektuellen auf einer Tagung in Potsdam." *Frankfurter Allgemeine Zeitung* 16 June 1990.

Joppke, Christian. *East German Dissidents and the Revolution of 1989: Social Movement in a Leninist Regime*. Basingstoke: Macmillan, 1995.

Kippenberger, Suzanne. "Der Olymp ist müde. Walter Jens in der Ost-Berliner Akademie der Künste." *Der Tagesspiegel* 8 December 1989.

Königsdorf, Helga. *1989 oder Ein Moment Schönheit. Eine Collage aus Briefen, Gedichten, Texten*. Berlin: Aufbau-Verlag, 1990.

---. "Bitteres Erwachen. Zwischenbilanz zur Lage in der DDR." *Frankfurter Allgemeine Zeitung* 4 January 1990. "Der Partei eine Chance geben." *Neues Deutschland* 22 November 1989.

---. "Deutschland, wo der Pfeffer wächst. Ein Beitrag zur Diskussion um die Literatur der DDR und ihre Autoren." *Die Zeit* 3 August 1990.

---. "Es lebe der Kapitalismus." *Neues Deutschland* 21/22 July 1990.

---. "Gedanken nach der Wahl: Links—nun doch oder jetzt erst möglich." *Neues Deutschland* 20 March 1990.

---. "In Sorge um meine Partei." *Neues Deutschland* 13/14 January 1990.

---. "Der Partei eine Chance geben." *Neues Deutschland* 22 November 1989.

---. "Der Schmerz über das eigene Versagen." *Die Zeit* 1 June 1990.

---. "Das Spektakel ist zu Ende. Und die Künstler werden wieder gebraucht." *Frankfurter Allgemeine Zeitung* 26 February 1990.

---. *Ungelegener Befund*. Berlin: Luchterhand 1990.

Kreuzer, Helmut (ed.). *Pluralismus und Postmodernismus: zur Literatur- und Kulturgeschichte in Deutschland 1980-1995*. Frankfurt am Main: Lang, 1996.

Kuhn, Anna. "'Eine Königin köpfen ist effektiver als einen König köpfen': The Gender Politics of the Christa Wolf Controversy." *German Monitor*. 31 (1994): 200-215.

---. "Rewriting GDR History: The Christa Wolf Controversy." *The GDR Bulletin*. 17 (1991): 7-11.

Lasky, Melvin J. *Voices in a Revolution: The Collapse of East German Communism*. New Brunswick: Transaction Publishers, 1992.

Liersch, Wolfgang. "... dann werden sie Häuser anzünden: Gespräch mit Stefan Heym." *neue deutsche literatur.* 480 (1992): 87-93.

Maetzke, E.O. " Ohne Spruchkammern." *Frankfurter Allgemeine Zeitung* 6 February 1990.

Martens, A. U. "Botschaft aus Schmollwinkel." *Die Welt* 5 April 1990.

Maron, Maron. "Die Schriftsteller und das Volk." *Der Spiegel* 12 February 1990.

Mohr, Peter. "Vom Anschluß überrollt. Stefan Heyms Erzählungen 'Auf Sand gebaut.'" *hannoversche allgemeine* 21 February 1991.

Mudrich, H. "Heym zur deutschen Lage. Sieben Geschichten zwischen Angst und Ironie." *Saarbrücker Zeitung* 15/16 December 1990.

---. "Unverdiente Partei-Priviligien abschaffen. Schriftsteller Stefan Heym in Saarbrücken. Ein Gespräch über die Entwicklung in der DDR." *Saarbrücker Zeitung* 24 October 1989.

Noack, Paul. *Deutschland, deine Intellektuellen: Die Kunst sich ins Abseits zu stellen.* Stuttgart: Aktuell, 1991.

"Nötige Kritik oder Hinrichtung? Spiegel-Gespräch mit Günter Grass über die Debatte um Christa Wolf und die DDR-Literatur." *Der Spiegel* 16 July 1990.

Oppen, Karoline v. *The Role of the Writer in the Unification of Germany 1989-1990.* New York: Lang, 2000.

Pankow, Klaus. "Gespräch mit Walter Jens." *Sinn und Form* 41 (1989): 309-319.

Paul, Georgina. "Text und Context: Was bleibt 1979-1989." *German Monitor* 29 (1992): 117-129.

Peitsch, Helmut. "Der 9. November und die publizistische Reaktion westdeutscher Schriftsteller." *Mauer-Show. Das Ende der DDR, die deutsche Einheit und die Medien.* Eds. Rainer Bohn, Knut Hickethier, Eggo Müller. Berlin: Sigma, 1992. 201-226.

---. "'Antipoden' im 'Gewissen der Nation'?: Günter Grass und Martin Walsers 'deutsche Fragen'." *Dichter und ihre Nation.* Ed. Helmut Scheuer. Frankfurt a. M: Suhrkamp, 1993. 459-490.

---. "'Vereinigung': Literarische Debatten über die Funktion der Intellektuellen." *German Monitor* 34 (1995) 39-65.

Reid, J.Hamish *Writing without Taboos: The New East German Literature.* New York: Berg, 1990.

Said, Edward W. "Foucault and the Imagination of Power." *Foucault: A Critical Reader.* Ed. D. Couzens Hoy. Oxford: Blackwell, 1986. 149-155.

---. *Representations of the Intellectual. The 1993 Reith Lectures.* London: Vintage, 1994.

Scheller, W. "Zahlt Miete für die Mauer! Ein Gespräch mit dem Schriftsteller Stefan Heym." *Stuttgarter Zeitung* 3 June 1989.

Scherpe, Klaus R. "Deutsche literarische Intelligenz nach der Wende." *Text & Kontext. Zeitschrift für germanistische Literaturforschung in Skandinavien.* 36 (1995): 108-126.

Schirrmacher, Frank. "Abschied von der Literatur der Bundesrepublik. Neue Pässe, neue Identitäten, neue Lebensläufe: Über die Kündigung einiger Mythen des westdeutschen Bewußtseins." *Frankfurter Allgemeine Zeitung* 2 October 1990.

---. "'Dem Druck des härteren, strengeren Lebens standhalten.'" *Frankfurter Allgmeine Zeitung* 2 June 1990.

---. "Wortführer." *Frankfurter Allgemeine Zeitung* 6 November 1989.

Schwilk, Heimo. "Die Mauer im Kopf. Revolution und Wiedervereinigung: Essays und Dokumente von Peter Schneider und Helga Königsdorf." *Rheinischer Merkur/ Christ und Welt* 5 March 1990.

Serke, Jürgen. "Das Letzte." *Die Welt* 10 October 1990.

Steinert. Hajo. "Deutsches Tempo. Stefan Heym und Günter Grass erzählen von der Wende." *Die Zeit* 16 November 1990.

Süskind, M.E. "Welche Kuckuckseier liegen in der DDR herum? Plauderei zwischen Bahr und Heym wird zum spannenden Dialog über Deutschland." *Süddeutsche Zeitung* 28 August 1989.

Süskind, Patrick. "Deutschland, eine Midlife-crisis." *Der Spiegel* 17 September 1990.

Weninger, Robert. "Literatur als mediales Ereignis: Eine Symptomatik deutscher Literaturdebatten seit 1945." *Colloquia Germanica: Internationale Zeitschrift für Germanistik* 3 (1998): 205-237.

Willms, J. "Die maßlose Empörung. Das deutsche PEN-Präsidium meldet sich zu Wort." *Frankfurter Allgemeine Zeitung* 4 July 1990.

Wolf, K.-P. "Die kleinen Betrüger. Interview mit dem Schriftsteller Stefan Heym." *Der Gewerkschaftler* 1 (1990).

ALISA KASLE

Everyday Stories of Hope and Despair in Eastern Germany: Kerstin Hensel and Ingo Schulze Write about Life after the *Wende*

> Die dritte Nachkriegsgeneration klappt das Große Buch der Geschichte einfach zu [. . .] Es gibt viele Geschichten, aber keine Geschichte mehr zu erzählen. Seitdem die Zentralperspektive Vergangenheit den Werken nicht mehr Kontur und Horizont verleiht, ist die Literatur unübersichtlich geworden. (Radisch, "Die zweite Stunde Null" 1)[1]

I. Introduction: German Literature and the Youngest Writing Generation

In 1994, Iris Radisch described a so-called *Generationsbruch* ("generational rupture") in contemporary German literature, in which young authors simply closed the first two chapters in the large book of German post-war literature and opened their own. The first chapter, written by the generation who went to school during the Nazi regime, either avoids all topics relating to Germany's past, or focuses on dealing with the war, the Holocaust, and one's own place in the rubble of Hitler's Reich. The second chapter, written by the children of those who had either been responsible for or tolerant of Hitler, is characterized by a general revolting against the generation of their parents and a quest for the truth about their parental generation's guilt. Both of the first two generations of post-war writers have history in common; a history they want to deal with, or forget, or make someone responsible for (Radisch, "Die zweite Stunde Null" 1).

The unification of Germany in 1989-90 brought about what some have called a second *Stunde Null* (Zero Hour) in German history. Suddenly, the German Democratic Republic disappeared and quickly became the five new states of the Federal Republic. After nearly ten years of unity, Germany has grown, more or (as some would argue) less, into one country—not just

1 "The third generation of post-war writers is simply closing the big book of history [. . .] There are many stories, but no history left to tell. Ever since the central perspective of the past has ceased to provide works with shape and form, the field of literature has become unclear."

politically or economically, but also culturally. Still, the issues of unification, the end of the GDR, and collective memory are central questions in almost all areas of cultural life in Germany today. In the decade since unification, much of German literature has, much like in the first Zero Hour in 1945, dealt with the past and the issues involved with this political and social unification process. The established authors of the former GDR such as Christa Wolf, Stefan Heym, or Volker Braun have written about the struggles involved with the loss of their country and the loss of utopian ideals, as well as the gain of new freedoms.[2] These authors have also been the focus of much of the literary critics' attention in their search for the perfect *Wenderoman* or unification novel.[3] A closer look at writers of the younger generation, however, indicates that they differ from their older colleagues in their treatment of history. Due to their age, they neither see themselves as victims of the socialist system, nor do they wish they could return to it. In an interview (1998), Ingo Schulze, perhaps the best-known writer of this generation, explained his feelings about unification:

> Ich bin sehr froh, daß die DDR zu Ende gegangen ist, und empfinde keine Trauer. Ich spüre eine starke literarische Generationsgrenze zu den vorherigen Generationen, die viel mehr in der DDR drinsteckten. Wir hatten das Glück, daß wir einen Anfang hatten, ohne richtig involviert zu sein. (Qtd. in Neubauer 15)[4]

This generation of authors only began to write literature around the time of unification and only became known as writers after the GDR became a part of the FRG. The young writers, therefore, experienced a different Zero Hour than the established authors of their parents' generation. The literature of this youngest writing generation, much like their western German counterparts, primarily focuses on the struggles and issues of everyday people in everyday life in unified Germany, not on communicating a political message. The actual unification as a historic event barely exists, but it is ever-present in its effect on ordinary people and their individual lives. Throughout these seemingly simple tales, national history is hidden behind the not so simple personal lives of characters that neither come to terms with the past, nor do they long for it. Kerstin Hensel, a representative of the youngest writing generation who grew

---

2 See Welzel 9 for more information about the established writers in the GDR and their literary and political reaction to unification. Also see Stephen Brockmann's extensive study *Literature and German Reunification*.

3 See Welzel 9. Iris Radisch claims to have found it in her article "Endlich! Der Wenderoman: Aber wer ist eigentlich Gert Neumann?" For additional information about the search for the perfect unification novel and the different focuses on Germany after unification see Kumphufer 17. Michalzik claims that with the publication of Schulze's *Simple Storys* the stereotypical call for the unification novel has finally disappeared (27).

4 "I am very happy that the GDR has ended and I do not feel sad about it. I sense a strong generation gap to the previous generations, who were more a part of the GDR than we were. We were lucky that we had a beginning without really being involved."

up in Eastern Germany, sees an interconnection between history and everyday life: "Geschichte kann weder aufgearbeitet noch bewältigt werden. Sie ist nur aus dem Alltag heraus zu begreifen. [. . .] Es sind Geschichten des Alltags, dem die Historie verwoben ist" (Billhardt/Hensel 7).[5]

Hensel and Ingo Schulze are two such young German authors writing about life after unification in Eastern Germany in the nineties. This essay examines what this third post-war generation born between the Elbe and the Oder rivers writes about in their post-*Wende* work, how the everyday is described, and how much of the past is present in their work. Both Hensel and Schulze have specific biographical information in common; both were born in the early sixties in the GDR and both were just beginning their careers as unification occurred. While most of Germany looks to Berlin for stories about unification, these two authors chose to set their stories in more provincial areas of Eastern Germany, in the fictional Leipnitz, a combination of Leipzig and Chemnitz (Hensel), and in the small town of Altenburg (Schulze). Yet despite their biographical similarities and the commonalities of their plot settings, their literary texts differ in the methods they use to depict everyday life. Hensel focuses on a single character's life, splitting up the plot into alternating pre-*Wende* and post-*Wende* chapters, whereas Schulze deals with a large number of characters after unification. While many of the struggles of Hensel's female protagonist are gender-related, Schulze's stories treat multiple issues, told from both female and male perspectives. Most of all, the stories presented in these two works give us two very different literary interpretations of the confusing complexity of life after unification, of which it seems no unified picture can be rendered.

Kerstin Hensel sees the search for the true picture of the former GDR as an impossible mission: "Es gab so viele Deutsche Demokratische Republiken, wie es Menschen gab, die dort gelebt haben. Wenn Typisches vorzuweisen ist, so kristallisiert es sich über Millionen einzelner Biographien heraus" (Billhardt/Hensel 6).[6] Life after unification can likewise be seen as a compilation of eighty million aspects, represented by the eighty million people in Germany and recorded, reflected, and lived in just as many different ways. In the same light, this generation of post-*Wende* writers does not identify itself as one coherent group writing literature with a specific program or sharing a similar goal (or enemy).[7]

---

5 "History can neither be reappraised, nor dealt with. History is only comprehensible in everyday life. [. . .] It is the everyday stories which make up history."

6 "There were as many German Democratic Republics as there were people who lived there. If there is anything typical about it, it is crystallized in a million single biographies."

7 Radisch, like many literary critics and writers, explains that this younger generation no longer has a common ground, since they no longer write towards or against a common goal (or enemy) or belong to a political program ("Die zweite Stunde Null," 1). Ingo Schramm, another young German writer from the East, also refuses to be seen as a part of a collective, as Müller states: "Er mochte überhaupt keinem Kollektiv mehr angehören [. . .]" (47) Müller—in response to a conference of young writers in Berlin entitled "Spät-Post-Pop-Hiphop-

If it can be said that there are common links among the writers of the third post-war generation, then it could be their focus on everyday life, their avoidance of themes that attempt to explain the country's past, their distance from joining together as a generation to fight for a common political goal, and their independence from the responsibility of trying to be the country's moral role-models as writers. This generation is too young to have been involved (as writers) with the Stasi in the past, and therefore they are not held accountable for the past situations that older writers from the GDR still confront. The younger writers are free to criticize the past or the present system in their literature, without being read as an explanation of their own personal past actions. Iris Radisch explains a further reason for the strength of this generation's literature:

> Für die Literatur ist das Verschwinden der Repräsentanten, zumindest im Augenblick, ein Gewinn. Wer immer seither versucht hat, Stellvertreter, allegorische Figuren oder soziologische Charaktermasken zu didaktischen Zwecken zu benutzen, endete schnell als schreibender Schulmeister. (*Die zweite Stunde Null* 1)[8]

The freedom to write or not to write about specific political topics enables Hensel, Schulze and many other writers of their generation to escape a prescribed role as a writer, which is not the case for the generation before them, whether West or East.[9] While this means that it is harder to pinpoint the commonalities of this writing generation, this freedom *is* in turn their common link. What their texts lack in providing moral lessons can be considered their strength as works of art. Because these works avoid being overly didactic, they are more open to wider interpretations by the reader and present a more accurate picture of the complexity of everyday life. In Hensel's narrative, as in Schulze's novel, the focus is on the subjective experiences of individuals lost in their everyday lives after unification, with no attempt to provide an answer for their misery or to place the blame on anyone specific.

Moderne," symbolizing the various conflicting directions young literature in Germany is moving in—explains that the young authors are only connected by a "post-modern ethic of the fragmentary," and instead of political reflections, the most they share are "anti-institutional discourses" ("[. . .] kaum noch Verbindlichkeiten, dafür eine 'postmoderne Ethik des Fragmentarischen,' und statt politischer Reflexion allenthalben 'anti-institutionelle Diskurse'"). For more information about young writers see Spiegel 41.

8 "For literature, the disappearance of representatives is, at least for the moment, a gain. Whoever has since tried to use representatives, allegorical figures or sociological character masks for didactic purposes soon ends up sounding like a writing school master."

9 Whereas the writers of the 1968 generation in the West often used their literary voice to deal with the past, break with their parents and criticize society, the established writers from the East (at least now after unification) are expected to exercise their role as writers in a similarly critical and political way, only 30 years later (confronting Stasi issues, explaining their own relationship to GDR regime in the past, etc.).

II. Kerstin Hensel: *Tanz am Kanal*

Hensel's 1994 narrative *Tanz am Kanal* tells the life story of thirty-six-year-old Gabriela von Haßlau growing up in the former GDR and living in the chaotic world of unified Germany. Through the use of two alternating timelines in the plot, the present (1994) and the past (1961-1989), the reader learns simultaneously about the personal history of this character as a young girl in the GDR, while constantly being reminded of her present post-*Wende* situation on the edge of society, where she writes her life story while sleeping under bridges and warming herself in run-down bars. Gabriela's daily fight in the present is the search for a piece of paper or a scrap of trash, which will serve to record her history. The story we read is neither a history of the GDR, nor a description of the political aspects of unification, nor is it an attempt to provide us with a message or a lesson about the two systems. Life, neither before nor after the fall of the Wall, is not particularly friendly to Gabriela, and no system is portrayed as good. Unification and GDR national history appear as background information, while the main focus is on the protagonist's struggles in the oppressive system of the socialist GDR and the harsh world of capitalism in the united Germany.

The oppression and restrictions imposed on Gabriele in her youth by the myriad forces in her life, including her authoritative upbringing, the socialist school system, the government, the SED, and later the Stasi, are skillfully communicated because they are revealed through Gabriela's eyes in the various stages of her youth. The details are often banalities, the descriptions of her childhood include the horrific and the hilarious in a single passage, and the language grows with the maturing of the main character. For example, in the beginning we learn about the various adults in Gabriela's life through their use of specific words. Gabriela's words are: "Violine, Pastete, Mozart" (10), Uncle Schorsch's words are all in dialect and considered poor German by her father: "Heiamachen, Ringelgehen, Muckschsein" (10),[10] her father's favorite word is the medical term varicose veins, or "Varizen" (9), and her nickname "Ehlchen" belongs to her mother (15). Gabriela's words represent what she should become: educated, cultured; her uncle's what she should not: uneducated, low class; her father's the seriousness of being a doctor; and her mother's the love she needed, but never truly received.

Gabriela's entire life is characterized by the fact that she is an outsider in society. At home, Gabriela *von* Haßlau, with her noble family name, is exposed to a world far removed from the socialist reality of her school. Her father introduces her to the conflict between the state and his own beliefs as he tells her that the government is against her family having a private cleaning lady:

10 "Violin, paté, Mozart"; "Going to bed, running in circles, being quiet."

> - Sprich nach: Staat, der ist dagegen, daß es Wirtschaftshilfen gibt.
> Ich begriff nicht, wieso jemand dagegen sein konnte, daß meiner Mutter Arbeit abgenommen, in den vielen Zimmern der Villa der Schmutz bewältigt würde. (35)[11]

Throughout her childhood, Gabriela never completely understands what the conflict between her father and the government is. There are no political discussions in the family, no explanations why Gabriela's mother should not have cleaning help, nor why Gabriela should not join the socialist party's young pioneer organization. Ernst von Haßlau, an ever-serious authoritative father, provides no further explanation for his decision not to let his daughter join, simply calling the youth group an "Affenzirkus!" (52)—"a farce." Later, when her school class trades their blue pioneer kerchiefs for the new blue shirts of the older youth group, the FDJ (Free German Youth), he once again sees to it that Gabriela is not a part of this organization. These clashes with the school administration later exclude her from the university, as "[g]esellschaftliche Organisation sei Voraussetzung für ein Studium an einer sozialistischen Universität" (61).[12] Her family's attempts to live outside of the system in East Germany ultimately fail: Uncle Schorsch is shot, her mother leaves Gabriela to flee to the West after divorcing her father, and her father escapes first through alcohol and then also to the West.

Though many of the terrible facts about Gabriela's childhood in the GDR are shockingly outrageous to the point of being too exaggerated to be believable, they are not presented as such, due to the simplicity of the cool, laconic narrative descriptions. Gabriela is not only deserted by her family, but by the entire system, which ignores her rape in the park by two men and their carving of a cross into her arm. The *Volkpolizei* accuses her of self-mutilation with a knife, in an attempt to slander the state. Gabriela is a female victim of male crimes in a male-dominated political system that will not acknowledge that crimes against women do occur. The rape scene is described in one single page in such an indirect manner that it would not hold up in a court of law, making it all the more brutal for the reader's imagination.[13] Likewise, the shooting of her uncle, the escape of her mother, and her only friend Katka's disappearance from school are mentioned in passing. Her father is the last person to leave her, and this too is explained in the typical short and effective Hensel style: "Nach vier Wochen erhielt ich eine Postkarte mit dem Bamberger Reiter. Er habe nicht anders gekonnt, stand darauf. Ich zerriß die Karte. Es gab keinen, dem ich sie zeigen konnte." (96)[14]

---

11 "- Repeat after me: The state is against us having cleaning help.
I couldn't comprehend why anyone could be against my mother being relieved of the work of fighting the dirt in the many rooms of the villa."

12 "[Membership in a] social organization is a prerequisite for studying at a socialist university."

13 See Leonhardt 8.

14 "After four weeks I received a postcard with a picture of the 'Bamberger Reiter.' He couldn't

When unification occurs, Gabriela is working on a farm in Mecklenburg, still hiding from the Stasi after her unsuccessful episode years prior as a spy in Leipnitz's *I-Werk* and art scene. Her remarkable run-in with the Stasi is just one more example of a witty and simple description of a shockingly outrageous situation that, described in any other way, would seem absolutely implausible. Yet, from a homeless writer-narrator who went from nobility to social outcast, unbelievable circumstances are expected. Gabriela manages to flee from a tricky and dangerous Stasi outing in a boat (we assume she is to be the victim of violence, rape or murder) by throwing the officer Queck and his chauffeur Manfred into the water and swimming to shore. Her escape from Leipnitz marks the beginning of her yearlong vagabond life, which is explained in only a few sentences ending with unification.

The brutality of the descriptive omissions by Hensel's writer-narrator Gabriela in connection with the major events in her life in the GDR strikes the reader all the more when seemingly harmless and often-irrelevant details are treated in paragraphs and even pages. Hensel's talent in describing in minute detail the only apprenticeship Gabriela was granted as a *Zerspannungsfach-arbeiterin* in the local *I-Werk* (83) has been praised by critics and literary scholars alike.[15] The descriptions of everyday events in Gabriela's childhood and her homeless adult life fill most of the 119 pages, relegating many of the major events in the protagonist's life and in Germany's history to the reader's imagination. Descriptive language combined with skillful omissions is where Hensel's stylistic strength lies. Hensel takes exactly three sentences to explain the unification process in 1989:

> - In Teterow sünd de Straten vull mit Lüd: de trekken dörch die Stadt, dat geiht los!
> - Wat geiht los?
> - Wat week ik, öwer wi möten dorbi sein! (115)[16]

In his critique in *Die Zeit*, Leonhardt terms this the most laconic, fitting description of the *Wende* known to him (8). More important than the actual political event of unification is the effect on Gabriela as an individual and the everyday conflicts she experiences in post-unification Germany.

Hensel uses unification as a meeting-point in the narrative structure, rather than making a political point of this major historical event. Unification marks the time at which Hensel's two alternating plot lines cross. Throughout the 27 sections, the plot alternates between the homeless, adult Gabriela and the

---

have acted any differently, was written on it. I tore up the card. There was no one I could have shown it to."

15 See Leonhardt 8; Hinck 36; and Wehdeking 96.

16 (This is in dialect:) "- In Teterow the streets are filled with people: they're marching through the streets, it's starting!
- What's starting?
- What do I know, but we gotta be there!"

protagonist's childhood and youth. The story Gabriela writes begins with a description of her fourth birthday in 1961 and ends in 1989 with unification. Only at the end of the entire narrative does the reader find out how the story written by the protagonist fits together with the story we read about Gabriela as an adult. This seemingly clear time structure, however, does contain confusing elements, which break up the otherwise smooth flow of events. The story is said to start in July of 1994, in a "summer of the century," "ein Jahrhundertsommer" (16). Yet the end of the story Gabriela writes (1989) also takes place in a "Jahrhundertsommer" (118). Not only does the reader not have any information about what the protagonist does between 1989 and 1994, but the story in 1989 also fits so well into the story in 1994 that we are led to believe it all occurs in the same year. Gabriela leaves Mecklenburg during unification and hitchhikes back to Leipnitz, ending up at the welfare organization Caritas, just where she is as the story in 1994 begins. The timeline is further confused by the fact that Hensel ends the narrative with the date 1993, making it clear that she wrote the story into the future.[17] Hensel purposefully leaves such plotline questions unanswered and forces the reader to decipher her texts for meaning. She explains:

> Ich will die Anstrengung der genußvollen Dechiffrierung von Texten; kein Rätselraten, aber die Mühe, hinter Geheimnisse zu kommen. Ich hoffe, der Leser geht auf die Vereinbarung ein: Hier wird scheinbar nichts zum Ende geführt, hier ist der Blick mit verstellter Kamera und temporalem Widerspiel. (Qtd. in Hammer 107)[18]

This "obscured view" of time and place in Hensel's narrative is at times so perplexing that, while most critics have noticed confusion in the timelines, many have incorrectly assumed that events that occur after the *Wende* occurred before.[19] Yet upon careful inspection of the chronological hints Hensel provides, it becomes clear that the inconsistencies and illogical occurrences all

---

17 One further example is the case of Noppe and Atze, characters Gabriela meets on the street when she is homeless, who die on page 67 and are then alive on page 77, though both events occur in what seems to be the same winter.

18 "I want the effort of a pleasurable deciphering of texts; no guessing games, but the trouble to uncover secrets. I hope the reader goes along with this agreement: Here, apparently nothing is brought to a close, here the view is through an obscured camera and in a temporal counter-play."

19 Wehdeking points to the difficulties in the chronological structure, though he incorrectly assumes that the episode with the magazine occurs before 1989, and therefore wonders how Gabriela's life story could have been printed in the eighties when she only just began to write it down in 1994. He reads this episode and the following Stasi episode as being at the same time before unification, missing the break between sections 19 and 20 on page 93. What he also ignores is that Gabriela knows the people in the bar "Die Drei Rosen" (90), she calls a bridge "hers" (91), and the factories have all closed "vorbei an stillgelegten Fabriken" (91), all situations that could have only occurred after the *Wende* (94-97). Two other critics, Hinck (36) and Leonhardt (8), notice the inconsistencies of time and yet assume the magazine episode is earlier than the opening of the story in 1994.

happen after the *Wende*. The complicated plot structure and its twisting and reversing of what occurs when, could be interpreted as the confusion of life after unification.

Through the alternating plot lines, various events in Gabriela's life before and after the *Wende* are set up against one another, creating parallels that a single chronological plot line would miss. The extraordinary events in Gabriela's childhood, from growing up in a noble family villa without love, to her outsider status in school, a brutal rape in the park, her job in the *I-Werk*, and her final job as a writer-spy for the Stasi, are juxtaposed with her daily post-*Wende* reality of homelessness and the attempt to get her life down on paper. Gabriela's writing career began with her Stasi reports and is mirrored by her discovery after unification by a western German women's magazine *MAMMILIA*, which reprints the first half of her life story. As Jürgen Berger writes in his critique, the parallel structure points to the fact that both the Stasi and the media are only interested in the acquisition and marketing of the written word (166). Despite the demands the communist and the capitalist systems place on her as a writer, writing is the only thing that Gabriela lives for and the only thing that gives her an identity. The events in Gabriela's childhood continually prove that her attempts to be a part of the communist society fail much in the same way as her homelessness as a young adult in the capitalist society bears witness to the fact that she does not fit into this new world. However, her life on the outside of society, with responsibilities only to herself, provides her with a certain freedom to write what she wants, which she would not have if she were a part of society. In the GDR she was forced to write reports for the Stasi, and if she were an established writer within the new capitalist society, she (or at least her publisher) would be more concerned about profits and what sold than with her desire to document her life. Instead, she relishes her newly acquired state of independence from all social and familial obligations.

> Ich bin frei. Heute, nachdem der unaufhaltsame Abstieg meiner Familie vollendet ist, erkenne ich: alles hat mich nur in den Zustand der Unabhängigkeit versetzt. Gewiß, ich bin allein und verludert genug, um in nächster Zeit keinen Menschen für mich beanspruchen zu können—was aber soll diese Abscheu, mit der die Leute mir begegnen, oder das Mitleid, das sie, schwitzend unter ihren Pflichten, aufbringen. Als ob es ihnen besser ginge. Keiner weiß mehr meinen Namen, keiner, was ich getan habe, wer ich war, wer ich bin. Was für ein Glück. (16-17)[20]

20 "I am free. Today, after the unstoppable downfall of my family is complete, I recognize: everything has just put me into a state of independence. Certainly, I am so alone and down and out that I can't place any demands on anyone else in the near future—but what is this disgust with which people confront me, or the compassion they spare, sweating under their obligations. As if they had it any better. No one knows my name, what I have done, who I was, who I am. How lucky."

Gabriela's independence as an outcast writer not connected to any part of society could be said to mirror Hensel's status as an author in this third generation in her freedom to write independent of a common political program. Yet the end of Gabriela's story in the apartment of a police officer by the name of Paffrath can be read as a resignation to join society and to give in to male desires. Not only was he the same person who had disbelieved her story of being raped when he was with the *Volkspolizei*, but also his repetition of "MeineGutemeineLiebemeineSchöne" (118),[21] as he tries to seduce her, is the same expression that the men who raped her in the park used (69). Life has not necessarily improved for Gabriela after unification, but she has come to accept her fate without protest.

Tanz am Kanal is as pragmatic and simultaneously as without hope as many of the books of this post-*Wende* generation, as Radisch explains:

> Diese Kindheitsbücher markieren einen Generationsbruch. So gelassen, so pragmatisch und gleichzeitig so hoffnungslos hat sich noch kein literarischer Nachwuchs selber beschrieben. [. . .] Die eigene Geschichte ist nicht mehr Anwendungsfall der Großen Geschichte. Die historische Kontinuität ist perdu. Keine Zeit für Tränen. ("Die zweite Stunde Null" 1)[22]

Like the characters in many other authors' books of Hensel's generation, Gabriela does not attempt to understand her past, nor does she try to explain why things happened the way they did—it is all just presented without a lesson or moral. Hensel defines herself as a writer of fiction, as opposed to history books: "Ich will keine Geschichtslehrbücher schreiben, das stimmt, mich interessieren die Menschen in ihrer Manipulierbarkeit und in ihrer Kraft, Geschichte mitzubestimmen" (Hammer 110).[23] Both in Hensel's narrative and in Schulze's *Simple Storys*, national political developments are not at the center of the fiction, but rather various aspects of individuals' complex and confusing, but nonetheless everyday lives. Hensel's strength in her short narrative is her alternating focus on the past and the present of a single character who is an outsider both in the communist GDR and the capitalist FRG. Hensel's protagonist Gabriela does not represent the typical biography of a young East-German woman coming of age at the time of the *Wende*, but rather an extraordinary story of the life of an individual who failed to fit into either system. Gabriela as an outsider, however, leaves the reader asking how this protagonist differs from the many everyday lives of other individuals

21 "Mydearmylovemybeauty."

22 "These books about childhood mark a generation gap. No new literary generation has ever described themselves so laid back, so pragmatic, and at the same time so hopeless. [. . .] One's own history is no longer exemplary for history with a capital H. Historical continuity is lost. No time for tears."

23 "I don't want to write history textbooks, that's true, I am interested in people and their susceptibility to be manipulated as well as their power to shape history."

dealing with the problems and issues surrounding unification. Ingo Schulze's *Simple Storys* provides some answers.

III. Ingo Schulze: *Simple Storys*

Ingo Schulze's 1998 *Simple Storys: ein Roman aus der ostdeutschen Provinz* tells everyday "Storys" about post-unification life in Eastern Germany. Critics and literary scholars have widely praised this best-selling book (which has already been adapted for the theater), propelling Schulze from almost complete anonymity to the status of one of the most famous writers of his generation (Seibt qtd. in *Deutsche Literatur 1998*, 227). In his novel, which at first glance seems more like a collection of 29 isolated stories than one coherent novel, no one character's life is explained from childhood to present. Instead, Schulze depicts bits and pieces from the lives of more than 35 characters from 1990 to 1997 as they attempt to adjust to the abrupt and difficult changes caused by unification and the demise of the GDR. Individually, each story is a simple tale of an everyday occurrence: There is nothing complicated or unusual about a couple breaking up and finding new partners, an unemployed academic who finds work as a salesman, a retired East German with a Stasi record, a West German real-estate agent, a struggling taxi driver, a local politician, two newspapers struggling for the same advertisement deals, a waitress whose restaurant always closes, a persecuted foreigner, a young nurse having an affair with an older man, an unemployed museum director, or a fatal bicycle accident. Yet the task of summarizing the complete plot of this novel is impossible: there are simply too many characters and too many stories. The figures and their stories are not only bound together through time (1990-97) and place (Altenburg), but also through intertwined personal connections and often a common history. It soon becomes clear that underlying the simple stories of everyday life, there are unspoken deeper dark histories.

Each of the stories told shows how the everyday lives of individuals after unification have suddenly become unmanageable, painful and hard to cope with—a phenomenon that could be referred to as *Wendeschmerz*.[24] Schulze reinforces the content with the form in his use of a series of jumbled-up, not totally complete, and simultaneously occurring short stories, coming together to create a novel. The cross-links between the characters and events in individual chapters become increasingly interwoven with each successive story, adding to the complexity of the prose for the reader, while creating

24 To my knowledge this term has not been used before, but I believe it best describes the painful process individuals in the new states of Germany have gone through in adapting to their new lives as members of the Federal Republic of Germany.

tension and a desire to discover the truth behind the past events alluded to in dialogues. There is no omniscient narrator; there is not even a consistent first-person perspective. The various characters in Schulze's novel move from playing the narrator of a particular story to later reappearing as a persona in another character's story and vice versa. While some characters narrate a story on their own, others have a story told for them, through their eyes in a figural narrative situation. Most of the information the reader is given about a particular character does not come to light in the chapters they narrate or have narrated for them, but rather in stories retrospectively told by others.

The reader must be attentive to the little details about each of the characters made in passing by other characters if he or she is to understand the connections and complex relationships between the characters. For example, the first chapter, narrated by Renate Meurer, introduces a past conflict between her husband Ernst and Dieter Schubert, without explaining exactly what it was about. "Auf dem Münchner Bahnhof werden Ernst und er sich erkannt haben. Ich bekam davon nichts mit. Woher sollte ich wissen, wie er aussieht? Nicht mal seinen richtigen Namen hätte ich angeben können" (16).[25] The details about Ernst Meurer's dark past in the socialist party only surface at the end of the book in his wife's conversation with his psychiatrist Barbara Holitzschek. Dr. Holitzschek on the other hand, has not killed a badger with her car (as she had originally believed and as had been presented to the reader: "Ich habe einen Dachs überfahren" [49]),[26] but rather a person, who turns out to be Andrea Meurer (the daughter-in-law of Ernst, wife of Martin). Though hinted at throughout the book, this only becomes clear in a conversation between two other characters Enrico and Patrick, as Enrico tells Patrick about his girlfriend Lydia's sudden disappearance after a fight with Barbara ("Babs") Holitzschek:

> Lydia sagte, daß sie Babs verstehen kann, daß sie aber nich behaupten soll, sie hätt einen Dachs gesucht, einen Dachs bestimmt nich. Aber wenn man schon jemanden totgefahren hat, wenn sowieso nichts mehr zu rettn ist, muß man sich ja nich auch noch selbst das Leben ruiniern. (192)[27]

Patrick, on the other hand, had been Lydia's boyfriend at the beginning of the book, and returns to her again at the end of the book after leaving Andrea's sister Danny, who now has custody of her sister's half-orphaned son Timo Meurer. *Simple Storys* then ends with an episode in which Ernst Meurer's unemployed son Martin (once an art historian) dresses up in a wet-suit and swimming fins as a part of a promotional campaign for a fish restaurant, is

25 "At the Munich train station Ernst and he must have recognized one another. I didn't notice anything. How should I know what he looks like? I couldn't have even said his real name."

26 "I ran over a badger."

27 "Lydia said that she could understand Babs, but that she shouldn't claim that she had looked for a badger, definitely not a badger. But if you have already run over a person, if there is nothing left to be saved, then you don't have to ruin your own life too."

beaten up and taunted by people on the street. As critic Christine Cosentino points out, the plot begins and ends with members of the Meurer family and moves out to other people from there. The relationships are all interconnected and events in one chapter affect characters in others. Seldom is a story complete and totally comprehensible on its own, and yet in their entirety, these stories still leave gaps for the reader to fill.[28] The reader never really knows everything about a character or a specific situation while reading a particular chapter, such as the aforementioned story with the badger, but is always just left to assume the connecting details through hints made by other characters in later chapters. The despair and the imperfect lives of the characters are mirrored in the reader's frustration with trying to sort out the puzzle of who is who. Readers must work to identify exactly who the characters are, in what context they have encountered them before, and what their histories are. Just as the pedantic reader of Hensel's narrative is likely to make a chart to sort out the confusing elements of time, Schulze's readers are almost forced to make notes of the "spatial" character relationships in these not so simple stories.[29]

A number of scholars claim that Schulze's style has been influenced by a variety of American writers from Hemingway (the sharp dialogues), Faulkner (the multiple narrators as in *Yoknapatawpha County*), and Richard Ford (the sentence structure), to Raymond Carver (the precise narrative perspective, tone, and cuts).[30] The quick cuts between episodes have likewise been said to call to mind the technique of "short cuts" as used in the film by the same name based on Carver's short stories directed by Robert Altman.[31] Schulze plays with his use of American influences in his choice of title. The misspelled English word "Storys" hints at an attempt at Americanization that was not quite successful—arguably an allusion to Eastern Germany's (even Germany's as a whole) move to use fashionable English words instead of German, as often as possible, even if the spelling is not correct.[32] The influence is

28 Cosentino comes to a similar conclusion when she writes: "Eine Pointe läßt sich bestenfalls in den Leerstellen finden, die der Leser füllen muß." ("A 'punchline' is most readily determined through the gaps which a reader must fill.") Michalzik points to the fact that especially West German readers have to "listen to that which is not said" in order to "understand the connections of this world" (30). The same could be said of all non-East German readers.

29 In the program "Literarisches Quartett" on the German television station ZDF, the critic Helmut Karasek commented that he used the same method when reading Schulze as he does with the "great Russians" in that he made a list of characters to keep them straight. Two ethnology scholars at the University of Cologne, Thomas Schweizer and Michael Schnegg, have studied the structure of the social network within Schulze's novel and provide complex diagrams and ethnological explanations of these structures on the internet.

30 See the excellent review on the internet by Missler. For a comparison to Richard Ford and Raymond Carver see Krekeler. Also see Winkels 17 and Cosentino.

31 See Lorenz and also Cosentino.

32 Michalzik calls the false plural form of the word *story* "einostdeutscht" (29). The word "Storys" is, however, acceptable in German as the plural form for the new German word "Story," just as "simple" is the plural form of the German adjective "simpel." Nevertheless, the American influence is obvious.

documented, but not criticized, not even commented on. America, also the setting for one of the episodes, is neither presented as a land of dreams, nor is it the "big bad world policeman." Schulze's best-selling book is a documentation of life after the *Wende*, without making a political statement. Although the characters in *Simple Storys* lead difficult lives and find themselves unable to adapt to the new situation, neither the cultural influence from America nor German politics are held responsible for the people's problems or criticized for unification.

Schulze sees the individual events that take place within these stories as plausible situations in most countries, with one important difference. In Eastern Germany, people all of a sudden lost the country they grew up in and were immediately confronted with the West.

> Ich denke, in "Simple Storys" habe ich Situationen beschrieben, die überall in der westlichen Welt so passieren können. Der Unterschied ist, ob Menschen von einer Woche auf die andere mit dem Westen konfrontiert wurden oder ob sie darin groß geworden sind. (Neubauer 15)[33]

This sudden confrontation with the West meant that people had no time to get used to the demands of everyday life in a competitive, capitalistic society with no guarantees. What had been the "everyday" suddenly became history and was pushed aside, forgotten, hidden, or perhaps even longed for. National GDR history, merely existing in hints and insinuations, slowly reveals itself in minor details as the chapters proceed. We learn about the Stasi desk furnishing the local newspaper bureau, the FDJ leader turned businessman, a school director firing a teacher due to pressure from the communist party, the new welfare office (*Sozialamt*) housed in the old Stasi building and the fact that "[a]m Ende wissen die mehr als die Stasi" (227).[34] Wolfgang Höbel, a critic for the magazine *Der Spiegel* makes the interesting observation that in these stories about life after unification West Germans play only a marginal role, remaining phantoms. Schulze's central focus is on the issues dealt with by those whose lives changed the most through unification, while West German characters are pushed to the sidelines.[35]

Schulze presents us mainly with the losers, only sometimes with the winners, of the unification process, with each side experiencing the chaos of everyday life and dealing with the past in their own way. One young girl, Connie Schubert, after being taken advantage of sexually by a West German real-estate agent, sees how things will develop in the East and decides to leave

---

33 "I think that I describe situations in *Simple Storys* that could happen everywhere in the Western world. The difference is if people are suddenly confronted with the West from one week to the next or if they grow up there."

34 "in the end they know more than the Stasi."

35 Michalzik goes so far as to say that Schulze was pedantically careful to put only one West German into the story—a real estate agent—and actually he would have preferred none (32).

Germany just after unification begins:

> Obwohl ich so naiv und blauäugig gewesen wäre, sagen sie, hätte ich bereits sehr früh – als sich die andern noch Illusionen hingaben—, bereits da hätte ich gewußt, wie alles hier kommen würde. Und damit haben sie ja auch irgendwie recht. (29)[36]

Another character, Renate Meurer, discusses the scandal around her husband's assumed Stasi-involvement and explains that after unification no one, neither the party he had served, nor Ernst himself, was interested in helping him clear up his records:

> Was sollte er denn unternehmen. Das ging so schnell, und plötzlich war Schluß. Plötzlich interessierte das keinen mehr. Hauptsache, Geld und Arbeit und Wohnung und EC-Karte und daß man sich auskennt mit Gesetzen und Formularen. Was anderes interessiert nicht, nicht die Bohne. (225)[37]

Although most characters take unification with difficulty, only few admit to missing things from the past. Hanni, in a midnight call to her friend Barbara Holitzschek, regrets that her former life and so many people from the past are gone: "Und das schlimmste ist, daß alles, was war, weg ist, die Leute, sie sind weg" (85).[38] Each character responds to unification differently—what they have in common is that their everyday life has dramatically changed and no one truly tries to come to terms with the past. Even the newspapers are no longer interested in writing about who did what in the past, as Renate comments to Babs:

> Wenn der letzte FDJ-Chef reich wird, weil er Aufträge für Baufirmen vermittelt, der kennt halt Tod und Teufel. Alles erfolgreiche Unternehmer, die Arbeitsplätze schaffen und Anzeigen bringen. Warum solln die Zeitungen den Mund aufreißen? Vorbei ist vorbei! (226-7)[39]

This attitude is typical not only of what the media often ignored after unification, but more importantly of what the average person failed to reveal. This can be attributed, on the one hand, to a desire to let the past be history and

36 "Although I was so innocent and naive, they say, I had very early—while the others were still full of illusions—I already knew how everything here would turn out. And somehow they are right about that."

37 "What should he do about it. It went so quickly and suddenly it was over. Suddenly no one was interested in it anymore. The main thing was money, a job, an apartment, and an ATM card, and that you knew your way around laws and forms. Nothing else interested anyone at all."

38 "And the worst thing is that everything that was is gone. The people, they are gone."

39 "When the last FDJ boss gets rich, because he secures orders for construction companies, he knows no fear. All of them are successful businessmen who create jobs and secure advertising deals. Why should the newspapers open their mouths? The past is past!"

focus on today and yet, on the other hand, to certain individuals' desire to have their own past kept secret.

The fall of the Wall and the end of the GDR forced ordinary East Germans to alter not only their lives, but also their perceptions of life. After unification, life has become the sum of all of the little everyday occurrences and things in each individual's life. Schulze's talent as a storyteller lies in his method of focusing on the "little" details in exact descriptions of situations and things, while barely mentioning the major events. As Höbel explains, Schulze's intense focus on everyday objects creates the feeling for the reader that these things in the newly conquered world of consumption are a threat to their users—as if the objects have conspired against their human owners. Just as in Hensel's narrative, the background information takes up the majority of the pages in the prose, leaving the extraordinary to merely a few sentences. The difference in the two methods, however, lies in Schulze's use of varying perspectives to tell the stories, while Hensel basically only tells one story and allows Gabriela to relate her entire story directly. The advantage of the complex narrative structure in Schulze's novel is that events in character's histories are portrayed through a variety of (often conflicting) perspectives, reinforcing the subjective nature of history. Ingo Schulze commented on his method: "Geschichten treffen Geschichte eben genauer. Ich konnte das [die Wende 1989] nur als 'Storys' wiedererzählen" (Neubauer 15).[40] Schulze skillfully connects passages of seemingly unconnected occurrences and characters into an unfinished mosaic of a plot in which each of the characters becomes a colored square forming a larger picture only visible in its entirety, though not ever complete. The final result is a tangled network of characters and events that form what history ultimately is: the subjective experiences of individuals.

Hensel's *Tanz am Kanal* and Schulze's *Simple Storys* represent two examples of responses to German unification from the perspective of young Eastern German writers. Neither writer is trying to create a new world, change the existing one, point fingers at the guilty ones in the past, or send a clear message to the reader. Events are told from an everyday and close-up perspective, apparently free of all political intentions. As many critics have commented, the literature of the post-*Wende* generation replaces national historical events with the subjective experience of individuals.[41] This is also true of the literature by Schulze and Hensel. Events are told and struggles are described, but some of the reader's questions about structure are left unresolved. Thus form and content reflect one another. The characters' insecurities mirror our own apprehensions as readers that not all of our questions are answered. Furthermore, literary genre distinctions are as unclear as the individual elements of content in these two books. The complexity of

40 "Stories tell history better. I could only tell that [unification 1989] through 'Storys'."

41 See Radisch, "Die zweite Stunde Null" 1, Schulze-Reimpell 19, and Winkels 5.

the *Wende* is expressed through the unclear *temporal* structure of Hensel's novel-like "narrative" and in the confusing *spatial* character relationships in Schulze's "novel" of short stories. Hensel and Schulze communicate through their literature that after the *Wende* time and space are no longer as simple as they appear to be.

In each of the two works introduced here, life in post-unification Germany is difficult, confusing, and at times unmanageable. Characters suffer through the painful process of *Wendeschmerz*, searching for their place in this new world of unemployment, materialism, and a quickly changing society. It is close at hand that the historical event of unification is much less the focus of literary writer's attention than subjective everyday experiences. In their focus on these everyday struggles, instead of larger political messages, it could be said that Hensel and Schulze show not a typical Eastern German perspective, but rather mirror a broader German-German *Lebensgefühl* ("feeling for life") characteristic of this entire younger generation in post-unification Germany.[42] This young generation is free from societal pressure to write for or against a specific political program and chooses instead to focus on everyday experiences of individuals, whether they live in the new states in the East, the old states in the West, or the new undivided capital, Berlin.

Works Cited

Berger, Jürgen. "Von der Euter- zur Tellerwäscherin. Eine sehr lebenstaugliche Heldin in Kerstin Hensels Erzählung 'Tanz am Kanal.'" Quoted in: *Deutsche Literatur 1994 Jahresüberblick.* Stuttgart: Reclam, 1995. 165-167.

Billhardt, Thomas, and Kerstin Hensel. *Alles war so. Alles war anders. Bilder aus der DDR.* Leipzig: Kiepenheuer, 1999.

Brockmann, Stephen. *Literature and German Reunification.* Cambridge: Cambridge UP, 1999.

Brömme, Bettina. *Sommerfinsternis*. Leipzip: Reclam, 2000.

42 This is not to say that the everyday struggles in the literature from Eastern and Western Germany are the same just—that they have the same focus—the everyday. While much of the literature from Eastern Germany written in the nineties (such as Hensel, Schulze, Alexander Osang's *Die Nachtrichten,* or Rita Kuczynski's *Staccato* etc.) deals with everyday issues related to *Wendeschmerz,* much of the recent literature of the generation in the West (such as the pop novels by Benjamin von Stuckrad-Barre like *Soloalbum,* Jane Hegers' *Willkommen in Chaos,* or Bettina Brömme's *Sommerfinsternis* etc.) ignores the fact that unification has taken place, yet still tells diverse everyday stories of individuals. The literature from Berlin (such as Tanja Dückers' *Spielzone,* Judith Hermann's *Sommerhaus Später,* M.G. Burgheim's *Future Pop,* Unda Hörner's *Unter Nachbarn,* or Elke Naters' *Königinnen*) takes on a special role as it focuses on the everyday lives of various characters in the big city of Berlin, in which unification is somehow ever present, even if never specifically mentioned. The history of this once divided city always plays a role as characters travel between former West and East Berlin, often commenting on how things have changed or how things used to be.

Burgheim, M.G. *Future Pop*. Frankfurt am Main: Eichborn, 1999.

Cosentino, Christine. "Wirres und Wahres in 'einfachen' Geschichten aus der ostdeutschen Provinz: Ingo Schulzes *Simple Storys*." *Glossen* 10 (2000) <http://www.dickinson.edu/departments/germn/glossen/heft10/cosentino.html>.

Dückers, Tanja. *Spielzone*. Berlin: Aufbau-Verlag, 1999.

Hammer, Klaus. "Gespräch mit Kerstin Hensel." *Weimarer Beiträge* 37.1 (1991): 93-110.

Hegers, Jane. *Willkommen in Chaos*. Leipzig: Reclam, 2000.

Hensel, Kerstin. *Tanz am Kanal*. Frankfurt am Main: Suhrkamp, 1994.

Hermann, Judith. *Sommerhaus Später*. Frankfurt am Main: Fischer, 1998.

Hinck, Walter. "Simplizissima unter der Brücke. Kerstin Hensels Schelmenerzählung 'Tanz am Kanal.'" *Frankfurter Allgemeine Zeitung* 2 Nov. 1994: 36.

Höbel, Wolfgang. "Glücksritter auf Tauchstation." *Der Spiegel* 28 Feb. 1998, <http://www.spiegel.de/kultur/literatur/0,1518, 27269,00.html>.

Hörner, Unda. *Unter Nachbarn*. Frankfurt am Main: Suhrkamp, 2000.

Krekeler, Elmar. "Nichts ist gefährlicher als das Leben. Ein Wenderoman und mehr: Der Berliner Ingo Schulze erzählt in vielen Masken von der ostdeutschen Provinz." *Die Welt* 13 Mar. 1998. <http://www.welt.de /archiv/1998/03/13/0313ku01.htm>.

Kuczynski, Rita. *Staccato*. Frankfurt am Main: Frankfurt Verlagsanstalt, 1997.

Kumphufer, Michael. "Der ganz große Stoff: Wo bleibt der Roman zur Einheit?" *Süddeutsche Zeitung* 30 Sep. 2000/ 1 Oct. 2000, section "Feuilleton": 17.

Leonhardt, Rudolf Walter. "Kerstin Hensels 'Tanz am Kanal.' Wo man 'nüsch' sagt." *Die Zeit* 7 Oct. 1994, section "Literatur": 8.

Lorenz, Dagmar. "Ingo Schulze. 'Simple Storys. Ein Roman aus der ostdeutschen Provinz.'" <http://www.carpe.com/buch/t_schulze_ingo_ simple.html>.

Michalzik, Peter. "Wie komme ich zur Nordsee? Ingo Schulze erzählt einfache Geschichten, die ziemlich vertrackt sind und die alle lieben." *Aufgerissen: Zur Literatur der 90er*. Ed. Thomas Kraft. München: Piper, 2000. 26-38.

Missler, Philip. "Weltgeschichte im Wasserglas. Ingo Schulzes 'Simple Stories' liefern eine tragikomische Fallstudie-Ost." <http://members.aol.com/hundspost/nr9/rez_schulze.htm>.

Müller, Lothar. "Barrikadenbau verschoben. Wenn Dichter sich verheben: Eine Tagung über Politik und Poetik mit jüngeren deutschen Autoren in Berlin." *Frankfurter Allgemeine Zeitung* 23 Feb. 1999: 47.

Naters, Elke. *Königinnen*. Köln: Kiepenheuer & Witsch, 1998.

Neubauer, Michael. "'Gefeit vor Utopien.' Thomas Brussig und Ingo Schulze, Erfolgsautoren der Nach-Wende-Generation, im Gespräch über die DDR und den Osten, über Literatur und die Schwierigkeit, den Westen zu verstehen." *TAZ—die Tageszeitung* 5 Oct. 1998: 15.

Osang, Alexander. *Die Nachrichten*. Frankfurt am Main: Fischer, 2000.

Radisch, Iris. "Die zweite Stunde Null." *Die Zeit* 7 Oct. 1994, section "Literatur": 1.

---. "Endlich! Der Wenderoman: Aber wer ist eigentlich Gert Neumann?" *Die Zeit* 25 Mar 1999, section "Literatur": 1.

Schulze, Ingo. *Simple Storys. Ein Roman aus der ostdeutschen Provinz.* Berlin: Berlin Verlag, 1998.

Schulze-Reimpell, Werner. "Neue Literatur aus Ostdeutschland." *Rheinischer Merkur* 18 Dec. 1998, section "Kultur": 19.

Schweizer, Thomas, and Michael Schnegg. "Die soziale Struktur der 'Simple Storys:' Eine Netzwerkanalyse." <http://www.uni-koeln.de/phil-fak/voelkerkunde/simple.html>.

Seibt, Gustav. "Die kleine Stadt. Hier entsteht die neue deutsche Literatur: Ein Besuch bei Ingo Schulze in seinem Altenburg." *Berliner Zeitung* 15 Aug. 1998. Quoted in: *Deutsche Literatur 1998 Jahresüberblick.* Stuttgart: Reclam, 1999. 225-231.

---. "Unsimplizissimus ostteutsch. Schreiben wie der Mauerfall: Ingo Schulzes 'Simple Storys.'" <http://www.berliner-kurier.de/kultur/lesen/belle/.html/belle.199803.05.html>.

Spiegel, Hubert. "Der Kranich hat niemanden, der mit ihm tanzt. Gemeinsame Interessen, aber kein gemeinsames Programm: Die junge deutsche Literatur bei den Kranichsteiner Literaturtagen." *Frankfurter Allgemeine Zeitung* 24 Nov. 1998: 41.

Stuckrad-Barre, Benjamin von. *Soloalbum.* Köln: Kiepenheuer & Witsch, 1998.

Wehdeking, Volker. *Die deutsche Einheit und die Schriftsteller: Literarische Verarbeitung der Wende seit 1989.* Stuttgart: Kohlhammer, 1995.

Welzel, Klaus. *Utopieverlust—die deutsche Einheit im Spiegel ostdeutscher Autoren.* Würzburg: Königshausen & Neumann, 1998.

Winkels, Hubert. "Zur deutschen Literatur 1998." *Deutsche Literatur 1998 Jahresüberblick.* Stuttgart: Reclam, 1999. 5-39.

JILL TWARK

"Ko . . .Ko . . . Konolialismus," said the giraffe: Humorous and Satirical Responses to German Unification

The 1989 revolution, also referred to as the *Wende*, and subsequent unification of Germany on 3 October 1990, drastically altered the lives of Germans living in the German Democratic Republic (GDR). While Western Germans bore the brunt of financing unification, Eastern Germans not only faced entirely new structures in their everyday lives, but they also had to deal with mass unemployment, the influx of Western cultural values, and a sudden rupture in their biographies. Given the weight of these issues, it may come as a surprise that a large number of Eastern German authors reacted to the *Wende* by producing humorous and satirical texts.[1] A few well-known representatives of this group are Volker Braun (*Der Wendehals*, 1995), Thomas Brussig (*Helden wie wir*, 1995), and Erich Loest (*Katerfrühstück*, 1992). But there are others less publicized—for example, Thomas Rosenlöcher (*Die Wiederentdeckung des Gehens beim Wandern. Harzreise*, 1991), Bernd Schirmer (*Schlehweins Giraffe*[2]), and Jens Sparschuh (*Der Zimmerspringbrunnen*, 1995)—who also belong in this category and deserve closer analysis.

All of these authors utilize humor and satire as literary modes to criticize the GDR and/or the unification process, while entertaining the reader. Traditionally, the intended functions of humor and satire have been to criticize, educate, conciliate, and/or entertain. A person who uses humor or satire distances him or herself from the object of this humor. In difficult circumstances, humor aids in bolstering morale. There are, however, also less apparent reasons for this phenomenon. These reasons have more to do with the origin and nature of humor, humor as a response to personal experience.[3]

Laughter is, according to Immanuel Kant, the result of an expectation which suddenly ends in nothing. He argues that everything which produces

1 Although I discovered this trend independently, it has been documented by Hartinger and Cosentino.

2 Bernd Schirmer, *Schlehweins Giraffe* (Frankfurt am Main: Fischer, 1994). This edition will be used for citations. The first edition appeared in 1992 with the Vito von Eichborn Verlag.

3 The following theoretical arguments for the proliferation of humorous and satirical texts following German unification have appeared in slightly altered form in Twark, "Wedel."

laughter is somehow paradoxical and, therefore, contrary to human reason.[4] Compared to the high expectations on both sides of the wall, the immediate results of unification indeed seem contradictory. Sigmund Freud's postulate that the higher the level of "Ersparung an Hemmungs- oder Unterdrückungsaufwand," the greater the enjoyment of humor, provides another, psychological explanation for a humorous reaction to the *Wende* (96).[5] Having lived under a repressive dictatorship all their lives, the fall of the wall provided GDR citizens the opportunity to release their pent-up emotions of anger, frustration, disappointment, etc. One way to do this was through humoristic and satirical writing, where they could suddenly lampoon and criticize freely, without fear of censorship or repression. Wolfgang Ertl's discussion of Rosenlöcher's and Sabrina Born's analysis of Brussig's and Schirmer's texts also support the thesis of humor being an act of liberation for GDR authors after unification. "[E]in trotz alledem befreiendes Lachen in schwerer Zeit," Ertl calls it (37).[6] Helmut Arntzen's observation that satire is often used as a literary form in transitional times to root out antiquated institutions and behaviors while ushering in the new also points in this direction (44-45). In releasing their emotions and criticizing society, artists and their public can speed up the process of coming to terms with the past.

Beyond these philosophical and psychological reasons a further explanation may be termed socio-historical. The clash of cultures brought about by German unification lends itself to humorous treatment precisely because of the contrasts between East and West German social, economic, and political structures. When two distinct cultures interact, cultural differences are highlighted, some of which are bound to appear odd or comical. The stereotypes and cultural differences embedded in Eastern and Western German society, developed over the course of forty years, could not have dissolved instantaneously, nor have they. In absorbing the GDR into the larger Federal Republic, the latter also turned GDR citizens into a denigrated and disadvantaged "Other." Being the economically and politically smaller and weaker of the two Germanies, the GDR was not able to assert itself during the unification process. Eastern Germans may thus use humor and satire to strike back at what appears to them

4 Kant writes: "Es muß in allem, was ein lebhaftes erschütterndes Lachen erregen soll, etwas Widersinniges sein (woran also der Verstand an sich kein Wohlgefallen finden kann). Das Lachen ist ein Affekt aus der plötzlichen Verwandlung einer gespannten Erwartung in nichts" (437). All translations are my own. ("There must be something contrary to reason [which cannot appeal to our common sense] in everything which provokes spirited, convulsive laughter. Laughter results from the sudden transformation of an anxious expectation into nothing.")

5 "energy not expended to inhibit or repress [one's emotions]." In other words, the fewer inhibitions or repressed feelings a person has, the more likely he or she is to laugh at something.

6 "A laughter that liberates in hard times despite all that has happened."

as new and obscure Western power structures that are replacing old, familiar ones.

Finally, literary historian Wolfgang Preisendanz described a tendency in post-WWII German literature to deal with the past using humorous means ("das Komische"). He argues that literary versions of historical events often appear humorous simply because they provide details of everyday life not normally included in official historical records (162-164). In striving to write objective chronicles of the past, historians focus upon broad socio-political movements, creating an abstract, one-sided view. Literary texts can fill in the gaps left by scholarly historical accounts by depicting details historians have rejected. One can thus conclude that nearly any detailed literary presentation of a historical event will appear *komisch* in the eyes of readers used to learning about history from history books and newspaper articles.

The range of explanations for humor and satire in literature is reflected in the variety of modes of humor found in each individual text. To elaborate upon some of these modes, I take a closer look at the three representative texts mentioned above: Rosenlöcher's *Die Wiederentdeckung des Gehens beim Wandern. Harzreise*, Schirmer's *Schlehweins Giraffe*, and Sparschuh's *Der Zimmerspringbrunnen*. Because these texts were composed soon after the wall fell (1990-1995), the humorous and satirical strategies the authors employ do not reflect a sovereign mastery of the subject as, for example, Günter Grass (*Die Blechtrommel*) or Edgar Hilsenrath (*Der Nazi und der Friseur*) do in their World War II satires, but rather they convey a stupefaction or helplessness as to how to put unification experiences into words. Thus their approach often appears more defensive than aggressive. In this essay I explicate these texts within the context of unification, thereby demonstrating them to be symptomatic literary responses.

To highlight similarities and differences between the three texts, I have divided my essay into four segments: The Comic Narrator, East vs. West, GDR Reflections: Only Ostalgie?, and Word Games and Scurrilous Forms of Humor. Each section deals with one major narrative device or theme, common to all texts, which is indicative of the times in which the texts were written.

I. The Comic Narrator

In engaging a first-person comic narrator, Rosenlöcher, Schirmer and Sparschuh supply a distinct lens through which unification is viewed. In each text, a forty-something Eastern German narrator faces difficulties adapting to recent changes. Like Cervantes' Don Quixote, his world has been turned upside down in the new, post-unification free market society, and his actions, thoughts and speech appear anachronistic, occasionally paranoid—definitely comical.

Whereas a healthy dose of self-irony helps Rosenlöcher's and Schirmer's protagonists maintain their optimism and eventually come to terms with the altered circumstances, Sparschuh's narrator, taking his situation too literally, gradually loses touch with reality and in the end faces a bleak, uncertain future. Despite their differences, the three narrators resemble each other in their bumbling fashion of dealing with unification's effects, their condemnatory attitudes toward Western German treatment of Eastern Germans, and their ironic, self-conscious perspective on the GDR.

In Rosenlöcher's twentieth-century *Harzreise*[7] the narrator, an unnamed author from Dresden, takes a three-day hike through the Harz mountains from Quedlinburg to Goslar "um wenigstens andeutungsweise wieder Gedichte schreiben zu können" (9).[8] The title is a double entendre on the narrator's wish to rediscover walking by taking a hike, as well as his need to get used to a new culture by moving within it. His departure date fatefully coincides with the West and East German currency union: 1 July 1990. Throughout his journey, he sees himself as an anachronism simply because he is walking and not driving a car. His absent-mindedness, clumsy behavior and shabby appearance—long, shaggy hair and beard, unfashionable clothing—also identify him as an East German and produce a comic effect. At the hotel where he spends the first night, he has serious trouble ordering a beer because the selection is so broad and all varieties are new to him. Finding a border guard still at his post at the supposedly open border in his first attempt to cross over to the West, he exhibits unnecessary paranoia by turning around and heading back East. The rude reactions he receives from nearly everyone he encounters add to his comical misery. Trying to pay for a meal at a *Ferienheim*, he accidentally pulls out an obsolete GDR hundred mark bill depicting Karl Marx's long-haired, bearded image and is ridiculed by the East German recipients: "Schaut euch das an. Der Karl Marx hier will mir einen Karl-Marx andrehn!" (64).[9] In depicting the narrator's difficulties getting used to the new circumstances, as well as the insulting reactions he receives from Eastern and Western Germans, Rosenlöcher convincingly depicts the rapid and complex cultural transformation which took place in Eastern Germany after the wall was opened. In the adjustment period, a person's actions and experiences often appear comical.

The unnamed narrator in *Schlehweins Giraffe* must also learn the hard way to deal with the changes in his world. As the narrative opens *in media res*, he has lost both his jobs (as a comma editor and as a recycling collector), his wife has left him for the third time, once and for all, and, on top of this, he has

---

7 For a detailed comparison of Rosenlöcher's *Harzreise* with Heine's and Goethe's works about a similar hike through the Harz mountains, see Grauert.

8 "in order to be able to write poems again, or at least hint at doing so."

9 "Look at this. This Karl Marx here wants to palm a Karl Marx off on me!"

agreed to adopt a giraffe as a favor to his friend Schlehwein. Despite extremely difficult circumstances, however, his persistence, self-irony and optimistic worldview prevent his fate from appearing truly tragic. Making the most of his situation, the narrator coopts the stuttering giraffe as a replacement partner in a mostly one-sided "dialogue." He writes the text itself as self-therapy, to chronicle and to come to terms with his circumstances, shifting back and forth between present and past events as he experiences unified Berlin together with the giraffe.

Similar to Rosenlöcher's narrator, Schirmer's protagonist displays shock and paranoia in his new circumstances. He believes the mailman is a former *Stasi* (GDR secret police) official. He feels he is being watched and pursued by the West German police because of his association with Schlehwein, who apparently engaged in criminal activities after unification,[10] and because he is harboring a giraffe, who supported the GDR regime, in his apartment. Through his protagonist, Schirmer depicts the fate of many East Germans after unification. Not only has the narrator's employment and social situation been altered, but his personal life has gone awry. Similar to the narrators in the other two texts, his clumsiness, naiveté, and fears make him laughable, but also likeable. As with Rosenlöcher's narrator, the reader easily empathizes with, but does not pity him; his ironic and humorous attitude marks him as a survivor. The laughter Schirmer produces is a "laughing *with*" rather than a "laughing *at.*"[11] Humor here, as in the *Harzreise*, helps the narrator to come to terms with his new situation, while entertaining and enlightening the reader.

Because of Jens Sparschuh's more critical, satirical stance, his protagonist Hinrich Lobek differs from the aforementioned narrators. This most likely results from the fact that the novel was written later than the other two: *Der Zimmerspringbrunnen*, published in 1995, depicts the Eastern German situation three years after unification. Hinrich Lobek, an unemployed Eastern German who has tried for years to find a job after being *abgewickelt* ("let go") from his former GDR Communal Housing Administration position, lives in Berlin with his wife Julia and their dog, Hasso vom Rabenhorst. A unification success story, with her full-time office job, feminist friend, and extramarital affair, Julia supplies a strong contrast to Hinrich, who putters around, as the first chapter heading describes it: "Eins zwei drei Jahre als Jäger in den eigenen vier Wänden" (9).[12] Likening his isolation to that of Robinson Crusoe on his deserted island, Lobek renames his dog "Freitag."

Three years of unemployment have left their mark on Lobek's personality. Lack of contact with other people has caused his communication skills to

---

10 Before fleeing the country, Schlehwein burned the property ledgers in his village in order to prevent former West German property owners from claiming their due after unification.

11 Hans Robert Jauss discusses the different types of laughter directed toward the comic hero, distinguishing between "lachen *mit*" and "lachen *über*" (109).

12 "One, two, three years as a hunter within my own four walls."

suffer, and he is unable to see through his delusions. These character traits appear blatantly comical in the job he finally lands as a sales representative for the West German "Zimmerspringbrunnen" company, PANTA RHEIn, hoping this will be the springboard to get himself back on his feet. Sparschuh intentionally selects this unnecessary, expensive item as the product which Lobek must sell door to door to (often unemployed and depressed) Eastern Germans to add to the grotesqueness of the situation. The company name, a Greek expression meaning "everything flows," is a pun on the Rhine location of the company headquarters as well as a jab at marketing strategies which use pompous advertising language to lend products a cultivated, elite aura.

One scene in particular illustrates Lobek's disturbed thought processes and pathological inability to communicate, even with his own wife. When Julia gets angry with him for not having cleaned up the dog's mess, Lobek does not argue with her aloud, but repeats the selling tips from one to eight from the PANTA RHEIn sales representative's manual in his head. When she finally storms out, not letting him reply to her barrage, he ponders: "Selbst ein gemeingefährlicher Verbrecher hat das Recht auf Verteidigung. [. . .] Das letzte Wort in einem ordentlich geführten Verfahren gebührt schließlich dem Angeklagten. Leben wir denn nun in einem Rechtsstaat, Julia, oder nicht? Es ist doch überhaupt nicht einzusehen, weshalb in einem Ehestreit nicht wenigstens die Regeln der Strafprozeßordnung gelten sollten" (66).[13] Here, the disparity between Lobek's "legalese" and the existential marital crisis demonstrates Lobek's humorous inability to communicate in *any* situation. Soon after this fight, Julia moves out. Lobek's communication problem, self-centered worldview, and *idée fixe* that if he can just be successful in his career, everything else will fall into place, are initially funny; however, since these personal issues are not resolved in the course of the novel, they lead to his demise.

As in the tradition of the picaresque novel, Rosenlöcher, Schirmer, and Sparschuh all evoke humor through exaggeration and the repetition of similar, epic narrative sequences. To be sure, Sparschuh's narrator-based humor is less conciliatory, more critical than Schirmer's or Rosenlöcher's. At first, the reader laughs more often *at* Lobek than *with* him, until his situation becomes so tragic that the laughter dies. Yet although Sparschuh's satirical critiques seem to be aimed at Eastern Germans and their attempts to conform to Western expectations (the novel bears the ironic subtitle *Ein Heimatroman*), Wolfgang Emmerich maintains that the real targets of Sparschuh's satire are the capitalist bluff society and its easily duped customers (505). In holding up a mirror to the West, Sparschuh presents a type of humor that both West and East German

---

13 "Even a common criminal has the right to defend himself. It is the just due of the defendant to have the last word in a properly conducted court proceeding. Do we live in a state under the rule of law or not, Julia? I can not understand why, at the very least, the code of criminal procedure should not be valid in a marriage fight."

readers can comprehend. By taking a humorous and/or satirical approach toward their protagonists, all three authors encourage the reader to sympathize with and to understand the particular East German predicament after unification.

II. East vs. West

Stereotypes and typical characters are another device meant to shed light on the East/West conflict. Although the narrators are presented largely as comical figures, in cultural confrontations their depictions of West Germans and the latters' attitudes toward Eastern Germany slide into the satirical. Whereas humor and the comic can be conciliatory, satire implies censure, and hence a more obvious attack. The narrators' negative opinions of Western Germans are a product of their observations of Western German behavior and verbalized opinions.

A specific example of Eastern and Western German differences that pokes fun at their problematic relationship is Bernd Schirmer's character, Uncle Alfred. Uncle Alfred from Munich represents the West German *Besserwisser*. Before unification, he had sent the narrator packages of chocolate, coffee, Uncle Ben's rice, and soap, but refused to visit because he was afraid of travelling to the East. As soon as the wall comes down, Uncle Alfred drives to East Berlin in his Mercedes, taking the narrator and his wife, Kristina, shopping for new clothes and to the most exclusive restaurant in West Berlin. Uncle Alfred is charmed by what he sees as Kristina's "natural," naïve behavior and attitude, but disappointed with the narrator's lack of ambition. He wants the narrator to return to the university and finish the German literature degree he had interrupted in 1968. He firmly believes the narrator was persecuted by the Stasi. The narrator laments: "Ich konnte sagen, was ich wollte, er war nicht davon abzubringen, ich war ein Verfolgter des Stasi-Regimes. Er arbeitete meine Vergangenheit auf, und ich war ein Opfer" (81).[14] In the figure of Uncle Alfred, as the narrator encounters him, Schirmer satirizes the "typical" wealthy, condescending, prejudiced Western German as he appears in an Eastern German setting.

Hinrich Lobek also has enlightening experiences with Western Germans. Before he can begin his new sales career, he must attend a training conference in the small town of Bad Sülz[15] in Baden-Württemberg. Learning a new

14 "I could say whatever I wanted, he could not be persuaded that I had not been persecuted by the Stasi regime. He worked through my past, and I was a victim."

15 "Bad Sülz," a fictional place name, also contains a hidden critique of West Germany. "Sülze" is headcheese, or pickled pork; the verb "sülzen" means to babble on about something.

profession has its pitfalls, and Lobek, the Eastern German greenhorn, has his own particular difficulties learning to become a sales representative à la Western Germany. Believing appearance to be the key to success, he dresses in a blackberry-colored suit, the epitome of business fashion in Eastern Germany in the early nineties, and carries an empty black briefcase in order to legitimate his presence. In his nervousness, he chokes on a piece of smoked ham when the company owner, a typical suave Western German business manager, Alois Boldinger, approaches to greet him. Choking prevents—and saves—Lobek from having to speak to Boldinger. When the time comes for him to role-play the salesman in front of the other representatives, however, his blundering saves the day. Sitting across from the acting "customer," Lobek, once again at a loss for words, presses the fountain's "on" button and accidentally squirts himself in the face. As Lobek wipes his eyes with a handkerchief, Boldinger comes to the front of the crowd and praises him for his ingenious sales tactics: "Boldinger sah mich bewundernd an, wie man eine exotische Pflanze ansieht: 'Herrschaften, das nenne ich östliche Ruhe und meditative Kraft! Ja, Mensch, auch wir hier im Westen können von Ihnen lernen. Durchaus!'" (52-53).[16] This meeting between an Eastern German and his new boss in a Western German setting further illustrates the comic clash of mentalities and cultures that unification produced. Whereas the sophisticated Western German businessman always produces articulate utterances, the uninitiated Eastern German is rendered speechless. In order to increase the comic effect of the meeting, Sparschuh has Boldinger respond entirely differently to Lobek's comic blunder than one would anticipate.

Despite Sparschuh's amusing satirical treatment, as with Schirmer and Rosenlöcher, the seriousness of Lobek's circumstances and the East/West conflict shine through. Sparschuh highlights Western German patronization of and disrespect for Eastern Germans in an encounter between Lobek and his salesman mentor, Uwe Strüver. The way Strüver treats Lobek is indicative of Western German attitudes toward Eastern Germans in general. First, Strüver inappropriately suggests they use the familiar *du* form of address, even though he is younger than Lobek. Lobek reflects upon the situation thus: "Er war, sah man genau hin, mindestens zehn, fünfzehn Jahre jünger als ich. Insofern hätte eigentlich ich ihm das Du anbieten müssen. Aber schließlich, er war der Westmensch; da hatte er bei mir wahrscheinlich gleich automatisch ein paar Jährchen von den 40 Jahren DDR-Leben abgezogen, denn richtig gelebt hatten wir ja nicht" (112).[17] By this time, Lobek has already absorbed and internalized

16 "Boldinger looked at me with admiration, like one looks at an exotic plant: 'Gentlemen, that's what I call Eastern calmness and meditative power! Yes, my man, even we in the West can learn from you. Most certainly!'"

17 "He was at least ten, fifteen years younger than me, if one looked carefully. Actually, I should have been the one to offer him the informal 'Du' address. But, in the end, he was the

Western German prejudices. According to Western Germans like Strüver, the Eastern German experience is not worthy of being considered "living" at all: "Das war ja kein Leben bei euch! Die Zeitungen waren keine Zeitungen. Die Wahlen waren keine Wahlen. Die Straßen keine Straßen. Nicht mal die Autos waren Autos" (112).[18] Lobek ponders Strüver's words: "Innerlich mußte ich ihm in allen Punkten recht geben. Aber, was zum Kuckuck war es dann, was wir die ganze Zeit getrieben haben? Wer weiß. Man muß es schon selbst erlebt haben, um es nicht zu verstehen [. . .]" (112).[19] Here, Sparschuh demonstrates poignantly how Western German attitudes can undermine the Eastern German collective self-image by calling Eastern Germans' entire life experience into question. Insulting behavior like this from the West, combined with accusations and prejudices, leads all three narrators to question their past lives and present identities.

Rosenlöcher echoes Schirmer's and Sparschuh's observations.[20] In his westward hike, Rosenlöcher's narrator exposes himself to many situations which amplify differences between Eastern and Western German cultures and attitudes. In the Eastern German town of Quedlinburg, Rosenlöcher's narrator overhears a Western German tourist: "'Das wird dauern, bis die hier im Osten gelernt haben, was eigentlich Arbeiten ist' bemerkte eine Kleinbildkamera spitz" (20).[21] The Western German tourists, looking at the run-down buildings, exclaim with indignation: "Was haben die hier aus unserem Deutschland gemacht!" (21).[22] They then turn to the narrator, as if he were personally responsible:

> Alle Apotheker sahn mich von der Seite an. Woher wußten sie, daß ich das aus Deutschland gemacht hatte? Ich allein hatte schuld, wo keiner sich erinnern konnte. Daß keiner sich erinnern konnte, war auch meine Schuld. Die Schuld, im Verfall keine Sprache für den Verfall gefunden zu haben. Denn wer eine Sprache fand,

---

Westerner; he probably just subtracted a few of the 40 years of life we spent in the GDR, since we really hadn't lived there."

18 "That was no real life there. The newspapers weren't newspapers. The elections were no elections. The streets weren't streets. Not even the cars were really cars."

19 "Deep down I had to admit that he was right on all points. But what the heck did we do the whole time then? Who knows. One had to have experienced it oneself in order not to understand it."

20 Despite his biting critiques of Western German behavior and attitudes, Rosenlöcher's narrator welcomes unification because it brings more freedom, higher quality goods, etc. Wolfgang Emmerich points out the contradiction in Rosenlöcher's critiques made apparent in the last scene of the text: "Die ironische Schlußpointe besteht im Kauf neuer Westschuhe (Marke 'Mephisto'), mit denen er sich nun den kapitalistischen Westen mühelos erwandern wird" (504). ("The ironic final point is made in buying a pair of new West German shoes [brand 'Mephisto']), which will now enable him [the narrator] to wander effortlessly through the capitalist West.")

21 "It's going to take a while before the people here in the East learn what it really means to work,' said a sharp-tongued 35-mm camera."

22 "What did these people here do to our Germany!"

> hatte das Land schon verlassen, das, doch als Kummerland meins, auf einmal den Apothekern gehörte (21-22).[23]

In using the metonymy of a 35-millimeter camera and the metaphor of the *Apotheker* (pharmacist) in referring to Western Germans while displaying their prejudices, Rosenlöcher creates a satirical picture of Western Germans and demonstrates how their (to them) apparently harmless comments provoke an identity crisis in the narrator. His reaction to their accusations represents the Eastern German dilemma when confronted with Western prejudices. Unable to slough the comments off, the narrator accepts the blame for the state of his country because he was one of those who stayed, both before and after the wall came down. The fact that his guilt is based upon his inability to remember *how* his country came to be in such a mess, that he was and is unable even to put his experiences into words, point to the difficulty Eastern Germans, in particular Eastern German authors, have in coming to terms with their socialist past and in communicating their biographies to Westerners.[24] Particularly significant in the German context where memory, forgetting and coming to terms with the past are major issues, Rosenlöcher effectively displays the confusion and speechlessness produced by the opening of the border when Eastern Germans were suddenly forced to explain how they could have allowed the development of—and survived within—an economically inviable, repressive dictatorship. Rosenlöcher portrays this communication barrier with comic irony but does not neglect to convey its serious nature.

Fredric V. Bogel describes satire as "that literary form that works to convert an ambiguous relation of identification and division into one of pure division" (46). By satirizing Western Germans, these authors erect a boundary between their narrators and Western Germans, whom the narrators see as intruding outsiders, contrary to official unification rhetoric that Western and Eastern Germans are *ein Volk* ("one people"). In making this division, these narrators (and authors) assert their identity as a defense against the larger, dominant Western German culture.

---

23 "All of the pharmacists looked askance at me. How did they know that I did that to Germany? I alone was guilty, when no one else could remember. The fact that no one could remember was also my fault. The fault, amidst the decay, of not having found a language to describe this decay. For whoever found this language had already left the country, which, as my worry-filled land, all of a sudden belonged to the pharmacists."

24 Grauert discusses Rosenlöcher's search for a new authorial identity.

III. GDR Reflections: Only Ostalgie?

The neologism *Ostalgie*, a contraction of *Ost* and nostalgia, has become a hallmark of East/West discourse. Many Eastern Germans, missing certain aspects of life in the GDR, look back sentimentally upon them, while Westerners often fail to understand how anything positive can be associated with their projection of the East German dictatorship. Emmerich has grouped together a large number of Eastern German literary works as "ostalgic," including Rosenlöcher's and Sparschuh's texts (502-505).[25] Yet Rosenlöcher, Sparschuh and Schirmer each has his own, unique ways of depicting and commenting upon the GDR past.

Although Rosenlöcher's text was written too soon after unification to display nostalgia in the way authors in later years have done, his narrator muses over the fact that the GDR as he knew it is rapidly desintegrating and points out unification paradoxes: "Ausgerechnet die neue Zeit war plötzlich die alte geworden. Während die alte Zeit, die längst überwunden war, plötzlich als neue Zeit neue Anfangsschwierigkeiten machte" (16).[26] Reflecting with irony upon aspects of GDR culture, he compares them with those in the Federal Republic, not always praising the Western ones as better. For example, Rosenlöcher appreciates the simplicity of mechanical GDR "Ruhla" pocket watches, preferring them to Western ones, which represent the "digital, western world" (36-37). West German watches have "pulsierende Ziffern, auftauchend im Nu und wieder verschwindend ins Nichts. Als wäre die Zeit abgeschafft zugunsten des blinkenden Kurzaugenblicks" (36-37).[27] A poet who receives his inspiration from moments of silence and contemplation, Rosenlöcher values the more "primitive" type of watch produced in the GDR, which depicted the passing of time as a slow and deliberate process. Emmerich interprets Rosenlöcher's text thus: "So ist ein intelligent, sensibel und munter erzählter Text entstanden, dessen leicht ostalgische Tendenz charmant und gar nicht störend ist" (504).[28] Because these authors present their emotions with irony and a solid sense of humor, the *Ostalgie* appears "charming" rather than "disturbing."

Schirmer encases *Ostalgie* in the form of a fantastical, nostalgic, talking giraffe. This giraffe, which the bankrupt East Berlin zoo sold to Schlehwein for

25 See also Sadowski-Smith.

26 "Of all things, the new times had suddenly become the old times. Whereas the old times, which had long been surpassed, suddenly produced new difficulties to adjust to, now being the new times again."

27 "pulsating numerals, appearing suddenly and then disappearing into nothingness. As if time itself had been abolished in favor of a brief, blinking instant."

28 "Thus an intelligent, sensitive, and lively text was created, whose faint *ostalgic* tendencies appear charming and not at all disturbing."

50 Marks and was then transferred to the narrator's Prenzlauer Berg apartment, has a long neck, gangly, uncoordinated movements and questionable intelligence. These physical attributes add a further grotesque ingredient to the narrator's out-of-joint world with a distinct allegorical significance. [29] In order to elaborate the giraffe's allegorical status and make the narrator's "dialogue" with her seem plausible, Schirmer gives her a voice, something which giraffes, who have no vocal chords, can never have. Her speech, however, is flawed: she talks with a stutter, saying "Ko", "Ko-ko-ko", "Konolialismus" instead of "Kolonialismus" and "Es lebe die dtsch demkrtsch Rupli."[30] These words alone make her suspect in post-unification Eastern Germany. But when a friend, Kleingrube, shows the narrator an old newspaper clipping of the giraffe in a circus tent licking the hand of the unnamed GDR First Party Secretary, Erich Honecker, her "guilt" as a government supporter is firmly established. Her twisted "Konolialismus" refers to the colonization of Africa which led to her mother's capture and importation to Europe but also echoes the resentment toward the Western German colonization of Eastern Germany.

As an allegory for Eastern German citizens trying to find their voice in a newly unified Germany, the giraffe's uncertain fate after the dissolution of the East Berlin zoo represents the uncertainty facing Eastern Germans after the absorption of their country into the Federal Republic. She must also readjust her behavior in the narrator's apartment—for example, learn how to turn the television volume down with her tongue—just as all Eastern Germans must learn new ways of thinking and acting. "Sie muß das endlich lernen," says the narrator. "Wir alle müssen viel Neues lernen in dieser Zeit" (14).[31] The suspicion surrounding her past recalls the furor which arose as the Stasi files were opened to public scrutiny in January 1992. Using a giraffe as a target for political accusations, Schirmer condemns the very real witchhunt against ordinary citizens. The giraffe's defective speech might represent the Eastern German voice, drowned out by a larger, more powerful Western German one which did not consider it worthy to be taken seriously. It may also stand for socialist rhetoric, which is no longer listened to or respected in most of the world today. In emphasizing her mechanical reactions and animal nature, Schirmer lampoons Eastern German nostalgic feelings without condemning them.

---

29 In German, a long neck can symbolize a "Wendehals," or "turn-throat," meaning in English "turncoat"or "opportunist."

30 "Long live the German Democratic Republic." Her choppy manner of speaking resembles that of Erich Honecker.

31 "She just has to learn this. We all have to learn a lot of new things now." In a similar manner in *Der Zimmerspringbrunnen*, Hinrich Lobek says his plants have to learn to adapt ("umlernen") to being watered regularly while he is unemployed and spending every day at home (19).

Sparschuh mocks *ostalgic* feelings by having Lobek create for the ex-GDR market a horrendous new type of indoor fountain guaranteed to assuage the bruised egos of Eastern Germans. After his dog drinks all the water from one of the various fountains set up in his apartment so that parts of it burn and melt, Lobek works desperately to undo the damage. The result is a new model. Proudly displaying a pen in the shape of the Berlin TV tower on top, the volcano-shaped fountain bearing a copper plate sawed in the shape of the GDR receives the name "Atlantis." This model proceeds to sell faster than Lobek can produce it, demonstrating the power of nostalgic feelings and mocking bad taste at the same time.

IV. Word Games and Scurrilous Forms of Humor

Schirmer and Rosenlöcher both produce humor through word games. Schirmer's narrator collects strange new words created during and after the *Wende*, as well as creating his own new compounds. Most terms he collects, for example "abwickeln" or "Altlast," are used to describe the dismantling and reorganization of the Eastern German infrastructure according to Western German guidelines. Together with his wife, the narrator creates his own words by combining two compound words with the same base to form a third word, comically blending the meaning of the original two, i.e. "Molotowcocktailparty" or "Pantoffelheldenstadt" (121).[32] While enter-taining to the reader, collecting and inventing new words also subverts the societal order. As these two examples demonstrate, some of these words are not completely apolitical and may be construed as a playful comment upon language and society. The alert reader will perceive in many of them resonances of suppressed anger and dashed hopes.

Like Schirmer's narrator, Rosenlöcher's author also enjoys creating amusing new compound words to describe his old and new environment. "Bedeutungsgewitter" is the effect produced by Western German newspapers upon their readers (11). This may be understood physically (their large size produces a loud rustle when read) and metaphorically (packed with information, reading them is like being bombarded by a thunderstorm). An East German pocket watch is a "Grobchronometer" (36) and an "Untergangsdenkmal" (37). "Schnürsenkelideen" are various disparate, often nonsensical ideas that occur to the narrator while hiking in the mountains (55).

32 The latter is a combination of *Pantoffelheld*, a hen-pecked husband, and *Heldenstadt*, a term used in the Soviet Union to exemplify a city with a heroic historical background. After 1989, the term *Heldenstadt* was applied to Leipzig as the city where the revolution began.

Schirmer introduces a further play on words, a traditional comic and satirical technique, in the *sprechende Namen* (meaning-bearing names) he provides for his narrator's friends in order to identify them with particular groups affected by and reacting in distinct ways to unification. Educated professionals, these characters held privileged positions in the GDR, but all have since lost their jobs. Bröckle, a history professor, plays the lottery, bets at the horse races, and enters various contests in an effort to win money, eventually opening a GDR nostalgia theme bar in the deserted house next door. A Marxist who believed in the progressive development of history, Bröckle now ironically allows his fate to be determined by the outcome of games of chance. *Bröckeln* in German is what happens when something decays and gradually falls apart—an appropriate name for an aging history professor struggling to survive, living in a dilapidated, old apartment in East Berlin. Kleingrube, an archivist, spends his days seeking out and exposing opportunists, i.e. East Germans who openly supported the GDR state but then became ardent capitalists in the Federal Republic, denying their past affiliations. *Kleingrube* means "little grave" or "little dug-out pit," implying the pedantic digging activities of the archivist. Schirmer colors his characters with irony, but their fates are drawn from reality.

The narrator's former career as a comma editor also carries symbolic weight. In his circle of academic friends, this job title is ironic because it requires a knowledge of language, yet is completely uncreative. The act of placing commas into a text can be viewed as a metaphor for Schirmer's own authorial activity. Commas make the reader pause; they fill in the gaps between words. Depending upon where they are placed, they can alter the meaning of a sentence. Schirmer's text functions as a comma, or reason to pause, in the flow of German history. It also fills in gaps left by media coverage and historical accounts of the 1989 revolution and its aftereffects. To Schirmer, external political events are just the backdrop: the incidents themselves are less important than his characters' reactions to them.

Rosenlöcher's calling as a poet can be seen in his frequent use of metaphors and metonymies to condense his descriptions and ironic attacks. [33] Most Western Germans are identified by their appearance: their assumed profession, clothing, cars, or tourist status. A Western German tour group he encounters in Quedlinburg is a group of "Kameras" (20), a man he meets in the hotel bar is a "Pullover" (32). They drive around in "Chromschiffe," which contrast with the "sogenannten Trabanten, die auch eine Stoßstange hatten und auch eine Kühlerhaube, so daß mit dem Wahrbild der Technik aller Gerätschaft

33 Rosenlöcher was best known in the GDR for his poetry collections *Ich lag im Garten bei Kleinschachwitz* (1982) and *Schneebier* (1988). Since 1989 he has also written a diary of the revolution *Die verkauften Pflastersteine. Dresdner Tagebuch* (1990) and another poetry collection *Ich sitze in Sachsen und schau in den Schnee* (1999).

Hinfälligkeit klappernd herangaloppierte" (26).[34] Here, the vivid description and onomotopoetic words bring to life a limping, sputtering Trabi. Rosenlöcher produces a comical effect by repeating these metaphors throughout the text. Like Bergson's jack-in-the-box, they pop up repeatedly in various contexts, as funny leitmotifs (105-110). They reduce, for example, Western German men to "Apotheker" (21), who have the reputation in Germany of being wealthy and charging high prices. He recognizes these "Apotheker" by their "Erwerbsblick" and the fact that they drive around in cars in order to experience the world. In German, this creates a pun: *fahren* (=to drive) in order to *erfahren* (=experience) the world (24). Once, he even mistakes a newly-rich East German driving a shiny new *Chromschiff* for one of these West German *Apotheker*: "Der plötzliche Auftritt von Ostapothekern machte mein Weltbild noch komplizierter" (25).[35] This admission demonstrates that the narrator does not condemn Western Germans per se, but rather the way they appear and act. The new attitudes and values entering his reality are unfamiliar and disturbing; he reacts to them by distancing himself through lending them humorous or ironic names.

One characteristic of metaphors and metonymies is their ambiguity: they connote more than just their surface meaning. Although the narrator uses the word *Apotheker* derogatorily, the word also has positive connotations. *Apotheker* play a necessary role in society, providing medicine for the ill. This implies that Western Germans (and certainly some Eastern Germans saw them this way, too) view themselves as the "cure" for the problems inherited from the socialist GDR. They are not doctors, i.e. not qualified to diagnose the illness; however, they are the intermediaries who provide a potentially curative medicine, in this case, a stable and powerful Western German economy and currency. The word *Apotheker* conjures up the image of a well-respected, self-confident, older man: a metaphor for what Western Germany, a successful state with experience in capitalism, represents for the GDR, the "sick patient" who needs to be cured.

The narrator also compares Western German men to Goethe. In doing so, he turns Goethe's image as a classical, canonical authority figure upside down, using him as ammunition to fuel his critique of Western Germans. Initially, as he walks, the narrator imagines he is Goethe: "Im Gehen zu denken, Goethe zu sein, brachte mich leidlich voran" (45), until he begins to tire.[36] Then he recalls Goethe's disdain for revolutionaries and freedom fighters and reconsiders: "Ach, war dieser Johann Wolfgang nicht das Urbild eines Großapothekers?"

34 "chrome ships"; "so-called Trabants, that also had bumpers and a hood so that, with that symbol of technology, the entire contraption's frailty galloped rattling along."

35 "The sudden appearance of Eastern German pharmacists complicated my worldview even further."

36 "To think while walking, to [pretend to] be Goethe helped me get along reasonably well."

(50)[37] With this rhetorical question, the narrator refers to Goethe's bourgeois conservatism, which he at this point connects with that of Western Germans. The more the narrator wanders and ponders, the more Goethe and the Western German *Apotheker* seem to have in common. By Chapter 16, they have blended into one single, hilarious, critical image: the Western German Mercedes driver. Because the Western German Apotheker-Goethe proceeds to drive past the narrator, not stopping to interact with him, the narrator perceives this as Western German arrogance and unwillingness to confront the Eastern German point of view. Figures of speech and images such as this one identify Rosenlöcher's text as the most critical of the three regarding Western German activities in Eastern Germany after the revolution.

Sparschuh also manipulates language in characterizing Hinrich Lobek. Not only does Lobek possess the communication barrier mentioned above, in order to compensate for it, he keeps a *Protokollbuch*, resembling a combination of both a personal diary and a Stasi report. The disjointed, paranoid language he uses reflects his own, depressed and detached self. In his protocol book, he calls his wife Julia "Observationsobjekt J." and, when she accuses him of spying on her, contradicts himself by writing: "Infame Vorwürfe!—Julia, sehr erregt (das entschuldigt aber nichts), behauptet heute: ich würde ihr nachspionieren und—wörtlich!—'in einem Protokollbuch' (!!!) jeden ihrer Schritte verzeichnen" (18).[38] Toward the novel's end, his speechlessness becomes acute: "Im Radio kam mein Lieblingslied, ein englisches: words are very unnecessary [. . .] In den Tagen seit ich wieder zu Hause saß, hatten sich die wenigen Wörter, mit denen ich meine letzten Vorweihnachtsverkaufsgespräche bestritten hatte, verloren. Sie waren verschwunden. Sie hatten wahrscheinlich ihren wohlverdienten Urlaub angetreten" (143).[39] Here, Lobek has become so alienated from spoken words, they appear to have taken on a life of their own, leaving him in silence.

Finally, scatological and sexual elements spice up and colloquialize these narratives. In *Der Zimmerspringbrunnen* and *Schlehweins Giraffe* the dog and the giraffe require constant care and clean-up. The narrator in *Schlehweins Giraffe* has bizarre sexual affairs with his (ex-)wife; his intense guilt about having had sexual relations alternately with her and his friend Bröckle's wife appears comically trivial within the context of larger world events. Hinrich Lobek, believing he is selling an indoor fountain to a physiotherapist,

---

37 "Boy, wasn't this Johann Wolfgang just the prototype of a big-time pharmacist?"

38 "Observation object J." "Outrageous reproaches!—Julia, very excited (that doesn't excuse anything), claims today: I am spying on her and—literally!—'in a protocol book' (!!!) am recording her every move."

39 "My favorite song came on the radio, an English one: words are very unnecessary [. . .] In the days since I was sitting at home again the few words with which I had conducted my pre-Christmas sales pitches had gotten lost. They disappeared. They probably went off on a well-earned vacation."

unwittingly winds up under the whip of Manuela the sado-masochist. In the course of his hike, Rosenlöcher's author, caught skinny-dipping in a creek, is accused of being a pervert, tries later unsuccessfully to use a vibrating, talking outhouse from which five people eventually exit, and mistakes a bird for a feces pile—until it flies away. These grotesque elements appear funny because they draw attention to the physicality of the narrators and their world, contrasting with the "higher," seemingly more important issues unificaton produced and lending these works a touch of the Rabelaisian carnivalesque.[40]

IV. Conclusion

Rosenlöcher, Schirmer and Sparschuh not only chronicle the events following German unification, they also offer commentary on these events through their humorous and satirical approaches. Using these modes in a fictional context, all three authors distance themselves from actual events, creating a Brechtian-like alienated space to reflect upon problems and conflicts created by unification. Their unusual texts play with, and thus break down, stereotypes about Eastern Germans both before and after Germany was united without assuming a plaintive or moralizing tone.

Satire theorists such as Helmut Arntzen have pointed out that there is often a utopia implied behind satire's extreme critiques. These three authors' concepts of utopia have shifted after unification. Whereas in socialism utopian hopes and visions were expected to be fulfilled by an improved societal order, these authors' narrators look to the private sphere—specifically, their (ex-) wives—as their source of happiness. In an interview conducted with Bernd Schirmer in Berlin on 15 June 1999, I asked him whether a humorous or satirical treatment may have helped his readers to deal with the time following unification. He replied:

> Das auf alle Fälle. Also das habe ich bei Lesungen gemerkt oder bei Briefen, die mir geschrieben worden sind. Das ist doch für manche sehr heilsam gewesen. Sie sind einfach dadurch mit manchen Dingen leichter fertig geworden, indem sie gemerkt haben, es geht nicht nur ihnen so. Und ihr Schicksal ist wert genug gewesen, literarisch behandelt zu werden. Das ist im Osten so gewesen. Und im Westen war es eigentlich ein Stück Aufklärung, ein gewisses Aha-Erlebnis, würde ich sagen: also *so* larmoyant und verbiestert sind die im Osten ja gar nicht. Die

40 Bergson writes: "Any incident is comic that calls attention to the physical in a person, when it is the moral side that is concerned" (93).

können sogar über sich selber lachen. Das war eigentlich sehr wichtig. (Twark, "Larmoyant" 41)[41]

Schirmer's, Rosenlöcher's and Sparschuh's humorous/satirical writings encourage the reader to identify with their protagonists, helping Eastern Germans to come to terms with their individual circumstances, as well as increasing the outsider's appreciation for and understanding of these. The authors' colorful descriptions definitely add a unique, creative twist to the giraffe-high pile of post-unification literature.

Works Cited

Arntzen, Helmut. *Satire in der deutschen Literatur: Geschichte und Theorie.* Darmstadt: Wissenschaftliche Buchgesellschaft, 1989.

Bergson, Henri. *Laughter.* Garden City, New York: Doubleday, 1956.

Bogel, Fredric V. "The Difference Satire Makes: Reading Swift's Poems." *Theorizing Satire: Essays in Literary Criticism.* Eds. Brian A. Connery and Kirk Combe. New York: St. Martin's Press, 1995. 43-53.

Born, Sabrina. "Frei sein wollen und frei sein können: Die Wende und ihre Folgen in der deutschen Erzählliteratur." Magisterarbeit Freie Universität Berlin, 1997.

Cosentino, Christine. "Scherz, Satire und Ironie in der ostdeutschen Literatur der neunziger Jahre." *Journal of English and Germanic Philology* 10(1998): 467-487.

Emmerich, Wolfgang. *Kleine Literaturgeschichte der DDR.* 2nd rev. ed. Leipzig: Kiepenheuer, 1996.

Ertl, Wolfgang. "'Denn die Mühen der Ebene lagen hinter uns und vor uns die Mühen der Berge': Thomas Rosenlöchers diaristische Prosa zum Ende der DDR." *Literatur und politische Aktualität.* Eds. Elrud Ibsch and Ferdinand von Ingen. Amsterdam: Rodopi, 1993. 21-37.

Freud, Sigmund. *Der Witz und seine Beziehung zum Unbewußten.* Frankfurt a. M.: Fischer, 1961.

Grauert, Wilfried. "Harzreise im Sommer (mit Heine im Herzen) oder Auf der Suche nach einer neuen (Autor-) Identität." *Weimarer Beiträge* 1 (1994): 103-119.

Hartinger, Walfried. "Texte nach der Wende: Versuch eines Überblicks." *Berliner LeseZeichen.* 6+7 (1995): 46-76.

Jauss, Hans Robert. "Über den Grund des Vergnügens am komischen Helden." Preisendanz and Warning. 103-132.

Kant, Immanuel. "Kritik der Urteilskraft," *Werke in sechs Bänden.* Vol. 5. Ed. Wilhelm Weischedel. Wiesbaden: Insel-Verlag, 1957.

41 "This [is true] in any case. I noticed this at readings or in letters written to me. It was really curative for some people. They could deal with some things more easily knowing that they were not alone. And their fate was important enough to be treated in literary form. In the East it was like this. In the West it was actually a bit of Enlightenment, an 'aha' experience, I would say: well, I guess those Easterners are not *that* plaintive and crotchety after all. They can even laugh about themselves. That was really very important."

Preisendanz, Wolfgang and Rainer Warning, eds. *Das Komische*. München: Fink, 1976.
Preisendanz, Wolfgang. "Zum Vorrang des Komischen bei der Darstellung von Geschichtserfahrung in deutschen Romanen unserer Zeit." Preisendanz and Warning. 153-164.
Rosenlöcher, Thomas. *Ich lag im Garten bei Kleinschachwitz*. Halle: Mitteldeutscher Verlag, 1982.
---. *Schneebier*. Halle: Mitteldeutscher Verlag, 1988.
---. *Ich sitze in Sachsen und schau in den Schnee*. Frankfurt a. M.: Suhrkamp, 1999.
---. *Die verkauften Pflastersteine. Dresdner Tagebuch*. Frankfurt a. M.: Suhrkamp, 1990.
---. *Die Wiederentdeckung des Gehens beim Wandern*. Frankfurt a. M.: Suhrkamp, 1991.
Sadowski-Smith, Claudia. "*Ostalgie*: Revaluing the Past, Regressing into the Future." *GDR Bulletin*. 25 (Spring 1998): 1-6.
Schirmer, Bernd. *Schlehweins Giraffe*. Frankfurt a. M.: Fischer, 1994.
Sparschuh, Jens. *Der Zimmerspringbrunnen*. Köln: Kiepenheuer & Witsch, 1995.
Twark, Jill. "So larmoyant sind sie im Osten gar nicht: Gespräch mit Bernd Schirmer." *GDR Bulletin* 26 (1999): 39-44.
---. "Mathias Wedel and Matthias Biskupek: Two Satirists 'im Wandel der Wende'," *glossen* 10 (2000). <http://www.dickinson.edu/departments/germn/glossen/heft10 /twark. html>.

GERALD A. FETZ

Theatrical Confrontations with the *Wende* and Post-Unification Germany: Strauß, Pohl, and Hein

I. Introduction

In the preface to his book *Deutsche Einheit als Herausforderung* (1990), the historian Christian Meier wrote:

> *Wahnsinn!* War in den Wochen des Umsturzes im Herbst 1989 wohl der häufigste, der kennzeichnendste Kurzkommentar zu dem, was in der DDR geschah und erlebt wurde. *Angst* scheint inzwischen längst zum zentralen Bestandteil der Zustandsbeschreibung der Deutschen Ost—aber wohl nicht nur ihrer—geworden zu sein. *Fremdheit* könnte sehr bald das wichtigste Stichwort zum mentalen Befund des Zusammenwachsens der beiden deutschen Staaten werden. (9)[1]

Four years later, Wolfgang Hardtwig and Heinrich August Winkler, in their *Deutsche Befremdung. Zum Befinden in Ost und West* (1994), reached a similar conclusion, based now on longer and more substantial observations of real developments, regarding the estrangement between Germans East and West in their now officially "unified" Germany:

> Der deutschen Vereinigung folgt [. . .] erst einmal eine neue deutsche Entfremdung. In den vergangenen vier Jahren hat sich gezeigt, daß die politische und rechtliche Einigung jene Trennung der Deutschen nicht kurzfristig aufheben konnte, die in den viereinhalb Jahrzehnten seit 1945 entstanden war. Die Spannungen und Krisen, die der so abrupt und unvorbereitet über die Nation hereingebrochene Vereinigungsprozeß mit sich bringt, legt vielmehr erst mit aller Deutlichkeit die tiefgehenden Unterschiede der Mentalitäten, Verhaltens- und Denkweisen in Ost und West frei. (7)[2]

---

1 Unless otherwise indicated, all translations are my own. "*Absolutely insane!* During the weeks of upheaval in the fall of 1989, that was the most frequent and most telling short commentary on what was happening and being experienced in the GDR. *Anxiety*, in the meantime, appears to have long become central to any description of the situation in eastern Germany—but not only there. *Strangeness* (or *alienation*) could very well soon become the most important descriptor of the mental condition of the process of growing together of the two German states."

2 "Following German unification has developed, for the present, a new German alienation (or estrangement). The last four years have demonstrated that the political and legal unification could not eliminate in the short term the division of Germany, which had developed in the four and one-

The scenes of euphoric joy and German-German togetherness which were at the center of virtually every eye-witness and journalistic report of 9 November 1989 and the next few days, even weeks, were apparently too good to last. In stark contrast, disturbing but undeniable signs of mutual distrust, ignorance, resentment, and other indications of estrangement "in the family" quickly became evident. By the time the official political unification of Germany took place in October 1990, there were more than a few voices who seriously questioned the validity of Willy Brandt's by-then famous assertion that "jetzt wächst zusammen, was zusammengehört."[3] Did (or do) Germany East and West really belong together after all? Even today, more than ten years later, one need only pick up one of dozens of German newspapers, journals, and magazines to realize that this question still looms large in the minds and hearts of many Germans and that unanimity about a positive answer to that question remains elusive.

Needless to say, many Germans have been busy during this past decade trying to explain why the estrangement continues to exist, why the Germans, now united politically, appear to be a rather dysfunctional family. The West Germans have, with some resentment, pumped billions of Marks into the reconstruction and modernization of the "new federal states," as they have come to be called. Anyone who has traveled through the former GDR in the past five or six years has had to recognize that at least this aspect of unification, "die äußere Einheit" ("external unity"), has progressed in most places amazingly fast. But the other side of unification, "die innere Einheit" ("internal unity") according to most observers and contrary to the rosy predictions frequently heard in late 1989 and 1990, is obviously going to take years, perhaps decades and generations, to achieve.[4] There is no simple explanation for this slow, sometimes imperceptible progress toward "innere Einheit," but the forty plus years—of living caught up in the antagonistic black and white thinking of the Cold War; of living in two political and social systems that were based on almost diametrically opposed assumptions and required profoundly different behavior patterns to attain success; of living in two societies that offered their respective citizens very different opportunities and

---

half decades since 1945. The tensions and crises, which the process of unification so abruptly and unexpectedly has brought to the nation, expose with far greater clarity the deep-seated differences in mentality as well as in behavior and thought patterns in East and West."

3 As reported, for instance, in *Der Spiegel* (25. December 1989) and cited frequently thereafter. "now that which belongs together is growing together."

4 Henning Ritter expressed this assessment in representative fashion: "Allenfalls wird man einräumen, dass die *äussere* Einheit— Privatisierung der Wirtschaft, Sanierung der Infrastruktur, Aufbau von Justiz und Verwaltung—zum Abschluss gekommen sei. Aber bis zur Herstellung, oder, wie es vornehm heisst, zur "Vollendung" der *inneren* Einheit, werde es noch Jahre, wenn nicht Jahrzehnte dauern." ("In any case, one will admit that the *external* unity—privatization of the economy, rebuilding the infrastructure, establishment of judicial and administrative entities—has been completed. But years, if not decades, will still be required before the bringing about or, as it is elegantly called, 'completion' of the *inner* unity.")

challenges; and of living in two cultures that propagated stereotypical images and unflattering distortions of the other—has clearly left its profound mark. This is a legacy, which, at best, will provide all Germans, East and West, with an abundance of challenges to work on for some time to come.

Although such prophetic visions were very few and far between at the time, Peter Schneider anticipated very accurately this difficult post-euphoria German-German condition in his novella, *Der Mauerspringer* (1982), a work in which his autobiographical protagonist tried to reach an understanding of why he, from the West, and his girlfriend Lena and other friends from the East eventually and inevitably confronted a *wall*, his now famous "Mauer im Kopf" in their relationships with one another. Some of his observations from 1982 provide indisputable insight into the various inabilities of Germans East and West to understand and empathize with each other still today. About his girlfriend Lena, for instance, we can read:

> Der Westen war ihr ein Knäuel von Widersprüchen, Halbheiten, leeren Versprechungen, ein anderer Erdteil, nur von Oberflächenhitze erwärmt, darunter ewiges Eis. Beziehungen wurden angeknüpft, um sie gleich wieder aufzugeben, Namen erfragt, um sie morgen schon zu vergessen. (83)[5]

Further, the narrator/protagonist asks himself what would happen if both German governments took a year off, went on vacation, if:

> [. . .] die Nachrichtensprecher und Kommentatoren ein Jahr lang schwiegen, die Grenzposten sich ein Jahr lang an der Adria und am Schwarzen Meer erholten und die Regierten anfingen, in Ost-West-Verhandlungen einzutreten [. . .] Sie würden—nach einer kurzen Umarmung—herausfinden, daß sie ihren Regierungen viel ähnlicher sind, als sie vielleicht hofften. (62)[6]

Finally, in the most famous line from the novella, the narrator asserts: "Die Mauer im Kopf einzureißen wird länger dauern, als irgendein Abrißunternehmen für die sichtbare Mauer braucht" (102).[7]

Schneider's prescience has clearly been born out by the developments in Germany over the past decade. Several critics have supplied insightful discussions of how many German writers, from both East and West, in poetry, prose, and

5 "For her the West was a tangle of contradictions, half-hearted gestures, and empty promises; another continent, eternal ice beneath a superficial warmth. Acquaintances were made only to be broken off; names exchanged to be forgotten the next day[. . .]" (99). Please note that all English translations of *Der Mauerspringer* are taken from *The Wall Jumper*.

6 "the journalists fell silent for a year; if the border police took a year to recuperate on the Adriatic and the Black Sea, and the people started their own East-West negotiations? After a brief embrace, they would discover that they resemble their governments much more closely than they care to admit" (72).

7 "It will take us longer to tear down the Wall in our heads than any wrecking company will need for the Wall we can see" (119).

drama, have reflected upon and struggled with all kinds of "walls in the head" and other forms of estrangement in this new and still mystifying "gesamtdeutscher Realität" ("unified German reality").[8] Other contributors to this collection of essays focus on various aspects of this new and challenging reality as it is dealt with in prose and film, for instance, but I will concentrate here on some of the ways in which dramatists, mostly from the West, have confronted the post-*Wende* German-German tensions and "unified German reality" in their works for the stage. Since there is a long and rather revered tradition in Germany of the theater being an "öffentliche Anstalt" ("public institution"), well-suited to and inclined to take up with political and social issues, it should be no surprise that numerous contemporary playwrights have tackled these current issues as well. Their plays, "Wendestücke," as they have been dubbed by at least one critic (Schalk), offer ample proof that the "Zeitstück" ("the contemporary political play") is still very much alive and thriving in Germany.[9]

Already in 1990 two plays were written and performed in the West that took up with post-*Wende* Germany: Herbert Achternbusch's *Auf verlorenem Posten* and Manfred Karge's *MauerStücke.* Written in haste, neither represents terribly good theater or presents sophisticated dramatic insights into the new German situation, but each of them introduces themes and critical attitudes, which will be expanded upon by other playwrights who follow them.[10] Achternbusch's play, written only a few weeks after the fall of the Berlin Wall and first performed in April 1990 in Munich, utilizes a loose structure and techniques learned from the Theater of the Absurd to underscore what he evidently saw as the rather bizarre nature of the sudden end to the division of Germany. Subtitled a "Revolutionsfarce," Achternbusch's play "cuts down to size a historic process stripped of its monumental jubilations and ceremonies" (Schalk 293) and lets his "liberated" East German "hero" stumble in a very confused state into the West, where he is drawn in typical German fashion to Italy, the "meeting place of the most banal of package-tourists" (293). Achternbusch's play is the first of many to assert that consumerism and capitalism, rather than political idealism or desire for higher freedoms, would prove stronger. "Wir sind das Volk." ("We are the people!") is shown to be a mere fleeting fancy; identity, if it exists at all, has to be found in more mundane ways. All signs of a renewed German national pride are

---

8 Among these critics, I would single out Brockmann (1994), Cosentino (1994, 1996), Ott (1991), Richard (1999), Sieg (1993), and Wehdeking (1995).

9 Other plays that deal with this topic include Elfriede Müller's *Goldener Oktober* (1991) Franz Xaver Kroetz' *Ich bin das Volk* (1994), Gundi Ellert's *Jagdzeit* (1994), the stage version of Thomas Brussig's highly regarded novel *Helden wie wir* (premiered in 1996), certainly the several relevant plays by Volker Braun, including: *Die Übergangsgesellschaft* (1988), *Böhmen am Meer* (1992), *Iphigenie in Freiheit* (1992), and *Der Wendehals* (1995), as well as Einar Schleef's trilogy, *Totentrompeten 1* (1995), *Drei Alte tanzen Tango* (1997), and *Deutsche Sprache schwere Sprache* (2000).

10 Keith Bullivant rightly sees Achternbusch"s play as setting "the tone for later dramatic works" (120).

shown to be grotesque and even frightening. Manfred Karge takes a similar point of view in his fragmentary *MauerStücke* where he also draws grotesque scenes to subvert and critique the still (at that time) prevalent mood of national euphoria mentioned above. Karge focuses attention on the phenomenon of the "Wendehals," the opportunistic East German who suddenly re-invents himself by doing a complete about-façe in order to take advantage of the new situation.[11] Karge also suggests how dangerous any revival of German nationalism would be, and he anticipates some of the tensions between "Ossis" and "Wessis" as Peter Schneider had done so accurately almost a decade earlier. Developments subsequent to November 1989 and to German unification less than a year later in October 1990, of course, would demonstrate how justified such prognoses were. A final noteworthy theatrical attempt to confront the profoundly unexpected new situation in Germany, also in 1990, was the Grips-Theater's *Auf der Mauer, auf der Lauer* which portrayed a German family, separated by the Wall somewhat earlier when the father fled to the West, suddenly caught between two worlds that refused to come together. Benjamin Henrichs underscored the play's description of the dilemma when he said about it: "Für die Deutschen-Ost ist Deutschland-West das Schlaraffenland des Konsums, nichts sonst. Für die Deutschen-West ist Deutschland-Ost eine einzige graue Wüste, nichts sonst."[12] Even though the production avoided an overly pessimistic conclusion, such views definitely pointed in the direction of the serious misunderstandings that constitute Schneiders "Mauer im Kopf."

II: Botho Strauß

It was Botho Strauß's enigmatic play from 1991, *Schlußchor*, however, that represented the first significant and widely discussed drama to confront questions and fears from post-Wall Germany. For some two decades, Strauß had been a veritable darling of countless German theater directors and critics. In 1993, two years after this play's première, Strauß ignited a cultural-political storm with the publication of his essay "Anschwellender Bockgesang." Written in a somewhat impenetrable style, the essay was nonetheless understood by many as an apology for reactionary and nationalistic, even xenophobic, sentiments. To what extent that was true, still remains unclear, but the perception that Strauß took a marked right turn politically has led certain left-leaning journalists and theater directors to shun him ever since. With *Schlußchor*, though, Strauß appeared just as perplexed and

11 Volker Braun later wrote a play titled *Der Wendehals oder Trotzdestonichts* (1995), in which he, too, took such "about-face" behavior to task, behavior that has been described as all-too-frequent among many formerly "committed" East German socialists.

12 "For the Germans-East, Germany-West is the paradise of shopping, nothing else. For the Germans-West, Germany-East is a total gray emptiness, nothing else."

just as skeptical toward the possible ramifications of the *Wende* as many artistic and intellectual colleagues on the left. Theater reviewers at the time, and many critics subsequently, found the play intriguing and meritorious.[13]

Schlußchor, a play in three only very loosely connected acts, combines highly stylized, surrealistic elements with concentrated, symbolic portrayals and (partially) discernible mythical figures, suggesting that there were obviously deep meanings and hidden problems in the very unexpected fall of the Berlin Wall, but also that one would be hard put to decipher exactly what all or even most of them might be. The first act exposes what is perhaps intended to be a group of representative West Germans on the eve of that momentous 9 November 1989, a group distinguished only by the gender and position in the group photo session in which they are engaged: "mann1" (M1) or "frau1" (F1), for instance. The stage directions to this act read as follows: "eine Schar von fünfzehn Frauen und Männern in vier Stufenreihen zum Gruppenfoto aufgestellt. Im Vordergrund der Fotograf, der drei Kameras...bedient." (9)[14] Not free to move much, the nameless figures toss sentence, thought, and conversation fragments at one another, but it is never clear who the intended addressee might be. Also uncertain is who in the group belongs with whom, if with anyone, or even what kind of group it is. At one point, after they have apparently beaten the photographer to death in a kind of mindless mob anger, seemingly born of impatience and frustration with his slowness, they suggest to a woman who has casually wandered by and whom they now ask to take their picture:

> M9: Wir sind ein kleines Betriebsjubiläum.
> F10: Wir sind ein kleiner Ausflug des Historischen Seminars.
> M3: Wir sind ein kleines Klassentreffen [. . .]
> Alle sanft: Wir sind der Chor [. . .] (30)[15]

Through these characters' conversation fragments, the reader or viewer is left with the unavoidable impression that these are superficial, vain, sometimes hate-filled individuals, egocentrically concerned only with themselves and thus unable to experience anything beyond very superficial relationships and feigned emotions. One figure, for instance, "F10," tells another: "ich kann diese Leute um uns nicht mehr ertragen. Häßlich sind sie und riechen sehr schlecht." (30)[16] But the most perplexing "high" point of the scene occurs when one of them suddenly yells out, totally without context, "Deutschland!" (15).

---

13 See, for instance, Richard, where he terms *Schlußchor* "das zentrale 'Vereinigungsdrama' der Deutschen" (7). ("the central 'unification drama' for the Germans.")

14 "a group of fifteen women and men in four bleacher-like rows, gathered for a group photo. In the foreground the photographer who is using three cameras."

15 "M9: We are a company anniversary party/ F10: We are a small excursion of the History Department/M3: We are a small class reunion/ All, softly: We are the choir [. . .]"

16 "I can't stand these people any longer. They're ugly and they smell terrible."

The second act is no less bizarre as it deals with the unexpected ramifications of an architect's unintentional intrusion on his female client as she, completely naked, is drying herself after a shower. Their subsequent attempts to discuss the blueprints, which he brought with him, are disrupted by this inadvertent happening. The second scene in this act takes place later at a social function in a villa, somewhere: the (formerly naked) client, now fully dressed, has apparently taken up with the Swedish competitor of the first architect. The latter, lovesick by now, waits in the entryway, talking alternately to himself, the mirror, and a series of strange passers-through, hoping all the while that she will pay him some attention. Finally, but not before "the Caller" ("der Rufer") enters and cries out—"Deutschland!"—, he discovers a pistol in a coat he puts on by mistake and shoots himself. Just before this happens, one hears a male voice from the social gathering in the next room, perhaps that of the Swede, assert: "also mich reißt es jedes Mal vom Sessel, wenn ich höre, was euch dies neue Deutschland kosten soll" (66).[17]

In the final act, the comings and goings of "the Caller" with his cries of "Deutschland!" increase, and there are now direct references to the fact that outside of the café where the scene is set, the Berlin Wall is falling: it is 9 November 1989. Here, too, as in the first two acts, the people who gradually fill the café can not seem to communicate with one another. Their conversations are all fragmentary and constantly interrupted, their attention distracted by someone or something else. "The Caller" enters with a young GDR couple, fresh from "drüben" (East Berlin), having just come West, like many others that evening for the first time, through the astonishing opening in the Wall. This "Caller," at least, appears euphoric as he adds to his "Deutschland" refrain the words: "das ist Geschichte, sag ich, hier und heute, sage ich, Walmy, sage ich, Goethe! Und diesmal sind wir dabei gewesen. Die Grenzen sind geöffnet! Die Mauer bricht! Der Osten [. . .] der Osten ist frei!" (86)[18]

All but two of the guests in the café follow him out into the street, but they seem to do so as if they were going out to see an accident or a building on fire. The historic magnitude, the historic significance of what is happening is completely lost on them. Anita, the rather bizarre daughter of one of the aristocratic officers who participated in the failed assassination attempt on Hitler in 1944 and was subsequently executed by the SS himself, flirts and argues with Patrick, the only other café guest who stays behind when the others exit to the streets. Patrick is a left-leaning history student who is critical of the "monarchist" act of resistance to Hitler of which Anita is so proud. His remarks provoke her, and she hits him, bites him, and, when she screams "Schwein" at him, he disappears just as the set transforms itself into a surrealistic park with a giant birdcage. Beethoven's "Schlußchor" to the Ninth Symphony is heard in the

17 "it makes me leap from my chair every time I hear how much this new Germany is going to cost you."

18 "This is history, I declare, here and now, I tell you, Walmy. Goethe, I say! And this time we've been present for it. The borders are open! The wall is crumbling. The East [. . .] the East is free."

background. This final scene displays a giant eagle (*Adler*) in the cage, a golden eagle of mythical proportions, either drugged or in a long, dark sleep. Anita talks to the feathered giant, cajoles him, and then insults the sleeping eagle: "kastrierte Chimäre! Wo ist dein Doppelbild? Schlappes Wappen! Erstarrte Ankunft! [. . .] du halbherziger, halbkröpfiger Greif!" (86)[19] She proceeds to cut open the cage, the "Adler" slowly gains consciousness, and there follows what appears to be an erotic battle between the two. Out of the dark, Anita emerges in a pile of feathers, bloody and all scratched up, but holding up a cut-off talon. The play ends with her calling out rather inexplicably: "Wald ... Wald ... Wald ... Wald" (98).[20]

Strauß's play is hermeneutically dense and difficult, to be sure, but there are some themes that become more intelligible after multiple viewings or readings. The West Germans one observes are caught up in trivial, sometimes mean and generally meaningless lives, and they are clearly incapable, with the exception of "the Caller," of grasping the significance of, let alone feeling genuine emotions about, the sudden turn of events in Germany. Even the "Caller" must be accused of succumbing to disturbing nationalistic pathos in his particular kind of euphoria. The East Germans, the innocent young couple in the West for the first time, are visibly baffled and out of place in this jaded, estranged setting. Resembling country bumpkins in the city for the first time, they even apologize to the motley group of café guests: "verzeihen Sie, wenn wir in unserem Benehmen etwas falsch machen" (86).[21] They are perhaps the only sympathetic figures in the entire play. The cry of "Deutschland," repeated throughout, seems equally out of context and place, and it has a jarring effect both on the figures in the play and the audience. One has been terribly unaccustomed since 1945, except perhaps in the context of soccer matches in which the German National Team is playing perhaps, to hear that word shouted with any enthusiasm. The mythical eagle, of course, suggests not too opaquely, a sleeping and very disoriented Germany that is being awakened. But Strauß, despite the ambiguous battle between the giant bird and the politically conservative (but hardly neo-Nazi) Anita, leaves all conclusions open: whether the rebirth and struggle are to be viewed with joy or concern, "Freude" or "Bedauern," as one critic has expressed it, is anything but clear. Anita, after all, is a strange and rather frightening figure, anachronistic in her political views and disconnected to life and contemporary reality. And her monarchism and emotional defense of earlier symbols and notions about a heroic Germany, at least heroic Germans, are convincingly refuted by the history student Patrick who relegates them to the distant past: "zu ihrer Zeit, vor der Zeit" (151).[22]

19 "castrated chimera! Where is your twin? You symbol gone soft! Calcified youth. You half-hearted, half-goitered griffin!"

20 "Forest ... forest ... forest ... forest."

21 "Excuse us, if we don't behave correctly."

22 "in their time, before time."

III: Klaus Pohl

The German playwright who has addressed the post-*Wende* and post-unification situation in his works most prolifically is Klaus Pohl. With differing dramatic strategies and styles as well as with varying perspectives and subject focus, Pohl has treated this current German "condition" in three plays: *Karate-Billi kehrt zurück* and *Die schöne Fremde*, both initially published and performed in 1991, and *Wartesaal Deutschland StimmenReich* from 1995. The first play, *Karate-Billi*, is set in a small East German town shortly after the surprising and abrupt end of the GDR, and focuses on the dislocations which those swift changes brought with them. The second piece, *Die schöne Fremde*, also set shortly after the *Wende* in a small German town, this one in the West, concentrates on the prejudices and latent, as well as not-so-latent, racist, xenophobic, and neo-Nazi attitudes which infect even citizens regarded as upstanding and come to the fore especially when they have or have had too much to drink. The third and later play, *Wartesaal Deutschland*, grew out of a *Spiegel*-project, which Pohl undertook that resulted in a three-part series in that magazine in August 1994 under the title "Planet Germany." For the play, Pohl used some of the interviews he had conducted and observations he had made on his travels throughout Germany, East and West, selected, concentrated, and reworked them for the stage. The play consists of 32 monologues delivered by a wide range of Germans from both parts of the newly unified but still very disparate country, but those 32 scenes were subsequently reduced to 20 for the premiere which Pohl directed himself in Berlin.

Karate-Billi kehrt zurück, a play in three acts and numerous scenes, concentrates microcosmically on a small East German town following the *Wende.* Most of the townspeople portrayed—the mayor and his wife, the pastor, a physician, a railway employee, and others—are intent on "revising" their pasts in order to adapt to the new situation and benefit maximally from it. Typical for this kind of citizen in the town (and, by implication, in the GDR in general) is the railway worker Waldemar Urban, who asserts at the outset: "Wir wußten ja nichts, wir wußten ja nicht, was da wirklich geht vor [. . .] Wir waren alle ahnungslos. [. . .] Und wenn du sagtest mal was, hieß es gleich: halt die Schnauze!" (9).[23] The "judgement" such assertions are seeking is clear: No complicity in any wrongdoings, no responsibility for anything negative that happened in the GDR. In fact, speaking for all of his fellow townspeople, even though none of them had contributed to bringing about the end of the GDR, the physician Ücker exclaims: "Trinken wir auf unsere Revolution!" And the pastor responds: "Jawohl, Franz. Auf die Revolution!" (30).[24]

---

23 "We knew nothing, we simply didn't know what was really happening [. . .] we were all without a clue... and if anyone said anything, then we heard immediately: shut up!"

24 "Let's drink to our revolution!" "Absolutely, Franz. To the revolution!"

Unfortunately for these revisionists and opportunists (*Wendehälse*), they are hindered from getting away with their hypocritical claims by Karate-Billi, a former star decathlete who was arrested years earlier, shortly before he was to participate in the Olympics, on trumped up charges of planned "Republikflucht" ("fleeing the republic"). He was subsequently incarcerated for 13 long years in the so-called "Irren-Villa" ("villa for the insane") in the town. Billi has now been "freed" from the sanatorium where his somewhat unnaturally devoted older sister, a psychologist, has been his caretaker for all of those years. Even though his mental state is, for good reason given what he has endured in the "Villa," somewhat precarious, he demands, first slowly and then with abandon, a confrontation with the truth behind his arrest and incarceration. The representative townspeople mentioned above initially think they can simply celebrate Billi's "liberation"—Ücker: "Wir trinken auf den befreiten Sohn der Revolution! Prost!" (27)[25]—, but gradually they are forced to try to make excuses and justify their purportedly benign actions and inactions. The railway worker Urban puts forward the all-too-familiar claim from after both 1945 and 1989: "Billi. Wir sind alle beschissen und betrogen worden. Und trotzdem. Ich will mich nicht mit dir vergleichen. Ich habe auf der anderen Seite gestanden. Aber ich bin immer anständig geblieben [. . .] Ich habe nur gewissenhaft durchgeführt, was die Gesetze verlangt haben" (59).[26] Not satisfied with such (traditional) self-justifications, however, Billi pushes further, and it becomes clear that, with a few exceptions, he is surrounded by former *Stasi-Spitzel* (snitches) and that it was even townspeople who, for no reason other than envy, had framed him and caused his downfall and arrest. Billi has now exposed them and gained some justice, at least. Or has he? The play ends after the "upright" citizens, pushed into a corner of potentially damaging truth by Billi, have summoned the police and the guards from the "villa." There is little doubt that they will return him to the asylum and thereby restore the new "order" of this post-*Wende* East German town. Those who can "revise" their not-so-clean pasts and "adapt" swiftly to the new situation and opportunities will apparently thrive. Those who cannot, or are audacious enough to seek truth and justice, might not fare so well, even in the German "Rechtsstaat" (state based on law) at least if Billi's fate is in any way exemplary.

Lest one think that the West German dramatist, actor, and director Klaus Pohl was taking a one-sided, myopic and self-righteous "Besser-Wessi" cheap shot at East Germany with this play, one needs only look at *Die schöne Fremde* from the same year, 1991. Here, Pohl turns his attention to Bebra, a West German "border" town, and it is quickly evident that he has ample criticism for his fellow "Wessis" as well. The *Stammtisch*-attitudes which Pohl has his figures display here are different only in kind from those of the East Germans shown in *Karate-Billi*: these

25 "Let's drink to the liberated son of the revolution! Cheers!"

26 "Billi. We were all crapped on and deceived. But nonetheless. I don't want to compare myself with you. I stood on the other side. But I was always decent, correct [. . .] I merely carried out conscientiously what the law required."

"solid" middle-class citizens, mostly men, are coarse, bigoted, self-important, and lewd. These detestable characteristics are heightened here, too, by the consumption of too much alcohol. One of the men, Ulrich Maul, entrepreneur and dog-breeder (German shepherds, of course), can be viewed as the mouthpiece for those who hold such views, whether they only mutter them in private or declare them boldly at the *Stammtisch*:

> Ulrich: Der Mittelstand! Du Drahtbürste! Das freie Unternehmertum! *Er rülpst.* Wir haben mit unserem Geld wie das Land noch geteilt war die Zonenrandförderung bezahlt! Und jetzt zahlen wir die Sozialhilfen für das Asylantenpack! Und jetzt ist der Scheißkommunismus am Ende und wir bezahlen die Leiche mit unserem Geld, daß die wieder auf die Füße kommt. (94)[27]

The play, constructed in five acts, is set in all but one act in the lobby and *Stube* of a small hotel in the provincial town of Bebra. A fierce winter storm has caused a train derailment outside of town, and one of the passengers, an attractive, young Jewish-American woman of German-Jewish origin—*die schöne Fremde*—and a young Polish man who has given her a ride to the hotel serve as the catalysts for the unfolding story. When the proprietress of the hotel shows the young woman to her room, she happens to see some fancy undergarments in her suitcase. Back in the *Stube* where several local men are drinking (one of them is also physically and verbally abusing his silent wife), the proprietress mentions what she has seen in the suitcase, igniting the men's lascivious imaginations. When the two Maul brothers are called out into the storm to look after their dogs, whose shelter has apparently collapsed, they discover that the Polish man's car is blocking theirs. An altercation ensues, and they beat him up badly after smashing his car. Christian Maul exclaims to one of the other men: "Lutter! Hau ihm die Polackenkutsche platt! Jetzt reicht es mir mit dem Gesindel aus dem Osten!" (103).[28]

When the brothers then leave to look after their dogs, Lutter goes with his own shepherd to the young woman's room, whom he mistakenly believes to be a prostitute. There, he proceeds to taunt her, threaten her, with the help of his dog, and sadistically force her to undress. When she threatens to call the police, Lutter "*lacht laut.* Die Polizei. Wäre ich vorsichtig. Ehrlich. An Ihrer Stelle. Polizei deutsch. Nichts jüdisch! Türkisch! [. . .]" (109).[29] That only warms him up and he escalates his anti-foreign commentary: "[. . .] Schlange! Polen. Russen. Rümanen. Juden! Vietnamesen! Neger! Es werden täglich mehr. Die wollen unser Deutschland zerstören. Die wollen unser Deutschland wegnehmen. Wenn wir

---

27 "Ulrich: The Middle Class! Holy Cow! Independent business! *He burps.* We paid for the upkeep of the border area with our money when the country was still divided! And now we're paying welfare for the pack of asylum seekers! And now that damned communism is finished, dead, and we're paying for its corpse with our money, just so it will be brought back to life again.

28 "Lutter, bash the heck out of his Polack wagon. I've had it with this riff-raff from the East."

29 "Lutter: *laughs loudly*. The police? I'd watch out. Honest. In your shoes. Police German. Not Jewish. Turkish."

nicht aufpassen" (112).[30] Finally, he threatens to rape her, but he is impotent and leaves as she mocks him and swears revenge.

After he was so brutally beaten, the young Polish man dies. *Die schöne Fremde* notifies the local newspaper of both events and summons a lawyer. The lawyer, however, warns her that her "reputation" (the men have spread the word that she is a whore, and Lutter claims that he paid for her "services") might undermine her attempts to press charges. The men return to the hotel, verbally abuse and manhandle the young woman for contacting the newspaper, and threaten to charge her with slander. The proprietress, Frau Mielke, who has sided with the men, announces to the young woman: "Gegen die Gebrüder Maul kommt in Bebra keiner an" (126).[31] Temporarily defeated, the *Fremde* leaves Germany and joins her boyfriend in Copenhagen, where, against his advice, she plots her revenge. In the final act, she appears again at the hotel in Bebra where she applies her seductive talent to manipulate and turn the men into fools. By promising that one of them can spend the night with her, she reduces them to animals. On her command, the brothers kill Lutter's dog, and he, in turn, stabs one of the brothers to death. When Lutter then turns on *die Fremde*, her boyfriend appears and whisks her away to safety. The play ends, though, on a rather haunting note when Ulrich Maul angrily confronts Lutter for killing his brother, and we hear Frau Mielke speak the ominous last words before the curtain falls: "Die Fremden. Das ganze Unglück kommt von den Fremden" (158).[32] Prejudice and bigotry die hard.

The Germans portrayed by Pohl in these two plays are, for the most part, a pretty wretched and despicable lot: petty liars and amoral opportunists in the East, vulgar "good old boys" and xenophobes in the West. And German society, in both parts, apparently does little to ensure that truth and justice prevail. With these characters, at least, the patina of civility, tolerance, and decency is frighteningly thin, requiring on either side of the former German-German border only a little alcohol to disappear completely. *Stammtisch* is apparently *Stammtisch* in both parts of the unifed country. A *Theater Heute*-discussion with two Berlin dramaturgs, dealing with contemporary theater in the recently unified Germany, appeared in 1993, carrying the title "Gemeinsam sind wir unausstehlich."[33] Pohl's two plays described above seem to suggest that (many? how many?) Germans are *unausstehlich*, even if they are dissimilar in other significant ways. Pohl's figures are stereotypical, clichéd representatives of some of the worst kinds of Germans, of some of the most disturbing traits and attitudes to be found among them.

---

30 "Snake! Poles. Russians. Rumanians. Jews. Vietnamese. Niggers. More and more of them every day. They want to destroy our Germany. They want to take our Germany away from us. If we don"t watch out."

31 "Nobody does anything against the Maul brothers in Bebra."

32 "Foreigners. All of our misfortune stems from the foreigners." (That this is a paraphrase of one of the Nazis' insidious assertions—"Die Juden sind unser Unglück!"/The Jews are our misfortune—with all of its implications is obvious).

33 "Together we're unbearable."

Theater often brings extreme situations, characters, and ideas onto stage; it often exaggerates problems in order to illuminate and call attention to them. After reading or seeing these two Pohl dramas, the question remains to what extent such characters without character; to what extent such hauntingly familiar attitudes and behaviors are representative of and common to a sizeable segment of Germans. Pohl does not appear to be very optimistic about the answer. A sufficient number of news reports from Germany over the past decade indicate that Pohl's portrayals in these plays are too close to real occurrences to be easily dismissed as exaggerated.

In the play from 1995, *Wartesaal DeutschlandStimmenReich*, Pohl treats both parts of Germany, or rather, he lets both parts of Germany, through both random and representative figures, express their attitudes, opinions, fears, and irritations about the "new" Germany directly. Although there are hints and signs of personal *drama* in some of their individual monologues, the play as a whole is decidedly undramatic in any traditional sense. An anonymous critic in *Die Welt* found the play, in its *Deutsches Theater Berlin* premiere production at least, irritatingly undramatic: "keine Geschichten, kein Leben im Wartesaal; nur Quatschen."[34] Yet, if one reads and looks more closely, one can not help but recognize that behind the shy or boisterous, coolly articulate or nervously confusing interview statements lurk the very dramatic upheavals that have profoundly altered the lives of these individuals and their fellow Germans. Michael Merschmeier accurately describes what these interview scenes in a railroad station represent: "Biographien und Bilder aus dem Bauch Deutschlands, aus allen Schichten, Ost wie West, unterm Strich rationale, emotionale und sentimentale Erklärungen und Beschreibungen dafür, warum noch nicht zusammenwächst, was (vielleicht doch nicht?) zusammengehört" (40).[35] The premiere production of the play in Berlin, reduced from 32 German characters and monologues to 20, brings first on stage a middle-aged administrator in a government agency and then the mayor of Bebra: next an old woman from East Berlin, followed by a schoolboy; then a Western insurance salesman who worked temporarily in the East, followed by a drunken fan of the Werder-Bremen soccer team, and so forth, one after the other, across the stage/ into the train station waiting room where they each stop, take a seat on a bench, and deliver a monologue. Some are terse and short, some are loquacious and lengthy. All provide a glimpse, a personal perspective on the events and their effect on individual lives and the society in general.

It is soon obvious from the statements and anecdotes of these figures that a big gap exists between Germans East and Germans West, in experience and perspective, in expectations and desires, in long-term goals and daily habits. Schneider's "Mauer im Kopf" is very much in evidence. The administrator, for

34 "no stories, no life in the waiting room; just chatter." *Die Welt* 28. October 1995.

35 "Biographies and images from the belly of Germany, from all classes, East and West, all in all, rational, emotional, and sentimental explanations and descriptions of why that which 'belongs together' (but perhaps not yet) still refuses to 'grow together.'"

instance, asserts with frustration that the West Germans who have come East to work simply do not understand East Germans or what enormous changes they have had to face: "Die wissen überhaupt nicht was hier läuft! Die begreifen die ganzen Probleme nicht! Die Bürger stören sie eigentlich!" (44).[36] The West German insurance salesman who temporarily worked in the East complains that he found the East Germans' way of speaking irritating, because their vocabulary was unlike that in the West. He also asserts that East Germans laughed too little, that their personal hygiene was terrible, and that (heaven forbid!) there was no Italian restaurant to go to after work: "Ohne Spaghetti al dente hat das für mich auf die Dauer keinen Sinn!" (46).[37] The reader or viewer is pulled back and forth between personal descriptions of genuinely significant problems and trivial complaints, between comical or sentimental anecdotes and heart-wrenching tales of real suffering and injustices. The latter is perhaps best represented by the *Malermeister* (painter) who delivers the final and longest monologue of the play. His life, in the East, in the West, back in the East, as an immigrant in Australia, and finally, after the fall of the GDR, back in the East, reflects in poignant terms the absurdities and traumas of postwar Germany and of those that ultimately led the East Germans to topple their Stasi-state.

Pohl's *Wartesaal Deutschland* is perhaps not great theater, but it does offer a genuine spectrum of German "stories" that make an impressive stage contribution toward presenting a differentiated, realistic, and compelling description of the post-*Wende* German condition. The individual characters are numerous and different enough, as are their opinions, attitudes, and life stories, especially in the longer published versions of the play, that any notion that two or three "types" can be representative of all Germans or their situations is dispelled. This play also avoids the rather one-sided polemical stances found in Hochhuth's play-in-a-series-of-scenes, *Wessis in Weimar* (1993), but it is certainly in the tradition of the *Dokumentartheater* (documentary theater) which Hochhuth pioneered in the 1960s and in which tradition his *Wessis in Weimar* is also to be understood.

IV. Christoph Hein

Christoph Hein, of course, had established himself as one of the leading writers of prose and drama in the GDR in the years prior to its abrupt end. He had been a committed socialist who was nevertheless very critical of the regime and its policies, both in his literary works and his numerous essays and public speeches. His drama, *Die Ritter der Tafelrunde*, written shortly before the collapse, took aim

36 "They have no idea what's happening here. They understand none of our problems. They citizens here actually make them uncomfortable."

37 "If there's no spaghetti *al dente*, there's no reason for me to stay here in the long run."

at the aged SED-leaders and satirized their outmoded political views and their pathetic distance from reality. Together with several other writers and cultural figures from the GDR, including Christa Wolf and Stefan Heym, during the hectic and confusing events of late 1989 and early 1990 Hein spoke out in favor of significant reforms within the GDR and against unification with the FRG. That, of course, was not what the people of the GDR wanted, nor was it what ultimately happened. Hein, and his other like-minded colleagues, were swept along by the tide. With his play *Randow*, written in 1994, some five years after the fall of the Berlin Wall, Hein turned his attention to the post-*Wende* and post-unification reality in eastern Germany. The play leaves little doubt that Hein's 1989 skepticism about unification has not been eliminated by post-unification developments.

Randow. Eine Komodie is a play that is written from the perspective of *eastern* Germany after the glow and high expectations of the immediate post-*Wende* period have worn off. His figures, now four years into unification, have had the chance and the challenge of adjusting to the new rules and realities–economic, social, and political—that had been installed from, and in large part by, the Western part of the new Federal Republic. Hein paints in *Randow* a rather bleak picture of the new situation, for many Easterners as well as for some Westerners. He both shows and implies numerous causes for this bleakness, but perhaps the main cause, as Schulze-Reimpell pointed out after the play's premiere, was that "die Menschen des Stuckes haben ihr Bezugssystem verloren—die Ossis wie die Wessis."[38] The play brings a wide range of topics and issues onto the stage. As Wolfgang Engler noted: "Fast alles kommt zur Sprache—Beziehungskisten, Umwelt- und Alkoholprobleme, Asylanten, alte und neue Nazis, Seilschaften jede Menge und, nicht zu vergessen, die Beziehung zu Frosch, dem heimlichen Hauptdarsteller."[39] Frosch, it should be noted, is a dog.

Randow, a rather idyllic valley near the Oder River and the Polish border, is also a main character in the play. A former East Berlin artist, Anna, moved to this valley shortly after the *Wende* with her second, meanwhile estranged, husband and her daughter from her first marriage. They had remodeled an isolated house in a hunting revier that was, during the GDR period, fenced off and used for secret military training. It turns out that those who sold her the house suffer from sellers' remorse, since bigger fish with more money are interested in her property and in the entire area. The local mayor and the re-assigned German border guard (there is no border in Lower Saxony any longer) try to pressure and frighten Anna, who now lives in the house alone with the dog, Frosch, into selling. But unknown to them, an even more powerful interest group from Cologne also covets the entire

38 "The characters in the play have lost their orientation—both those from the East and from the West."

39 "Almost everything is expressed—relationship entanglements, environmental and alcohol problems, asylum seekers, old and new Nazis, collaborations of all kinds, and, don't forget, the relationship to Frosch, the secret main character."

area, and, because this cartel is willing to promise jobs to the local population, succeeds in purchasing and once again fencing off the entire valley. Very reluctantly, Anna decides to sell and flee back to the city, but only after someone has poisoned Frosch.

Hein's depiction of the powerlessness of the individual, ironically, even of the little schemers, over money (from the West) is clearly intended to underscore the plight of many in the East as they faced what in some regards looked very similar to colonization. With the exception of Anna (and Frosch), the characters in the play are all manipulators (privately, as in the case of Anna's estranged, alcoholic husband, and in society writ large and larger, as in the case of the local mayor and the real estate broker from Cologne, respectively), or they are among the manipulated and exploited. Sometimes they are one and the same—that is what the new conditions appear to generate: a hierarchy of manipulators and manipulated.

Once again in Hein's play, as in those of Strauss and Pohl, the reader or viewer is confronted with stark portrayals of dysfunctional personal relationships (Anna's with her ex-husband and petulant and smart-alecky teenage daughter); of classic good-old-boy connections that disadvantage others; and of hierarchical business relationships where boss and employee are on extremely unequal terms. There are unsolved murders of foreign border-crossers with subsequent cover-ups, a disturbing abundance of "Wendehälse," and shadowy connections between Nazi and/or Stasi pasts, on the one hand, and contemporary forces that are ruthless and politically reactionary on the other. The play is, as Friedrich Dieckmann has pointed out, "[. . .] ein soziales Panorama des östlichen Deutschlands im Jahre 4 seiner postrevolutionaren Existenz."[40]

One might be tempted to argue that Hein overstates and exaggerates, thereby creating caricatured people and situations rather than presenting the complex reality of life in this new Eastern Germany. Can this (eastern) German reality be as crass as it is shown here to be? In the first place, literature and theater are not charged with the responsibility of presenting reality in all of its nuances and colorations, and overstatement and exaggeration are frequent and well-regarded theatrical strategies. So, even if Hein were guilty of overstatement and exaggeration here, one should not be too quick to hold him to a "reality" standard that is inappropriate for literature. But does he really exaggerate? Numerous journalistic reports of people and towns in the "new federal states," as well as many social science analyses of the difficulties faced by countless unemployed, uprooted, and disillusioned eastern Germans, present portraits and conclusions very similar in kind and tone to what Hein sets on stage in this play. Perhaps more importantly, one can view Hein's play as realistic because it portrays very real perceptions of reality, perceptions that reflect justified anxieties about having little or no control over one's life, one's environment, and even one's livelihood in a

40 "a social panorama of eastern Germany, in the fourth year of its post-revolutionary existence."

society where many personal relationships are dysfunctional and governed by the desire for self-centered gain. Just as the characters in Hein's play, Anna and even "the small sharks," do not understand the mechanisms that turn them into pawns and victims, so too did (and perhaps still do) many eastern Germans find it impossible to comprehend the forces that so dramatically altered their lives, certainly not always for the better, in some rather inscrutable ways.

V. Conclusion

As the foregoing discussion of these dramas about the *Wende* and post-*Wende* German situation make abundantly clear, despite the euphoric excitement and hope of the weeks immediately following the fall of the Berlin Wall in November 1989, the political unification of Germany has been extremely difficult. Today, some ten years later, Schneider's "Mauer im Kopf" remains for many a challenge and a hurdle as Germans from East and West seek common ground, try to find understanding for very different pasts and disparate present conditions and perspectives. "Ossis" and "Wessis" continue to mistrust one another, the "Ossis" often expressing resentment over what they perceive to be arrogance, disinterest, and colonizing attitudes on the part of the "Wessis" and their often unjust and cold-hearted systems, while the "Wessis" still complain frequently about what they perceive to be laziness, inflexibility, and an unrealistic, post-GDR attitude on the part of the "Ossis" whereby they still expect the state to support them and solve all of their problems. The description offered by Henning Ritter in the *FAZ* five years ago of German unification seems to still be valid after ten years, despite some important progress, namely that the **external** unity is complete, whereas it may take decades to achieve **internal** unity. Similarly, Schneider's prophecy from 1982 appears to be valid still. The "neue deutsche Befremdung," of which Hardtwig and Winkler spoke in 1994, remains a significant problem. But troubled German-German relations, "Ossi-Wessi" tensions, are clearly not the only topic on which these and other dramatists have concentrated. In explaining the range of themes found in Christoph Hein's *Randow*, Wolfgang Engler, we will recall, noted that just about everything is expressed: relationships, environmental concerns, alcoholism, asylum, Nazism and Neo-Nazism. All of these topics and problems, along with others, are found throughout these plays, underscoring the extent to which they are viewed to be serious impediments to achieving the promise of the late 1989 euphoria as well as the promise of social justice, tolerance, economic well-being, and enlightened citizenship of which the Federal Republic, as a democratic society, boasts.

The plays which I have chosen to discuss here, selected in part because they are both unique *and* representative, in part because of the stature of their respective authors, and in part because they present a good range of topics, perspectives, structures, and styles, provide valid insight into what we might rightly call **the** German *Zeitstück* of the 1990s. The extent to which any of these plays will achieve and retain a place in the repertoire of contemporary German-language theater remains to be seen, of course, but there can be no doubt that as imaginative dramatic and theatrical attempts to confront the challenges of this unanticipated new Germany, as *Zeitstücke* and literary *Zeitdokumente*, and as the most recent contributions to German theater as "öffentliche Anstalt," they are distinctly worthy of our attention.

Works Cited

Balk, Wolfgang & Sebastian Kleinschmidt, eds. *'Denk ich an Deutschland...' Stimmen der Befremdung*. Frankfurt a.M.: Fischer, 1993.
Braun, Volker. *Der Wendehals oder Trotzdestonichts*. Frankfurt a.M.: Suhrkamp, 1995.
---. *Die Übergangsgesellschaft*. Frankfurt a.M.: Suhrkamp, 1988.
---. *Böhmen am Meer*. Frankfurt a.M.: Suhrkamp, 1992.
---. *Iphigenie in Freiheit*. Frankfurt a.M.: Surhkamp, 1992.
Brockmann, Stephen. "German Literary Debates after the Collapse." *German Life & Letters* 47/2 (April 1994): 201-210.
---. *Literature and German Unification*. Cambridge: Cambridge UP, 1999.
Brussig, Thomas. *Helden wie wir*. Frankfurt a.M.: Fischer, 1998.
Bullivant, Keith. *The Future of German Literature*. Oxford: Berg, 1994.
Cosentino, Christine. "'Die Gegensätze Übergänge': ostdeutsche Autoren Anfang der neunziger Jahre." *The Germanic Review* LXIX.4 (Fall 1994): 146-156.
Dieckmann, Friedrich. "Grosse und kleine Gier." *FAZ*. 23. December 1994. 35.
Ellert, Gundi. *Jagdzeit. Theater heute* 9 (September 1994): 28-42.
Engler, Wolfgang. "Froschs Ende." *Die Zeit*. 6. January 1995. 15.
Hardtwig, Wolfgang & H. A. Winckler. *Deutsche Befremdung. Zum Befinden in Ost und West*. Munich: Beck, 1994.
Hein, Christoph. *Randow. Eine Komödie*. Berlin: Aufbau, 1994.
---. *Die Ritter der Tafelrunde und andere Stücke*. Berlin: Aufbau, 1990.
Henrichs, Benjamin. Review of *Auf der Mauer, auf der Lauer*. *Die Zeit* 11. May 1990.
Hochhuth, Rolf. *Wessis in Weimar. Szenen aus einem besetzten Land*. Munich: dtv, 1994.
Jarausch, Konrad, ed. *After Unity. Reconfiguring Germany Identity*. Providence: Berghahn, 1997.
Krajenbrink, Marieke. "'Da mach ich mir ein historisches Eselsohr': Tradition und Aktualität in Botho Strauß' *Schlußchor*." *Literatur und politische Aktualität*. Eds. Elrud Ibsch & Franz v. Ingen. Amsterdam: Rodopi, 1990.
Kroetz, Franz Xaver. *Ich bin das Volk. Theater heute* 10 (October 1994): 44-51.
Meier, Christian. *Deutsche Einheit als Herausforderung*. Munich: Hanser, 1990.
Merschmeier, Michael. "Von deutscher Vereinigung." *Theater heute* 12 (1995): 40.
Müller, Elfriede. *Goldener Oktober. Theater heute* 5 (May 1991): 44-54.
Ortheil, Hanns-Josef. "Die Dramaturgie der Wiedervereinigung." *Merkur* 519/46-6 (1992): 481-496.

Ott, Friedrich. "GDR Literature and the German 'Wende.'" *World Literature Today* 65.2 (1991): 232-236.

Pohl, Klaus. "Planet Germany." (Parts I, II, III). *Der Spiegel*. (15.8.94, 22.8.94, 29.8.94): 96-110, 96-111, 107-125.

---. *Karate-Billi kehrt zurück. Die schöne Fremde. Zwei Stücke*. Frankfurt a.M.: Verlag der Autoren, 1993.

---. *Wartesaal Deutschland Stimmenreich. Theater heute* 12 (1995): 44-55.

Ritter, Henning. "Endlich oder unendlich? Die deutsche Einheit nach fünf Jahren." *FAZ* 2 Oktober 1995.

Richard, Jörg. "Die deutsche Wende und der Wandel des Theaters (1989-1999)." *glossen* H.8, an electronic journal (1999).

Schalk, Axel. "*Wendestücke*: German Plays for Today - Theater after the *Blitzkrieg*." *The Individual, Identity and Innovation. Signals from Contemporary Literature and the New Germany*. Eds. Arthur Williams & Stuart Parkes. Bern: Lang, 1994): 273-296.

Schleef, Einar. *Totentrompeten I* and *Drei Alte tanzen Tango. Vorhänge. Stücke I.* Frankfurt a.M.: Suhrkamp, 2000.

Schneider, Peter. *Der Mauerspringer*. Berlin: Rotbuch, 1982. English edition: *The Wall Jumper* New York: Random House, 1983.

Schulze-Reimpell, Werner. Review of *Randow*. *Stuttgarter Zeitung* 30. December 1994.

Sieg, Katrin. "The Revolution has been Televised: Reconfiguring History and Identity in Post-Wall Germany." *Theatre Journal* 45 (March 1993): 35-48.

Strauß, Botho. "Anschwellender Bockgesang." *Der Spiegel*. 8. February 1993. 202-207.

Strauß, Botho. *Schlußchor*. Munich: Hanser Verlag, 1991.

Wehdeking, Volker. *Die deutsche Einheit und die Schriftsteller: literarische Verarbeitung der Wende seit 1989*. Berlin: Kohlhammer, 1995.

Cinematic Responses

ROBERT D. LEVY AND RICHARD W. MCCORMICK

Mastering the Past and Present: Problems of Memory in Postwar and Post-*Wende* German Cinema

Comparing Kurt Maetzig's 1947 film *Marriage in the Shadows* and Helke Misselwitz's 1992 film *Herzsprung*, one notes some significant thematic similarities but also some important differences.[1] The contrasts between the two are illustrative of important distinctions to be made between the historical contexts in which they originated: the aftermath of the collapse of the Nazi-led German state, the Third Reich, at the end of World War II; and the aftermath of the dissolution of the East German state, the German Democratic Republic (GDR), and its unification with West Germany, the Federal Republic of Germany (FRG), in 1990 as the Cold War between the Soviet bloc and the West was coming to its end.

Those two contexts are obviously different, for, in spite of the GDR's totalitarian aspirations, it was very different from the Third Reich; certainly it was not as criminal as the latter, for one thing not having attempted genocide of any particular ethnic minority. In addition, its existence as a German experiment in (Stalinist) socialism right next to, and in competition with the capitalist German state, the FRG, made for many obvious contrasts with the Third Reich, which was the only German state from 1933 to 1945.[2] When the Third Reich collapsed, it did so by losing the most awful war humanity has ever known, a war that it, of course, had started. The amazingly peaceful end of the GDR—voted in essence out of existence by its own people in the first free election ever held there—cannot be compared to 1945, nor can the economic difficulties experienced in the former GDR long after unification compare with the destitution, ruin, and misery of Germany in 1945.

---

1 "Herzsprung" is the name of a real town in eastern Germany, although the credits at the end of the film state that one will not find it as it is depicted in the film. Because it is a place name, it will not be translated into English, although readers who do not understand German should also know that the two components of the compound word "Herzsprung" mean in German "leap of the heart," and this is a meaning to which the film obviously alludes.

2 As much as the German exiles proclaimed an "other Germany" (a claim the GDR would also make), there was no government in exile, as well as very little internal resistance to the Nazi state.

There are many similarities between the fascist Nazi State and the Socialist East German State: both were obviously undemocratic one-party states that pretended to rule on behalf of the people. Citizenship in Nazi Germany was defined in racial terms and in terms of Marxist-Leninist ideas about class by the GDR's leading party, the Socialist Unity Party (*Sozialistische Einheitspartei Deutschlands*, or SED). Both states developed an internal security apparatus led by a secret police service that both tyrannized citizens and depended on them informing on each other. Both states drew strength from and fostered that aspect of the German national character long defined as authoritarian.

The two films we are discussing also have a number of things in common. They were both made by *Deutsche Film-Aktiengesellschaft* (DEFA), which for most of its history was the state film production company of the GDR; yet both *Marriage in the Shadows* and *Herzsprung* were made at a point when the GDR did not exist. Maetzig's film was made in the Soviet zone of occupation in 1947, before the GDR was created (in 1949), and Misselwitz's film was made in 1992, after the GDR had ceased to exist.[3] Both filmmakers were at one time citizens of the GDR. Maetzig would become a citizen in 1949, and he went on to become one of the new state's most important filmmakers. Misselwitz, who was born, as it happens, in 1947, was a citizen of the GDR until 1990. Most significant, of course, are the similarities between the narratives of the two films. Thematically, romantic relationships in the films act as plot devices to reveal the story of two traumatic periods in German history: a marriage in *Marriage in the Shadows*, and a love affair in *Herzsprung*. Both relationships, furthermore, have even more symbolic/allegorical significance politically and socially because of their status as sexual relationships between Germans and others defined in racist terms as somehow non-German.

The contrasts are equally telling. On the one hand, Maetzig's film is an early attempt at *Vergangenheitsbewältigung*, or mastery of the Nazi past, although its indictment of the apolitical artist and its depiction of solidarity between a Jewish doctor and his working-class patients hint at its agenda for postwar Germany. On the other hand, Misselwitz's film is more properly a work of *Gegenwartsbewältigung*, or mastery of the present, that is coping with the economic, cultural, and social disarray in eastern Germany in the wake of unification. *Herzsprung* does, however, make connections between the xenophobic violence of the early 1990s (which it depicts and analyzes) and the claustrophobic and racist provincialism of the GDR, which had long stymied the dreams of its citizens to travel and kept foreign workers from Africa and Southeast Asia strictly segregated from the rest of the population. The film also

3 The *Deutsche Film-Aktiengesellschaft* (German Film Corporation or DEFA) was founded with the approval of the Soviet occupation forces in East Berlin in 1946. It became the state film production company of the GDR after the latter's founding in 1949. It continued producing films after unification in 1990 until 1992, the very year *Herzsprung* was made, when DEFA ceased to exist. See Schenk.

alludes to the crimes of fascism, and to the hypocrisy of the GDR's antifascism and internationalism.

The events of 1989, and reunification in 1990, brought to the surface memories of the initial division of Germany in 1949.[4] The creation of two separate German states in 1949 actualized the two dominant notions of what it meant to be German in the immediate postwar period. On the one hand, the three western zones of occupation coalesced to create the Federal Republic of Germany; and on the other hand, the Soviet-occupied eastern zone evolved into the German Democratic Republic.[5] The FRG, dominated by advocates seeking closer relationships—social, economic, and political—with the West, sought to fashion itself as a Western-style liberal, bourgeois democracy.[6] In contrast, the returning exiles of the German Communist Party (*Kommunistische Partei Deutschlands, KPD*) quickly gained control under the tutelage of the Soviet occupation forces and encouraged closer ties with the Soviet-controlled socialist world. For both the FRG and the GDR, the recent National Socialist past served as an ideological backdrop to advance the contested national identities within Germany in the years leading up to the creation of two German states in 1949.

The trauma, severity and intensity of National Socialism and the Holocaust, in particular, offered German filmmakers an important opportunity to highlight the differences between competing visions and orientations for the future. The early films in the postwar period recollecting the immediate past and the necessity to reconstruct the nation physically and psychologically, the so-called rubble films (*Trümmerfilme*), are emblematic of the attempts to grapple with the tensions of the postwar situation (Schobert 5-6). These films often appropriated either explicit or implicit references to the recent past, while at the same time distilling the ideological possibilities for the future. These early postwar German filmmakers were sensitive to one of the more dynamic

4 The FRG, which came into existence on 23 May 1949, minimized the opportunities for a single, autonomous German state. After the creation of the FRG, the GDR was tenuously created on 7 October 1949, following the developments in the West and treading lightly around Soviet concerns.

5 It should be remembered, however, that despite the various plans among the Allies, the postwar plans for Germany did not include a hardening of the zones of occupation, much less the division and creation of two new states.

6 The rise of Christian Democracy in Germany, as throughout postwar Europe, sought to balance the demands of a social welfare state ("Christian socialism") and a liberal, parliamentary democracy. The frequently cited fact that the FRG did not have a constitution, but rather a "Basic Law" (*Grundgesetz*), also suggests the postwar (West) German desire to unify the western and eastern zones of occupation, a built-in component to the Basic Law. Declaration of the autonomous FRG in the late Spring of 1949, however, squelched the debates about unifying the four occupation zones into a single state. In the East, the GDR's, and particularly the SED's, interest in unifying the two German states after 1949 seemed unlikely as well. The question of unifying the two halves of Germany, however, appeared to have been sealed by the building of the Berlin Wall on 13 August 1961.

qualities of the cinematic medium: its ability to manipulate time, which recreated and created the past and the future through the lens of the present. Time, of course, remains one of the most contested domains in recent German history. We refer here to the discussions surrounding continuities and discontinuities in the German past, the so-called *Sonderweg* thesis.[7] Because the returning KPD, and its successor party, the SED, consistently positioned itself as the true resistance to National Socialism, the Nazi past was bracketed out of the GDR's past, and Western, capitalist Germany was equated with fascism, particularly after 1945 (Herf 14). Under the rubric of "another Germany" (*anderes Deutschland*), the GDR built a myth of resistance, opposition to and struggle against not only National Socialism, but also opposition to the emerging FRG, which openly claimed the problematical political heritage of the German past.[8] Although couched in the language of the People's Front (*Volksfront*) characterized by class solidarity and a desire for international peace, the GDR's myths of resistance and opposition served the vital function of legitimizing the interests of returning ardent communists and eventually the SED. Film, however, was counted among the more important spheres in the evolving ideological contest between the competing and different views of the past, present, and the potential future within the GDR, but also between the evolving divided German states.

The manipulation of time in film, while neither innovative nor unique to postwar East German filmmakers, helps to construct the myth of antifascism eventually promulgated in the GDR. The past, present and the future blur together in film to create a unique sphere of (literally) an "imagined community" (Anderson 37ff.).[9] The world, thus represented in film, not only acts as the reflective mirror of its social reproduction, but also operates powerfully as a projector re-fashioning its audience's social world (Said 40-41).[10]

---

7 The *Sonderweg* ("special path") thesis, which actually has its origins in the pre-World War I era, began as an accounting for the German uniqueness among the more "advanced" and industrialized nations of Europe, and the superiority of German *Kultur* (a term whose literal translation is "culture," but carrying strong connotations of German nationalism) over European "civilization." National Socialism, of course, reconstituted the uniqueness of the German "special path," and in the post-World War II era the uniqueness of a *Sonderweg* became an embarrassment, in both the East and West.

8 Myths in this sense are not wholly fabricated or made-up notions of the collective past; rather, myths rationalize and function as an agent of collective memory.

9 Anderson's focus on the interplay between "print-capitalism" and the constructions of national consciousness are, of course, directly applicable to the role of film as a vehicle ("mode of production") of national identity. In this respect, the films of the GDR (similar to other national cinemas) contribute to popular or mass consciousness of what it means to be an (East) German.

10 Film, as with other "literate" discourses, "contains" and "represents" aspects of the social world. These opposing forces articulate ways in which the world is made meaningful, and in the process "made"; that is, socially constructed.

Marriage in the Shadows: Eastern Memories and Myths before the *Wende*

Marriage in the Shadows (*Ehe im Schatten*, 1947) in many respects is a conventional narrative film, and is based loosely on the life of the actor Joachim Gottschalk.[11] The film's narrative follows a linear chronology, and is divided into three periods—or acts—1933, 1938 and 1943. The choice of these representative periods bears some similarity to the events in the final years of Gottschalk's life, but these selected years immediately stand out in retrospection for other historical events; this would have been even more the case for contemporary German audiences. 1933, of course, is the year the Nazis came to power in Germany; 1938 is the year of the Night of the Broken Glass (*Reichskristallnacht*), the first open Nazi pogrom against Jews; and 1943 represents the turning point in the Nazi war against the Soviet Union with the collapse of the Sixth Army and the German defeat at Stalingrad.

The first act of the film (1933) opens with the closing scene from Schiller's play *Kabale und Liebe* (*Love and Intrigue*) in a small Berlin theater. The actors who play the main roles in the staged drama, Elisabeth Maurer and Hans Wieland, are also the film's protagonists. Following the closing curtains and the audience's adulation for Elisabeth and Hans, the remaining main characters are introduced in the next few scenes: Herr Fehrenbach, the theater owner and director; Dr. Herbert Blohm, a playwright and publisher; Kurt Bernstein, a minor actor in the theater, but significantly more important for the film; Dr. Louis Silbermann, a physician and Elisabeth's uncle; Elisabeth's maid; and Herr Gallenkamp, a functionary in the Nazi Ministry of Culture.

Symbolic of the events of 1933, and allegorically, the film's opening act moves quickly from the play to the entry of Blohm—in the film and as a love interest for Elisabeth—to a brief vacation off the Baltic coast at Hiddensee and to the revelation that Elisabeth is Jewish. This coincides with the changing mood in the country as an old man hammers a sign into the ground near the beach reading "Jews not welcome!" ("Juden unerwünscht!"). Elisabeth and her entourage return to Berlin in late February 1933 to hear about the burning of the *Reichstag*, and to discover that she cannot return to the theater.

The opening temporal act also sets the stage for the resolution of the complicated love triangle between Elisabeth, Hans, and Blohm. After the announcement by Gallenkamp to the theater group about the new artistic and cultural aesthetics, Elisabeth's maid tells Hans that she will be protected

11 *Ehe im Schatten* (*Marriage in the Shadows*), D: Kurt Maetzig. Script by Kurt Maetzig (104-minutes, 2845 meters; Black and White. DEFA: (East) Berlin, 1947). Based on the Hans Schweikart novella *Es wird schon nicht so schlimm* (*It won't be so bad*). The film premiered in all four sectors of Berlin on 3 October 1947: at the *Filmtheater am Friedrichshain* in the Soviet zone, the *Cosima-Filmtheater* in the American zone, the *Prinzenpalast* in the French zone and the *Kurbel* in the British zone.

because her husband is an Aryan.[12] Resolved to show his love, and to protect her, Hans rushes off to find Elisabeth. Outside of her apartment, however, he encounters his rival suitor, Blohm. Hans bows out of the competition. Inside, Blohm excitedly attempts to show Elisabeth photographs from their recent holiday, and in the process a Nazi party pin falls out of his pocket. He attempts to explain why he was forced to join the Nazi party, and also why he has accepted a position in the state cultural ministry. "I can help to prevent the excesses," he pleads to Elisabeth. After all he does know that she is Jewish, and then he boldly suggests that perhaps he can help her "fix her papers." Elisabeth turns him out, and they part. It appears that the love triangle has completely collapsed; but in the closing scene of this opening act Hans indirectly asks Elisabeth to marry him and she accepts.

Many of the essential themes, tropes, and cinematic elements of the antifascist genre are already present in this film. In this respect, the film becomes more than a vector of memory. It is an active agent of memory. That is, *Marriage in the Shadows* helps to create the varieties of memory about the German past in the GDR, not only in films but in the larger social consciousness as well. Films such as Wolfgang Staudte's trilogy of *Antifa* films *Die Mörder sind unter uns*, *Rotation* and *Der Untertan*,[13] are among the more famous early efforts, and Konrad Wolf's films, from the 1950s through the 1970s, such as *Ich war neunzehn* and *Mama, ich lebe*, characterize the patterns of East German cinematic memories of the National Socialist past and the official party (SED) line of opposition and resistance.[14] *Marriage in the*

12 The nuance of this reference in the film refers to the often-contorted Nazi definitions of citizens ("Aryans") and the racial definition of Jews. "Mixed" (*Mischlinge*) categories continued to exist in the so-called Nuremberg Laws of 1935 and its revisions until the collapse of the regime in 1945. Gradually, and predictably, the position of "mixed" persons grew worse and worse. In February 1943 a Berlin protest by "Aryan" women married to imprisoned Jewish men stunned officials; the situation, of course, is reversed in the film and suggestive of the problematical conceptions of gender in Germany under the Third Reich and even (if not more so) after.

13 *Die Mörder sind unter uns* (*Murderers Among Us*), D: Wolfgang Staudte. Script by Wolfgang Staudte (91-minutes, 2475 meters; Black and White. DEFA: Berlin, 1946). The film premiered in the Berlin *Staatsoper* on 15 October 1946; *Rotation*, D: Wolfgang Staudte. Script by Wolfgang Staudte and Erwin Klein (84-minutes, 2297 meters; Black and White. DEFA: Berlin, 1949). The film premiered in the Berlin *Babylon* on 16 September 1949; *Der Untertan* (*The Subject*), D: Wolfgang Staudte. Script by Wolfgang Staudte and Fritz Staudte (109-minutes, 2963 meters; Black and White. DEFA: Berlin, 1951). The film premiered in the Berlin *Babylon* and *DEFA-Filmtheater Kastanienallee* on 31 August 1951. Based on the 1918 Heinrich Mann novel of the same name.

14 *Ich war neunzehn* (*I was Nineteen*), D: Konrad Wolf. Script by Konrad Wolf and Wolfgang Kohlhaase (120-minutes, 3262 meters; Black and White. DEFA: Berlin, 1968). The film premiered in the Berlin *Kosmos* and *International* on 1 February 1968; *Mama, ich lebe* (*Mama, I Live*), D: Konrad Wolf. Script by Wolfgang Beck, Günter Klein, Klaus Wischnewski and Dieter Wolf (103-minutes, 2820 meters; Color. DEFA: Berlin, 1977). The film premiered in the Berlin *International* on 24 February 1977.

Shadows links together the socialist vision of the postwar and future Germany—before a divided Germany became a reality—through its narrative and character development, and simultaneously provides a twist to the standard perspective of the so-called antifascist (*Antifa*) genre of GDR filmmaking. The *Antifa* films of the later fifties and onward extended the historical referent of fascism, according to the KPD's inclusion of Western capitalism as a variation of fascism.[15]

According to this doctrine, already established in the exile years of the 1930s, those who were not Nazis or Nazi supporters (*Mitläufer*) were classified as either "fighters against fascism" (*Kämpfer gegen Faschismus*) or "victims of fascism" (*Opfer des Faschismus*), in order of preference and deference (Herf 87ff.).[16] Accordingly, this schema privileged the communist "victims" of National Socialism as "fighters against fascism." The category of "victims of fascism," on the other hand, lumped together the "apolitical" enemies of the Nazi state, including German-Jews and other persecuted religious and "racial" groups. Most of the *Antifa* films produced from the 1950s forward readily accepted these ideological presuppositions. *Marriage in the Shadows*, however, specifies the victims of the National Socialists as Jewish, a rarity in the naming of Nazi victims in the GDR and the socialist world of Eastern Europe (as far as naming the victims specifically as non-communists). The film, however, problematizes the evolving hierarchy of victimization. The film's subtle ideological perspective, the development of characters, and a variety of cinematic techniques—particularly, close-ups, dissolves, and the adoption of a more documentary or realistic perspective in key scenes—blur the fact that the primary victims of National Socialism were racial. The fate of the Jewish characters (Elisabeth, her uncle and Bernstein) is depicted as tragic and inevitable; but it is Hans's failure to grasp the implications of the political situation until it was already too late that becomes the dominant focus of the

---

15 The 1935 adoption of the "popular front" strategy of resistance to fascism modified Ernst Thälmann's (the leader of the KPD) 1930 declaration that the governments in Weimar Germany were fascist. This populist strategy opened the way to include Western governments as allies in the fight against fascism. In the postwar struggle for identity between East and West Germany, a return to Thälmann's earlier, more dogmatically anti-capitalist doctrine can be noted.

16 This hierarchy, coincidentally created in 1947 by the SED and concretized by the GDR after its founding in 1949, carried a "pension" paying "fighters against fascism" more than "victims of fascism." The distinction of "fighter against fascism" is, of course, a political distinction and emphasizes the communist resistance and opposition against National Socialism in Germany. An interesting addition to the complications in this hierarchy is the relationship of Jews in "mixed" marriages during the Third Reich. The distinction of "privileged marriages" (that is, Jews living legally in Germany married to non-Jews) prevented East German Jews from claiming official status as "victims of fascism!" And even in the official language classifying victims, references to Jews were either non-existent or marginalized using euphemistic expressions, such as "victims of the Nuremberg racial laws" or "those who wore the Yellow Star."

film's identification with the victims of the Nazi state.[17] Particularly in the final scene of the film, depicting Hans and Elisabeth's burial, the title over this scene dedicates the film to the memory of Joachim Gottschalk and other victims (of fascism), without referencing the victims as either racial or political.[18] No mention is made of a distinction between political and racial victims of the Nazis; they are all simply victims. As this final example within the film demonstrates, the Jewish victims of the Nazi reign remain somewhat disembodied and unnamed, both in the emerging ideology and mythology of the GDR and what would become the antifascist cinema. *Marriage in the Shadows* nevertheless stands out as one of the earliest attempts by German filmmakers to grapple with the postwar consequences of racism and anti-Semitism. The film sheds light on the deeply embedded prejudices in National Socialist thought and action, and the uniquely Jewish nature of the Holocaust.[19]

Maetzig's attempt to deal with the Jewish victims of Nazi persecution sheds light on one of the more slippery questions of modernity, and especially in modern Germany: identity, and in *Marriage in the Shadows*, what it means to be a German. Perfunctorily, the sub-questions of religious identities are subsumed in the framework of a German national identity. Elisabeth and Bernstein's Jewishness is important—that is why, after all, they are targeted as victims—but that is only one aspect in the matrix of identification created in the film. Initially, the primary source of character identification is the theater. The main characters are all actors or workers in the theater. That is, they are all artists. The Nazi relation to art, and particularly through Joseph Goebbels's Ministry of Popular Enlightenment and Propaganda (*Ministerium für Volkserklärung und Propaganda*), provides the unstated background to one of the more moralizing qualities of the film: fascist/capitalist versus socialist aesthetics of art.[20] The second source of identity in the film is actually that of being German. Again this is played against the backdrop of the Nazi attempts

---

17 This is at once a scathing critique of other "apolitical" persons and groups who failed (missed the opportunity) to oppose or resist the Nazis and the Nazi state. However, it is also a highly sympathetic reconfiguration of such "apolitical" persons, such as Hans, as victims, mostly of their own failure to act, but also of National Socialism.

18 "Dieser Film ist dem Andenken des Schauspielers Joachim Gottschalk gewidmet, der im Herbst 1941 mit seiner Familie in den Tod getrieben wurde, und mit ihm zugleich all denen, die als Opfer fielen." ("This film is dedicated to the memory of Joachim Gottschalk, who in the Fall of 1941 committed suicide [literally, 'driven to death'] with his family, and to all other fallen victims.")

19 While Jews were targeted as racial victims of the Holocaust, if not the primary victims, the creation of a "scale of victimization," with Jews at the top, is problematical. This said, however, Jews were specifically targeted as "racial enemies of the state" indiscriminately of class, age or gender, whereas other groups, such as the communists, were more narrowly targeted as political enemies, along the lines of Barbara Harff and Ted Gurr's categorization of "politicide" as a distinct variation of genocide (359-71).

20 See Rentschler and Schulte-Sasse. These studies emphasize and analyze various aspects of the ideological sources in the creation of a Nazi aesthetic, specifically in film.

to define Germanness. And finally, *Marriage in the Shadows* helps to establish many of the central characteristics of what would become the defining genre of the GDR: the antifascist cinema. This is the least tangible and most slippery source of identity, and yet we would argue that this is the essence of what holds the film together in style, theme and content. Although the GDR was still two years from coming into existence, *Marriage in the Shadows* seeks to articulate ideas that would become the founding myths of the GDR: that it was simultaneously a victim of National Socialism, and also a fighter against fascism, past and present.

Consequently, Hans Wieland is the focus of attention throughout the film, and not Elisabeth Maurer. While the racist and anti-Semitic persecution Elisabeth suffers is central to the film's overall narrative, Hans's internal and moralized struggle subsumes Elisabeth's situation. In the consolidation of internal and external persecutions, *Marriage in the Shadows* flattens the distinctions between the Nazi persecutions of Elisabeth and the psychological persecutions endured by Hans. Without reading too much into the film's title, perhaps, it may not be too far to stretch the aspects of "marriage" and "shadows" to suggest the film's amalgamation of subjects and narrative elements in an uncertain or nebulous formation. That is, through the shifting emphasis between Elisabeth and Hans, the film complicates the category of "victim of fascism," and by extrapolation also certainly problematizes the category of "fighter against fascism." The turning point for Hans in resolving his internal conflict is his return from military service. This pivotal moment clearly breaks the film's depiction of Hans (Elisabeth and the future GDR by extension) as "victims of fascism," as they take their fate into their hands and thereby become "fighters against fascism."

Marriage in the Shadows does not answer the identity question. The film's ending, in fact, ironically recalls the notoriously Nazi propagandistic film *I Accuse* (*Ich klage an*) through the replication of the motif of a woman (Elisabeth) at the piano, nearing her end, dramatic lighting (reminiscent of Weimar expressionist filmmakers' use of shadows) and music highlighting the cumulative tragedy in a series of increasing afflictions, and the suicide turned inside-out as a socially responsible or at least acceptable act.[21] All these aspects return to the question of time in the film. *Marriage in the Shadows*, while foreshadowing the *Antifa* films of the GDR, provides a link between the cinemas of the German past, including the Nazi cinema! The questions of identity raised in the film are provocatively left up to the audience, albeit with

---

21 *Ich klage an* (*I Accuse*), D: Wolfgang Liebeneiner. Script by Eberhard Frowein and Harald Bratt (Black and White. Tobis-Klangfilm: Berlin, 1941). This film was given an "artistically especially worthwhile" (*Künstlerisch besonders wertvoll*) rating by the Nazi film chamber of the cultural ministry.

powerful suggestions and cues from within the film and the settings in which the film was shown.

Herzsprung and the Post-*Wende* Identity Crisis: Ethnicity, Nationality and Gender

Herzsprung opens with a close-up shot of what first appear to be snowflakes floating downward, but which are then revealed to be goose feathers as the camera pans down to a close-up of a dead goose.[22] Over that image we hear women singing; in the next shot they are shown to be factory workers plucking geese. One woman compliments another, Elsa, on her singing voice, telling her that she should have been a singer, only the first evocation of the trope of missed opportunities in the lives of the people who live in this somewhat desolate provincial town in the former GDR. This makes the choice of her next song all the more ironic, in which she sings about *Heimat, süße Heimat* ("home, sweet home" or "homeland, sweet homeland").[23] A younger woman, Johanna, is called away to the office, where she learns that she is being laid off. Her husband is an agricultural worker who has already lost his job; in his despair, he is drinking away the little money they have. Early in the film Johanna finds him dead in the barn where he had worked: first he shot all the cows and then himself.

But before Johanna, the film's female protagonist, comes upon this gruesome scene, she has already met the male protagonist of the film, a man of African heritage who speaks flawless German, and thus is probably an Afro-German from the FRG, although he's never given a history, let alone a name in the film; in the credits he's called simply *Ein Fremder*, a "stranger," or

---

22 *Herzsprung,* D: Helke Misselwitz. Script by Helke Misselwitz (87-minutes, 2389 meters; Color. DEFA, Thomas Wilkening Filmgesellschaft and ZDF: Potsdam-Babelsberg, 1992). The film premiered in Berlin on 19 November 1992.

23 The German term *Heimat* is often considered untranslatable; its meaning encompasses not just "home" but also "homeland," "the place where one grew up," as well as the region and indeed the nation of one's birth. Furthermore, it has historical associations with conservative, anti-modern groups in late nineteenth-century Germany who glorified the rural areas of Germany and rejected the "degenerate" modernism of the growing urban centers, above all Berlin. There was an associated literary movement from the turn-of-the-century into the 1930s that tried to produce *Heimatliteratur*, and some types of nature films in the 1920s, including the "mountain film," were also considered part of this tendency. All things connected with *Heimat* were considered positively in the 1930s under Nazi rule, including these types of literature and film. And of course the genre of technicolor film romances set in the provinces that became so popular in the FRG in the 1950s was also called the *Heimatfilm*. See, e.g., the discussion of the term in Silberman 115-17 and 127.

"foreigner."[24] Accompanied by her two children, she gives him a ride in her red car; it is clear from their encounter that the two adults are attracted to each other. The Afro-German man characterizes himself as someone who is always on the move, something that obviously intrigues Johanna.

After the death of her husband, we see Johanna at the funeral dinner. Next Johanna visits her friend Lisa, a hairdresser, and asks to have her hair dyed red like Lisa's. Johanna and Lisa then drive to a nightclub where they meet a businessman from the West who is attracted to Johanna. He invites her to visit him at his chocolate factory; Johanna, hoping for a job, makes the trip. While he does offer her lots of free chocolates for her children, he has no job to give her; the factory needs to be strictly rationalized. After telling her this, he continues trying to seduce her with champagne, which she pours in his lap, dumping all the free chocolates on him as well before walking out.

Some of the rowdy, unemployed young men in the town who went to school with Johanna are attracted to neo-fascist ideas and are gradually becoming skinheads. Johanna's father, originally a Pole who was confined in a German concentration camp, is shown standing shocked in front of a graffiti slogan about the need to send "foreigners to concentration camps"; at this moment, the Afro-German, who has just returned to the area, joins him in front of the graffiti. The two feel bonded by their reaction to the slogan, go drinking together, and have a good time until the Afro-German says that he has come to the town to find a blonde woman with two children and a red car; a change comes over the father when he realizes that the stranger is interested in his daughter. He abruptly leaves the bar.

Johanna and the Afro-German man meet again, and their interest in each other is obvious. They dance together at a local bar, infuriating Soljanka, one of the town's young rowdies who is obviously infatuated with Johanna. The Afro-German man gets a job at a new café that is being established just off the freeway in an old trailer. The café is then named, seemingly in his honor, *Onkel Toms Hütte* (Uncle Tom's Cabin). To threaten him, the local rowdies hang a baby doll from the roof of the café, a doll with supposedly African features that has a noose around its neck. To intimidate Johanna, they spray-paint her window with the message that she is a *Negerhure* ("a nigger's whore"). Meanwhile the Afro-German "stranger" and Johanna have consummated their love after an erotic encounter in the shower notable for its depiction of a female gaze of desire (Johanna's, to be specific). The "stranger" is by no means faithful to Johanna. She learns this on New Year's Eve, when, after

24 "Foreigner," however, is usually expressed in German as *Ausländer*. To be fair to the film, he is not the only character who is defined in such a vague, or rather allegorical/expressionistic way. One woman in the film is called by the credits *Die Verrückte*, the "crazy woman," a designation appropriate to her mysterious, not specifically defined role, which seems to be that of both a "village idiot" and a "holy fool" who witnesses many of the most important scenes.

dressing like a bride, she comes to visit him at the café, and finds him kissing another employee. A stereotypical roving male, he tells her that his body is his, but that she owns his heart. This she accepts, and it seems they will spend the evening together. He tells her to wait while he goes outside to empty the trash; at the dumpster he is jumped by the rowdies, who gag him and tie him to the tree, set fire to the café/trailer, and toss knives at the tree where he is bound. Gagged, he can't tell them that Johanna is in the burning trailer; she runs out of it to find safety but instead is hit by one of the knives being tossed at her lover. Scared by what they have done, the rowdies run away; Soljanka cries out that this was not what he had intended. The film ends with feathers floating in the air and a pan across Johanna's pale corpse, evoking the dead goose at the beginning of the film. As the camera pans away from her body toward the freeway, the noise of the traffic in the early morning is heard and the credits begin to roll.

When Johanna's father abruptly leaves the bar after drinking with the Afro-German, he is obviously upset at the "stranger's" sexual interest in his daughter. He goes home and announces to Johanna that "Ein Neger ist für dich gekommen" ("A nigger has come for you"). Johanna then argues with her father about the appropriateness of the term *Neger* for the Afro-German man who has come to the town of Herzsprung, maintaining that one should call such a person an African, or an African-American, or an African-German. Her father, however, answers simply that he has nothing against *Neger*; he does not seem understand her distinctions, because, of course, his real concern is due not "just" to racism but to a combination of racism and sexism, a patriarchal interest in controlling his daughter's sexual autonomy when it threatens his assumptions about appropriate partners.

It is not just in this one relatively short debate that one notes the film's insistence on a nuanced, differentiated look at ethnic and national origin that settles for no simplistic, stereotypical, monolithic conception of such categories and identities. The film in general creates a complex picture of national/ethnic identities. Not only is the idea of a simple and single identity for anyone of African heritage rejected, there is also no monolithic Germanness that is represented or postulated in the film, either. As one of the rowdies sits having his hair shaved off by Lisa, he jokes about sending foreigners to concentration camps. Lisa tells him that Johanna's father was a Polish inmate of a German concentration camp during the war. Not only is their joke thus linked concretely to German actions during the Third Reich and World War Two, but also their unspoken assumptions about the equivalence of whiteness and German identity are called into question. Indeed, one could make the point that under Germany's restrictive citizenship laws, the "stranger's" legal status as a German may be much more secure than Johanna's father: if "Afro-German," the "stranger" has at least one parent who is a German citizen, which makes him one too. This is not the case for Johanna's father, who was born in Poland,

and may well be a citizen now, but his daughter's citizenship would ultimately depend on her mother's status as a German, not on her non-German father's status.[25] These distinctions are of course lost on the skinheads, and this too would seem to reflect accurately anti-foreigner sentiment in Germany, which is actually driven more by concerns about race and ethnicity than by the technicalities of legal citizenship. Nonetheless it is satisfying to watch Johanna angrily take the razor from Lisa and continue shaving the young man in a much more threatening manner, scaring him into a realization of how his bigoted threats—and his callous allusion to the darkest legacies of German history—might offend someone whom he considers to be clearly and unproblematically German.

But even the town's young rowdies with their skinhead sentiments are depicted in a way that explains their behavior with some sensitivity, although not in any way apologizing for it. Johanna stresses that they went to school with her, and while this bond in a sense makes her underestimate the threat they pose to her, nonetheless they are portrayed as being in many ways as disoriented by the post-unification malaise in eastern Germany as Johanna herself is. Indeed, Soljanka, the young rowdy Johanna seems to know best, is portrayed by the same actor as the one who played her husband, Jan, an allegorical/expressionistic touch that implies a common type of young East German male whose brutality (whether racist or sexist) is criticized but whose disorientation and despair are depicted sympathetically.

At the same time, the portrayal of Jan/Soljanka does not posit any stereotypical German or even East German identity, because a crucial part of what is criticized in these two characters is sexism. This characteristic links all of the male characters in the film, from Jan/Soljanka to Johanna's father to the West German factory owner to the Afro-German "stranger." This sexism is not portrayed in a simplistic way as monolithic, nor are men in the film generally portrayed without sympathy. In their one scene together early in the film, Jan the drunken husband forces Johanna to kiss him, and when she bites him instead, he slugs her. Then he weeps after she leaves; the next time we see him, he has committed suicide. Soljanka's inability to accept Johanna's sexual interest in the Afro-German is a complicated mixture of jealousy as well as sexist and racist ideas about controlling (protecting/policing) German women, and it leads to the tragedy at the end of the film, which he unwittingly causes and then very clearly regrets. Johanna's father, who is much more politically progressive, but who is also characterized by his voyeuristic spying on Lisa, displays similar attitudes. At the same time he is shown as capable of

25 The FRG's rather archaic (and racist) citizenship laws, still primarily based on bloodlines, have finally been reformed by the new Social Democratic-Green governing coalition. These 1999 reforms, while welcome, are however at best partial, which unfortunately seems to be the limit of what is politically possible in Germany today.

developing an equitable (and almost ideal) relationship with Elsa, a woman of about his own age who is a friend of Johanna's from the poultry factory.

The West German capitalist is perhaps the least sympathetic character, with his assumptions about Johanna's vulnerability and his ability to impress her with his wealth and good taste, as well as his insensitivity to her actual economic situation, but even he is given some depth; his loneliness and eagerness to please seem genuine. The Afro-German appears uninterested in a committed relationship, but his love for Johanna seems genuine. While his implied promiscuity might be interpreted as reminiscent of older racist/anti-Semitic tropes about the rootless cosmopolitan, we would argue that through these flaws his character becomes less idealized and gains realism and depth. This in turn works against the character's otherwise problematic lack of a name and a history.

That Johanna and not the "stranger" dies at the end is also perhaps problematic, should we read the film as a simple allegory in which it is the East German woman who seems to be the ultimate victim of German unification. But it would be an even more problematic idealization of the "stranger" to make him the victim at the end of the film. We would interpret Johanna's unexpected death as another way in which the film complicates the story and avoids the most clichéd ending.[26] The complexity of the characters and the story in this film militate against any too simplistic allegorical interpretation.

Memory and the (East) German Past, Present and Future

It is perhaps the depiction of the West German factory owner in Herzsprung that would be most objectionable to those critics who found many of the German films dealing with post-unification eastern Germany to be too critical of the West and unification and too uncritical of the GDR, not sufficient in their attempts to deal with the GDR's past.[27] Critics who make such arguments often imply that the moral necessity for East Germans to come to terms with the GDR's past is to be equated with the need for all Germans to deal with the

---

26 We must admit, however, that the actual means by which she is killed—running between the rowdies and the Afro-German, seemingly unaware of what is happening, and then getting a knife in her back—seems overly contrived. A more plausible, if also more horrible, ending would have been to let her die in the fire that engulfs the café.

27 See, e.g., Hughes and Brady 208; with regard to *Herzsprung* specifically, see Boy. Also negative in their evaluations of the film, although not for its depiction of East-West tensions, but rather for the most part for its aesthetic failures (especially with regard to its use of the symbolical and allegorical): Renke, the reviewer in the *Kölner Stadt-Anzeiger* ("Reale Verzweiflung"), and Körte. Predominately positive were reviews by Voss, Rhode, Lenz, Koll, Schönemann and Wetzel. Lenz and Rhode mention the film's success at the Hof Film Festival in early November 1992.

Nazi past; that the second dictatorship in the German twentieth-century history demands the same treatment as the Third Reich.[28] But the latter's crimes are not exhausted by its having been a dictatorship, and as stated above, they far exceed anything committed by the GDR. Furthermore, dealing with the history of the GDR cannot mean simply to treat it as another, distinct anti-democratic episode in German history, if only because its relationship to the Nazi state is far more complex; indeed, many of the crimes of the GDR were justified by its ruling elite precisely with reference to antifascism, one of the pillars of the dominant state ideology. That this antifascism had its limits, above all with its overvaluation of the Communist resistance and its relative silence about the main victims of fascism, the Jews, cannot be denied. It was obviously used opportunistically by the governing elite (whose experience in the resistance to Nazism was nonetheless genuine). Indeed, the elevation of this official antifascism to a somewhat hollow state religion is arguably one of the reasons that many of the disaffected in the wake of the state's demise were so receptive to neofascism.

Helke Misselwitz's film makes definite and crucial connections both to the GDR past and to its complex relation to the Nazi past. This is done most effectively with the character of Johanna's father as a one-time Polish inmate of a German concentration camp, a fact that positions the loose talk of concentration camps by the rowdies and their xenophobia in a very critical light. But Johanna's father, besides being a character whose relationship to antifascism and the fascist past is no empty abstraction, is also a character who speaks most clearly of his dissatisfaction with the GDR: he tells the Afro-German that he had wanted to work as a sailor and see the world but instead ended up a worker on a collective farm in the provinces, a statement that resonates both as a critique of a system that allowed its citizens very little freedom and as a critique of the regime's restrictive travel policies. His initial attraction to the Afro-German man is not just due to solidarity with another outsider in a still-xenophobic Germany, but also to his fascination with this man's experiences as a Westerner who has traveled a great deal, who has done what the father had always wanted to do. And perhaps also there is an attraction to this dark-skinned outsider because his very appearance symbolizes the diversity (and the exoticism) denied to the population of the GDR, especially in the provinces, due both to the travel restrictions mentioned above but also to the strict segregation of most Third-World migrants in the GDR. At

28 For a discussion of the various labels of "totalitarian state" and "dictatorship," see Jarausch. Two particularly useful chapters, from a comparative perspective of placing the GDR within the main of German history, are Jürgen Kocka, "The GDR: A Special Kind of Modern Dictatorship" and Christoph Kleßmann, "Rethinking the Second German Dictatorship" in the same volume.

this level, the attraction the father feels toward the Afro-German man is very similar to his daughter's attraction to him.[29]

This constellation also carries an implicit critique of the hypocrisy of the GDR's vaunted internationalism. Combined with the film's analysis of the susceptibility of the young rowdies to neo-fascist and xenophobic ideas, there is a complex critique both of the GDR past and the present and future within unified Germany, specifically of the potential for serious racism and xenophobia, the very problems that over the course of 1992, the year of the film's premiere, became so virulent that at least one critic (Lenz) found the film prophetic. This constellation of problems—racism, anti-Semitism and xenophobia—remains a serious concern for the present and the future, and not just in unified Germany, as events in the U.S. and in England recently have shown us.

Conclusion[30]

Prefiguring the creation of the GDR, and in light of the reunification of the two Germanies in 1990, the power of *Marriage in the Shadows* lies in its direct confrontation with a difficult past, as *Herzsprung* compels viewers to engage with a troubling present. At the same time, however, *Marriage in the Shadows'* manipulation of time suggests not only a reflection about the National Socialist past, but the realities of the immediate postwar present conditions and the possibilities of the future, all with strong connections to the experiences in post-unification Germany. Without diminishing this powerful aspect of the film, it should be remembered that *Marriage in the Shadows* was produced and distributed in the context of the emerging worldview of East German communism. Maetzig's affiliations with the communist party (he had been a member of the KPD since 1944) and the Soviet-controlled censorship and distribution practices in the late 1940s (as the "Cold War" was heating up) create the constellation of contexts within which the film operates. In this respect, *Marriage in the Shadows* prefigures the *Antifa* genre of GDR films by several years and helps to establish critical aspects shaping East German memory—the myths of resistance and opposition—about National Socialism.

29 It must however be noted that Afro-Germans were present in the GDR, and, as citizens of that state they were not segregated the way migrant workers from Angola, Mozambique, or Vietnam were. But this does not mean that they were especially "visible" in GDR society, or that other GDR citizens knew any more about them than citizens of the FRG did about Afro-Germans in West Germany.

30 We would like to thank Kristie Foell for her many positive and encouraging comments and suggestions, and especially for her insights to improve the concluding section of this chapter; needless to say, however, all faults and limitations remain ours.

Similarly, the matrix of *Herzsprung*'s production and release, as one of DEFA's final productions following the collapse of the GDR and the reunification of Germany, establishes a unique link between the two films beyond superficial comparisons. Both films problematize and grapple with the complexities of German memory and identity.

One significant contrast between Maetzig's *Marriage in the Shadows* and Misselwitz's *Herzsprung* is gender—not merely the gender of their directors, that is, that Maetzig was a man and Misselwitz is a woman—but, much more significantly, the gendering of the German versus the non-German partners of the depicted heterosexual relationships. Depicting the Jewish character (Elisabeth) in *Marriage in the Shadows* as a woman makes the female protagonist in that film doubly powerless in ways that make the story of her suffering perhaps more poignant yet also conflate stereotypes about Jews with stereotypes about women in an especially problematic fashion. Depicting the German character as a woman in *Herzsprung* (Johanna) complicates the power relationships in the interracial relationship in some interesting, if not entirely unproblematic, ways: she has a more secure status as German than her Afro-German lover, but as an East German in comparison to someone who is a Westerner (and more cosmopolitan) and as a woman in a Germany that is sexist east and west (if in somewhat different ways), she is less powerful. This more complicated constellation is characteristic of Misselwitz's film, which in our opinion demonstrates an admirable complexity in dealing with the contemporary German identity crisis in all its troubling aspects: tension between Westerners and Easterners, racism and anti-foreigner sentiments.

Both films deal with racism, of course, but *Herzsprung* does it more forthrightly. *Marriage in the Shadows*, while being one of a few DEFA films that actually address anti-Semitism, ends with a dedication that downplays the importance of the Jewish character in the film (as do the gender dynamics indicated above). Thus, the film foreshadows the neglect of the racist/anti-Semitic component of fascism that would become typical of the GDR, a failure in its *Vergangenheitsbewältigung* that would become all too evident in the xenophobia that erupted in the early 1990s in the aftermath of German unification. This is a problem that is not exclusively limited to eastern Germany and the new *Länder* of the reconstituted FRG, but after more than a decade continues to plague the political and social climate in the East.

Works Cited

Anderson, Benedict. *Imagined Communities: Reflections on the Origin and Spread of Nationalism*. London: Verso Press, 1991.

Boy, Christof. "Ich hab' die Nacht geträumet," Rev. of *Herzsprung*. *taz*. 19 November 1992.

Harff, Barbara and Ted Gurr. "Toward Empirical Theory of Genocides and Politicides: Identification and Measurement of Cases Since 1945." *International Studies Quarterly* 37.3 (1988): 359-71.

Herf, Jeffrey. *Divided Memory: The Nazi Past in the Two Germanys*. Cambridge: Harvard UP, 1997.

H. Hughes and M. Brady. "German Film after the Wende." *The New Germany: Social, Political and Cultural Challenges of Unification*. Eds. D. Lewis and J.R.P. McKenzie. Exeter: U of Exeter P., 1995.

Jarausch, Konrad H., ed., *Dictatorship as Experience: Towards a Socio-Cultural History of the GDR*. New York: Berghahn, 1999.

Körte, Peter. "DDR Adé." *Frankfurter Rundschau*. 20 November 1992.

Koll, Horst Peter. Rev. in *Film-Dienst* 45. 24 November 1992: 29.

Lenz, Eva-Maria. "Skinheads, Schneeflocken, Sterntaler." Rev. of *Herzsprung*. *FAZ*. 20 November 1992.

Maetzig, Kurt, dir. *Ehe im Schatten* (*Marriage in the Shadows*). DEFA, 1947.

Misselwitz, Helke, dir. *Herzsprung*. DEFA, Thomas Wilkening Filmgesellschaft and Zweites Deutsches Fernsehen (ZDF), 1992.

"Reale Verzweiflung." *Kölner-Stadt-Anzeiger*. 21 November 1992.

Renke, Klaus. "Vom Sterben aller Hoffnung." *Neues Deutschland*. 19 November 1992.

Rentschler, Eric. *The Nazi Ministry of Illusion: Nazi Cinema and its Afterlife*. Cambridge: Harvard UP, 1996.

Rhode, Carla. "Schwarz, weiß, rot." Rev. of *Herzsprung*. *Tagesspiegel*. 21 November 1992.

Said, Edward W. *Orientalism*. New York: Vintage Books, 1994.

Schenk, Ralf, ed. *Das zweite Leben der Filmstadt Babelsberg. DEFA-Spielfilme 1946-1992*. Berlin: Henschel Verlag, 1994.

Schobert, Walter, "Vorwort." Hilmar Hoffmann and Walter Schobert, eds., *Zwischen Gestern und Morgen. Westdeutscher Nachkriegsfilm, 1946-1962*. Frankfurt am Main: Deutsches Filmmuseum, 1989.

Schönemann, Hannes. Rev. in *Film & Fernsehen*. 6 (1992) & 1(1993): 135-36.

Schulte-Sasse, Linda. *Entertaining the Third Reich: Illusions of Wholeness in Nazi Cinema*. Durham: Duke UP, 1996.

Silberman, Marc. *German Cinema: Texts in Context*. Detroit: Wayne State UP, 1995.

Voss, Margit. "Rot wie Blut, schwarz wie Ö." *Berliner Zeitung*. 20 November 1992.

Wetzel, Kraft. "Böse Deutsche? Rechte Gewalt im Spiegel neuerer deutscher Filme." *Film & Fernsehen* 3 (1994): 4-11.

MASSIMO LOCATELLI

Ghosts of Babelsberg: Narrative strategies of the *Wendefilm*

The fall of the Berlin Wall led the East German culture to a fast and dramatic epistemic reorganization. By identifying the main narrative functions upon which this culture was founded, both on the level of hegemonic power and on the oppositional one, in accordance with Brecht's "language of the slaves" (*Sklavensprache*), this paper investigates how these figures broke down or survived the clash with the age of mediated reality and what function they have taken on in the new social system.

To begin with, film practice, metatextual reflection and filmic self-representation show that film narration before and even after the *Wende* was part of an openly word-obsessed cultural discourse. This obsession took the form, on the one hand, of a glorification of the scriptwriter—who was overrated as the *Autor*[1] of the whole film text—and on the other of the privileged positioning of the *Literaturverfilmung* (the adaptation of a literary text) in the DEFA genre system as a means of interpreting history and society. The True Word, the *pravda*, provided a solid foundation for the symbolic order and still legitimizes any signifying praxis. Therefore a critique of the ideology informing these practices shall start from a textual analysis with a semiotic toolbox. As just one example, the theater-in-film fiction of *Stilles Land* (Andreas Dresen, Maxfilm 1992) clarifies the paradoxes of the encounter with the western word (world). This film tells of the debut of a young theater director who stages Beckett's *Waiting for Godot* on a forgotten stage in the sad and lifeless Mecklenburg area, while the Wall falls in the distant capital Berlin. One can immediately see that *Stilles Land*, like many other titles of its generation, openly stresses the problem of authorial status in the GDR era and in the following years.

1 Faithful to the classic traditions of pre-war German cinema, GDR critics referred to well-known scriptwriters like Wolfgang Kohlhaase as the *Filmautor* or *Autor*; this distinguishes East German use of the term from the West German concept of *Autorenfilm*. This notion was more commonly tied to its literary origin: the author (lat. *artifex*), as a sign for an institutionalized ideology of self-expression, was in this more general sense not only the writer, but the director as a film-maker and film-creator.

Based on the symbolic construct of the word *Autor* itself, the ideology of the author simultaneously served the inner and exterior legitimization of the state-subsidized and party-controlled cinema as well as satisfied any oppositional will of expression.[2] Even after unification, the authorial shadow looks like a firm ground for texts that articulate an East German regional identity and yearn for the enunciatory power of the past.

In effect, the DEFA film constructed an innocent and unaffected model of spectator, who was to trust the enunciational source in all questions of believing and knowing. The rupture between knowing and believing in the socialist society undermined this strategy during the last decade of socialist realism, at least after *Solo Sunny* (Konrad Wolf, DEFA 1980). But only a few *Wendefilme* are really aware of this break and seek to propose new communicational contracts. One of these happy few is *Letztes aus der DaDaeR* (Jörg Foth, DEFA-Gruppe “DaDaeR” 1991). To be sure, the majority of film texts are based on the classical closed enunciation mode of an objective narration and visualization, in other words on the objectivity of the voice and of the gaze. An alternate way of establishing narrative authority has also been found by making the objective gaze explode in a poetic will of absolute self-expression, as in the dreamlike visions of director Herwig Kipping. On the one hand, he consciously recalled the dreamlike mode of Romanticism in the pretentious bio-pic *Novalis—Die blaue Blume* (Thomas Wilkening prod. 1993). On the other hand, in his diary of the GDR-foundation days, *Das Land hinter dem Regenbogen* (DEFA-Gruppe “DaDaeR” 1992), the tortured corporeality of the children and the landscapes of Stalinism literally blow up.

Films of the *Wende* often go back to a precise definition of space and time in the GDR, which is founded on pre-*Mauerfall* DEFA-discourses about national identity. Such chronotopic narratives (the Wall is the exemplary case) work as the visual representation of a collective consciousness and at the same time as a sign of the discursive construction of participation. The most impressive confrontation with the GDR-chronotopy is the work of Jörg Foth, his DEFA technical team “DaDaeR,” and two well-known underground cabaret-actors, Steffen Mensching and Hans Eckard Wenzel, who produced the aforementioned *Letztes aus der DaDaeR*. The film follows the theatrical *personae* of Mensching and Wenzel, i.e. the clowns Meh and Weh, into a journey through the most representative locations of the GDR after the fall of the Wall. By incorporating into the narrative historically meaningful places, like the cement plant in Rüdersdorf where dissidents were forced to work, this film challenges the spectator to take a more complex view of the social existence of both GDR and the new *Bundesländer*. In fact, *Letztes aus der*

2 I refer here not only to the often-invoked function of art as a “*Ventil*” for dissident artists, but also to the repressed oppositional will or feeling that characterized many people working in the GDR-institutions although they did not actively oppose the government. This was the case of many DEFA-*Angestellten* (employees).

DaDaeR employs the classical cognitive structure used in the "road movie" genre, which balances a weak narrative with the implicit strong narrativity of the filmed locations and bodies.

It is curious that the regional TV-channel, ORB, presented this ninety-minute long feature film at the beginning of its late-night program, not as a *Spielfilm* (a feature film), but as a performance of two cabaret artists, that is as a happening to be seen as pure entertainment: a warning for the spectator not to take the cinematic reflection too seriously. Certainly, the film is based on a succession of sketches, most of which show their theatrical roots: indeed, the tradition of satirical theater, in the GDR strictly bound to the utopian possibility of an oppositional self-expression, serves here to legitimize the enunciational source and to guarantee high recognizability for the film itself. The dominant objective visual construction, a total lack of focalization, the careful respect for verbal statements, musical pieces and burlesque acting, define the artists as reliable narrators and the filmmaker as a half-documentarian witness; but the chronotopic narrative trajectory opens new spaces, sometimes even in spite of the main enunciational strategy.

The locations where the sketches take place are connotative spaces of discourse: the spectators themselves have to recognize them and relate them to their own experience of GDR and the *Wende*, to interpret these free spaces, as they like. This cognitive reception process begins immediately with the first episode, "Es ist mir eine besondere Ehre" ("It is a special honor"), a parody of the sad and hypocritical party ceremonial, which is located in the auditorium of the old Academy for State and Law in Potsdam-Babelsberg. This was the academic institution where new *apparatchiks*[3] were educated and therefore the designated place for impressive state ceremonies. The dialogue between official speakers Meh and Weh shows the emptiness of the institutionalized word: the socialist rhetoric is deconstructed through ironic assonances (e.g.: "Epidemie der Künste," or "epidemic of the arts," instead of "Akademie der Künste," "Academy of the Arts"), until the verbal emptiness itself destroys the acting bodies upon which this word was written. At this point, the reciprocal exchange of honors devolves into a sadistic duel, where the assigned medals are no longer signs of value but reveal themselves as slashing weapons. Both protagonists are thrown into a garbage container.

The construction of this scene seems to support the cognitive work of the spectator. Meh and Weh themselves are but postcards from the DaDaeR, activating the viewer's narrative capability, memory, and expectations. Their duel of stinging medals is a pantomime based on the visualization of the bodies: when they are containerized into the garbage truck, the allegorical meaning of their corporeal presence becomes excessively clear. They are not only functions of the narrative metaphors, but they are also subjected to the

---

3 Russian term for politically reliable Communist party functionaries.

complete control of the camera: Meh and Weh, while lying in the rubbish, are suspended in the air by means of a slow camera movement that turns the image upside down. They not only have no right of looking or moving, they also lose any weight or consistency.

Emblematic in this sense is a pantomime played by Meh, in which he tells his companion the events of his life. He communicates through facial expression and gesture, while his make-up and costume as a clown erase every individual trait. Like the locations, the actors' bodies are taken as functional elements of the visual construction of the scene, shapeable profilmic material, places like any other in the imagery of the film.

Even if the fools' lack of corporeality is emphasized by filmic codes and genre rules like the continuous slapstick gags, the fact that the theatrical figures of Weh and Meh were already well-known to Berlin audiences transforms their iconic appearance into phantasmagoric indices of GDR history, leading the spectator along a narrative trajectory of parodied party ideology and through spaces of memory or *Gedächtnis* loaded with meaning. Contaminating filmic cognition of socio-historical formations with a literary and theatrical parodic mood, *Letztes aus der DaDaeR* satirizes mercilessly the structural discourse of GDR state ideology, that is of the socialist myth of collective participation and of the national spaces or chronotopic formations where this mythology was enacted.

Andreas Dresen's *Stilles Land* also goes back to the problem of the East German post-socialist identity, beginning with the protagonist's interpretations of Beckett's *Godot*. The search for identity during and after the Wende thus begins with an exploration of both theatrical traditions and a provincial location. The filmmaker wrote in an introductory note to his original screenplay:

> Dies ist kein Film über Theater, auch wenn er fast ausschließlich an einem Theater spielt. Es ist auch keine wie auch immer geartete Provinzsatire. Provinz ist ja bekanntlich immer woanders und man selbst hat damit natürlich am allerwenigsten zu tun.
>
> [. . .] Es ist letztendlich das Land meiner Kindheit, meiner Jugend, von dem hier erzählt werden soll. Das Theater, die Stadt, die Landschaft—lauter uneingelöste Versprechungen, Dornröschens Schloss, das hinter der verstaubten Dornenhecke auf den rettenden Prinzen wartet. Stilles Land der nicht eingelösten Träume und Hoffnungen, graues Land, das in seiner Abgeschiedenheit und Kargheit eine eigene Poesie hat. Es ist die DDR, aber nicht nur, es ist auch dieser Landstrich dort oben im Nordosten mit seiner Weite, seiner Spröde, Eintönigkeit.[4]

4 Excerpt from the introduction to the screenplay of *Stilles Land*, unpublished:
This is not a film about theater, even if it is placed almost completely on a theater stage. Neither is it a provincial satire of any kind [. . .]
It is ultimately the land of my childhood, of my youth, which I want to speak about. The theater, the town, the country—these are nothing but broken promises, the castle of Sleeping

These premises notwithstanding, the story never gives up a paternalistic, caricature-like tone in its representation of the narrow-minded inhabitants of the Mecklenburg province. Intellectual theater director Kai keeps on crashing against indifference and apathy towards any cultural proposal, as in the beginning scene of his arrival in the little town:

> Kai: Hallo, koennen Sie mir sagen, wo hier das Theater ist?
> Passant: Hier gibt's kein Theater.
> Kai: Doch. Hier muss es.
> Passant: Weshalb fragen Sie, wenn Sie alles besser wissen?[5]

The amusing sequence of Kai's dinner at the *Volkshaus*, the old institutionalized meeting place for the socialist community, illustrates the clash between high culture and provincialism. What remains of the one and only recognized structure of interpersonal communication and popular culture in the region are but drunken and quarrelling villagers. Kai ends up being beaten because he dared to order a cup of tea instead of sharing in the local traditions of the habitual customers, i.e. consuming excessive quantities of beer. The visual rhetoric emphasizes, as in many other films of the *Wende,* the threatening aspect of corpulent provincial people: one of them looks at the protagonist from the menacing height of his massiveness and is looked at by little, shuddering Kai—the primary identification source—through a strong *contreplongeé*, a point of view shot filmed from bottom to top.

The spectator is clearly invited to fear the rough hostility and the provincialism of the common people, a curious phenomenon after forty years of DEFA tradition, during which one of the most debated aesthetic goals was a politically correct representation of the worker and peasant classes accompanied by an effective communication strategy aimed at reaching the so-called *gewöhnliche Leute* (ordinary people). The paradox of this caricatured view of ordinary people is a sign of the social distance between urbanized, high-cultured filmmakers and ordinary, *kleinbürgerlich* filmgoers, which results in the aforementioned longing for enunciational strength and for the authorial miracle. In this sense, the chronotopic representation of the East German countryside is reduced to a self-referential narrative space of identification, by means of stressing differences and superimposing the

---

Beauty, who waits for the prince to rescue her. The still land [Stilles Land] of unfulfilled dreams and hopes, a gloomy land that could find in its seclusion and meagerness a poetry of its own. It is the GDR, but not only, it is also this wide, austere, monotonous expanse of land in the Northeast.

5 Kai (to a passer-by): Could you please tell me where the local theater is?
Passer-by: There is no theater here.
Kai: On the contrary. There has to be.
Passer-by: Why do you ask, if you know everything better?

author's views on the background of urban legends about the province. If so, the bond with the DEFA heritage is actually more strengthened than betrayed. The DEFA productive apparatus would have liked to tell stories about the working classes and ordinary heroes. This utopian goal was mainly unachieved; instead, DEFA films depicted the struggle of the *intelligentsia* or remained limited to optimistic romances about idealized factory workers. Interestingly, the series of Berlin films written by scriptwriter Wolfgang Kohlhaase can be compared with the West German *Heimatfilme* for its potential for cultural identification. This is not because of a thematic or ideological similarity, but for the evident attempt to outline a national identity that includes the popular classes by imagining social reality as a community, in this case a young urban *Kiez* (the typical Berlin district) community. For the GDR filmic culture the province, not involved in politics and anchored to the good old traditional wisdom, was an unsolved problem. Films after the fall of the Wall tried sometimes to discover new spaces in the economically underdeveloped and ecologically wasted country regions of the new *Bundesländer*, but they ended up as narcissistic self-reflections without real references to society.[6]

Apart from the authorial construction of non-urban spaces, another reason for filming provincial locations and residents as objects of cruel satire is the general semiotic truth that they offer a full range of stereotyped characters and popular caricatures. By using these stock figures, the filmic sign system achieves a non-traumatic portrayal of radical changes in social and cultural habits. This would explain the taste for horrific melodramatic commonplaces that characterizes films like Helke Misselwitz's *Herzsprung* (Thomas Wilkening prod., 1992) and *Engelchen* (Thomas Wilkening prod., 1996).

As Andreas Dresen noted, we are talking about the GDR, but not only the GDR. It is also a strip of pan-German land, it is the provincial idyll intended as a space of childhood and of never-realized dreams, as a space of immobility and timelessness. The visual construction of the locations around the anonymous village of Anklam in *Stilles Land* undertakes this task: it freezes and hinders the action, setting the narrative free from temporal structures and conditions, at least for a while. Indeed, the film uses a series of short, motionless, deep shots of country landscapes as punctuation marks. The first one is a subjective shot showing Kai's point of view from the train compartment when he arrives in Anklam. The second is the most suggestive, taken during a rude argument within the theater ensemble. The leading actor Horst cries out his disappointment at the moral collapse of the socialist nation with theatrical impetus: "Das-Land-ist-still!" ("The land is silent!"). Cut, a panoramic view of the Mecklenburg fields follows silently and echoes this laconic utterance, as it were framing the sound.

6 Clearly, the same cannot be said of documentary productions.

Unavoidably, the succeeding similar panoramic views, like dots and colons of the montage, let the desperation of the foolish actors sound anew: some of these shots underline topical events in Kai's relationship with scriptwriter Claudia; one celebrates at dusk the fall of the Wall; one shows the dark night of disappointment at the lack of an audience for the theater premiere. In parallel runs a sequence characterized by the presence of the actors' bodies within the landscape, specifically the industrial harbor, always by night, always loaded with light and loneliness. This shall be the place for expressing melancholy, sensitivity, longing for love. At the end of the film Horst and Kai, whose name means "pier," meet here, and without a single word, turn their eyes towards the sheds and the cranes reflected in the sea. The factory, the sea, the countryside establish the unabridged borders of the diegetic world.

By this I mean not only the geographic borders, but also the syntactical limits of the discourse flow. The end of this flux is obviously fixed by the last scene, where Kai seems to accept his limitations. As Claudia leaves with a West German journalist, the film shows us a thoughtful Kai on the stage. A cut takes him onto a country road lost within the elegiac horizon: it is the first time that the film visualizes a way of escaping. Kai looks with curiosity at the far-off shores, turns around, looks at the village and goes back. After another cut he stands again on the stage, but this time the curtains open, the spotlights turn on, a musical comment starts over and the story freezes definitively within a frame stop. The narrow limit of the stage should be sufficient for Kai to fulfill his desire for self-realization. These limits are enforced in the next example, a film from 1990 that works on the symbolic value of the traditional, provincial and not-yet-divided German *Heimat* during World War II.

Maxim Dessau's *Erster Verlust* (DEFA, 1990) tells a story about the cruelty of the war and about femininity within the traditional discourse of *Heimat* literature and film production, going back to 1942, when a young farmer is called up into war. His wife Kathrin and his sister Frieda get help with the farm from the Nazi state: a Russian war prisoner. Alexej needs to be nursed back to health and Kathrin falls in love with him. When a *Wehrmacht* soldier discovers them, Alexej is taken away.

The film begins with a non-diegetic *Knabenchor* ("a boy's choir") and a complete view of the village, but the camera looks immediately for Kathrin and finds her asleep in the cemetery. The title sequence ends with another panoramic view shot from the church tower. After learning the chronotopic coordinates, we see the farmer working in the fields; the camera moves then towards him and goes around him: he looks to the camera, panting loudly. The camera leaves him, panning across the whole width of the scene and ending by showing a panoramic view of the valley at his feet. A feminine voice-over introduces a fade, which transforms the landscape into a big close-up of a hand, putting a stethoscope on a nude shoulder. "Breathe out, breathe in. [. . .]" repeats the woman. The camera first follows the hand, which is crossing the feminine body of the patient and reaches the chest for the check up; then it goes on examining her and discovers Kathrin's tender face. Cut.

I would like to underscore the symbolic function of this fade within the first sequence, which at first glance serves the thematic introduction of the film as a presentation of both characters and locations. The fade sublimates the landscapes into a body; this means that, through fading, the narration hypostatizes the native country, the *Heimat*, in the form of the feminine body. This symbolic connotation is not to be forgotten throughout the whole examination, and overdetermines the last words of the doctor: "You are absolutely healthy, Kathi, you only need to rest."

The film continues in a dark room. A door opens and two women enter. The camera moves back and zooms to a close-up of Kathrin. She enters the room, followed by the panning camera, and hunches over a bed, looking for something. Cut. We see in a close-up a picture book, then the camera pans until it frames the body of a uniformed, sleeping girl. A musical commentary starts over the close-up of her face, upon which the camera stops and zooms. A cut back to the preceding close-up of Kathrin follows. Although this scene apparently has been built as a subjective shot, it works according to the rules of the shot/reverse shot, because the camera remains in one position between takes and one has only the impression of observing the quietly sleeping girl from the same angle as Kathrin's: I prefer to describe this apparent point-of-view shot as a false subjective one.

After having established the main narrative figure's visual perspective, the film concedes a complete view of the room, i.e. of the narrative space. The spectator shares the angle of the girl's mother, who has been standing at the door the whole time, but the camera is positioned behind her shoulders and her back is visible within the frame. This take is nothing but a half-subjective shot, confirming again that the film is not willing to allow any character complete autonomy of sight. In narratological terms, it means that no character assumes the task of focalizing the story.

This last note has to be related to stylistic elements like the coarse-grained black and white photography and the elegant writing of fine camera movements and symmetrical cutting. While this aesthetic choice lies in the best DEFA tradition of classical historical films, like the prize-winning *Jakob der Lügner* (Frank Beyer, 1974) and *Die Frau und der Fremde* (Rainer Simon, 1985), it certainly contributes to establishing a distance between the enunciation source and the story being told. The presence of an enunciational point of view was already underlined during the first scene: firstly by the strong *plongeé* at the beginning, in other words by a panoramic view from God's angle, then by the metafilmic view from the dark top of the church tower—taken through a window and from behind the chiming bells—and finally by the farmer's look into the camera, as the camera itself approaches him. All these shots, though diegetically functional, reveal an external, extradiegetic point of view, a narrator focalizer, which requires the spectator not to share his gaze with the characters.

Kathrin's role, as I already noted, is to be the object of the spectator's gaze, an untouched landscape to be observed, full of the yearning on which the enunciation relies. Continuing the aforementioned scene, she stands up from the girl's bed and steps to the left: the camera moves slowly into the room together with the second woman in order to follow Kathrin. Cut. We go to a close-up of the protagonist's hands taking a photograph from another picture book. A teddy bear dressed like a *Hitlerjunge* (a member of the Nazi youth organization) is also clearly visible. The camera zooms closer, so that one can recognize the girl's family in the photograph, and it pans down while Kathrin puts down the photo and takes a drawing from a picture book named *The First Battles on the Western front.*

The accuracy of these details, here and in the following sequences, and the narration time dedicated to them, show how the film takes care of the re-establishment of the mythic world of the German *Heimat*. It is a sort of little showcase of the accessories of a past time, in many cases of old playthings reminding us that the dream of the leisurely homeland could be pleasurable, similar to the dream of a lost childhood.

Set like *Stilles Land* in the present time, the modern *Heimatfilm*, *Neben der Zeit* (Andreas Kleinert, Ö-Film 1995) relates in many ways to *Erster Verlust*. This film looks at the East German provinces as a region where differences and shifts are not admitted in the self-image of pre-unification villagers, telling the story of a Mecklenburg family composed of an aging mother and her twenty-something son and daughter. The central role of the daughter, a railway station master expecting to be fired as regional trains are being cancelled after the *Wende*, is played by Julia Jäger, the same actress who played Kathrin in Max Dessau's wartime film. She "again" falls in love with a Russian soldier, Sergej, this time a member of the retiring troops of the Warsaw Pact who does not want to return to Russia and hides in the ruin of a former Red Army military base. Julia's brother Georg, emotionally and economically dependent on the mother, is desperately jealous and kills Sergej. Julia leaves the village for good, taking the last train to leave her little station for Berlin.

Despite the nervous character of Georg—played by Sylvester Groth, whom we are going to meet in another disturbing role in *Abschied von Agnes* (Michael Gwisdek, Ostfilm 1993)—one has a foreboding of the possible traumatic ending when the whole story of the mother is revealed. She once fell in love with another Russian soldier and drove her German husband to suicide, causing her frustration and social banishment. The falsely idyllic family picture presented at the beginning of the film blows up when Julia innocently takes Sergej home: the visual construction of the dinner scene openly underscores the narrative re-establishment of the oedipal structure, whose strength shatters Georg's unstable equilibrium between the childish role he plays and the desire he feels towards both mother and sister. At first he reacts hysterically and violently, forcing the mother to dance with him like a puppet; significantly, he obtains her consent. Supported by this sort of agreement, he waits until Julia has consummated her first night of love to suffocate the exhausted Sergej with a pillow. The incestuous drama told in this film mirrors the fracture that the failing of the patriarchal order of Prussian socialism inflicted on the would-be-objective view of Germany implied by common-sense filmic rhetoric. Thus the closing shot of *Neben der Zeit*, which shows Julia looking sadly at her *Heimat*, is a mirror image of the final shot of Kai in *Stilles Land*, but with one notable difference: Julia breaks out of her circumscribed landscape while Kai accepts it.

Upon the rhetoric of a German national identity, specified and identified in the case of DEFA films through particular connotations that we named the "GDR chronotopy," the socialist ideological apparatus built its state mythology, legitimizing itself through antifascism and brilliant antifascist movies, like *Fünf Patronenhülse* (Frank Beyer, 1960). The figures of socialist rhetoric became self-sacrificing workers in the *Gegenwartsfilme* (films about the present), through which the stable order of the community imagined by the party ideologists had to be represented. Curiously enough, it is precisely the stability of affective relationships dictated by DEFA that shows today how much the Oedipal iconography marked the socialist imagination. The desirable corporeality was that of the working man, while the body of the woman walking beside him stood for generative capability and symbolized national unity (the few exceptions were, in the 1980s, *Solo Sunny* and the works of filmmaker Evelyn Schmidt), while many *Jugendfilme* (films about youth) helped to situate their children in an educational project, which wanted them to guarantee the sunny future of the socialist enterprise.

The figures of the socialist Holy Family—the worker, his wife, their son—hypostatize both state reason and a transcendental collective subjectivity, legitimized by the aforementioned enunciative strategies: literariness; authorship; the address to a weak model-spectator; belonging to the German *Heimat*; position within the chronotopic coordinates of the GDR. In the GDR, their cinematic bodies served the "re-personalization of totalitarianism,"[7] but after the *Wende* many films restored this narrative place, trying to individualize anew the ghostlike, frightening collective experience of being reunified with capitalism. A film obsessed with the banishment of the East German Holy Family is *Jana und Jan* (Helmut Dziuba, DEFA 1992).

Helmut Dziuba directed some of the most ambiguous DEFA-*Jugendfilme*—e.g., *Erscheinen Pflicht* (1984), *Verbotene Liebe* (1989)—and apparently could not abandon his favorite figures. *Jana und Jan* tells the love story between two teenagers locked up in a reformatory a few months before the fall of the Wall.

---

7 I refer to an unpublished suggestion of Klaus Finke at the Oldenburg University.

Jana seduces Jan, and gets pregnant; but when she tells him that she is willing to abort, the little man beats his little woman with anger. She repents, just in time to refuse an abortion. They meet again and flee the reformatory for the open spaces of unified Germany: when they arrive at the old border, walking through the ruins of the Wall in the middle of the Thuringian forest, she finally gives birth to the child.

The film openly assumes the penal institution as a representative microcosm through continuous reference to the 1989 events, but otherwise makes the cruel experience of being imprisoned unreal by an uncritical use of prison film genre conventions and by portraying secondary characters according to common stereotypes about bad boys, bad girls, and hypocritical educators. Even the enunciational point of view gets its embodiment in the sensitive character of Julia, a nice lesbian girl, who suffers at the miseries of the community and ends up committing suicide. Corporeality itself, despite being at the center of the narrative trajectory, is negated by its own broken visualization: exemplary in this sense are the love sequences. In the seduction scene, when Jana silently enters the men's shower and undresses slowly in front of a naked Jan, the editor employs a rude spatial and temporal fracture: as Jana stands finally denuded in front of the camera, she slightly turns her head, timidly. A cut shows the corresponding take of Jan staring at her, but suddenly her hands enter the frame to caress the boy's trunk, in spite of a distance of four or five meters that seems to separate the lovers. In the next scene she sits upon him and embraces him before the lascivious gazes of Jan's pals. This radical temporal ellipsis, like the contradictory exposures and angles of the eye-line shots of Julia's shy love declaration to her androgynous friend Lady, undercuts the abashed discovery of feminine physicality by both Jana and Julia, and compels them back to their narrative roles.

The last frames reinforce the strong symbolic value of the last scene—the birth of the child in the unified no-man's land: The pains start. Cut. Panoramic view of the Thuringian forest, through which the border crosses. In voice-over, Jana is shouting Jan's name. Fade. Extreme close-up of Jana shouting, but now she is lying on a hospital bed. Frame stop, credits. What if she had aborted?

More significant than the male rhetoric of this final ethical question is the desperation underlying these doubts, showing how the enunciation yearns for the solidity of old narrative structures and tries to rebuild the feminine hypostasis of the young amorous mother as a glimmer of hope in a time where things become anarchic and chaotic. The medium *Wendefilm* renounced even such DEFA virtues as the representation of work: in *Jana und Jan* there are only two one-minute scenes showing the girls plucking chickens. Both scenes are functional to the narrative as they show the cruelty of Jana's colleagues in the face of her pregnancy; on the other hand, they do not know how to relate to their own physicality, so that the *Mater Dolorosa* depicted by fading and stopping the frame can only be a phantasmatic representation of the great *manqué*, the lack of male creative power left by the *Wende* under the ruins of the Wall.

Last but not least, I would like to stress the textual work of the filmic discourse of the *Wende* on this *manqué*, after having tried to fill it with the apparent iconographic fullness of the old socialist Holy Family. Many *Wendefilme* thematize, in one way or another, this ghostlike experience of (cultural and existential) dissolving that emerges as the deep structure of the East German self-representation on the screen.

In *Letztes aus der DaDaeR*, the ghosts emerge while Meh and Weh participate in the reunification celebrations on Walpurgis Night 1990, in the middle of the Harz Mountains, again on the old border. The protagonists' performance does not fit with the enthusiastic atmosphere, as they recite critical texts comparing past illusions with future ones. Through continuous dissolves, they are immersed into the singing, beer-drinking, dancing masses that keep the federal German flag flying. Nonetheless, they do not succeed in overlapping the western witchery with the spirits of the eastern past: a drunken patriot attacks them and shouts directly into the camera, having unknowingly recognized the symbolic value of the clowns. The half-documentary modality permits the spectator figure to escape the control of the enunciational source, causing a wound in the narrative organism.

Even if this may be the only case of metafilmic spectrality, many other *Wendefilme* play with the ghosts of the GDR's imagined community on the thematic level. Whereas Herwig Kipping tortures, crucifies and blows up the actor's bodies, Rainer Simon in his *Im fernen Land Pai-tsch* (Studio Babelsberg, 1993) burns the heresy of the new order at the sacrificial stake of the last fire sequence. The identity crisis was more clearly depicted in his *Der Fall Ö.* (1989), a complex, metafilmic war film, where the failure of the German patriarchy leaves an absolute, dreamlike state of confusion and desperation.

A very sharp description of the grounding experience of this feeling—the memory of the GDR secret police (*Staatssicherheit* or *Stasi*)—has been given in *Abschied von Agnes* (Michael Gwisdek, Ostfilm 1993). This sort of modern *Kammerspielfilm* tells the story of Heiner (Gwisdek himself), an aging writer left alone by the death of his beloved wife, Agnes; he survives by recording memories and impressions of life in order to write again. One day a mysterious man, fleeing from annoying journalists, gets into his apartment. Stefan (Sylvester Groth) imposes his own presence and remains hidden there, letting Heiner take care of him. The young Stasi agent gradually reveals to Heiner that his wife had spied on him; Heiner was so naïve that he also became an informer without knowing it. Finally, Heiner reacts, suddenly throwing Stefan from the window, and regains the weak balance he had won by killing Agnes—as we can now understand.

The fine psychological description of this confrontation between a man searching for emotional stability after the *Wende* by closing himself into his own four walls and the frightening intruder who profanes this sacred place (the ghostly appearance of his would-be-forgotten past failure) is underscored by the optimal framing of the typical Berlin apartment and its claustrophobic perimeter. The way that the rooms of Heiner's apartment surround the courtyard (typical of a Berlin apartment), as well as the camera movements along the gloomy corridors, create an intricate choreography of looking, glancing, peeping, which results in an ambiguous game of rejection and fascination.

Abschied von Agnes openly suggests a homoerotic attraction of the writer for his guest, prisoner and kidnapper, leaving Agnes as an icon of idealized femininity in Heiner's imagination. Stefan dresses in her old clothes and asks his blackmailed housekeeper to go for a walk with him. Heiner is tenderly seduced and agrees, commenting that it would be the first time he goes out with a woman since Agnes' death. The dialogue alludes to Heiner's homosexual desires, which Agnes, a declared lesbian, had spoken about in the Stasi files. In this respect Gwisdek's film, after having satirized the misanthropy and weakness of a word-obsessed, Berlin-centered, authorial modality of narration, stresses also the perversion of the socialist Holy Family and its ghostly existence in this new age of electronic communications. In other words, this film takes the consequences in these narratives, on which the discourse of the *Wende* is based, to the extreme.

As we have seen, those narratives were the constitution of a GDR-chronotopy as a shared diegetic world of any *Wendefilm*, a world structured by the dichotomies urban spaces/countryside, author/spectator, high culture/low culture, oppositional expression through art versus the anonymous ideological control of the SED through mass entertainment and participation. The GDR-chronotopy is depicted on the one hand by recycling the iconographies of the German *Heimat* and of the imagined socialist community on the other. The last type of narrative emerged as the principal source of inspiration for old and young filmmakers even after the fall of the Wall: I showed how the rhetorical device of the classical Holy Family helped immensely to imagine a Cold War Prussian socialism in the past as well as a common identity for betrayed *Ossis* (the inhabitants of Eastern Germany) in the present.

I presume that the *Wendefilme* employ mainly recognizable remains of the GDR-chronotopy which have lost the ideological function imposed by official discourse, and that they try to rebuild the codified commonplaces of Prussian socialism into a new post-socialist identity, imagining East Germany as a community based on both German and socialist memories. But in times of globalism and electronic communication, the hypostatic substitutes (*Ersatzfiguren*) for dreaming oneself untouched, i.e. the Worker, his Wife and the Holy Child, have lost any congruence or reference to reality. The films of the *Wende* choose between two possible answers: disguising any social change by declaring sacred the DEFA-experience or blowing up the corporeal presence of these ghosts of an ambiguous past. Neither communication strategy has reached a wider public. The *Wendefilme* themselves, not shown and not even known, are only phantasmatic apparitions of a long, long, legendary time ago.

Filmography

Abschied von Agnes (Michael Gwisdek, Ostfilm 1993)
Engelchen (Helke Misselwitz, Thomas Wilkening prod. 1996)
Erster Verlust (Maxim Dessau, DEFA 1990)
Die Frau und der Fremde (Rainer Simon, DEFA 1985)
Herzsprung (Helke Misselwitz, Thomas Wilkening prod. 1992)
Jakob der Lügner (Frank Beyer, DEFA 1974))
Jana und Jan (Helmut Dziuba, DEFA 1992)
Das Land hinter dem Regenbogen (Herwig Kipping, DEFA-Gruppe "DaDaeR" 1992)
Letztes aus der DaDaeR (Jörg Foth, DEFA-Gruppe "DaDaeR" 1991)
Neben der Zeit (Andreas Kleinert, Ö-Film 1995)
Novalis: Die blaue Blume (Herwig Kipping, Thomas Wilkening prod. 1993)
Solo Sunny (Konrad Wolf, DEFA 1980)
Stilles Land (Andreas Dresen, Maxfilm 1992)

JENIFER K. WARD

German-Germanness: On Borders, Hybridity, and Sameness in Margarethe von Trotta's *Das Versprechen*

The compelling story of the symbolic erasure of the Berlin Wall on 9 November 1989, a move that led to the unification of two sovereign states or to the reunification of long-lost parts of a whole, depending on the political lens of the observer, begged for a movie. And in some ways, Margarethe von Trotta and Peter Schneider, who collaborated on the screenplay with the help of Felice Laudadio, were the ideal pair to make that movie. Von Trotta has long been fascinated with the love-hate relationships between pairs of siblings, friends, institutions, and ideas in a German context, and Schneider has positioned himself (or been positioned) as a kind of spokesperson for the German psyche in general, and as a commentator on the politics of the Wall, in specific. *Das Versprechen* is the resulting work: a film that chronicles the division of Germany beginning with the construction of the Berlin Wall in 1961 and ending with its opening on 9 November 1989. Here von Trotta uses the love story between Sophie, who had escaped to the West in 1961, and Konrad, who did not or could not leave the East, as a melodramatic allegory for the division of Germany. The son that the two conceive in Prague, on neither West German nor East German soil, is named Alexander, an evocation of that important plaza where East meets West in Berlin. He is the "hybrid" resulting from their union. Certainly the story of the Wall as a border separating East and West (and all of the other divisions which led from that primary distinction) has the potential to evoke the currently popular theoretical lens of hybridity, and it is against this backdrop that I wish to consider *Das Versprechen.*

The discourse of hybridity in contemporary cultural studies recognizes that "[. . .] in the complex reality of postcoloniality it is [. . .] vital to assume one's radical 'impurity' and to recognize the necessity of speaking from a hybrid place" (Trinh 1). Hybridity in this sense, then, is most often associated with the struggle of social entities in postcolonial or diasporic contexts to account for the complicated and intertwined facets of their identities, which have evolved from the straddling of two or more borders or cultural heritages. It is often a struggle fraught with questions of power and hegemony, as individuals work to protect one facet of their cultural heritage from being co-opted or effaced by the other. As such, then, hybridity is an argument for radical resistance against an environment that demands sameness. More recently, critics have pointed to the problematic aspects of this argument, reminding us that at the heart of a notion of hybridity is, in fact, an assumption that there are *purities* to speak of. In a recent article in *The German Quarterly*, Todd Herzog refers to the discourse of hybridity—as formulated chiefly by Homi K. Bhabha—as the "theoretical flavor of the day" (1). While I certainly do not wish to contest Herzog's assertion, I do want to suggest that some of the building blocks of a notion of hybridity—borders and complicated identities—have been present in German cultural production in the earlier films of von Trotta since the late 1970s.

In these works, von Trotta played with the components of a discourse of hybridity by invoking the concept of what I would call "incomplete" identities. For example, she often groups two or more women characters who display individually different features of an "ideal" hybrid personality. When, in several of the films, the characters find that the supply of available characteristics in a German context is woeful, the women cross borders into various southern climes to secure supposedly "un-German" traits (warmth, emotion, affinity for nature-not-culture) from peasants in Portugal, schoolgirls in Egypt, etc. The resulting encounters are ultimately little more than a touristic consumption of exoticism.

Das Zweite Erwachen der Christa Klages (1977), for example, arose out of the late 1970s hysteria in Germany about terrorism. This atmosphere, still palpable into the early 1980s, also was present in two subsequent von Trotta films, namely *Die bleierne Zeit* (1981) and *Heller Wahn* (1982). Into the atmosphere of this political turmoil, then, von Trotta's earliest films were released. Self-actualization of women, empowerment, and finding an authentic voice—all high on the agenda of the women's movement at that time—against such an overwhelming political backdrop must indeed have seemed impossible, and, it seems to me, that the journeys of von Trotta's protagonists must also be read as much in light of 1980s feminism as in terms of an "orientalist" maneuver, to use Edward Said's designation. The dilemmas and quests of these characters stand in for similar dilemmas faced by women in general: how to find a "room of one's own" in the "master's house," particularly when the house is in such a state of internal chaos.[1]

In *Christa Klages* the journey is to Portugal. Christa has robbed a bank in order to save a financially troubled day-care center, and finds that she is unable to find a way to get the money into the proper hands. People are unwilling to implicate themselves in the affair by serving as liaisons, one of her accomplices is shot dead during their escape, and the situation for Christa becomes

1 I have conflated, or at least combined, here two emblematic metaphors from Western feminism, the first coined by Virginia Woolf, and the second by Audre Lorde.

untenable. She leaves Germany in frustration and heads south. What she considers to be the archaic and nature-bound lifestyle of her Portuguese hosts, their warmth and emotion, allows Christa to suspend rational thought and escape from the downside of *culture* in Germany into the soothing balm of *nature* in the South. Similarly, in *Die bleierne Zeit*, one recalls that there is a brief sequence in which Marianne is shown in the Middle East. Even though the segment is designed to introduce us to the context in which Marianne is trained as a revolutionary, it further serves the purpose of contrasting Marianne's Germanness to the dark-haired children fascinated with her blonde hair, and allows Marianne to articulate her desire to leave everything German behind, as well as a belief that the revolutionary leaders in her camp are somehow more egalitarian in their thinking about women.

The film *Heller Wahn* was completed in 1982, five years and two films after *Christa Klages*. Whereas Christa began her "awakening" almost by accident—she was, after all, primarily interested in saving a day-care center—*Heller Wahn* centers more overtly on the developing relationship between two women, and the effects and results of that relationship. The two women, Ruth and Olga, are characterized by dichotomies. Ruth is dark, brooding, fragile, dependent, and voiceless. Olga is light, cheerful, self-assured, independent, strong, and capable. After a series of unfortunate events, which bring Ruth to a psychological crisis, Olga suggests that they escape Germany—the site of Ruth's trauma—and head south to Egypt to teach at the Goethe Institute. Egypt is represented, of course, as being what Germany is NOT: chaotic and not ordered, warm and not cold, and full of psychologically healthy citizens. Olga and Ruth's Egyptian host points out to them that, in spite of great famine and deprivation in Egypt, there is no suicide to speak of; that suicide is a German phenomenon. Ruth prospers in this new climate, surrounded by Egyptian schoolgirls eager to learn about Karoline von Günderrode and German women writers.

In all three of these films, then, von Trotta makes heavy use of the transgression of borders, allowing her female characters to move across national cultures in order to "shop" for characteristics, attitudes, and attributes which are apparently not patriarchal and, therefore, also "un-German." Only by physically leaving German soil is it possible for these women to cobble together an identity, which will allow them to return as whole people. While von Trotta no doubt means for these excursions to be implicit critiques of patriarchy and of Germany, one must ask how these representations are different from the type of classic *Bildungsreise* which pits a rational German against a sensual "Other" of some southern nationality.

Perhaps it is no accident that the making of *Das Versprechen* comes after a period of several years in which Margarethe von Trotta herself did what so many of her female characters had done before—leave Germany, in this case to live in Italy, where she made three films. Von Trotta's return to a "German" film dealing with the history of the divided and then reunified Berlin is itself an evocation of the movement in and out of national cultures, both in the extent to which von Trotta's own positioning vis-à-vis the material is informed by her distance from Germany and her immersion in a different culture, and, of course, the degree to which the story of Berlin in postwar Germany is itself a narrative of contested borders, multicultural hybridities and struggles for identities. Even the process of filming reflected a kind of amalgam of various influences: a German-Swiss-French co-production, with a cast intentionally comprised of film workers from both the former east and former west, and co-written with Peter Schneider and Felice Laudadio, the idea to do the film had actually come from von Trotta's Italian friend Francesco Laudadio, who had celebrated New Year's Eve in Berlin in 1989. "That I've returned to Germany with *The Promise* is just as much a coincidence as the one that an Italian would celebrate New Year's in Berlin in 1989. But I feel as if it was meant to be for me. I had to return to Germany but with a new way of seeing things. [. . .] From a distance, I have learned to like a lot of things about Germany that I would never before have viewed positively."[2]

If the making of this film represents a kind of homecoming for von Trotta and a post-mortem of the divided Germany, it also serves as a curious return to the origins of the question of that division in German cultural production. The opening of the film is historical footage of August 1961, with a voice-over proclaiming that in that year the world was divided. Further, as we learn that the narrative of this film will revolve around a couple of East German lovers, one of whom is a scientist and one of whom will flee to the west, leaving the other behind, it is impossible not to recognize the film as a citation of Christa Wolf's 1963 story "*Der geteilte Himmel,*" even though the genders of the protagonists are reversed.

The "divided-ness" and "postwar-ness" of Berlin is inescapable in this film, as is the thematic and formal preoccupation with hybridity, with sometimes permeable and sometimes impenetrable borders and barriers. The medium of film itself is a hybrid art, using word and image to tell its story, and this film in particular plays with the juxtaposition of historical footage and fiction, for example, as the opening voice-over points out that the divided Germany itself was a hybrid: it was the child of Moscow's concept and execution and West Germany's barbed wire. Scenes are frequently shot from the perspective of the border towers, and the wall itself—with graffiti representing the march of world history—serves as the backdrop for any number of scenes, as does the *Kaiser Wilhelm Gedächtniskirche.* Rather than clean editing cuts between scenes, we are often led from one segment to another through the use of a straight-on shot of the S-Bahn heading west or east. Scenes of personal interactions are often filmed through the iron bars of a bed's headboard or

---

2 http://www.flf.com/promise/allnotes.htm (Fine Line Features).

through fences, and even Sophie's warehouse apartment has a view of the wall. We see parallel representations of trucks broadcasting propaganda driving back and forth on either side of the wall, and we watch as Konrad watches west TV and Sophie east. Alexander throws a ball across the wall, and without fail his unidentified counterpart throws it back. And finally, when the border is finally breeched at the end of the film, champagne is shared back and forth across the checkpoint fence.

Likewise, the similarities and differences between the east and the west are foregrounded in virtually every scene. On the one hand, when Sophie and her friends emerge in the west from their escape through the sewers—one of her friends points out that at least *shit* cannot be divided—they do not recognize it as the west. Only when they see a Ford automobile with a license plate BRD, do they realize they have reached the Promised Land. On the other hand, the film makes ample use of the many stereotypes about the differences between the west and the east perpetuated back and forth over the years: the west is represented by high fashion and crass consumerism; by the drug addicts and panhandlers of Bahnhof Zoo; and by the specter of terrorism as depicted in "wanted" posters lining the walls of the subway station. The east fares no better: in the film we see parents turn their children in to the *Stasi*; cynical citizens who advocate parroting the SED party line to gain personal freedoms or privileges; a church turned into a gathering place for rowdy, drunken malcontents; and citizens being forcibly detained, removed, or even shot for the most minor of infractions. Even a child's toy calls up the inferiority of the east: when Alex meets his new half-sister Lene, he gives her a stuffed panda bear and promises to take her to see real pandas at the zoo. Konrad and his wife Elisabeth realize what the children can not: that Lene will never be allowed to accompany Alex to West Berlin's zoo. Konrad steals, therefore, into Lene's room that night and takes the panda from the sleeping child. So that she may have a toy more representative of the drab, but available brown bears in the eastern zoos, Konrad sadly attempts to cover the panda's white face with brown paint.

In addition to the attention paid to the border between East and West Germany, there is a similar preoccupation in the film with the productive possibilities of *places and people apart*: that is, spaces and individuals somehow exempt from the untenable nature of Konrad's or Sophie's worlds: the sun is often evoked as standing in the middle of two orbits; Sophie's French lover is one of the few characters in the film to demonstrate any kind of intact sense of self; the man Sophie hires to go east to attempt to help Konrad escape is of undetermined foreign extraction; and the place where Alexander is conceived is on neither East nor West German soil, but in Prague. Similarly, Konrad's sister Barbara, a minister, spends her time working in a church which serves as a kind of unfettered space through which Sophie and Konrad's letters are filtered. The only exception to this pattern of showing neither-East-nor-

West as positive comes when Harald, Barbara's husband, is deported to the West. Unable to face life without Barbara and in such a spiritually barren location as West Berlin, he attempts to return to the East. He climbs fences and crosses over into the so-called no man's land. Into this place that is neither east nor west, but perhaps the most unsettling physical demonstration of the contested border between both Germanies, Harald walks deliberately and without hesitation. When the border guards' spotlights illuminate him, and when the order comes: "*Halt! Oder ich schiesse!*" Harald continues walking toward the guard's tower and is shot dead.[3]

In *Das Versprechen* then, we see consistent use of the various components of the discourse of hybridity, just as we did in von Trotta's earlier "German" films. I would like to argue that while this may be the case, von Trotta fails to fulfill the discourse's radical potential: while all of the relationships she draws may seem to be undergirded by a kind of complication of a unitary identity, the process must be understood as hybridity's opposite: the starting point is not the desire to account for the richness of an existing, multi-faceted identity in a postcolonial reality, and to insist on retention of each of its lineages, which would be the conventional understanding of the theoretical notion of hybridity. Put simply, von Trotta has attempted to illustrate what happens when a people discovers that its belief in a unitary identity has been disappointed. The two lineages diverged over the course of a brief history, and the new historical circumstances are not enough to undo that fact. When Alexander, at the end of *Das Versprechen*, stands between his parents at the breeched Berlin Wall, he tries to link the three in a kind of recuperation of what never was. From his perspective, he is bridging the gap between his mother and father and, thus, between the two halves of his own national heritage. And since the physical reality of the closed border has been erased, he does not understand his mother's refusal to meet his father halfway. He dismisses her desire to wait with the words "*Warten?! Das Wort kannst du streichen*!"[4] For Alexander, after all, the story of his divided parents has always been simply one of an externally determined barrier. Once the wall is breeched, there is more sadness than ever, because the very fact of the division had provided the identity for their relationship.

In spite of his parents' earlier assertion that "*Liebe geht durch Beton*,"[5] Alexander's existence is the product of a *mythologized* love that has been frozen in time. When the border finally opens, he fully expects that he will broker the reunion of his parents. He recognizes, on the one hand, that he might never have been born if his father had accompanied his mother to the West—which begs the question of what "new" Germany has been born as the

3 "Stop, or I'll shoot!"

4 "Wait!? You can forget that word!"

5 "Love goes through concrete."

allegorical counterpart to Alex—and on the other hand, he maintains a naïve belief that the acknowledged love his parents still share should be reason enough for them to pick up where they left off in 1961. Sophie points out to him that, love notwithstanding, she and Konrad had never actually lived together. The dailiness of so many years of separate evolution has trumped the timeless quality of love deferred, for Konrad and Sophie in particular, but for Germany and Germany, by extension. Alexander's German-German hybridity, therefore, is of no use at the advent of a (re)unified Germany, which so desperately wants to see itself as a unitary culture finally put together again. A hybridity of historically determined differences performing sameness offers nothing, and the film ends with the figure of Sophie in the paralysis of a freeze-frame over which the final credits roll.

Melodramatic as such an ending may be, and as heavy-handed as some of the allusions are in this and other of von Trotta's films about Germany, they do provide a kind of shorthand and easily recognizable map of personal grapplings with German history in the twentieth century. When Alex tries to understand his parents' relationship to each other and this history at the advent of a new era, or when Jan (in the film *Marianne and Juliane*) tears up his mother's picture and demands that the story of her life begin to be told, audiences resonate with the struggles these young people face and the responsibilities they will carry in a Germany for which sorting out complicated identities is not only the flavor of the day, but the very real legacy of a century of contested borders and evolving definitions of what it means to be *German*. Particularly in the two examples just cited, it is the "hybrid" children who are left to sort out the dichotomous legacies of their parents. Jan must decide whether his identity will be shaped by the legacy of his terrorist mother or his liberal, but law-abiding aunt. And Alexander must somehow be both "East" and "West," when both are becoming officially superseded. Both children are given narrative agendas in the films as creators of a new Germany, a task at which their parents failed. Perhaps it is no accident that von Trotta ends the films and paralyzes her images at the very moment at which the youngsters are given this responsibility.

Critics have certainly been quick to point out, fairly consistently, that von Trotta's films about Germany suffer from a concentration on the personal destinies of individuals, rather than on political or historical accuracy. With *Das Versprechen*, she has the added burden of having made **THE** film about the fall of the Wall. In an interview with Mariam Niroumand, she laments: "Als wir 1991 das Drehbuch schrieben, hatten wir ja noch damit gerechnet, daß wir einer unter vielen Filmen über die Mauer sein würden. Jetzt ist es der einzige, und da wird nun alles von erwartet."[6] In this instance, though, personal

6 "When we wrote the screenplay in 1991, we thought that we would have one of many films about the wall. Now it is the only one, and thus everything is expected of it."

destinies mirror a political reality. Even over ten years since the fall of the Wall and the reunification of Germany, the border exists, not only "im Kopf," but also in the distinctions between the landscapes and cityscapes of East and West. Jan's admonition to Juliane to begin to tell the story of her sister, and Alexander's frustration at his parents for standing still when the concept of waiting has just been stricken from the vocabulary of postwar German-German consciousness with the opening of the border—these are the stuff of questions. The answers, if Jan and Alexander are any indication, likely do not simply sort themselves out by virtue of hybridity. In some sense, then, von Trotta's ending to *Das Versprechen* as a metaphor for the unification of Germany is the only legitimate one: a static and fuzzy image, where all outcomes and promises are in question.

Works Cited

Die bleierne Zeit. Bioskop Filmproduktion, 1981.

Heller Wahn. Bioskop Filmproduktion, 1982.

Herzog, Todd. "Hybrids and *Mischlinge*: Translating Anglo-American Cultural Theory into German." *The German Quarterly* 70.1 (Winter 1997): 1-17.

Niroumand, Mariam. "Die Mauerspringer: Margarethe von Trottas Ost-West-Liebestragödie eröffnet heute abend die Berlinale. Ein Gespräch mit ihr und Co-Autor Peter Schneider." *die tageszeitung*. 9 February 1995.

Trinh, Minh-ha T. "From a Hybrid Place" (Interview with Judith Mayne). *Framer Framed*. London: Routledge, 1992.

Das Versprechen. Bioskop Filmproduktion, 1994.

Das Zweite Erwachen der Christa Klages. Bioskop Filmproduktion, 1977.

KRISTIE A. FOELL[1]

History as Melodrama: German Division and Unification in Two Recent Films

Media, history books, and those who experienced the transformations alike agree that the events of 1989/90 in Germany were "historic" events: the peaceful but persistent demonstrations in what had been perceived as a repressive, totalitarian state; that very state's decision not to use force against the demonstrators; the fall of the Berlin wall on 9 November 1989; and, of course, German unification itself. Many of the events were ready-made "television events," providing a drama and suspense that were effective in the moment but that become somehow difficult to tell with the same effect in the past tense, I believe for two reasons. First, the element of Cold War suspense that made German partition and unification a good "story" at the time has now vanished; the outcome is known. Second, the main "character" in the events of 1989/90 was a collective, "the people" (*das Volk*). The experiments of some left-wing dramatists notwithstanding, using "the people" as anything but a backdrop for a more personalized story has always presented dramaturgical difficulties.[2] A solution to both difficulties is offered by melodrama.

It is a commonplace that history can best be portrayed in art through the personal, but "the personal" need not be melodramatic. In the following, I will argue that German unification finds its commensurate expression in melodrama, that the German experience of division and unification was by its nature melodramatic and therefore lends itself especially well to melodramatic representation. German unification and its portrayal correspond to the preexisting topoi and methods of melodrama, in particular a concern with revolution, a tendency towards a black-and-white moral view, the use of family relationships and romantic love as mechanisms of identification, and the potential for either affirmative or critical portrayal of events. It is no accident that the only two feature films shown in a 1999 Berlin retrospective on the fall

1 I would like to thank the Fulbright program for an initial grant that sent me to Berlin to begin this research and my department at Bowling Green State University for allowing me to take advantage of that grant.

2 Erwin Piscator's experiments in "mass theater" in the twenties arguably had as much to do with reaching a mass audience and employing a collective mode of production as with the use of the crowd as a character, while Elias Canetti's use of the crowd in his plays led many critics to consider them unstageable. See Stieg.

of the wall fall into this genre, albeit in very different ways.[3] While Frank Beyer's *Nikolaikirche*, based on the eponymous novel by Erich Loest, adheres to many of the formulas of traditional, cathartic melodrama, Margarethe von Trotta's *Das Versprechen*, I argue, is much closer to the critical or "sophisticated" melodrama described by Thomas Elsaesser.

Melodrama

Melodrama was born of revolution. Well before it became a central term within feminist and psychoanalytic film studies in the 1970s, even before the great Hollywood melodramas of the 1940s and 50s were made, the theatrical melodrama "originated in France with the overthrow of the *ancien regime*. As a form of theater, it is legally the offspring of the French Revolution." As Daniel Gérould notes, "Since the poor and the downtrodden are its protagonists of choice, melodrama tends to favor the cause of the dispossessed rather than of those in power, even when its plot structure ultimately brings about accommodation to the reigning order" (185).[4] As evidenced by the work of D.W. Griffith and, I contend, by the two films under discussion here, melodrama is a highly appropriate genre for times of revolution and change.

Both artistically and morally, melodrama works with stark oppositions: good and evil, dark and light, contrasts that can be expressed both visually and in terms of character. George Bernard Shaw enumerated some of these character contrasts when he described the melodrama as

> depending for variety of human character, not on the high comedy idiosyncracies which individualise people in spite of the closest similarity of age, sex, and circumstance, but on broad contrasts between types of youth and age, sympathy and selfishness, the masculine and the feminine, the serious and the frivolous, the sublime and the ridiculous, and so on. (93)

Such characters never stand simply for themselves; rather, as Martin Meisel has written, "One result of such oppositions and contrasts is immediate recognition, an easier, quicker match to existing cognitive schema; a process that vision itself is primed to serve" (66). As we shall see, German division and unification map all too easily onto the "existing cognitive schema" of the oppositions of the Cold War, the discourse of the GDR as an "*Unrechtsstaat*"

---

3 The *Berliner Morgenpost* reported that the *"Veranstaltungsreihe '10 Jahre Maueröffnung'"* showed twelve documentaries plus *Nikolaikirche* and *Das Versprechen* ("Festspiele").

4 Gérould continues, "Thus melodrama's central theme of oppressed innocence has regularly been perceived as an incitement to rebellion against tyranny by audiences suffering similar victimization [. . .]
As at a tribunal, evil was punished and providence justified. Pixérécourt's friend and champion Charles Nodier, in his defence of the genre, declared that 'Melodrama was the morality of the Revolution'" (185).

(with West Germany and all of the West representing the Rule of Law), and capitalist triumphalism in contrast to perceived socialist economic failures. Moreover, portrayals of the East German past itself tend to indulge a black-and-white view of history, with the actors clearly divided into "bad" representatives and collaborators of the government and their "good" victims and opponents. The Cold War offers a convenient backdrop for what Elsaesser called the "Manichean conflicts" of melodrama (73).

In fact, it is hard to imagine an era better suited to melodramatic portrayal than the Cold War. The Berlin wall, as an absolute social division, practically invites melodramatic representation, as Christa Wolf seems to have almost immediately recognized with her 1963 novel, *The Divided Heaven*, which appeared just two years after the Berlin Wall was built in 1961. In Wolf's reworked "feminist" melodrama, the forces separating the main characters, the lovers Rita and Manfred, are indeed the external social forces of the divided Germany, but reinforced by the personal ambitions and political convictions of the protagonists. Very melodramatically, Rita suffers a nervous breakdown as a result of losing Manfred to the West; in this socialist melodrama, however, she recovers and the reader expects that she will enter into a more politically harmonious relationship with Wendelin, a convinced socialist.[5]

Melodrama's situatedness in the family appeals to well-known mechanisms of identification, enabling it to appear relevant to a broad spectrum of society. The German drama of division was itself a family drama, often enacted quite literally and melodramatically for the press as blood relatives waved at one another across an impassable border (a gesture von Trotta takes as the visual emblem of her film). It is precisely this appeal to presumably common denominators of human experience that led pre-cinematic melodrama to be equated with "the non-literary, the popular and the 'low' in the high/low cultural binary opposition on both sides of the Atlantic" (Mulvey, "Obsession" 123). Melodrama's "personalization" has been "frequently condemned as a key feature of ideological domination in popular culture." Yet, as Bratton, Cook, and Gledhill recently asserted:

> Rather than displacing the political by the personal, melodrama produces the body and the interpersonal domain as the sites in which the socio-political stakes its struggles. [. . .] In this context, the notions of excess, sensation, spectacle and affect by which melodrama is most commonly characterized become key terms in a debate about how the form engages with and processes the complexity of modernity and the politics of cultural change. (1)

Indeed, these authors go so far as to contemplate "melodrama's key role in modernity as a mediator of social and political change through the diverse and

5 Peter Schneider notes that he and von Trotta frequently thought of Wolf's novel during their work on *Das Versprechen*; in fact, they tried to convince Christa Wolf to work on the film with them (Schneider 135).

personalized forms of popular culture" (8). It remains to be asked whether the traditional or the critical melodrama is more effective in this regard.

As a genre, melodrama has the potential to provide either reassurances or critical perspective. The essential ingredient of the Hollywood cinematic melodrama of the 1950s was a woman denied personal (usually sexual) satisfaction by the strictures of a regimented and judgmental society. In many of these melodramas, there is a happy ending, usually in the form of a marriage, as Mulvey and many other critics have noted "like many traditional European folktales, the Hollywood narrative tends to resolve itself around marriage" ("Obsession" 127). This form of resolution is used in *Nikolaikirche* and is in keeping with its basically optimistic and affirmative view of the peaceful revolution (*sanfte Revolution*) of 1989.

It was Thomas Elsaesser's 1972 essay "Tales of Sound and Fury" that first singled out for attention the exceptions to this rule and as Klinger notes:

> invented a category of films called the "sophisticated family melodramas" of the 1940s and 1950s, largely comprised of the works of Sirk, Nicholas Ray, and Vincente Minnelli. This label defined the potential of some melodramas to surpass the genre's cathartic aims and reactionary tendencies to achieve aesthetic complexity and social commentary. Thus, the sophisticated family melodrama realized the genre's historical capability to act as a revolutionary form during times of cultural struggle [. . .] Sirk, the most self-consciously Brechtian of these directors, emerged from Elsaesser's essay as a filmmaker whose oeuvre demonstrated how melodrama, often considered a trivial genre, could achieve the status of a serious artistic and cultural form. (xii)

The émigré Douglas Sirk has arguably been the most influential of these three directors for the German cinema, particularly in his importance for R.W. Fassbinder and others of the New German Cinema generation, to which von Trotta also belongs.[6]

In her treatments of both Douglas Sirk and R.W. Fassbinder, Laura Mulvey discusses a particular critical version of melodrama in which, even when the separated lovers are united at the end of the film, there is often some remaining impediment or obstacle. The two films I will discuss draw on this tradition to varying degrees. Mulvey illustrates her point with reference to Douglas Sirk's *All That Heaven Allows*, in which the lovely and still-youthful wealthy widow,

---

6 Of course Nicholas Ray had major significance for Wim Wenders, but neither of these directors was especially interested in the domestic melodrama; both fall rather into the "masculine" melodramatic genres, gangster movies and westerns.
Only recently has the significance of von Trotta and other female directors of her generation for the New German Cinema begun to be considered. At the time, women directors were almost completely excluded, both from the movement's formal expressions (Oberhausen manifesto) and its reception. As Julia Knight writes, "Although the work of women directors forms an important part of the New German Cinema, women's filmmaking has developed along a course different from that of their male colleagues, and this has contributed significantly to its marginalization in most studies of the new cinema" (25). See also Möhrmann and Fischetti.

Carrie, falls in love with her young gardener, played by Rock Hudson. The two are separated not only by social class, but also by the stigma attached to an older woman's sexuality; her children have already selected a "suitable" partner for her twilight years, a wealthy and boring older neighbor. At the end of the film, Carrie and her gardener are together—but he has been paralyzed in an accident and she is more his caretaker than his lover. Thus the melodramatic heroine both does and does not overcome the social boundaries set for her: she gets the younger lover, but his "damaged" state returns her to a mothering, care taking role (Mulvey, "Notes," 40-43 and 46-47). This partial, not entirely satisfactory resolution is one of the main features separating the traditional, cathartic melodrama from its more critical, "sophisticated" variant. In the following, I will show that, while Beyer's *Nikolaikirche* by and large adheres to the traditional formula, von Trotta draws consciously on the high-impact emotional potential of the genre without providing the same sense of release.

Nikolaikirche

Frank Beyer's film version of Erich Loest's *Nikolaikirche* splits the difference between melodrama and the nineteenth-century historical novel, undertaking to show a cross-section of GDR society through one family: the surviving widow, son, and daughter of Albert Bacher, one of the "true believer" communists who helped found the society. Bacher, as we learn in a series of flashbacks, shot a German "fascist" soldier during World War II and fled to the Soviet Union, where he again had to prove his loyalty to the Soviet-Communist cause by shooting a German P.O.W. The heroism, or at least the extreme physical and emotional exertion, of a young man turning his back on his country and fleeing such a great distance on foot, all because of his belief that the communist solution was a better alternative than the Nazis, provides essential background for understanding why *this* generation, the founding generation of the GDR, believed in its cause so strongly that a wall and a highly developed system of spying did not seem measures too extreme to protect what they had begun. But the generation of the sons and daughters is already distanced from this experience; as a speaker at the ceremony naming a street after Bacher says:

> Als Albert Bacher zum ersten Mal in einem sowjetischen Wald auf einen faschistischen Soldaten schoß—was da in ihm vorging, möchte ich begreifen. Ein Deutscher war sein Feind, ein Ukrainer oder Usbeke aber sein Genosse. Wir lesen Bücher und sehen Filme, doch Vorstellungen kann nur jeder für sich selbst entwickeln. (37)[7]

---

7 "When Albert Bacher first shot at a fascist soldier in a Soviet forest—I would like to understand what was going on inside him then. A German was his enemy, but a Ukrainian or Usbeki was his comrade. We read books and see films, but each of us must imagine how it was for ourselves." Unless otherwise noted, all translations are my own (KF).

As signified by the ceremony itself—the street naming—Albert Bacher has become a myth.

Bacher is contrasted with his son, Alexander "Sascha" Bacher, who is a career Stasi officer. Alexander is motivated, not by true belief in the goodness of his cause, but by sheer ambition with an Oedipal component. The son of General Albert Bacher, as the novel opens, Sascha is obsessed with being promoted from Captain (Hauptmann) to Major, an ambition he finally achieves in the fall of 1989. In the meantime, he carries out every command: spies on his own mother, fills out the required papers on his budding romance with the young Claudia, and abruptly terminates the relationship when he learns that she is active in the oppositional Church and environmental movements. Sascha is a good illustration of Mulvey's observation that "Father/son rivalry, conflict and different forms of reconciliation make up by far the most frequent form of Oedipal narrative, a negotiation into the patriarchal symbolic, which is supposed to involve the subordination of desire to the patriarchal symbolic" ("Obsession," 128). Sascha's particular tragedy is that the patriarchal order to which he aspires—the career ladder of the Stasi—evaporates just as he has succeeded in becoming his father; however, because Sascha is such a careerist, engaged more in a compliant, sycophantic self-abasement to his father's image than in an agonic Oedipal struggle, the reader or viewer is more likely to react to his downfall with *Schadenfreude* than sympathy. In the mapping onto familiar cognitive schema, Sascha is clearly the "bad guy" in the family, the conformist or *Mitläufer* willing to sacrifice everything to the prevailing order although, paradoxically, his father's intention in establishing that order was rebellion. Claudia, far from becoming a melodramatic heroine holding out for the forbidden man, finds happiness in the arms of a more politically appropriate bedfellow.

The apparent heroine of both novel and film is Astrid Protter, whose life initially seems to follow some of the recipe for melodrama, but with a difference: while Astrid is dissatisfied in her marriage, this is not the major ingredient in her mental breakdown. Rather, her professional frustration and her suffering at the environmental degradation she sees around her drive her into a depression. An architect by training, Astrid sees herself caught in a bureaucratic "planning institute" that never has the means to carry out its projects, ignores serious problems of infrastructure or blames them on the inheritance of capitalism ("*das kapitalistische Erbe*"; in the case of broken toilets, obviously a ridiculous claim forty years into the GDR), and quashes all protest or initiative from employees like Astrid. Indeed, after Astrid refuses to sign a report because it does not address the decay of several local schools, Astrid's supervisor sends her on medical leave, while thinking to himself, "Vor zwanzig Jahren hätte solches Aufmucken mit einem Parteiverfahren geendet: Selbstkritische Rücknahme und strenge Rüge, Ausschluß bei fortgesetzter

Meuterei" (28).[8] After she falls in a strip mine—partly shocked by the destruction of nature, partly suicidal—Astrid lands in a psychiatric clinic, where she meets Frau Heit, a woman active in the church movement, which, in this context, stands for authenticity.

It is important to note that the Leipzig Nikolaikirche, and, by extension, "the church" presented in this novel, is a Protestant church with its emphasis on individual conscience and accountability and the priesthood of all believers. Within GDR society, the church provided one of the few democratic and individualistic alternatives to official society. It is this aspect of the church movement, rather than any specifically Christian dogma or ritual that seems to touch and transform Astrid Protter. In finding the courage to engage in protest against the environmental policy of the GDR, she regains not only her equanimity and her own sphere of personal and political expression, but also saves her marriage. Her husband, himself long resigned to the conditions in the GDR and tending towards alcoholism, accompanies her to observe the May 1989 elections, and discovers that courage makes her beautiful ("Mut machte schön," 415).

Astrid's reconciliation with her husband fits the traditional melodramatic mold; indeed, the woman who "saves" her husband from despair and debauchery through her own spiritual strength and virtue is a common Victorian motif. But far from being subsumed in a social order unquestioningly affirmed by the narrative, Astrid's return to her marriage and family is made possible only by the fact that she first goes through a process of individuation with regard to both her family and the larger society. Astrid is tempted by the comfort of belonging to something larger; the novelist represents this with a flock of seagulls:

> Möwen waren Kameraden, Freunde, die würden niemals auseinandergehen. [. . .] Es wäre gut, Möwe zu sein. Unterschreib hier, Astrid, wir anderen unterschreiben doch auch. [. . .] Die Möwe Astrid konnte sich als eine unter vielen fühlen, nicht verfolgt ihrer Buntheit wegen. Möwen sehn sich alle gleich. (276)[9]

As she breaks free from the pressures to conform and stands up for what she herself thinks—in particular for environmental protection—Astrid loses this protection of the group; she is kicked out of the party. This exclusion is in fact a triumph of individuation; when her boss assures her that he, too, will vote for her exclusion, his word choice indicates emancipation, as the German expression for kicking someone out also means, "to fly."[10] While Astrid has

8 "Twenty years ago this kind of trouble-making would have ended with an investigation by the Party: self-critical recanting and strict critique, or being kicked out of the Party if the rebellion continued."

9 "Seagulls were comrades, friends, they would always stick together. [. . .] It would be good to be a gull. Sign here, Astrid, all the rest of us are signing, too. [. . .] Astrid the gull could feel like one among many, not persecuted for her bright colors. Gulls all look alike."

10 "Wetten, Astrid [. . .] daß **ich** dafür stimmen werde, daß du endlich fliegst?" (427).

many of the characteristics of the melodramatic heroine—entrapment in social circumstances, mental instability, ultimate reconciliation in marriage—her self-emancipation, standing for that of all GDR citizens, breaks the mold.
The unreconciled melodramatic heroine of the novel, the remaining figure of lack whose presence casts a shadow on Astrid's happy ending, is her mother, Marianne Bacher, widow of the communist hero. Marianne's adult life has been lived almost entirely in the shadow of the wall, which also played a decisive role in her personal life. Her former lover, the "Cold Warrior" Linus Bornowski, reappears after the death of her husband. Linus's phone call from West Berlin provokes a flood of memories:

> Linus, Linus, Linus Bornowski. Ihr erster richtiger Liebhaber, der Mann vor Albert. [. . .] Linus, der verrückte Motorradfahrer mit der wilden Mähne. [. . .] Der wieder in ihr Leben eingedrungen war, als Albert in Moskau studierte. Auch als Liebhaber verrückt. [. . .] Also nicht nur der Mann vor Albert, sondern auch der dazwischen. Ihr einziger Seitensprung, der zählte. (44-45)[11]

The flickering of this old flame between Marianne and Linus provides the real erotic tension in the novel and the film. In part this is due to suspense (will they or won't they rekindle their romance?), but it is also undeniably because of the implicit melodrama of the Wall as a separating device. As Georges Bataille has extensively argued, eroticism lies in the transgressive act. The wall and the ideology behind it once ripped this pair apart, and the passions of ideology became intermingled with the passions in the love triangle over the years, at least for the two men involved.

The film both minimizes Marianne's role and heightens its inherent melodrama; it reduces the number of meetings between Linus and Marianne to one, but has Marianne's son, Sascha, bugging that one meeting. Having placed a microphone on the restaurant table he reserved for them, Sascha listens to their entire conversation in another room. He does not like what he hears. Marianne, it appears, was pregnant by Linus when the latter disappeared; with the father of this child gone without a trace and no possibility of attributing the pregnancy to her husband, who was studying in Russia at the time, Marianne had an abortion. As this was before Sascha's birth, Sascha suddenly realizes the contingency of his life: had his father not incarcerated Bornowski, his mother might possibly have fled with the Westerner and Sascha himself, product of Marianne and Albert, would never have existed. Sascha seems reduced to hysteria when he confronts his mother with his new knowledge, railing that the whole Bacher family is a product of chance. Much like Konrad in *Das Versprechen*, Sascha spends the rest of the film trying to assert his masculine and authoritarian identity against this affront, only to find himself

11 "Linus, Linus, Linus Bornowski [she thinks to herself]. Her first real lover, the man before Albert. [. . .] Linus, the crazy motorcyclist with the wild mane. [. . .] Who had reappeared in her life while Albert was studying in Moscow. A passionate lover, too. [. . .] Not only the man before Albert, then, but also the one in between. Her only indiscretion that really counted."

impotent against the people's revolution at the end of the film. The film ends with one of the Stasi officers stating, "Wir waren auf alles gefaßt, nur nicht auf Kerzen und Gebete."[12]

The novel itself does not reduce Marianne Bacher's role to reproduction; neither her former lover nor her son learns of her abortion after Linus's disappearance, a secret to which only the reader is privy. In a faint echo of Günter Grass's allegorical treatment of Oskar Matzerath's possible German and Polish fathers in *Die Blechtrommel*, the novel alludes to questions of biological lineage, but only tangentially, with the abortion seeming to stand in for many "aborted" attempts at reunifying East and West Germany or at least opening the iron curtain.[13] Of more concern to the novel's protagonists, however, is ideological lineage. Sascha frequently asks Astrid what their father would think of her involvement with the church, pacifists, and environmentalists: "Was meinst du wohl, wie Vater das fände: Ein Schild, auf dem diese windelweiche pazifistische Losung aufgemalt ist, und seine Tochter trottet hinterher" (324).[14] In Sascha and Astrid's generation, this patriarchal argumentation no longer convinces; Astrid can only laugh at the decaying structures of the Stasi: "'Ihr versteckt euch in eurer Burg mit Decknamen und Geheimnistuerei und laßt keine Frau hochkommen, denn die könnte eines Tages den ganzen Zirkus komisch finden und absurd sowieso. Sascha, ihr spielt Indianer" (325).[15]

The great secret of the triangle Albert-Marianne-Linus is not biological lineage, but the fact that Marianne's husband, Albert, was directly involved in kidnapping Bornowski from West Berlin shortly after his emigration in 1957. Albert has every reason to cooperate in this unsavory affair, in which Bornowski is drugged during a meal at a restaurant and driven away unconscious, for his own commanding officer has threatened to use Bacher's wife, Marianne, as "bait" for Bornowski. The latter's offense was the possession of unflattering photos of Stalin; his refusal to disclose their origins earned him 11 years in Bautzen, the infamous East German prison. After an interrogation at which Albert is present, Linus indulges in sexual fantasies that have as much to do with getting even with Bacher as they do with his lust for Marianne.

Just as the two men know nothing of Marianne's abortion, neither Albert's rival/victim nor his wife is aware of the extent of his involvement in

---

12 "We were prepared for anything except candles and prayers."

13 The date of Marianne's abortion, 1957, was just one year after a 1956 democratic uprising in Hungary was put down and many of its leaders executed.
In her essay in this volume, Jenifer Ward refers to the East/West-German parentage of Alexander in *Das Versprechen* as "German-German hybridity"; it is interesting that *Nikolaikirche* alludes to this possibility as well.

14 "What would father think: a sign with this milktoast pacifist slogan painted on it, and his daughter trotting along behind."

15 "You hide in your fort with code names and all kinds of secrets and won't let any women climb the ladder, since they might find the whole circus funny and absurd, which it is. Sasha, you're playing cowboys and Indians."

kidnapping Linus. In the novel, the event is told in flashback from Albert's perspective just as he suffers a fatal heart attack; he shares his memories with no one. When Linus "reveals" Albert's complicity in his disappearance to Marianne, he has no idea that he is telling the truth; he is motivated solely by a desire for revenge that now takes Marianne as its object instead of its means. When she asks him why he has to be so cruel, his internal, accusatory answer makes Marianne herself responsible for the fact that the Stasi tried to lure Linus with a stand-in for Marianne's daughter.[16]

Proof or no proof, Marianne walks out on him in a scene that provides one of the emotional high-points of the film. "Für einen Augenblick fürchtete er, Marianne würde ihm ins Gesicht schlagen. Da wendete sie sich ab und war eine Sekunde später hinter einem Raumteiler verschwunden. Aus, eine Tür war zugeschmettert, dahinter lag gelebtes Leben" (453).[17] Marianne Bacher, like Sophie, is confronted with a life unlived: the "what if" of a possible life with Linus. Unlike Sophie, however, she emphatically closes the door on that life and, more particularly, on the reasons why it became impossible. The aging Marianne Bacher simultaneously condemns herself to perpetual lack, shows her own independence, and personifies the repression of the GDR past. Erich Loest and his omniscient narrator, by carefully controlling who knows what with certainty, seem to indicate that the actual details of wrongdoing, betrayal, kidnapping, and espionage during the Cold War are not themselves central to the continued existence of the "wall in the head," particularly for the older generation; instead, different experiences and allegiances combine with suspicions and bad consciences to make dialogue impossible.

In a Hollywood melodrama, Marianne Bacher might have rekindled her affair with the lame, aged, and married Linus, his physically damaged state and only partial availability a reflection of the vicissitudes of aging and society's ambivalence towards the sexuality of older women. At the personal level, it is clear that Marianne Bacher would have nothing against such an outcome; as she prepares for her first meeting with Linus, she thinks to herself, "Alter schützte bekanntlich nicht vor Torheit, und ein Mann Mitte sechzig war heutzutage in allerhand Fällen durchaus ein Mann" (149).[18] In the context of the Cold War past and German reunification, Marianne Bacher is left instead without even this partial living man and a damaged memory of her husband.

As befits both the title of the film and the East German origins of its creators, the dramatic climax occurs not on 9 November, the date remembered by most of the world as the fall of the Berlin wall, but with the Leipzig Monday

---

16 In the German original Linus shifts from the second person singular to plural in the same sentence.

17 "For a moment he was afraid that Marianne would slap him in the face. Then she turned away and disappeared behind a room divider. It was over. A door was slammed shut; behind it lay a life lived."

18 "Age is no protection against folly, and a man in his mid-sixties is most certainly still a man in certain situations."

demonstration of 9 October 1989.[19] The crowd comes close to acting as a character during this climactic scene, but not until the audience has been introduced to individuals belonging to each of its various factions. Thus the viewer is privy to the motivations and emotions of church leaders and members (Pastors Ohlbaum and Reichenbork; Vockert and Frau Heit), protesters (Astrid and her husband), the Stasi, who survey the situation (Alexander/Sascha), and the militia (*Bereitschaftspolizei*) who are charged with keeping order and faced with the prospect of having to subdue or arrest friends and relatives (Frau Heit's son, Horst). The fact that the viewers have been drawn into identification with individual "good guys"—and probably feel some ill-will towards Sascha, the Stasi officer who spies on his own mother—assures that we will be "rooting" for the success of the peaceful revolution and cheering when the Stasi officers are left holding the bag.

Nikolaikirche thus ends on a very affirmative note; the peaceful revolution has succeeded and none of the heroes has been harmed. Through her confrontation with East German working conditions and her contact with resistance groups, as well as an interval of therapy, Astrid has found a new confidence in herself and rekindled her marriage. Truth and justice have triumphed, marital happiness has been restored, and the Stasi villains have been punished in the most appropriate way possible: by the thwarting of their ambitions. The only thing missing from this melodrama is the piano accompaniment.

Das Versprechen (The Promise)

Margarethe von Trotta's film *The Promise*,[20] with screenplay by Peter Schneider, at first glance seems to follow the melodramatic recipe with very few exceptions updated for the nineties. Indeed, if one understands "melodrama" to mean the personalization of history, then von Trotta herself recognizes that she is known for this type of film: "Mein Name verband sich [. . .] mit einer bestimmten Erzählweise: deutsche Geschichte über persönliche Schicksale darzustellen" (Matthies 140).[21] The force separating the lovers, Konrad and Sophie, is the wall itself and the prohibitions and expectations

19 Asked about this in an interview, Beyer replied, "Nach meiner Meinung—und nicht nur nach meiner—ist der 9. Oktober in der neueren deutschen Geschichte ein ausserordentlich wichtiges Datum [. . .] Im Rueckblick ist das ein Eckdatum in der deutschen Geschichte. Was dann kam, der 9. November '89 und der 3. Oktober '90, waren die Folgen" (Pflaum). ("In my opinion—and not only mine—October 9 is an extraordinarily important date for recent German history [. . .] In hindsight, it is a cornerstone of German history. What followed, 9 November 1989 and 3 October 1990, were the results."

20 The film was shot in 1993, had its festival premiere late in 1994, and was released to the general public in 1995; it also opened the *Berlinale* film festival in February of 1995.

21 "My name was associated with a certain way of telling a story: representing German history through individuals."

explicitly articulated by the East German government. For von Trotta, known for her feminist films in which women ignore, break free of, or even kill men (*Sheer Madness/Heller Wahn*), this story centered on romantic love is a departure.[22] But a couple separated for the duration of the Berlin Wall (1961-1989) is an especially apt metaphor for the Cold War.

The film opens with documentary footage of the building of the Berlin wall; the grainy, black-and-white quality of this footage along with the 1960s tanks, barbed wire, and uniformed soldiers connote historical reality. At the end of this sequence, a white-clad bride waves her handkerchief to people we presume are her relatives on the other side of the wall. The image freezes on a close-up of the waving handkerchief over which the credits run. The frozen handkerchief serves as an emblem of the German family melodrama, a gesture of isolated femininity.

The narrative opens with a student dance in the 1960s. Konrad and Sophie are dancing a slow dance when the signal is given by one of their group; the students meet by a sewer cover and climb in one after the other. But Konrad trips over his shoelaces; we see him splayed flat on the cobblestones as police sirens approach. Instead of joining the others, Konrad replaces the manhole cover and hides as the police car goes by. This is the first of many turning points when Konrad is prevented from joining Sophie by either chance or cowardice; the film's central question is which one of these forces is really foremost. Even at this point, we can imagine him returning to the sewer and joining his friends below the city, but his father suddenly appears on the scene, tipped off by Konrad's sister. Konrad's father not only chastises him for not thinking of his family—families of those who fled to the West were routinely considered suspect, often demoted or denied privileges—but he calls the authorities and turns in his son, saying that it's better to go to them before they come to you.

Konrad is interrogated and then must prove himself by serving his time in the military, where he is trained as a wall guard. The class motif so common to melodrama enters the picture when it emerges that Konrad has ambitions to study; as his father warns him, only in the GDR will he be allowed to do so. Sophie, meanwhile, has taken up residence with her wealthy aunt, a fashion representative. To paraphrase Mulvey, "The lower antinomy in the polarisations"—in this case male/female, Western *haute bourgeoisie*/East German—"creates an unexpected parallel between the two terms" ("Fassbinder," 47). In effect, Konrad is feminized, both by his failure to break free of the East and by his status as administrated, spied-upon East German citizen from whom obedience is required. Konrad, without insight into these mechanisms, on the one hand allows himself to be buffeted by Cold War

22 The director noted that she relied on Schneider to provide the "male" perspective previously absent from her films: "Ich hoffte auch—zu Recht—, daß Peter mir den männlichen Aspekt 'entschlüsseln' würde, der in meinen Filmen bisher zu kurz gekommen war" (Matthies 142). ("I hoped that Peter would help me to figure out the male aspect that had been missing from my previous films, and he did not disappoint me.")

political forces, but also remains in East Germany precisely in order to regain his lost manhood through a career achievement only possible for him in socialism.

When Sophie tries to get Konrad out by paying a smuggler, Konrad does not come; in this one instance, the audience is kept in the dark about the reasons for his non-appearance. Did he fail to show up because he was more dedicated to his own future than to Sophie, as his rival claims? Or was he tipped off that the ring had been exposed? Sophie seems to believe the former, and we see her shedding her tears alone after a fashion show, still dressed in the provocative red dress she modeled. She is the very picture of the melodramatic heroine: the unfulfilled woman in the midst of superfluous wealth. Over-the-top images like this one—Sophie is completely alone in a dark room, sprawled on a divan in her sequined evening gown; the camera not only lingers on her, but gives a close-up of her tear-stained face—invoke the excessive emotions of melodrama through a conscious appropriation of the iconography of Hollywood glamour.

Sophie and Konrad finally get a chance to meet when Konrad attends an astronomy conference in Prague in 1968. As they sit in a café, Sophie reproaches Konrad that she was the price he paid for his academic success in the East. Konrad seems to want to disprove this when he allows their lovemaking to make him late for his presentation at the international astronomy conference. A long tracking sequence of the lovers running up the stairs to their hotel room emphasizes the joy and dizziness of their reunion, with Sophie's red dress again coding for her passion.

Sophie and Konrad agree that she will join him in Prague if he can complete his studies there; in the conditions of the Prague spring, Sophie finds Prague more congenial than East Germany, and there is some brief discussion of "socialism with a human face." When the Soviet tanks roll into town, however, that dream is gone; Sophie forces her way out of the hotel and into the street, while a soldier restrains Konrad. Again, Sophie appears more competent and assertive than Konrad.

This is the second instance where von Trotta inserts documentary footage into her film; the grainy, black-and-white images of rioting mobs and Soviet tanks are clearly distinguishable from the clean, color photography of the main diegesis, creating a difference that is hard to ignore. Is history merely a backdrop for the personal here and elsewhere, or is it in fact the decisive force in the film? Are the main characters subjects or objects of history? Author Peter Schneider seems to label them objects with his question, "Was macht die Geschichte aus Individuen, die sie gewissermaßen als Geiseln genommen hat" (Matthies 142),[23] but the answer is not so easy even for him.

Exactly what it is that keeps the two lovers separated is a point of contention throughout the film: has Konrad really been kept away from Sophie by political and historical forces beyond his control, or is there something in

23 "What does history do with people it has more or less taken hostage?"

him that has placed his own interests above his relationship with Sophie? Similarly, is Sophie truly the "woman scorned," the helplessly abandoned female powerless to do anything to reunite the pair, or has she also placed her own interests above love, as Konrad accuses: did Sophie become enamored of her aunt's consumer world of villas and high fashion and therefore fail to return to Konrad when he could not escape?

Paradoxically, each appears more "innocent" if s/he is a passive object acted upon by the forces of history, a melodramatic hero/ine tied to the railroad tracks of historical process, as it were. By contrast, to the extent that each has actively chosen his or her own fate, each is responsible for the couple's separation, for the lack of closure in the melodramatic narrative. Admirably, neither Schneider's narrative nor von Trotta's visual realization unties this knot and offers a clear answer; rather, by inviting the viewer to "take sides" in the cinematic divorce court represented by this personal narrative, they also potentially engage the viewer in questions of national complicity in and responsibility for Germany's persistent division.

Konrad's weakness of character, if it is one, is represented by the untied-shoelace motif: his untied laces trip him up during the first escape attempt; we see him bend to tie his shoelace while waiting for Sophie in Prague; later in the film his son, Alex, lovingly binds up his father's shoelace. Schneider is aware of the ambivalence of the gesture: "Ist Konrad aufgrund einer lächerlichen Lappalie—weil er im entscheidenden Moment über seine Schnürsenkel stolpert—im Osten geblieben? Wie wird das Paar mit diesem Zufall fertig, ist es überhaupt ein Zufall?" (Matthies 142).[24] From Sophie's perspective, it appears that Konrad has done exactly what he wanted to do, pursuing his career within a society that financed his studies. But the viewer is privy to Konrad's reality, while Sophie is not. The subplot involving Konrad's sister, Barbara, who becomes a Protestant minister and leader in the church movement, underlines the oppressive circumstances under which the entire family must live. When Konrad's father is not admitted to Barbara's trial (for protesting the Prague invasion), he cries out, "Sogar in der Nazizeit, als ich abgeurteilt wurde, durften meine Eltern an der Verhandlung teilnehmen" (Schneider 70).[25]

Sophie, meanwhile, finds that she is pregnant following the couple's encounter in Prague; but during her visit to Konrad to tell him this, she clearly shows that she has no understanding of what conditions in East Germany have become. She offers to come back to be with him; he counters that she would surely be imprisoned and interrogated for months, and proposes that they meet in Sweden, where he is soon to go for a conference. Sophie does not understand why he turns on the radio during their conversation; he signals that the room is bugged. The viewer sees how Konrad must decide to leave his

24 "Did Konrad stay behind in the East because of a stupid chance event—because he tripped over his shoelaces at the decisive moment? How does the couple deal with this accident of fate, or is it even an accident?"

25 "Even in the Nazi period my parents were allowed to take part in my trial."

dying father in order to join Sophie, and is ready to do this; but at the last minute the government denies his visa, possibly because someone has gotten wind of his plan. Sophie, of course, cannot be aware of this and continues to blame Konrad for his failure to join her. Once again Konrad appears emasculated; but to Sophie, the problem seems to be his lack of character and commitment to her, while the viewer is aware that he is the subject of a paternalistic state. When Sophie is turned away at the border one more time, after many attempts to visit Konrad, she writes to him that they must live separate lives now.

If the emotional attachment truly ended here, there would be no film. From the viewer's perspective, it may be that Sophie and Alex are Konrad's weakness, and that Sophie's continuing attachment to Konrad is her weakness, keeping her from fully living her own life. In the political allegory the film propagates, it was, paradoxically, the desire to maintain peace and some sort of connection at all costs that kept the two Germanys separated.[26]

We see the costs of this ongoing connection when, in the late 1970s, Konrad again appears at Sophie's doorstep while attending a convention in West Berlin. Sophie appears to have detached from him—she is living with a French reporter named Gérard—while Konrad has married and has a child, but their interaction is wistful. As Elsaesser noted, a "recurrent feature" of melodrama is "desire focusing on the unobtainable object" (85). "A sequence of substitute actions creates a kind of vicious circle in which the close nexus of cause and effect is somehow broken and—in an often overtly Freudian sense—displaced" (79). Konrad gets Sophie's permission to have their son, Alex, visit him; Konrad's affection for Alex, the symbol of the ongoing (displaced) connection between the two, proves Konrad's undoing.

Under pressure from the political authorities, who know they can keep him from seeing his son, Konrad signs a statement that his interview with *Le Monde* (an interview he granted to Sophie's partner, Gérard) was a fabrication. The Stasi officer makes the equation perfectly clear: "A signature for a son."[27] Konrad persists in thinking that he can maintain his own individual happiness if he collaborates with the system. Only when this bargain no longer works—when the authorities revoke Alex's permission to travel to East Berlin some years later—does Konrad emphatically resist, but in a pitifully ineffectual way: he seeks out his Stasi officer at a local bowling alley and decks him. Konrad

26 Whether this was "really" (historically) the case depends on one's view of the effects of Willy Brandt's *Ostpolitik*. There have been numerous arguments that Western actions such as paying hard currency for the release of East German political prisoners may have kept the independent East German state afloat longer than might otherwise have been the case.

27 East German scientist Jens Reich finds this action of Konrad's both realistic and understandable: "Das ist überzeugend. Er rettet sich mit dieser Unterschrift und schadet niemandem. Im Westen wußte ja jeder, daß ein Dementi wie in diesem Fall erzwungen war" (Reich 138). ("I find it convincing. He rescues himself with his signature and doesn't hurt anybody else. In the West everybody knew that denials like this one were given under pressure.")

gains nothing from this and certainly does not seriously threaten the state, but does lose his job and his family, and is demoted to working in a janitorial position. Konrad now stands doubly emasculated: by his continued residence in the East, and now by the loss of the outward prestige and achievement that society had granted him. It is in this situation that the wall comes down.

Sophie and Konrad approach each other in the tumult of the night the wall fell, but the film stops before they meet, halting on a shot of Sophie's face that expresses all her misgivings about the damaged man she is now being offered. Unlike Sirk's Carrie, Sophie does not immediately show herself willing to assume the role of consoler, caretaker, nurse for this broken man; the viewer is left without the satisfying closure of the happy wedding, or even embrace.

A woman being interviewed seems to speak for Sophie: "Für mich kommt es zu spät. Wenn nach dreißig Jahren der Käfig aufgemacht wird, kann man nicht mehr fliegen" (Schneider 128).[28] Sophie, although outwardly successful—she has raised her child, has a job, has had other lovers—is clearly in the position of the melodramatic heroine even at the end of the film, an unusual ending for the feminist von Trotta. To me this demonstrates that the film is "really" about German history and how it has robbed individuals of their happiness, and not primarily about the relationship problems of an individual man and woman.

As Mulvey notes, "discussions of the differences between melodrama and tragedy specify that while the tragic hero is conscious of his fate and torn between conflicting forces, characters caught in the world of melodrama are not allowed transcendent awareness or knowledge" ("Notes," 41). The questions about personal and societal responsibility that this film raises come up in every love story—indeed, in every life—but are particularly poignant against the background of the divided Cold War world. The question of what keeps the lovers apart is also, of course, the question of what kept the two Germanies apart for so long: the polarity between the Soviet "evil empire" and "capitalist imperialism," or the combined cowardice and selfishness of individual German citizens?

Conclusion: Critical Melodramas?

Paradoxically, the objections of many critics to *Das Versprechen* centered on its (perceived lack of) verisimilitude. Discussion of the film frequently centered on whether it portrayed "things as they were," and von Trotta's own lead actress, Corinna Harfouch, criticized the film for not accurately depicting GDR

28 "It's too late for me. When your cage is opened after thirty years, you've forgotten how to fly."

reality.[29] By contrast, several critiques of Beyer's film erroneously (wishfully?) referred to it as a docu-drama, while the *Süddeutsche Zeitung* approvingly titled its review "So war es wirklich" (Heims).

East-West identity politics played a role, though not a very rational one, in the negative reception of von Trotta's film within Germany: as Schneider points out, "Margarethe wird immer dafür angegriffen, daß sie nicht hier war, sondern in Rom, als die Idee entstand; man streitet ihr das Recht ab, so einen Film zu machen. Dabei wird leicht unterschlagen, daß ein gewisser Peter Schneider schon seit dreissig Jahren hier lebt und sich ja schon im *Mauerspringer* mit dem Thema beschäftigt hat" (Niroumand).[30] Indeed, before writing his novel, Erich Loest, who had not lived in the GDR since 1981, had to engage in a research process very similar to Schneider and von Trotta's extensive background reading and interviewing of participants.

Both *Nikolaikirche* and *Das Versprechen* reach their narrative climax in a moment of mass revolution: the Leipzig demonstrations in the former, the fall of the Berlin Wall in the latter. In *Nikolaikirche* the triumph of the people's revolution is itself the cathartic high point. The title of book and film confirms this; by focusing on the church as a site of opposition, Loest proclaims his clear standpoint on the side of the oppressed and persecuted, thus following the traditional melodramatic formula. Schneider and von Trotta, by contrast, portray the fall of the Berlin Wall as something that happens to their main characters, not as a revolution in which they have actively participated. Sophie and Konrad thus become objects, not subjects, of history. While this does not necessarily release them from responsibility for the personal choices they have made, the revolution of 1989 provides them no cathartic release or resolution, but only new uncertainties.

The portrayal of opposites in the two works follows similar patterns: while *Nikolaikirche* makes clear distinctions between good and bad, perpetrators and victims, with those individuals and institutions associated with the GDR state generally on the negative side of the balance, *Das Versprechen* allows itself no such moral clarity. Gender partisanship aside, Konrad and Sophie appear

---

29 "Ihre ehemalige Heimat koenne sie in dem Film nicht wiedererkennen, was im Drehbuch noch glaubhaft erschien, wirke im Film platt und unglaubwuerdig. Der ostdeutschen Schauspielerin missfallen vor allem 'die duesteren Bilder' und 'der harte Ton der Gespraeche.' Die Reduzierung der DDR-Wirklichkeit auf einen staendigen Konflikt mit der Staatssicherheit treffe nicht die historische Wahrheit" ("Negativwertung"). ("She said she couldn't recognize her former homeland in the film; things that seemed convincing in the script came out flat and unrealistic in the film. The East German actress was especially critical of 'the gray images' and 'the hard-edged tone of the conversations.' She claimed that the reduction of GDR reality to a state of permanent conflict with the state security system did not reflect the historical truth.")

30 "Margarethe has been criticized for the fact that she was in Rome, not Germany, when the idea took shape; her right to make such a film is disputed. It's too easy for these critics to forget that a certain Peter Schneider has been living here for thirty years and already wrote about this topic in *The Wall Jumper*."

similarly victimized and sympathetic, but also similarly responsible for and thus complicit in their own destinies and separation.

In its use of the family as a focal point, *Nikolaikirche* follows the recipe of the nineteenth-century novel more than that of the melodrama, exploiting the family and relational ties of the Bachers to shed light on many niches of GDR society. It does, however, rely strongly on the Oedipal component of melodrama in the tense relations around Marianne Bacher (her husband and his rival on opposite sides of the Cold War; her son jealously guarding and competing with his father's work and reputation). *Das Versprechen*, with its strong focus on the romantic couple, invites greater emotional identification from the viewer and thus appears to be the more melodramatic text; however, the lack of romantic resolution places it closer to the "sophisticated family melodrama."

Finally, on the whole *Nikolaikirche* is a reassuring text while *Das Versprechen* is an unsettling and critical one. Both films are critical of the situation during the Cold War and the actions of the East German government in particular, but this goes without saying in the post-Wall period. It is more interesting to ask what attitude these films display towards German unification. *Nikolaikirche* celebrates the triumph, not of the West, but of East German opposition, and affirms this through its use of the melodramatic formula: the 68ers Astrid and Harald are happily reconciled, having found their way back to their authentic, protesting selves, while the younger environmentalist Claudia seems poised to follow in their footsteps with an appropriate, church-movement love of her own. One reviewer noted the proximity of this resolution to socialist iconography:[31] "Politik kittet die Ehe, die privaten Schwierigkeiten heben sich in der grossen Gesamtloesung auf—ein noch von frueher vertrautes Motto" (Westphal).[32] Only the irreconcilable differences between Marianne and Linus allude to the difficulties inherent in the project of German unification; the relegation of these difficulties to the older generation indicates that they will be quickly overcome. *Das Versprechen*, by contrast, portrays the fall of the wall itself as an ambivalent moment, confronting Konrad and Sophie with the possibility of an uncomfortable relationship they might have preferred not to face; the historical turn cannot redeem their individual fates.

Das Versprechen, with its focus on the unfulfilled romantic couple, is only superficially the "more melodramatic" of the two films in the traditional sense; moreover, it does not reward the viewer's identification with the romantic couple, but instead leaves the viewer in a state of Brechtian alienation by refusing to resolve the romantic tension. In every other way as well—its questioning portrayal of revolution, its relatively non-moralizing deployment of dichotomies, and its critical rather than reassuring perspective—it is the more

31 In his essay, "Ghosts of Babelsberg" for this volume, Massimo Locatelli points out the central role of the Socialist Holy Family in DEFA film cinography; Beyer, of course, had extensive DEFA experience.

32 "Politics mends the marriage, private difficulties are transcended by the Great Societal Solution—a motto familiar from earlier times."

"critical" melodrama of the two, mobilizing the viewer's emotions to question received truths rather than sigh in relief at the triumph of the good.

Works cited

Bataille, Georges. *Erotism: Death and Sensuality*. Tr. Mary Dalwood. New York: Walker, 1962.

Beyer, Frank (Dir.). *Nikolaikirche*. Made-for-TV film, 1995.

Bratton, Jacky, Jim Cook, Christine Gledhill, eds. *Melodrama: Stage, Picture, Screen*. London: British Film Institute, 1994.

Brooks, Peter. "Melodrama, Body, Revolution." Bratton et al 11-24.

Bruckner, Jutta. "Für Margarethe von Trotta." Schneider 150-159.

Elsaesser, Thomas. "Tales of Sound and Fury." *Imitations of Life: A Reader on Film and Television Melodrama*. Ed. Marcia Landy. Detroit: Wayne State UP, 1991. 68-91. Originally published in *Monogram* 4 (1972) 2-15.

"Festspiele erinnern an den 10. Jahrestag des Mauerfalls." *Berliner Morgenpost*. 27 Oct. 1999.

Fischetti, Renate. *Das neue Kino: acht Porträts von deutschen Regisseurinnen*. Frankfurt: Tende, 1992.

Gérould, Daniel. "Melodrama and Revolution." Bratton et al. 185-198.

Heilman, R.B. *Tragedy and Melodrama*. Seattle: U of Washington P, 1968.

Heims, Hans-Joerg. "So war es wirklich. Frank Beyers eindrucksvoller Zweiteiler Nikolaikirche," *Süddeutsche Zeitung*. 30 October 1995.

"Jens Reich im Gespräch mit Peter Schneider." Schneider 135-139.

Klinger, Barbara. *Melodrama and Meaning. History, Culture, and the Films of Douglas Sirk*. Indiana UP, 1994.

Knight, Julia. *Women and the New German Cinema*. London: Verso, 1992.

Loest, Erich. *Nikolaikirche*. Leipzig: Linden-Verlag, 1995.

Matthies, Otto. "Interview mit Margarethe von Trotta und Peter Schneider." Schneider 140-145.

Meisel, Martin. "Scattered Chiaroscuro: Melodrama as a Matter of Seeing." Bratton et al 65-81.

Möhrmann, Renate. *Die Frau mit der Kamera. Filmemacherinnen in der Bundesrepublik Deutschland*. Munich: Hanser, 1980.

Mulvey, Laura. "Fassbinder and Sirk." *Visual and Other Pleasures*. Bloomington: Indiana UP, 1989. 45-48.

—. "'It will be a magnificent obsession': The Melodrama's Role in the Development of Contemporary Film Theory." Bratton et al. 121-133.

—."Notes on Sirk and Melodrama." *Visual and Other Pleasures*. 39-44.

"Negativwertung," *FAZ*. 17 February 1995. 39.

Niroumand, Mariam. "Die Mauerspringer." *taz*. 10 February 1995: 15.

Pflaum, H.G. "Als der Staatsmacht das Rückgrat brach. Regisseur Frank Beyer über seinen Zweiteiler Nikolaikirche, den er nach dem Roman von Erich Loest drehte." *Süddeutsche Zeitung*. 25 October 1995.

Reich, Jens and Peter Schneider. "Jens Reich im Gespräch mit Peter Schneider." Schneider 135-139.

Schneider, Peter and Margarethe von Trotta unter Mitarbeit von Felice Laudadio. *Das Versprechen oder Der lange Atem der Liebe*. Berlin: Volk & Welt, 1994.
von Trotta, Margarethe (director) and Schneider, Peter (screenplay). *Das Versprechen*. Bioskop Film, 1994/1995.
Shaw, George Bernard. *Our Theatres in the Nineties*, Standard Edition (London: Constable, 1954), vol. I.
Stieg, Gerald. "Die Masse als handelndes Subject." *Frucht des Feuers. Canetti, Doderer, Kraus und der Justizpalastbrand*. Vienna: Edition Falter, 1990. 81-158.
Westphal, Anke. "Postprotestantische Anrufung." *taz*. 12 April 1996: 19.
Wolf, Christa. *Der geteilte Himmel*. Berlin: Aufbau, 1963.

HELEN CAFFERTY

Sonnenallee: Taking Comedy Seriously in Unified Germany

Es wird Zeit, daß man darüber spricht, was die DDR noch war außer Mauer, Stasi und Zentralkommitee. In der DDR gab es z.B. Menschen, die es woanders nicht gab, wie Pionierleiter und Westverwandte. Im Westen hatte man wiederum vieles, was man im Osten nicht bekam: Stones-Platten, Friesennerze und Krönung. Einige Dinge teilten Ost und West aber auch miteinander. Wie zum Beispiel die Sonnenallee. Im Westen lag das längere und im Osten das kürzere Ende. Die Mauer ging mittendurch. (Press material for *Sonnenallee*)[1]

Sonnenallee, a surprise box-office success, premiered in movie theaters on 7 October 1999, the fiftieth anniversary of the founding of the German Democratic Republic. "Ein ironisches Datum," says director Leander Haußmann: "Es ist nicht der Mauerfall, das wäre was Ernstes" ("Im Theater").[2] The book by former East Germans Thomas Brussig and Haußmann had received the prestigious German screenplay prize (Der Drehbuchpreis des Beauftragten der Bundesregierung für Angelegenheiten der Kultur und Medien) in February 1999. Both Brussig, born in 1965 and author of the best-selling novel *Helden wie wir* (1995) and Haußmann, born in 1959, and named best young director by *Theater heute* in 1991 and Director of the Schauspielhaus in Bochum in 1995, are representatives of a new generation of East Germans who have risen to prominence after the *Wende.* Haußmann states that after ten years, enough time has passed to allow for a different and comic reflection on life in the GDR: "Es musste so lang dauern, weil die Ossis noch keinen Abstand hatten. Und diesen Film durfte nur ein Ossi machen" ("Im Theater").[3]

1 "It is time to talk about what the GDR was in addition to the wall, the Stasi and the Central Committee. In the GDR, for example, there were human beings you couldn't find anywhere else, like Pioneer directors and relatives from the West. In the West, on the other hand, there was a lot of stuff you could not have in the East: Stones records, Friesian anoraks, and Krönung-brand coffee. But East and West did share some things with each other. For example, the street Sonnenallee. The longer end was in the West and the shorter end in the East. The wall went right through the middle."

2 "An ironic date [. . .] It is not the fall of the wall, that would be something serious."

3 "It had to take so long, because the Ossis (Easterners) hadn't gained any perspective yet. And only

The comedy's ostensible trivialization of the differences and commonalities between East and West, its supposed taking the side of the East against the West, and its claimed lack of *Regimekritik* ("criticism of the regime")[4] landed it in the middle of a contentious discourse about East German identity and deformation under *die DDR-Diktatur* ("the GDR-dictatorship"). Moviegoers apparently went to the comedy to laugh and be entertained, however. With over two million viewers by the end of the year, *die Mauerkomödie* ("wall comedy"), as it was labeled, had become the most popular German film in the year 1999.[5] Not all viewers were from the East; numbers show one third of the audience to have been in the former West.

To say that the film struck a nerve is an understatement. Responses by cultural critics and reviewers ran the gamut from high praise to condemnation. Praise generally centers on the excellent acting[6] and sound track, the well-made comedy, pace, youthful high-energy, wit, and entertainment value, but also on its treatment of the GDR past; e.g., Kerstin Decker claims that the film represents an "Entdämonisierung" ("undemonizing") of the GDR (278). Critics focus on comedy as trivialization (*Verharmlosung*) of the *DDR-Diktatur*-and/or dismiss it as an example of *Ostalgie*.[7] Bizarrely enough, the Berlin magazine *Tip* even compared the film to comedy produced under the Nazis (Decker 277), despite the

---

an easterner could make this film."

4 "Regimekritik bietet der Film nicht, obwohl das [. . .] einmal so geplant war. So wollte Haußmann, dass eine Hauptfigur von Grenzsoldaten erschossen wird [. . .] Aber er verzichtete dann doch auf sein Gewaltopfer, weil die Geschichte 'sich nicht mehr erholen würde' [. . .] und verkehrte das traurige Ende in sein ostalgisches Gegenteil [. . .]" (Wellershof). ("This film offers no critique of the system, although that [. . .] was planned at one time. For instnace, Haußmann wanted one of the main characters to be shot by border guards [. . .] But he then decided not to sacrifice the character, since the story 'wouldn't have recovered' [. . .] and transformed the tragic ending into its 'ostalgic' opposite.")

5 Although audience share for German films rose in 1999, U.S. hits garnered the highest numbers of visitors, e.g. "Star Wars: Episode Bedrohung" with 7.9 million.

6 Well-known former East German actors Katharina Thalbach (Mother) and Henry Hübchen (Father) are joined by celebrated former West Germans actors Ignaz Kirchner (Heinz), Margit Carstensen (school director), and Detlev Buck (ABV Horkefeld). Micha and his friends are played by newcomers Alexander Scheer (Micha), Alexander Beyer (Mario), Teresa Weißbach (Miriam), and Elena Meißner (Sabrina).

7 One critic dismissed early "ostalgic" enthusiasm in the East by offering "Die West-Perspektive: [. . .] die Story [. . .] ist unbedeutend [. . .] So bleibt ein Film, dem garantiert kein großer Erfolg beschieden sein wird. Irgendwie fehlt einfach jenes Moment, das ihn sehenswert machen würde" (Filmspiegel Kommentar Wolfgang). ("From the Western perspective: [. . .] the story [. . .] is lightweight [. . .] What remains is a film that will certainly not be a big success. The film simply lacks anything that would make it worth seeing.") Claus Löser says that the film was made with "eine zumindest fahrlässig zu nennende politische Unbekümmertheit" (*Film-Jahrbuch 2000*, 333). ("a political carelessness that can almost be called criminal neglect.") Hans Buch also criticizes the film: "Die DDR war zwar unfreiwillig komisch, ihren Opfern aber nicht zum Lachen zumute" (*Film-Jahrbuch 2000*, 334). ("The GDR was unintentionally funny, but its victims didn't feel like laughing.")

fact that Nazi comedy never satirized representatives of the regime, as does *Sonnenallee.*

The question as to whether comedy can be an appropriate vehicle for something as serious as life with the wall in the GDR was raised most emphatically by *Help, e. V.*, an organization dedicated to the support of victims of violence. It filed suit against Haußmann on behalf of those whose escape attempts at the wall resulted in injury, imprisonment, or death, explained board member Alexander Hussock. "Beleidigung von Angehörigen einer Gruppe, die unter Willkürherrschaft verfolgt wurde," is a crime punishable under Paragraph 194 of German penal code ("Die Mauer ist nicht zum Lachen").[8] Specifically, the insult was felt to consist in no serious consequences being shown from the border policemen's behavior at the wall, in the film's portrayal of the border police as ordinary human beings or as the butt of jokes, and in the character Wuschel, who is not afraid after he is shot at in front of the wall but is anguished because his Stones record has been shattered. For several months Brussig had a response on the official *Sonnenallee* web site stating that the insult to victims of the wall lay "Außerhalb des Films" (www.sonnenallee.de).[9] The suit has since been dropped but not the criticism that "die Verbrechen der DDR-Diktatur bagatellisiert werden"("*Sonnenallee* jetzt ohne Strafanzeige").[10]

Spiegel-Online reported in their coverage of the lawsuit against *Sonnenallee*: "in den neuen Ländern gilt er sogar als neuer Kultfilm, der von vielen Besuchern mehrfach angesehen wird" ("Haußmann nach Anzeige").[11] Both the soundtrack CD and the video single showing the Dynamo 5 (five members of the film's cast) singing "The Letter" were bestsellers.[12] The film's web site includes a computer game and a page where clicking the hand of actress Katharina Thalbach as she reaches for *Bückwaren* (scarce goods) behind a virtual counter brings you to a list of *Sonnenallee*-items for sale: t-shirts, combs, posters, etc. Despite the mass-

8 "Insult to members of a group persecuted under totalitarian rule."

9 "outside of the film." The full text read: "Sehr geehrter Alexander Hussock vom 'Help, e.V.'-Vorstand, einer dpa-Meldung entnahm ich, dass der 'Help e.V.' gegen den 'Sonnenallee'-Regisseur Leander Haußmann Strafanzeige wegen 'Beleidigung der Maueropfer' stelle. Da ich derjenige bin, der zu diesem Abenteuer anstiftete, können Sie auch gegen mich Strafanzeige stellen. Zu reden ist von einer Beleidigung, kein Zweifel–es gibt sie. Doch die 'Beleidigung der Maueropfer' besteht nicht darin, was 'Sonnenallee' zeigt. Die Beleidigung liegt außerhalb des Films." ("To Alexander Hussock of the 'Help, Inc.' board of directors: I learned from a German press agency report that 'Help, Inc.' is filing suit against Leander Haußmann, the director of *Sonnenallee*, for alleged 'insult to the victims of the wall.' Since I am the one who incited this episode, you may add my name to your suit. It is certainly correct to speak of an insult; there is no doubt of that. But the 'insult to the victims of the wall' does not consist in what *Sonnenallee* shows. The insult is outside of the film.")

10 "the crimes of the GDR dictatorship are trivialized."

11 "in the new states it has the status of a cult film seen multiple times by its fans."

12 The clever use of diagetic and extradiagetic music, some of which was composed for the film by Stephen Keusch, Paul Lemp, and the Einstürzende Neubauten, has lead to comparisons to the musical films *Hair* and *Saturday Night Fever*; and it has been called an "East Side Story." Veronika Hall calls it "eine Kreuzung aus Kammerspiel und Musical" (*Film-Jahrbuch 2000*, 335). ("a cross between a chamber play and a musical.")

marketing appeal to *Ostalgie,* Haußmann and Brussig, along with other proponents of the film, react negatively but not necessarily consistently to the characterization of the comedy as an expression of or as a pandering to *Ostalgie.* The word itself appears to be contested, sometimes being used as a neutral term meaning a form of nostalgia, a kind of homesickness for a lost era, in this specific case, the GDR or aspects of it, and sometimes as a negative term implying selective amnesia and misplaced sentiment. Critics seem to interpret the word to mean *Ostalgiker* want the GDR back while *Ostalgiker* themselves appear to place emphasis on their right to remember formative experiences and their own past.

Haußmann critiques the word: "Entweder ist man nostalgisch oder nicht. Wie heißt das denn bei den Westlern? Westalgie? Das ist eine Form der Verächtlichmachung" ("Im Theater").[13] In the same interview, he claims that when some Ossis state drastically that they want their wall back,[14] they don't mean it literally: "Das Wort [*Ostalgie*] kommt von denen, die sich ärgern, dass sich andere an eine schöne Zeit erinnern, während sie meinen, es war eine totalitäre Zeit, und die kann gar nicht schön gewesen sein [. . .] Sie wollen nur ein Stück Heimat wieder haben, um das sie sich betrogen fühlen" ("Im Theater").[15] In this case, Haußmann is pointing out that the dominant discourse makes the western phenomenon the norm, *Nostalgie,* and the eastern phenomenon an inferior subcategory, *Ostalgie.* Difference is created that simultaneously renders illegitimate the memories and emotions involved. In fact, arguments about legitimate difference are central to a discourse on the erasure of East German identity. The problem is mirrored, for example, by the continued propensity in the *Volksmund* ("vernacular") of some West Germans to refer in the year 2000 to the old Federal Republic as "Deutschland," for example, in the statement, "we left Germany yesterday for Berlin."[16] As in the case of U.S. citizens who erase the existence of most of the western hemisphere by referring to themselves as Americans, such erasure reflects the economic and cultural dominance assumed unconsciously by the speaker. Haußmann obviously sees the film as working against such exclusion and erasure. Beyond the *Volksmund,* public discourse on political structures of control in the *DDR-Diktatur,* and East and West German psychoanalytic theories of deformation because of that control, have also tended

---

13 "Either you are nostalgic or not. What do they call it when it applies to Westerners? Westalgia? It is a way of making something contemptuous."

14 At this writing, personal opinion surveys still show that 20% each of former East and West Germans say they would like to have the wall back.

15 "The word comes from those who are irritated that there are others who remember a nice time, which the first ones think was a totalitarian time and cannot have been good in any way. They only want a bit of homeland back, so as not to feel betrayed."

16 This habit may be a Cold War leftover reflecting guidelines in West German schools that recommended "Deutschland" as the preferred designation for the *Bundesrepublik.* Even Chancellor Schroeder was not immune to linguistic lapse when in May 2000 while addressing the *Bundestag,* he said in reference to the number of firm-sponsored job training opportunities that in the East there were not as many as "bei uns"—meaning the West (Stadlmeyer).

to obliterate the remembered, lived experience of the individual in favor of a reductive discourse of deformation and wasted lives.[17]

Brussig takes a somewhat different tack from Haußmann and makes a distinction between the *Ostalgie* practiced by the radio-TV station MDR and the *Sonnenallee* material:[18] "Das Unterhaltungsprogramm des Senders wisse nichts von dem Gefühl, daß es 'von vorn bis hinten zum Kotzen war, man hat sich aber prächtig amüsiert'" (Sundermeier).[19] Brussig clearly believes that the film presents a differentiated picture of life in the GDR, that there are "good guys" and "bad guys" in this film.[20]

Although there have been general claims about the liberating effect of laughter and comedy, as well as charges of political bad taste and worse, I would like to take a more differentiated look at how comedy functions in the film.[21] The following discussion of *Sonnenallee* is intended to sort out the different comic strategies at work, to speculate about how some of these comic techniques may be working for the East and West German viewers I posit,[22] and to make the case that on the popular level, the film may have knocked a small chunk out of *die Mauer im Kopf.* I also want to consider what traditions the creators of this *Mauerkömodie* drew upon in their contribution to post-unification discourse on life in the GDR.

The possibility that East and West Germans are laughing at some of the same things but having different liberating experiences has to do with the role of context in the construction of meaning: what experiences, needs, and expectations viewers bring to the text. Obviously, audiences from the new states bring varying degrees of first-hand experience or connections with life in the GDR, which audiences in the old states generally cannot have had. A portion of the East German audience also brings varying levels of need for public affirmation of an erased East German

---

17 See the section, "Ostdeutsche Psychogramme: Anpassung und Neubeginn" (Glaser, 131-146). See also "Die Ostdeutschen sterben aus" (Decker 9-22).

18 There are three different versions of the *Sonnenallee* story: the film itself, Brussig's best-selling novel *Am kürzeren Ende der Sonnenallee* (1999), which was serialized in the *Berliner Morgenpost* the summer before the film opened, and *Sonnenallee: Das Buch zum Farbfilm* (1999), which contains an earlier version of the screenplay. Brussig's first novel *Wasserfarben* (1991) has its main character living in the Sonnenallee, but the street has little importance in the novel.

19 "The entertainment programming of the station knows nothing of the feeling; it was enough to make you throw up all the time, but you could have terrific fun anyway."

20 Kühl underscores this point: "Hier mault keine PDS, dass früher die Welt eine bessere war und man sein Stückchen wiederhaben will." ("This is not a case of the PDS whining that the world was better before and we want back our piece of it.") The PDS, or Party of Democratic Socialism, is the successor party to the SED, or Socialist Unity Party, which was the official state party of the GDR's one-party system. Hence the PDS is routinely suspected of wanting East Germany back.

21 For an excellent discussion of the role of laughter as resistance in literature and film, see Christine Haase's dissertation.

22 Research has generally theorized spectatorship in terms of class, race, gender, and sexuality while at the same time acknowledging that in practice, a single, stable viewer does not exist in these terms. I am positing East and West viewers whose instability in these terms intersects with the instability of the categories former East and former West. See "Introduction," *Viewing Positions* 3-4.

past; some may already be constructing a new German identity based on these needs while others may be experiencing other forms of *Ostalgie.* Of course, some East and West Germans may reject the film altogether. However, for those it entertains and amuses, I will claim that *Sonnenallee* constructs a dimension of remembered experience in the GDR that has been erased by discourses on the GDR-Dictatorship. The youthful high jinks engaged in by the adolescents, the slapstick, the resourceful trickery of the positive characters, the fast-paced editing reflecting a youthful pace, and the high-energy acting in the film make an argument for the intensity and fullness of lived experience in the GDR. Simultaneously, the film uses the same comic means to normalize, to deconstruct the Ossi as deformed Other for a western audience. The film also satirizes the GDR state and its representatives, although I would claim that former East Germans may experience greater or at least a different recognition of the satiric mode in the GDR context. The comedy works to obliterate "otherness" for a West German viewer while preserving the "difference" that makes visible the memory of lived experience in the GDR.

> For thy sweet love remember'd such wealth brings
> That then I scorn to change my state with kings.
> (Shakespeare)

Set in East Berlin in the seventies, the story is a romantic comedy about teenage first love and coming of age in the GDR. Micha and his gang of sixteen-year-olds are obsessed with music and girls, want to form a resistance group one minute and worry about not being allowed to study at the university the next. They grow up at the wall near the *Sonnenallee* border crossing only a stone's throw away from "dem goldenen Westen" (the golden West). Perhaps the strongest normalizing features are the genre of romantic comedy itself and the structural elements of the "new film romance" *Sonnenallee* incorporates: the wrong partner, the troubled period of getting to know and trust one another that dispels initial hostility, and the final coming together in the perfect moment (Neale 70). The business of mainstream romantic comedy is to produce a heterosexual couple. *Sonnenallee* produces not just one or two old-fashioned heterosexual couples: the main romantic plot concerns Micha and Miriam; a subplot treats Micha's best-friend Mario and the "Existentialistin" Sabrina; a new romantic couple emerges from a formerly domestic one as Micha's father and mother renew romance and sexual passion after the mother decides to abort her attempt to cross over into the West. Finally, with the sister-caricature, Sabine, who is "allen Männern hörig," we get a comic repetition of heterosexual coupling: her first boy friend is a party member, the second an aspiring actor, and the third, a Catholic. A "knutschendes Pärchen" ("a pair necking") is usually part of the background when Micha's gang gathers at their meeting place at a playground nearby.

The minimum level of generality required by romantic or domestic comedy has a normalizing effect. Gender runs to traditional type. Although more than 90% of working-age women in the GDR were employed, none are shown in untraditional roles in the film. Micha's mother Doris is depicted as an over-protective mother in the home. After some second thoughts about abandoning her family for the golden West, she turns back from her escape-attempt to rejoin them; her one risky deed affirms family ties when she smuggles her brother's ashes over the border to be where their mother is buried. The GDR-hippie, Sabrina, is not shown working, and despite her active role in seducing Mario and her first protestations against marriage, in the end, she uncharacteristically wants to marry and be protected when she gets pregnant. Whether Micha's father Hotte and Doris work or not is never mentioned. Viewers, depending on how much they know about the GDR, can assume that both work or only Hotte. Here the filmmakers take the safe way out; the genre does not require specificity here, so the touchy issue of women's roles before and after the *Wende* is simply avoided in favor of a homogenizing effect. In a similar simplifying manner, the presence of other ethnicities is avoided in favor of two binaries: East Germans versus West Germans, and representatives of the state versus Micha's circle of family and friends.

Miriam is portrayed almost exclusively through Micha's eyes and is a projection of his desire. She is not only "die Schulschönste," she is also "die wunderbare, sagenhafte, anbetungswürdige, unerreichbare Miriam"[23] who makes the world stop on Sonnenallee when she steps from her apartment building onto the sidewalk. Border guards, street workers, and the disoriented "man on the street" pause in wonder to stare at this blond, long-legged apparition. The camera shows her walking into a bigger-than-life close-up, in a slower-than-life, heart-stopping moment, and frames her as spectacle; an Elvis-like voice croons, "Stay, because you are my dream." Shot in soft focus and golden light, she appears even more inaccessible, like a saint or Madonna in short blue shorts and a white blouse. Micha's rival is a West Berliner who works as a page in a hotel and drives his customers' fancy cars over the border. Like a hero of medieval romance, Micha must perform extraordinary deeds to win her: in this case, an inspired FDJ speech and the invention of his diaries.

Little marginal space is found to deviate from the heterosexual norm. At the blowout party, a lesbian couple arrives among the many crashers and appears later in the bathtub as one of a series of quick intershots showing happy carousers. A second example is the surprise kiss during the credits between Olaf and Udo, the "FDJ-Freunde" (Free German Youth friends) from Dresden whose mind-boggling first contact with West-TV, the credits cutely suggest, may have had an awakening effect beyond the story. Marginal notes aside, this relentlessly mainstream comedy overlaps emphatically with the emplotment of first love in male heterosexual

23 "the most beautiful girl in the school... the wonderful, legendary, enchanting, inaccessible Miriam."

desire, a dominant mode familiar to everyone, East and West.[24] At the same time, the exaggeration and comic repetition pushes the film in the direction of parody and self-consciousness, which heightens the sense of playfulness without going so far as to denaturalize the paradigm of heterosexual desire. In addition, so much repetition of sex and sexual desire underscores the first pillar of a tripartite obsession of GDR youth of the seventies: sex, drugs and rock and roll.

"Es gibt ganz furchtbare Ossis und sehr angenehme"
(Haußmann)[25]

The treatment of character in *Sonnenallee* follows a general comic principle. The lighter the irony and milder the satire, the more distance is overcome to create sympathy with the characters. The more mocking and hard-edged the satire, the more distance is created to impede sympathy. Physical humor and slapstick are employed in both categories. The characters treated with a loving satirical touch include Micha and his fellow adolescent friends, male and female, his parents, his Uncle Heinz from the West, and the local cop on the beat, ABV Horkefeld. Those treated with varying degrees of mocking satirical bite are the border soldier and the school director, who appear as the most powerful representatives of the system, as well as the western observers at the border.

The domestic comedy centers on the Ehrenreichs, Micha's family, which, it is important to note, is a statistically typical GDR family. Despite all the attention given by public discourse to those in the SED, to those in the Stasi, and to IMs or *Spitzel* ("informants") in the population, the overwhelming majority of East Germans were none of these things and neither is this family, as the name "Ehrenreich" ironically suggests.[26] The Ehrenreichs are not heroes but ordinary conformists; the father, Hotte, is reluctantly so, wanting to register *Eingaben* ("official written complaints") about all the inconveniences the family puts up with. The logic of comic absurdity satirizes the structures that control by fear, e.g. as Hotte explains to Onkel Heinz why they think the neighbor is a member of the Stasi. Hotte states that this neighbor hangs out the flag. Onkel Heinz counters that the Ehrenreichs also hang out the flag. Hotte's answer: "Because the neighbor's in

24 In interviews on the film, Haußmann uses male heterosexual experience as a standard and assumes a male viewer: "Wenn ein Junge zum ersten Mal ein Mädchen sieht — das ist etwas, was jeder versteht. Das hat jeder ähnlich und doch unterschiedlich erlebt" ("'Sonnenallee'—eine Mauerkomödie," 21). ("When a boy sees a girl for the first time—that's something everybody can understand. Everyone has had this same experience, but with individual differences.") Much has been made of Brussig and Haußmann remembering different aspects of their own youth in the GDR. As Brussig put it, he was not building a museum for the GDR but "eher dem eigenen Erwachsenwerden" ("rather to his own adolescence") (24).

25 "There are really terrible Ossis (Easterners) and quite agreeable ones."

26 For statistics on numbers of Stasi and IMs in various years, see Engler, 289-290. The name "Ehrenreich" translates as "rich in honor."

the Stasi." The father resists allowing the neighborhood policeman, ABV Horkefeld, to recite police ranks, an empty exercise, and takes control of the conversation by reciting the naval ranks, also without purpose. He finally gets a telephone, a rarity in the GDR, by claiming he has epileptic episodes. His illusory sense of agency within the system is expressed by his motto: "Rin in die Organisation und von innen ufmischen."[27] Hotte is most involved in the attempt to make the *MUFUTI* (*Multifunktionstisch* or multifunctional table) work. His battle with the unmanageable piece of furniture is punctuated with "Scheiß-Ostding" ("East German piece of crap"). He is the most outspoken in the family but to no political effect. The *Mufuti* produces generalized laughter because of Hotte's slapstick struggle with it. For viewers from the former East, there is the added ingredient of recognition and recollection of the object.[28] In addition, one can read the collapsing Mufuti as concretizing, in a comical way, the promises of the GDR to deliver a cleverer, more technically avant-garde society and its failure to do so. On another level, it stands for everything that did not work right in the GDR.

Micha's mother is more conforming and cautious than his father. Her favorite word is "vorsichtig" (:careful"), Micha tells us. She is so because she wants her son to have a future and tries to impress the supposed Stasi neighbor with their *Systemfreundlichkeit* ("system friendliness"). Exaggerated as her anxious conformity is, she is also the most desperate character in the family and plans an escape when she finds the lost passport of a West German woman. She turns back when she loses courage but she also hears the impatient words of the Westerners behind her: "Wir wollen auch nicht vergammeln in der Zone." Turning back, she takes this as a provocation "nicht zu vergammeln in der Zone" and seduces Hotte in a reaffirmation of her love for him.[29] The family's *Westverwandtschaft* ("western relative") Uncle Heinz, whose exaggerated fears about crossing the border lead him to smuggle only legal items like candies and underwear, is as helpless a character as his sister and brother-in-law, no smarter or more sovereign than the Ehrenreichs. Still, he sticks by the family and resists being referred to by the boyfriend as someone "aus dem nichtsozialistischen Ausland": "Ja, wir sind alle Deutsche. Es gibt solche und solche, aber alle sind Deutsche."[30] His obsession with asbestos appears ridiculous, and he eventually dies mysteriously of lung cancer himself. Onkel Heinz, the West German, is the only one to die in this film

27 "You've got to get into the system and agitate from within."

28 Haußmann believes that the "Ossis" laughed at places the "Wessis" could not because of sheer recognition. "Aber als wir diesen Film einigen Leuten vorgeführt haben, gab es einen Unterschied zwischen West- und Ost-Zuschauern—die lachten an unterschiedlichen Stellen. Bei den Ossis ging das dann so: 'Ey, guck mal, den Kassettenrecorder hatte ich auch mal!' ("'Sonnenallee'—eine Mauerkomödie," 21). ("But when we showed this film to some people, there was a difference between the eastern and western viewers—they laughed in different places. The easterners had this sort of reaction: 'Hey, look, I had that same cassette player!'")

29 "We don't want to rot in the Eastern zone either [. . .] not to rot in the Eastern zone."

30 "from the nonsocialist part of the world [. . .] Yes, we're all German. There are good ones and bad ones but they are all Germans."

and it is hard to miss the anachronistic reference to the decision to close the Palast der Republik because of asbestos, seen by some in the East as another erasure of their past. Nevertheless, the incongruities in this family constellation produce a sympathetic, not mocking laughter.

Mario's friend Sabrina, swathed in black, is a caricature of the GDR version of disassociated hippie youth seeking individuality. Her room is decorated in black with existentialist sayings; she spouts Sartre without understanding him. She says to Mario as she seduces him "Du kannst Dich nur befreien, wenn Du auch alle anderen frei machst."[31] "Are you sure that's what he meant?" Mario asks, without a clue, however, to what Sartre might have meant. "Er war doch Franzose" ("he was French"), she answers. Despite misunderstanding Sartre, Mario and Sabrina discover the freedom of "hit-the-road pur" after he is kicked out of school. They are shown on their moped driving the back roads of the GDR to the refrain: "This land is your land, this land is my land, from Karl-Marx City to Rügen Island." "Da begann die schönste Zeit seines Lebens,"[32] Micha tells us with the proviso that the GDR may have seemed so large because their moped was so slow. Sabrina also introduces the gang to a substitute drug at the wild party where they mix Asthmakraut Halle with Club Cola. Wuschel, on the other hand, is addicted to Mick Jagger and the Stones and visits a "dealer" who sells illegal records from the West. When Wuschel is shot, he is more heartbroken that his record is shattered than he is grateful that it shielded him from the bullet. The incongruities emerging from the youthful attempts to create a counter-ideological self-image of "Underground"— sex, drugs and rock and roll— are handled with a sympathetic irony that forecloses distance, brings the characters closer, and makes them seem more human.

Physical humor underscores sympathy with Micha when he gets drunk on Asthmakraut Halle at the party. A point-of-view shot shows a wavering, unclear Miriam through his drunken perspective. Then, when she leaves in disgust, besmirched with the chocolate torte he has unwittingly smeared on her blouse, the camera captures him in a long shot as he sinks like a cartoon character to the sidewalk, proclaiming: "wir sind geistig miteinander verbunden."[33] Detlev Buck's broad comic characterization of ABV Horkefeld makes the policeman more sympathetic as his demotion in rank and loss of power unfold over the course of the film.

The above characters are attempting to experience pleasure, freedom, individuality, and to preserve human ties; they are pursuing happiness in spite of the *DDR-Diktatur*. Harder-edged characterization is reserved for representatives of the system who wield power over the others. For example, the school director's juxtaposition to Honecker's portrait in a close-up underscores her identification with the state. She gives a self-righteous speech about the boys urinating on the

31 "You can only free yourself when you set everyone else free."
32 "And so began the most beautiful time of his life."
33 "we are bound to one another spiritually."

anti-faschistische Schutzwall[34] but unwittingly ends up making the ultimate reduction by equating the GDR-state with the wall: “Sie urinieren auf unseren Staat.”[35] Her dismissal of Mario from the *Erweiterte Oberschule Wilhelm Pieck*, a pre-univeristy secondary school, also has its consequences. After a short period of freedom, he becomes vulnerable to pressure from the Stasi to become a *Mitarbeiter* or collaborator. The border soldier, who is convinced that the West has “keine Schangse” (“no chance”), is presented as a total ignoramus. Physical humor becomes repulsive when he is shot in a close-up with open mouth showing his teeth full of “amalgam”: “Hauen hie hal. Hie im Hesten glauen, haß man dahon Hebs hekomm. Aber ich habe noch nie Krebs. Noch nicht ein Mal.”[36]

The treatment of the West in the film is differentiated. Uncle Heinz is ridiculous but beloved, and the caricature of Micha’s playboy rival from the “Golden West” with the J.F. Kennedy School T-shirt is fairly benign. The visiting school class from the West, who mock Micha from the tourist platform on the other side of the wall, is mocked in return when Micha screams that he is going to blow them to bits when he comes back from his three years in the army. Despite the nonsense of the remark—East, not West Germans were shot at the wall—a stunned silence ensues until we hear the teacher say in a falsely calm voice: “Und jetzt der geordnete Rückzug.”[37] By now the audience’s sympathy is with Micha and the laughter is directed at the retreating Westerners. Although the ludicrousness of the mutual infinite regress of constructing the Other on the other side of the wall comes across, the film does not avoid the binary in this payback and interestingly enough, uses the term “Ossi” as well as “Zoni” at the beginning of the film, an anachronism, which suggests that the cycle continues in the present. Here, comedy reveals and underscores the problem. The most mercilessly satirized GDR characters, the school director and the border policeman, do not get to take part in the dance that will eventually bring down the ridiculous *Antifaschistische Schutzwall*; she is absent and he stands helplessly by as the ordinary people gyrate their way toward the wall.

> Ein Leutnant und zwei Mann vom VEB Meinungsforschung hatten endlich die Quelle der politischen Witze ausfindig gemacht. Wie sich herausstellte, stammten sie alle von einem Alten im Erzgebirge, früher Bergmann bei der Wismut, dann Holzschnitzer; er erfand sie alle und setzte sie in Umlauf, Stück für Stück, indem er sie mal bei einem Schnitzabend, mal in der Wirtschaft beim Bier erzählte. Und von da fanden sie dann allein ihren Weg, zu Fuß sozusagen. Der Leutnant hatte mit den Witzen schon viel Ärger gehabt, aber nun sah er seine Bemühungen von einem schönen Erfolg gekrönt. Du erfindest alle politischen Witze, sagte er dem Mann auf den Kopf zu, und der Alte stritt gar nicht erst ab. Das habe ich schon beim Kaiser gemacht, sagte er. Der Leutnant

34 “anti-fascist protective barrier.” This was a standard euphemism employed by the GDR.

35 “You urinate on our state.”

36 “shee here. ey elieve in the est, you et ancer. But I’ve never had cancer. Not once.”

37 “and now an orderly retreat”

konterte: Damals war das auch eine fortschrittliche Sache, ich meine, den Militarismus und die historisch längst überlebte Feudalkaste dem Gespött breiter Bevölkerungsschichten preiszugeben. Das habe ich schon bei Adolf gemacht, fuhr der Alte sich zu rechtfertigen fort.
Der Leutnant fand auch das ganz in Ordnung: Das war antifaschistischer Kampf mit den Mitteln der politischen Satire, sagte er, setzte aber mit aller Schärfe hinzu: Bloß jetzt geht sowas nicht mehr, heute, wo wir den Sozialismus aufbauen.
Der ist aber nicht von mir, der ist nicht von mir, rief der Alte da erregt und sprang auf, sodaß die beiden Männer, die den Leutnant begleiteten, ihn auf seinem Schemel festhalten mußten.

(*DDR-Witz*, from *Novembermärchen*)
Otto Emersleben[38]

Political jokes were told all over the Eastern block in various versions, and GDR variants have been compiled in several collections. Disagreement reigns as to the socio-political role of comedy, whether it functions subversively or not.[39] This lack of unanimity is mirrored by views on the role of the political joke in the GDR. It seems clear that, except in a few cases, political jokes did not constitute political resistance.[40] Stefan Wolle treats them as part of his chapter on *Ersatzöffentlichkeit* or "substitute public discourse" (253). Ernst Röhl, in his essay on political humor in the GDR, discounts them as "intellectual resistance": "Sie sind, wie mir scheint, eher eine unterhaltsame Form der Anpassung. Der Untertan läßt Dampf ab, er macht sich lustig über seine Obrigkeit, ohne ihr den Gehorsam aufzukündigen" (56).[41] Haußmann claims, on the other hand, that humor was necessary to exist in the GDR: "Die DDR war eine einzige Klamotte, glauben Sie mir, und man brauchte ziemlich Humor, um zu bestehn" ("Im Theater").[42]

---

38 "A lieutenant and two men from the Stasi had finally discovered the source of political jokes. As it turned out, they all came from one old man living in the Ore Mountains. A miner for a while and then a wood carver, he invented all the jokes and put them into circulation one by one by telling them at a meeting of woodcarvers, then at a pub over beer, and so on. And from there they made their own way, on foot you might say. Political jokes had given the lieutenant a lot of trouble, but now he saw that his efforts would be crowned with success. You invent all political jokes, he said right in the old man's face. He did not deny it. I was doing it already under the Kaiser, he said. The lieutenant countered: But at that time, it was a progressive thing to do, I mean, to make militarism and the historically defunct feudal caste vulnerable to the ridicule of a broad cross-section of the populace. I did it under Adolf too, the old man continued.
The lieutenant also felt that was O.K. It was anti-fascist struggle using the means of political satire, he said, but then added with all severity possible: But now you should not be doing it, not now when we are building socialism.
That's not my joke! That's not my joke! the old man yelled and jumped up and the two men accompanying the lieutenant had to hold him down in his chair."

39 See Neale's summary of the arguments made by theorists on both sides (71).

40 The GDR regime defined them as resistance in a few cases by sentencing some people to prison for telling a joke.

41 "They appear to me to be more of an entertaining way of conforming. The subject lets off steam, he makes fun of his superior, without renouncing obedience to him."

42 "The GDR was a piece of work, believe me, and you needed quite a bit of humor to survive."

Haußmann's own view is not always consistent here,[43] but it seems clear that he has a different understanding from Röhl and is placing a different emphasis in the film. More than just an entertaining way of conforming but perhaps less than "intellectual resistance," humor offered its consumer a momentary confirmation of an identity separate from the absurdity represented in the joke and an affirmation of resilience reinforced by laughter in an interwoven pattern of pun and trickery. One example is Doris' idea of smuggling Heinz's ashes across from West to East in a coffee can. The family expects western coffee, but what can be in there? Punchline: Onkel Heinz.

A related wily practice in the GDR was "reading between the lines" of official discourse in public ideological pronouncements in the press or other media. One can read Micha's FDJ speech as a comic version of this phenomenon. His repeated and exaggerated emphasis on Marx's *love* for the *Arbeiterklasse* ("working class") creates an intensity that Miriam reads correctly as Micha's passion for her. As in the case with GDR jokes, this does not represent political resistance but rather resilience: the capacity to partake deeply and fully in what constitutes the coming of age despite the strictures of the GDR dictatorship.

Röhl recounts GDR jokes according to themes in the film that they satirize: the absurdity of state discourse, scarcity of consumer goods and *Südfrüchte* ("citrus fruits"), and police jokes. For example, the "dumb"-jokes about policemen are even more specifically recalled by the stupid actions of the neighborhood policeman and the border soldier. Horkefeld cannot figure out which button to push on the tape recorder, for example, and even more stupidly, the border soldier acts out his belief in the GDR as the victor of history: "Wir kommen" ("We are coming"), he yells as he moves the border marker two feet. The above joke about the creator of all jokes illustrates in its structure the self-reflexivity of the film as well: A joke about jokes and the GDR-system as the biggest joke of all. I would argue that former East German viewers' laughter resonates with recognition of these joke-like structures and patterns. But the East German audiences are not only laughing at the GDR past as a way of liberating themselves from it. Indeed, laughter produced by various levels of recognition, from familiar objects to joke-like structures, is also stimulating resilience in the face of a contemporary unification discourse that invalidates memories of the past. For many East German viewers, the experience of erasure and exclusion is momentarily suspended. It is clear why potentially tragic moments are not allowed to endanger this high. The two major exceptions are Micha's loss of Mario's friendship, which is treated sentimentally and is sadder than Uncle Heinz's death, which is treated more comically, and of course, Wuschel's brush with death at the wall, suggesting the stupidity and brutality of the regime. However, fast-paced editing sweeps the audience into the next sequence. Wuschel lives to get another chance at his album, and at the end, in a fast intercut we see Mario and Sabrina stumbling out of the

43 See his comments on "das Heldenhafte" ("the heroic") in his Vorwort to *Das Buch zum Film*, 7.

justice of the peace as bride and groom; he has been domesticated but will escape the Stasi.

In addition, *Sonnenallee* is indebted to the popular work of Ulrich Plenzdorf, whose *Die neuen Leiden des jungen W* (1973) was performed in theaters in both East and West. Edgar Wibeau's fascination with rock music, jeans, and popular culture represented the youthful desire for individuality and self-expression in the early seventies. The film *Die Legende von Paul und Paula* (1974), one of the most popular films in DEFA history,[44] is alluded to directly. Winfried Glatzeder, the actor who played Paul in Plenzdorf's film, makes a cameo appearance as Paul. He lives in Miriam's building and stands on the stairs in front of his door, which has the names Paul and Paula on it. As Micha rushes up the stairs to bring Miriam his diaries, Glatzeder asks "Ein Beilchen gefällig?"[45] referring to the scene in Plenzdorf's film in which Paul assails Paula's apartment with an axe. To underscore the reference, the Puhdys intone in their caveman voices "Geh zu ihr und lass Deinen Drachen steigen,"[46] an original text by Plenzdorf for his own film, also an inflated celebration of masculine desire. *Sonnenallee,* however, represents a departure from the treatment of male desire in Plenzdorf's *Die neuen Leiden* and *Paul und Paula.* Edgar can not stop and presses on with Charlie after a first kiss, frightening her away, which contributes to his own self-loathing and desperation. Paul's hacking away at Paula's apartment is part of a syndrome that cannot take no for an answer. However, the door is already open for Micha and the next shot shows him already in Miriam's bedroom, where she joins him in the initiation of sex after he "lays his life at her feet" by giving her his diaries: "Und ich habe geglaubt, die im Westen küssen besser."[47]

Both of the Plenzdorf texts claim a death: Edgar's self-destructive accident with his invention and Paula's death in childbirth because she desires another child in spite of the doctor's admonition. There is no youthful death in *Sonnenallee.* Unlike Plenzdorf's later dark prose work "Kein runter, kein fern" (1984), which deals with a lost, confused youngster's obsession with Mick Jagger and the Stones, Wuschel is saved by his Stones album as well as endangered by it. The death of Edgar was meant to puncture the optimistic rhetoric of the GDR with a critique of the school system and produce dialogue on the problems and needs of youth. *Sonnenallee* avoids death because its comedy has a rhetorical purpose: to challenge assumptions about deformation in the GDR by showing that the absurdity of the state was a breeding ground for "youthful craziness" which could be lived as resilience as well as deformation.

44 Almost everyone in the East would be familiar with the film, which has been a continuous repeater on TV and in theaters.

45 "May I help you with an axe?"

46 "Go to her and let your dragon-kite go up"

47 "And I thought they kissed better in the West."

The entire action of *Sonnenallee,* a quintessential *Berlinfilm,*[48] takes place on a single set especially constructed for it in Babelsberg representing the end of the street at the very margin of the *Grenzgebiet* ("border area") adjacent to the border crossing. The East Berlin set has been created with great attention to accurate detail.[49] At the same time, it draws attention to its studio-constructedness. Tumbleweed drifts across the street, suggesting ironically the lack of vitality *im wilden Osten* ("in the wild East"), but it also suggests a fictional landscape and imagination. The set tells us that we will learn the truth to be found in fiction, not in history. Micha's other story, made possible by the inspiration of love, is his own development from a noncommittal youngster who does not know how he feels about the system to open resistance by refusing the army. In the process of inventing his "unzählige Tagebücher" ("countless diaries") in order to lay a fictional life before Miriam's feet, he becomes the person he wants to be for her. His attempts to assume a younger self in writing the "frühe Jahrgänge" ("earlier years") are funny. He writes how happy he is finally to be able to have learned the "ß," because he is able to write his favorite word, "Scheiße," shit. However, as he grows with the writing, he has poetic insights into the limitations of the GDR: "Dieses Land drückt wie zu enge Schuhe. Man kann sich nicht bewegen, nur träumen."[50] On a personal level he is dreaming of Miriam, but on another level, this dreaming refers to his invention of himself through his diaries, and his growing desire to come of age with integrity. However, when the lights go out and an alarm is sounded outside, his writing about standing up to the machine guns of the Soviets is reminiscent of the writer in *Schtonk* (1991), who feeds off his surroundings in order to create his fake Hitler-diaries. Wuschel's close call with death limits Micha's fiction-making, but paradoxically, it is also his fiction that prepares him for understanding that everything is not just "Spiel" ("play"); he defies the state's expectations by refusing the enlistment that will ensure his future, even before he knows whether Miriam will accept his diaries. And it is clear that he will never be a border policeman; his refusal represents a repudiation of his angry threat to blow the "Wessis" away.

Micha tells us his story of first love in the GDR in a voice-over commentary that punctuates the film throughout. He uses present tense at the beginning of the story—"Ich lebe in der DDR"—but ends it in the past tense: "Es war einmal ein Land [. . .] es war die schönste Zeit meines Lebens. Ich war jung und verliebt."[51] Micha labels the last installment of his diary "Gegenwart" ("present") before he refuses military service. The past tense at the end of the film lets the viewer know

---

48 This term is in current use, also in advertisements for *Sonnenallee*, and refers to films whose action and themes make Berlin the only possible setting. Barton Byg discusses the traditional importance of the Berlin film as a sub-genre of DEFA film in "The Berlin Film."

49 See Lothar Holler's comments on building the set in "Grenzübergang Sonnenallee."

50 "This country is tight like too narrow shoes. You can't move, just dream."

51 "I live in the GDR." Once upon a time there was a country [. . .] it was the most beautiful time of my life. I was young and in love."

that he has continued to write a diary beyond this last installment. The film continues beyond the happy ending of the romantic comedy, leaving genre behind. Instead, it progresses in condensed, allegorical time from the seventies of the love story to the dance of the people toward the wall, which signals the opening of the border, an event to which the older Micha looks back from some future point. The fusion of writing and desire, familiar to us in many works written by GDR authors,[52] is reiterated on the adolescent level of popular culture as a fusion of pop music and desire. When Wuschel discovers that his "unberührte Musik der Stones" ("untouched music of the Stones") is a fraud, Micha persuades him to play his *Luftgitarre* ("air guitar"). The two pretend so intensely that they are soon producing the sounds of the Stones and the people of *Sonnenallee,* infected by the desire in that music, begin their comic dance toward the wall as the border police look on helplessly. Time springs ahead as the boys jump from the balcony into the next decade. The dance is an old motif for revolutionary passions (the dance around the guillotine, for example). However, when the wall actually fell in November 1989, there were no executions on either side; people danced joyfully in the streets. The comic dance in *Sonnenallee* celebrates the people's desire to conquer the wall and suggests in retrospect the disappearance of fear in November 1989.[53] Here the film works against a simplistic *Ostalgie* that wants the GDR back again. When Micha refuses the army, he says "Ich bin raus, ganz raus."[54] The joke, it turns out, is on the GDR recruiter, who replies: "Das denken Sie–Wir zeigen Ihnen was die Diktatur des Proletariats bedeutet."[55] Instead, the wall comes down. In this sense, the film presents a triumphant post-wall recollection of the comic side of GDR absurdity without the fear that was so much a part of it.

After Micha says "Ich war jung und verliebt,"[56] the color begins to fade from the set as all the paper and trash from the people's demonstrations and the opening of the wall blow across the scene. The flash-forward into a devastated future recalls Wolfgang Staudte's *Der Untertan* (1951), where the absurdities of the system have brought about the end of the state. However, unlike *Der Untertan,* where the militaristic deformation created by the system is satirized in a negative main character, the comic approach to Micha and the positive characters in *Sonnenallee* makes them sympathetic figures. The color that represents Micha's

52 Examples are Anna Seghers' *Der Ausflug der toten Mädchen* (1946), Jurek Becker's *Jakob der Lügner* (1969), Wolfgang Kohlhaase's short story "Die Erfindung einer Sprache"(1977) and Christa Wolf's *Nachdenken über Christa T.* (1968). Wolf fuses desire, fiction, and imagination in order to affirm the role of human imagination and longing in creating socialism; Kohlhaase and Becker identify it with survival under fascism, Seghers with her longing to go back to her mother and to a Germany before fascism had taken hold.

53 In Berlin, this loss of fear is usually associated with the mass demonstration on Alexanderplatz on 4 November 1989 with its now famous, satirical *Losungen* ("slogans"). Actress Katharina Thalbach, who plays Misha's mother in the film, says in an interview that after the fear was gone it was possible to see how funny people were (www.sonnenallee.de).

54 "I am out, totally out."

55 "That's what you think. We'll show you what the dictatorship of the proletariat means."

56 "I was young and in love."

youth, all the intensity, vitality, resourcefulness, and resilience we have just witnessed, drains from the frame to leave a drab black and white empty set without any trace of the remembered experience of those who lived there. Haußmann underscores this point with Nina Hagen's DDR hit, which Wolf Biermann has characterized as a "genialer Schlager."[57] "Du hast den Farbfilm vergessen"(1973) thus returns the viewer to the decade of Micha's story. The song is a comic lament in which she expresses anger and sadness at her boyfriend's thoughtless use of black-and-white film to take snapshots of their vacation in Hiddensee on the Baltic:

> Du hast den Farbfilm vergessen, mein Michael
> Nun glaubt uns kein Mensch wie schön's hier war.
> Du hast den Farbfilm vergessen bei meiner Seel'
> Alles blau und weiß und grün und später nicht mehr wahr.[58]

Instead of letting black-and-white signal an authentic past, Haußmann underscores the one-dimensionality of documentary black-and-white here and equates it with the reductiveness of the depictions of life in the GDR in contemporary discourse.

It seems clear that the ten years elapsed since the *Wende* are not long enough to allow everyone to laugh at life in the GDR. It is no coincidence that Haußmann and Brussig belong to the last generation of former East German artists who came of age with the wall still standing. Perhaps for this reason they were able to use comic means to construct their recollections of the GDR past and simultaneously to explode the popular caricature of the *Jammer-Ossi* ("complaining Easterner"). Instead of complaining about erasure, they have indeed done something about it. By combining the elements of western mainstream popular comedy with GDR traditions, they have created a unification-text about the GDR past that speaks to large numbers of viewers from both former Germanys, East and West.

---

57 "clever hit." Biermann describes: "Das war ja ihr erster Hit. Damit wurde sie populär auf einen Schlag. Im Grunde ein vollkommen beknackter Text, aber sie hat ihn so intelligent gesungen, daß alle hingerissen waren, die dümmsten Leute und die klügsten Leute, die Leute mit der höchsten Kultur und die Banausen. Alle waren begeistert" (76). ("That was her first hit. She became popular with it overnight. It was really a stupid text, but she sang it so intelligently that everyone got carried away, the dumbest people and the smartest people, the most cultivated people and the philistines. Everyone was crazy about it.")

58 You've forgotten the color film, my Michael
No one will believe now how nice it was here
You've forgotten the color film, my dear.
All the blue and white and green, and then no longer true.

Works Cited

Byg, Barton. "The Berlin Film," Introduction to *Berlin, Divided Heaven: From the Ice Age to the Thaw. A Series of Thematically Linked Films for Festival and Classroom Screenings*. Amherst: DEFA Film Library at the University of Massachusetts Amherst and ICESTORM International Inc., n.d.

Brussig, Thomas. *Am kürzeren Ende der Sonnenallee*. Berlin: Verlag Volk & Welt, 1999.

---. *Helden wie wir*. Berlin: Verlag Volk & Welt, 1995.

---. *Sonnenallee*. Drehbuch. *Sonnenallee. Das Buch zum Farbfilm*. Ed. Leander Haußmann. Berlin: Quadriga, 1999

---. *Wasserfarben*. München: Deutscher Taschenbuchverlag, 1994. First published in Berlin by Aufbau-Verlag, 1991.

Das Buch der Unterschiede. Warum die Einheit keine ist. Ed. Jana Simon, Frank Rothe, Wiete Andrasch. Berlin: Aufbau, 2000.

Decker, Kerstin & Gunnar. *Gefühlsausbrüche oder Ewig pubertiert der Ostdeutsche. Reportagen, Polemiken, Porträts*. Berlin: Das Neue Berlin, 2000.

DDR-Witze: Walter schützt vor Torheit nicht, Erich währt am längsten. Ed. Reinhard Wagner with collages by Andreas Prüstel. Berlin: Dietz Verlag, 1994.

Der Untertan. Directed by Wolfgang Staudte. Screenplay by Wolfgang and Fritz Staudte based on Heinrich Mann's novel. DEFA, 1951.

Die Legende von Paul und Paula. Directed by Heiner Carow. Screenplay by Ulrich Plenzdorf. DEFA, 1973.

"Die Mauer ist nicht zum Lachen," Interview with Alexander Hussock conducted by Barbara Bollwahn de Paez Casanova. http://www.taz/de/tpl/2000/05/10.fr/serviceBox?

Drozdzynski, Alexander. *Der politische Witz im Ostblock*. Düsseldorf: Droste Verlag, 1974.

Emersleben, Otto. *Novembermärchen: keine bleibende Stadt*. Schwerin: Thomas Helms Verlag, 2000.

Engler, Wolfgang. *Die Ostdeutschen. Kunde von einem verlorenen Land*. Berlin: Aufbau, 1999.

Film-Jahrbuch 2000. Ed. Lothar Just. München: Wilhelm Heyne Verlag, 2000.

Filmspiegel Kommentar Wolfgang: *Sonnenallee*. Http://www.filmspiegel.de/start/standard.html

Glaser, Hermann. Ed. *Die Mauer fiel, die Mauer steht: Ein deutsches Lesebuch 1989-1999*. München: Deutscher Taschenbuch-verlag, 1999.

Haase, Christine. *Das gehängte Lachen: Lachen als Widerstandsform in Literatur und Film*. Diss. University of Virginia. 1996.

"Haußmann nach Anzeige: 'Anschuldigungen sind banal'" 27. Januar 2000. Spiegel-Online. http://www.spiegel.de/kultur/gesell schaft/0,1518.62083,00html

"Im Theater sitzen die Spielverderber." Interview with Leander Haußmann by Peter Zander. Http://archiv.berliner.archiv 1999/991006/feuilleton/story01.html

Holler, Lothar. "Grenzübergang Sonnenallee: Ansichten des 'Mauerarchitekten' von 'Sonnenallee.'"*Sonnenallee. Das Buch zum Farbfilm*. 64-71.

Kühl, Christiane. "Sex und Substitutionsdrogen." 7.10.1999 taz http://www.taz.de/tpl/2000/05/10.fr/serviceBox?

Neale, Steve. *Genre and Hollywood*. London and New York: Routledge, 2000.

Plenzdorf, Ulrich. *Die neuen Leiden des jungen W*. Frankfurt/M: Suhrkamp 1973.

---. *Kein runter kein fern.* Frankfurt/M: Suhrkamp, 1984.

Röhl, Ernst. "Schlechte Zeiten—gute Witze: Polithumor in der DDR." *Sonnenallee. Das Buch zum Farbfilm.* 50-58.

Schtonk!. Directed by Helmut Dietl. Screenplay by Helmut Dietl and Ulrich Limmer. Producer, Günther Rohrbach.1992.

So lachte man in der DDR. Witze und Karikaturen. Berlin: Eulenspiegel Verlag, 1999.

"*Sonnenallee.* Auferstanden aus Ruinen." www.kinonews.de1999_/kino/html-k/10-18V.html

Sonnenallee. Das Buch zum Farbfilm. Ed. Leander Haußmann. Berlin: Quadriga, 1999.

Sonnenallee. Directed by Leander Haußmann. Screenplay by Thomas Brussig and Leander Haußmann. Boje Buck Productions, 1999.

"*Sonnenallee*—eine Mauerkomödie. Interview mit Leander Haussmann and Thomas Brussig geführt von Sandra Maischberger." *Sonnenallee. Das Buch zum Farbfilm.* 8-25.

"*Sonnenallee* jetzt ohne Strafanzeige." taz Berlin lokal Nr. 6130. Http://www.taz.de/tpl/2000/05/10.fr/serviceBox?

Sonnenallee. Official web site. www.sonnenallee.de

Stadlmeyer, Tina. "Eine blanke Zumutung." taz Nr. 6140. 12.5.2000.

Sundermeier, Jörg. "Erklärt Brussig." taz Berlin lokal Nr. 60007. Http://www.taz.de/tpl/2000/05/10.fr/serviceBox?

Viewing Positions: Ways of Seeing Film. Ed. Linda Williams. New Brunswick, N.J.: Rutgers University Press, 1995.

Wellershof, Marianne. "*Sonnenallee.* Musik der Freiheit." 4. Oktober 1999. Spiegel-Online. www.spiegel.de/ kultur/kino/0,1518,45232,00.html

Westphal, Anke. *Die DDR als Hippie-Republik.*. 28.8.1999 taz. Http://www.taz.de/tpl/2000/05/10.fr/serviceBox?

Wolf Biermann: Ausgebürgert. Fotografien von Roger Melis. Mit abschweifenden Anmerkungen und wichtigen Nichtigkeiten von Wolf Biermann. Ed. Oliver Schwarzkopf and Beate Rusch. Berlin: Schwarzkopf & Schwarzkopf, n.d.

Wolle, Stefan. *Die heile Welt der Diktatur. Alltag und Herrschaft in der DDR 1971-1989.* Econ & List Taschenbuch Verlag, 1999.

Notes on Contributors

Helen Cafferty is Kenan Professor of German and the Humanities at Bowdoin College in Brunswick, Maine. Her major research interests include 20th Century literature and culture; women's studies; post-World War II film; Berlin; and GDR literature and culture. She served as coeditor with Jeanette Clausen of *Women in German Yearbook* (1989-91). Recent publications include: "What's Feminist About It? Reflections on Collaboration in Writing and Editing," with Jeanette Clausen, in *Common Ground: Feminist Collaboration in the Academy* ed. Elizabeth Peck and Joanna Stephens Mink (SUNY, 1997) and entries in *The Feminist Encyclopedia of German Literature* edited by Friedericke Eigler and Susanne Kord (Greenwood Press, 1997) and *Encyclopedia of German Literature* edited by Matthias Konzett (Chicago: Fitzroy-Dearborn, 2000).

Carol Anne Costabile-Heming is currently Associate Professor of German at Southwest Missouri State University. She received her MA (1989) from the University of Pennsylvania and her PhD (1992) from Washington University in St. Louis. Her research interests include the role of the Stasi in literary circles in the GDR; censorship mechanisms in the GDR; images of Berlin; and the authors Günter Kunert, Jürgen Fuchs, and Peter Schneider. Recent publications include *Intertextual Exile: Volker Braun's Dramatic Re-Vision of GDR Society* (Olms, 1997), as well as articles in *Mosaic* and *Monatshefte*. She has also contributed to *The Feminist Encyclopedia of German Literature* (Greenwood Press, 1997), *Encyclopedia of Contemporary German Culture* (Routledge, 1999), and *Encyclopedia of German Literature* (Fitzroy-Dearborn, 2000). She is currently preparing a book that examines the various censoring mechanisms in the GDR.

Gerald A. Fetz is Professor of German Studies and Dean, Davidson Honors College at the University of Montana. His publications include a book on Martin Walser (Metzler, 1997), numerous articles and book chapters on: Walser, Thomas Bernhard, Max Frisch, Franz Innerhofer, Kafka, History and Drama. He is currently writing book on W.G. Sebald. He has been the recipient of research fellowships from DAAD, Fulbright, NEH, and APA.

Kristie A. Foell is Assistant Professor of German at Bowling Green State University. In 1999-2000 she directed her university's study abroad program in

Salzburg and produced a documentary about the program. She received her Ph.D. from the University of California at Berkeley in 1992 with a dissertation on Elias Canetti; since that time, her research focus has shifted to literary responses to German unification. She has published or presented on Stefan Heym, Christa Wolf, Christoph Hein, Monika Maron, Günter Grass, and Thomas Brussig. She has repeatedly spent time in Berlin, most recently as a Fulbright scholar.

Rachel J. Halverson is an Associate Professor of German at Washington State University. She specializes in post-war German literature and culture. Her publications include *Historiography and Fiction: Siegfried Lenz and the "Historikerstreit"* (Lang, 1990), as well as articles on Jurek Becker (in *Monatshefte*, 1993), Günter de Bruyn (*Rocky Mountain Review*, 1996 and *glossen*, 2000) and Wolfgang Hilbig (*Seminar*, 2001). She is currently working on the interplay between narrative strategies and identity in autobiographies published by East German authors following the *Wende*.

Rolf Jucker is a Senior Lecturer in German at the University of Wales Swansea. He is particularly interested in contemporary German literature, literary theory and all aspects of the relationship between literature, history, ecology and the economy. His publications include: *"Dem Chaos anarchisch" begegnen. Zur Rekonstruktion der Utopiekonzeption in Stefan Schütz' Roman Medusa anhand der Figuren Gorga Sappho und Naphtan* (Lang, 1991), and edited volumes on Volker Braun (1995), Peter Bichsel (1996) and Stefan Schütz (1997).

Alisa Kasle is a PhD student at the Universität Paderborn. She received her B.A. from the University of Vermont (1992) and her M.A. from the Universität Paderborn (1998). Currently, she is a freelance English instructor at the Humboldt-Universität zu Berlin, the VHS Schöneberg, Berlin and other institutions. Her dissertation focuses on "Der Alltag nach der Wende in der deutschen Literatur: Wie die jüngste Generation den Alltag nach 1989 (be)schreibt."

Robert D. Levy is a doctoral candidate in history at the University of Minnesota, Twin Cities Campus. His thesis deals with the recreation of film-going activities in Germany after the Second World War (1945-1961), and the interplay between the cinema (*Das Kino*) as a metaphor for the nation and the sources of national identification. His publications include a volume entitled *Coming to Terms with "What" Past? New Perspectives on the Holocaust and Its Place in the Twentieth Century* that he is editing with William Brustein (Praeger).

Maximo Locatelli is a Teaching Assistant for the History of Film Theories at the Catholic University of Milan. At the present time he is working on themes related to German and Chinese cinema. His main publications include *Béla Balázs.Uomo visibile* (Euresis, 1998) and *Béla Balázs. Die Physiognomik des Films* (Vistas Verlag, 1999) as well as edited volumes: *La periferia dell'impero. Appunti sul cinema non hollywoodiano* with C. De Falco and A. Ostini, (Euresis, 1997); *Huang Tu Di—Terra Gialla. Appunti sul cinema delle tre Cine* with B. De Marchi (Euresis, 1999) and *Camicie nere, camicie brune* with B. De Marchi (Euresis, 2000).

Richard W. (Rick) McCormick is an Associate Professor of German at the University of Minnesota. His research and teaching focus on German cinema and twentieth-century German literature and culture. He has written on New German cinema, German feminist cinema, Weimar cinema, and West German cinema of the 1950s. He is the author of *Politics of the Self: Postmodernism, Feminism, and West German Literature and Film* (Princeton UP, 1991) and a coeditor (with Sandra Frieden, Vibeke Petersen, and Laurie Melissa Vogelsang) of *Gender and German Cinema: Feminist Interventions* (Berg, 1993), 2 vols. His book on Weimar literature and film, currently titled *Identities in Crisis: Gender, Sexuality and "New Objectivity" in Weimar Film and Literature*, is forthcoming with Palgrave/St. Martin's Press.

Karoline von Oppen is a Research Fellow in German Studies/Historical Studies at the University of Birmingham, UK. Her research interests include Writers and Politics Post-1945; the Politics of German Unification; Literature of the 1980s and 1990s; and German Media. She is the author of *The Role of the Writer and the Press in the Unification of Germany 1989-1990* (Lang, 2000).

James Reece is Associate Professor of German at the University of Idaho. His main research interests include literature of the former GDR and literature and autobiography. He has published on Günter Kunert, Wolfgang Hildesheimer, Wolf Biermann, Peter Schneider, and Volker Braun.

N. Ann Rider is Associate Professor of German and Women's Studies at Indiana State University. Her main research interests include East German Literature and Culture; 20th Century German Literature and Culture; Critical, Gender and Feminist Theory; Multicultural Pedagogy. Her publications include: "The Critical Difference: Meeting the Challenge of Multicultural Pedagogy" (*GDR Bulletin*, 1997), and articles on Günter de Bruyn (*The German Quarterly*, 1995) and Walfriede Schmitt (*Contemporary Theater Review*, 1995).

Stuart Tabener is Lecturer in German at the University of Leeds, UK. His main research interest is the relationship between politics and aesthetics in post-war Germany. He has written on Günter Grass, Martin Walser, Stefan Heym, Uwe Johnson, literature and the Holocaust, and on the role of the intellectual in Germany pre- and post-unification. He is currently writing a book about the normalization debate in post-1990 Germany and developments in aesthetics and literary fiction in the 1990s. His publications include *Distorted Reflections: The Public and Private Faces of the Author in the Work of Uwe Johnson, Günter Grass and Martin Walser* (Rodopi, 1998); articles in *Monatshefte* (1999), *Deutsche Vierteljahrsschrift* (1999), and *German Life and Letters* (2000).

Jill Twark is writing her dissertation at the University of Wisconsin-Madison. Her main research interests include twentieth century German literature and culture, GDR literature, post-reunification literature. Her publications include articles on Eastern German Cabarettists, and on Mathias Wedel and Matthias Biskupek.

Jenifer Ward is Associate Professor of German and Chair of the Department of Modern Foreign Languages and Literatures at Gustavus Adolphus College in Minnesota. Her research interests include Twentieth Century German Literature and Cinema, Women and Cinema, Cinematic Adaptations of Postwar German Novels. She has published on Peter Henisch, Jurek Becker, and Margarete von Trotta.

Index of Names

Page numbers refer to text and footnotes. Numbers with "n" refer to notes only.

Humanities from de Gruyter

1870/71–1989/1990 German Unifications and the Change of Literary Discourse

Edited by Walter Pape

1993. VI, 382 pages. Hardcover.
• ISBN 3-11-013878-6
(European Cultures - Studies in Literature and the Arts, Vol.1)

Renowned historians and Germanists from Britain, the USA and the Federal Republic of Germany examine reactions to the imposed unification of 1871, which has already been the subject of much historical and literary discussion, and the unification of 1989/90. The cultural and intellectual changes linked with these unifications are analysed using central historical and literary problems and authors (for the 19th century Spielhagen, Raabe, Fontane, Hoffmann von Fallersleben, Freiligrath and Herwegh). Problem-oriented papers deal with the question of national identity and with nationalism and education after 1870. A number of contributors compare cultural and literary change after the founding of the first and second German national states: these include the image of Berlin, historical narratives, together with the functions of lyric poetry and the dream of 'a different Germany'. British and American perceptions of literary and cultural change post-1990 are demonstrated using the attitude of intellectuals to unification, the 'case' of Christa Wolf, and the GDR avant-garde of the Prenzlauer Berg.

Sabina Schroeter

Die Sprache der DDR im Spiegel ihrer Literatur

Studien zum DDR-typischen Wortschatz

1994. X, 241 pages. Cloth.
• ISBN 3-11-013808-5
(Sprache, Politik, Öffentlichkeit, Vol. 2)

The authoress examines the lexis of 35 novels and stories written in the GDR between 1949 and 1989 to discover typical GDR elements in the present-day German vocabulary. The study aims to illuminate the relationships between language and society and between language and ideology, using the GDR as an example.

From the contents:
Word-formation - Post-war vocabulary - Occupational and personal designations for women - Compounds with *Volk-* - The vocabulary of Marxist-Leninist ideology - Representation of Stalin in the novels - Index of words.

WALTER DE GRUYTER GMBH & CO. KG
Genthiner Straße 13 · D-10785 Berlin
Telefon +49-(0)30-2 60 05-0
Fax +49-(0)30-2 60 05-251
www.deGruyter.de

W DE G

de Gruyter
Berlin · New York

Linguistics from de Gruyter

Dieter Herberg /Doris Steffens / Elke Tellenbach

Schlüsselwörter der Wendezeit

Wörter-Buch zum öffentlichen Sprachgebrauch 1989/90

1997. X, 522 pages. Cloth.
• ISBN 3-11-015398-X
(Schriften des Instituts für deutsche Sprache, Vol. 6)

The short period around the Wende ('turning point') of 1989/90 saw the creation of around 1,000 new words, symbolising the shift from Menschen in der Gerade-Noch-DDR ('People in the rapidly disappearing GDR') to künftige Bundesbürger ('future citizens of the Federal Republic'), and including items such as Flüchtlingsmassen ('masses of refugees') and Massenflucht ('Mass escape'), the Aktenwaschanlage ('Share laundry') and – of course – the Wendehals ('Turncoat'). Everything you need to know about these is contained in the new 'Book of words'. The authors record the various word formations and their meanings and provide the requisite background knowledge. Numerous examples show how the words were used – or still are being used.
"Schlüsselwörter der Wendezeit" is a work of reference and at the same time a reader for all those who want to find out more about this recent chapter in the history of the German language.

Sprache im Umbruch

Politischer Sprachwandel im Zeichen von "Wende" und "Vereinigung"

Edited by Armin Burkhardt and K. Peter Fritzsche

1992. XXI, 314 pages. Cloth.
• ISBN 3-11-013613-9
(Sprache, Politik, Öffentlichkeit, Vol. 1)

Linguistic and politological examiniation of political language in the GDR before and after the "turning point". Linguistic analyses in the context of German unification and the first elections in united Germany in 1990.

From the Contents:
Politische Kultur in der DDR - "Macht des Worts - "Wir sind das Volk" - Sprechchöre bei der "Montags-Demo" in Leipzig - Christa Wolfs Streit mit dem "großen Bruder" - Sprache des Umbruchs und ihre Übersetzung - Sprache der Volkskammer - Schulbücher in der DDR - "Haus Europa" - Die Deutschen und das Deutsche - Gesamtdeutsche Bundestagswahlen - Sprache der Vereinigung

WALTER DE GRUYTER GMBH & CO. KG
Genthiner Straße 13 · D-10785 Berlin
Telefon +49-(0)30-2 60 05-0
Fax +49-(0)30-2 60 05-251
www.deGruyter.de

de Gruyter
Berlin · New York